Critical Perspectives on Diversity in Organizations

Decades of investigations into diversity in the workplace have created mixed answers about what kinds of effects it has on employees and teams, and whether or not it can be managed effectively to generate positive outcomes for organizations. In contrast to mainstream work from management and psychology, critical views on workplace diversity have emerged that seek to grasp more fully the messy social and political realities of workplace diversity as they operate in context.

Critical Perspectives on Diversity in Organizations therefore seeks to review, integrate, and build upon emerging critical perspectives on workplace diversity to help give a fuller understanding of how employee differences affect workplace interactions, relationships, employment, inequality, culture, and society. Critical perspectives help to fill in and openly recognize many of the more far-reaching issues that pure management and psychology approaches can leave out – issues of power, inequality, politics, history, culture, and lived experiences. If organizations do not try to take these issues into account and critically reflect on them, then diversity management is likely to remain a relatively blunt instrument or worse, a hollow piece of rhetoric.

This book will be of interest to international graduate students and researchers working on topics associated with equality, diversity, and inclusion in organizations, as well as various organizational practitioners and activists engaged with these issues.

Thomas Calvard is Senior Lecturer in Human Resource Management in the Organization Studies Group at the University of Edinburgh Business School, UK.

Routledge Studies in Organizational Change & Development

Series Editor: Bernard Burnes

For more information about this series, please visit: https://www.routledge.
com/Routledge-Studies-in-Organizational-Change–Development/book-
series/SE0690

Critical Perspectives on Diversity in Organizations

Thomas Calvard

Routledge
Taylor & Francis Group

NEW YORK AND LONDON

First published 2021
by Routledge
52 Vanderbilt Avenue, New York, NY 10017

and by Routledge

2 Park Square, Milton Park, Abingdon, Oxon, OX14 4RN
*Routledge is an imprint of the Taylor & Francis Group, an
informa business*

© 2021 Taylor & Francis

Library of Congress Cataloging-in-Publication Data
A catalog record for this title has been requested

ISBN: 978-1-138-63378-0 (hbk)
ISBN: 978-1-315-20713-1 (ebk)

Typeset in Sabon
by MPS Limited, Dehradun

Contents

Acknowledgments

I would like to thank my wife Jacklyn, father Stephen, sister Sarah, and dog Odin, as well as other close friends and relatives, for providing diverse forms of love, support, and encouragement as I developed this book.

I would also like to thank the editorial and commissioning team at Routledge for their support and patience as I developed this book. In this regard, I extend my appreciation to David Varley, Brianna Ascher, and Naomi Round, as well as their respective teams and colleagues.

Finally, I would like to acknowledge and express my appreciation for all the diverse colleagues and collaborators I have had the pleasure and privilege of knowing and working with over the last decade. They have shaped my thinking on diversity and organizations, and nurtured my enthusiasm and learning on the subject. These include Kate Sang, Michelle O'Toole, Kristina Potočnik, Nick Oliver, Tinu Cornish, Debora Jeske, Rob Briner, Maryam Aldossari, and Dawn Chow, among many others, and the many fantastic scholars and authors cited in this book.

Introduction

Like many areas of the social sciences, diversity can be a daunting subject to think and write about. The fact, idea, or even the mere suggestion of the idea that we *differ* in many fundamental ways as humans, employees, professionals, and managers may seem as blindingly obvious as the fact that we share similarities and have things in common. However, while our similarities may be relatively taken-for-granted, harmonious, or easy to appreciate, our *differences* are perhaps more likely to be met with mixed feelings, to say the least. Differences and diversities can surprise or provoke, prompt reflection and elaboration, and fundamentally keep relocating us anew within a complex social landscape of shifting, intersecting, and conflicting identities.

Historical, cultural, and legal developments in the latter part of the twentieth century have meant an increasing drawing of attention to the inequalities, discrimination, and characteristics surrounding human diversity that require greater recognition and protection from harm. Similarly, a greater awareness of diverse struggles, voices, experiences, and achievements now infuses public and corporate consciousness in various ways around the world. Often, diversity itself has a self-organizing quality, in that difference begets more difference, as well as catalyzing the formation of new solidarities, and even the re-formation of old ones. The navigation of human difference poses fundamental philosophical and social questions about what we are to 'do with' our differences and when – put them aside, tolerate them, celebrate them, transcend them, perform them, and so on. In short, these seem to be questions about how we should best 'organize' and 'manage' diversity. This in turn brings us back toward recognizing the power, politics, and inequality inherent to diversity; if we are to manage and organize it, then we might do well to ask, in whose interests, and who is this 'we'?

Diversity is therefore a complex phenomenon in various senses – in terms of its many attributes, its operations, and its relations to institutions, organizations, powerful actors, structures, and inequalities. Furthermore, in some instances, diversity can appear to be overwhelming, messy, contradictory, ironic, and to defy easy social, political, or cultural explanation. Three brief examples might be helpful in illustrating this point.

First, in the summer of 2016, months ahead of Donald Trump's winning of the US presidential election, Trump's wife Melania made a speech at the Republican Party's national convention, a speech subject to a minor scandal of being allegedly plagiarized in part from a similar 2008 speech given by the then First Lady Michelle Obama (McCarthy & Jacobs, 2016). In relation to this item, a wry social media comment circulating online noted 'the irony of a Slovenian immigrant with a thick accent regurgitating a Black woman's speech while being cheered by a room full of people who believe Black people and immigrants are ruining this country' (Roy, 2016). Despite this example not taking place in an overtly organizational setting, it shows how a single incident can carry particularly rich, complex resonances for institutions, organizations, and working lives. A single social media comment hints at elements of hypocrisy, irony, the historical race relations climate of the US, immigration policy, diversity of political opinion, gendered media representations, and the delicacies of speechwriting, not to mention the communicative practices of diverse social media audiences.

Second, in another recent case, Oxford University and its equality and diversity unit came under widespread criticism – again, largely through social media – for writing a staff guidance newsletter emphasizing that avoiding eye contact or not speaking with diverse others can constitute 'everyday racism' and 'racial micro-aggression' that is tiring and alienating to racial minorities (Gray, 2017). However, it was widely criticized for being insensitive to the fact that people with a learning disability on the autism spectrum, or even just shy or anxious individuals, would also show some of this behavior, despite not being racist in the slightest. One response even accused the University of 'ableism', presumably in terms of its disregard for the legitimate lived experience and conduct of those with autism, and its privileging of a certain set of behaviors as normal, expected conduct. The communication also stressed the need to avoid jokes and questions that might draw undue attention to different nationalities and exclusionary stereotypes (Gray, 2017). In this case then, we see the irony and complexity of diversity totally foiling a presumably well-intentioned item of organizational communication. The experience of one diversity characteristic (race) comes into interactive contact with the expression of another difference (disability/autism), and diversity management finds itself caught in a contradiction as it tries to shape the local, everyday conduct of its employees in a uniform manner.

To take a third and final example from beyond the West, consider work, employment, and organization in relation to Arab men in the Middle East and Africa. The Economist (2017) published an article on the 'sorry state of Arab men', describing evidence supporting a 'crisis of masculinity' over lack of work and income, despite men clinging to patriarchal attitudes for comfort and many still generally dominating homes, families, offices, and state departments. The article goes on to interpret evidence in terms of it reflecting a mixture of issues; men determined to be financial providers, a backlash against assertive women, a climate of religious conservatism, violence, harassment, female genital mutilation, NGO activism, and the changing of some biased laws but a lack of official support or role models. Again, as well as the complexity of these environments, we also see contradictory, ironic, and unexpected turns of events relating to diversity and ripe for critical interpretation. Whether, for instance, it is Lebanon appointing a man as its first-ever women's affairs minister (The Economist, 2017), or a heroic young Saudi woman defying a gendered driving ban to save a man's life by driving him to hospital (Al-Tuwalah, 2017).

In the constant, media-rich environment of the twenty-first century, one could find any number of similar examples to choose from in any given week, covering many other equally complex issues relating to societal and organizational diversity, framed in positive, negative, neutral, or ambivalent ways. This book will continue to draw on and present such examples wherever possible. At the same time, the book is seeking to make the foundational argument that by deploying various critical perspectives on diversity in organizations, we can help to better uncover these issues, articulate them, and indicate political and ethical paths for key actors to resist abuses of power. Such paths can help minorities emancipate themselves from harm and indignity and re-construct their diverse identities and sense of well-being.

Taking this approach of course means attempting to be clear and inclusive about what constitutes an organization and what does and does not constitute a critical perspective, as well as reflecting on the conceptual language and meanings surrounding diversity and diversity management. This book will make many attempts to answer these questions, although typically not claiming such answers as definitive or authoritative. Rather the reader is a fellow traveler coming to their own conclusions about diversity in organizations, in the hope that they find the chapters at least a workable and consistent presentation of a series of related critical themes, thinkers, and topical areas. The consistent thread lies in the presentation of a critical, self-questioning mindset on organizations and diversity, and reviewing how that has been conveyed, and can be applied, to various degrees in management and organizational research and theory, drawing on influences across philosophy and the social sciences.

This critical approach can mean adopting – at least temporarily – fairly pessimistic assumptions, or at least ones that are inconvenient to prevailing interests and orders. For example, considering where organizations are not necessarily well equipped to deal with diversity at all, whether it relates directly to their working objectives or not, and how their power structures may actively suppress it and undermine its expression. This indeed means questioning the more rosily optimistic, rational, managerial views that managers can clearly perceive, manage and direct diversity towards improving performance. Even management research that is only slightly critical of this view and starts talking to managers directly soon finds that so-called diversity management is 'easy to say, difficult to do' (Foster & Harris, 2005).

As with critical management and organizational research more generally, this also means taking a critical approach on what qualifies as an organization, and what an organization is for, and how it operates as an entity. In abstract terms, this might seem unhelpful, but there are definitely at least several ways to advance this questioning process that are likely to prove more fruitful than simply assuming organizations simply 'are' limited to ordered buildings, offices, factories, for-profit businesses, and so forth. First, because there are many competing images and metaphors of organization that are themselves highly diverse (Morgan, 1997). From skyscrapers to oilrigs to sweatshops, arguably, organizational forms extend as far as the human imagination can conceive of them, although for many modern workers, they also can often seem like a necessary evil, or "these rather recent and far from natural forms of human collectivity" (Gabriel, 2000, p. 94). A related point is that while obvious images and prototypes of organizations may readily come to mind, it is also worth critically challenging these mainstream ideas of organization to find a wider range of more exotic or colorful 'alternative' forms of organization. These alternatives might serve to reveal and enlighten us about various positive and negative departures from the obvious or status quo (Parker, Cheney, Fournier, & Land, 2014a). Finally, there is no need to assume that organizations exist as fixed objects or things in any concrete sense at all. Instead, we might opt for a more critical perspective on organizations by seeing them as representing an ongoing process or processes of *organizing*, swapping the noun for a verb (Bakken & Hernes, 2006; Hernes & Weik, 2007; Weick, Sutcliffe, & Obstfeld, 2005).

Perhaps the common denominator of critical perspectives on organizations and diversity, as defined rather loosely and inclusively in this book, is that they do ask fundamental questions about power, context, knowledge, reality, form, and process. By implication, the extent to which any perspective neglects to ask these questions or tries to simplify them away with taken-for-granted assumptions and one-sided generalities suggests that such a perspective is relatively lacking in criticality. Critical questions are, almost by definition, difficult to formulate, to measure precise and simple answers to, and often raise more questions and problems rather than generalizable wisdom. This, however, should not detract from their importance and their appeal to those studying and experiencing organizations and diversity. Indeed, building a critical theoretical understanding of a social and organizational issue may require several attempts, but where successful, is likely to provide rewarding answers akin to solving a profound puzzle or mystery (Alvesson & Kärreman, 2007). Stuart Sim (2004, p. 165) closes his humorously illustrated, accessible introduction to critical theory with the assertion that "critical theory helps to promote the cause of democratic pluralism, and is therefore an integral part of the current political scene. Theory is power. This is not merely an academic exercise for "intellectual mandarins", but a perspective on awareness and a talent well worth developing for all of us." Critical theory (in theory at least) can also therefore uphold values that are truly in sympathy with diversity – democracy, empowerment, consciousness raising, and so on.

This book is therefore an exploration of the value of critical theories and perspectives as applied to diversity in organizations, drawing on real-world examples (global and international ones as often as possible), organizational and management research, and other relevant interdisciplinary and theoretical resources as appropriate. However, it does not pretend to be an authoritative source on critical thinkers and original texts. This would be both daunting and counterproductive – the roots of critical texts and thinkers' ideas are often far-reaching and difficult to decipher in their exact details and intentions, despite many experienced writers reading them and re-reading them. The purpose here is to treat various critical figures and concepts in a general, exploratory fashion in terms of some of their key concepts and worldviews, speculating on how they might relate to diversity in organizations.

That said, this book does seek to contrast its critical intent and contribution with more 'mainstream' management, research, which often takes a rather functionalist, rationalist approach rooted in psychology, economics, and the implementation of human resource management (HRM) practices. Of course, 'mainstream' and 'critical' research is not a sharply defined dichotomy – it would be uncritical to assume otherwise – and there are many shades of grey in between these two poles, although it seems fair to assert that there is some polarization in the use of theories, methods, and journals across them. Such polarization makes this book worth writing – as many books on workplace diversity tend to fall more in the 'mainstream' camp rather than squarely in the critical one. One aim of the book then is to prompt reflection and questioning on what critical perspectives on diversity in organizations consist of, and the value and quality underpinning such perspectives over so-called 'mainstream' alternatives.

Partly this is an issue of different paradigms, and foundational perspectives on ontology and epistemology, again ironically representing a diversity of viewpoints unto themselves. This is also an interdisciplinary issue, in that different paradigms may be more likely to originate in part, and derive from, different disciplines or areas of academic study (Oswick, Fleming, & Hanlon, 2011). Using a diversity of disciplinary material to investigate diversity itself is the concern here, and doing so successfully being likely to lead to more radical, original, and influential contributions (Oswick et al., 2011).

That said, it is impossible to cover everything, and the mainstream versus critical distinction made here does mean giving more attention to some disciplines over others. Namely, mainstream views will tend to favor more mathematical and pure scientific disciplinary influences for their presumed objectivity and realism, whereas critical views will tend to favor more arts and humanities-based disciplinary influences for their philosophical, experiential, and social interpretations of phenomena. Here, the more critical positions associated with social constructionism, postmodernism, and post-structuralism and the like will be favored over the more positivistic, scientist, managerialist perspectives of the mainstream. While there are some more inbetween positions such as 'post-positivism' and 'critical realism' that temper their scientific objectivity with some pragmatic social and political subjectivity, a central argument of this book is that more mainstream, positivistic approaches struggle to deal with the complexity of diversity as provided in the three examples previously. In some ways they have not evolved their theories and statistical procedures to explain them satisfactorily. In any case, they can appear to erase the context and the rich pluralism of issues hiding beneath the surface of demographic trends and patterns of inequality.

The aim here is not to devalue positivistic contributions, however. For the most part, it is perhaps more constructive to assume that they act as complementary to – albeit slightly separated from – critical perspectives on diversity – in a sort of surface-deep or figure-ground relationship. It doesn't seem especially fruitful to get bogged down in the notion of 'paradigm wars' or 'paradigm incommensurability' in pitting incompatible assumptions against each other in ways that are difficult, if not impossible, to resolve in any straightforward fashion (Jackson & Carter, 1993). What does seem to matter here is a related sense of being able to be reflexive and self-aware about navigating and intervening in meaningful ways in social relationships where paradigmatic beliefs and dimensions are in play (Holland, 1999). In a sense, histories of disciplines and paradigms relate profoundly to diversity, if we choose to see them as changing diversities of worldviews.

C.P. Snow's notion of 'two cultures' of science and literature struggling to build bridges instead of remaining in opposition is one that has endured since the mid-nineteenth century (James, 2016). In the twenty-first century, upon the death of the sociologist Zygmunt Bauman, we can reflect on his career and contributions to seeing the world in new ways, despite his work tending to avoid data and facts in favor of sweeping impressions and imaginative visions of our times and lives (Gross, 2017).

Gibson Burrell and Gareth Morgan's model of sociological paradigms remains important to framing conversations about multiple, partial views that may be put forward about organizations – concerning the relative influence of free will versus deterministic factors, and how subjective versus objective certain realities and assertions are considered to be (Deetz, 1996). Although this book presents critical perspectives on diversity in organizations as worthy of greater attention relative to more mainstream ones, it shares Deetz's (2000) concern that writing on organization should be more focused on sorting out the quality of knowledge claims in general, rather than assigning blame to various paradigmatic communities, or seeking to discredit their worldviews (Deetz, 1999). These issues and claims are important for diversity – they shape what the implications are if we approach it with the aim of studying it like an exact 'diversity science' (Plaut, 2014), and how we decide what counts as 'evidence' we can use to inform and guide decision-making and diversity agendas (Morrell, 2012).

In Part I, this book starts by defining and considering mainstream diversity management literature in terms of its contributions (Chapter 1) but also as a point of departure for the remaining chapters, which focus on a range of more critical perspectives, where the meaning and definition of a critical perspective on organizations is considered in chapter two. Both chapters will seek to present exemplary authors, pieces of theory, research, and scenarios surrounding mainstream versus critical views of organizational diversity.

Part II of the book covers a series of three proposed 'defining aspects' of a critical perspective on diversity in organizations more specifically. First, Chapter 3 looks at the 'historical turn' in management and organization theory, and the value of history and historiography as part of a critical approach to diversity in organizations. Second, Chapter 4 addresses the defining themes of power, and the inequality inherent to social power relations in organizations, as underpinning and explaining diversity and the experiences it generates. Third, Chapter 5 rounds this off by considering the importance of adopting critical perspectives on institutions in relation to diversity, in terms of trying to foreground it against a societal and temporal context that is as complete as possible.

Part III of the book contains five chapters, this set of five representing selected topics that provide ways of elaborating on critical perspectives on diversity, together making up most of the body of the book itself. The structure of the five chapters is by no means exhaustive or absolute, but the intention is to capture as many of the most important, relevant and written-about critical aspects of diversity in organizations. First, Chapter 6 looks at the critical theoretical and methodological lens of intersectionality as a way of acknowledging the messy complexity of diversity in organizations. Second, Chapter 7 looks at discourse and the influential role of language in determining how diversity in organizations is constructed and experienced. Third, Chapter 8 looks at multiculturalism and the relatively neglected critical debates in sociological and political theory and philosophy that can help us understand how organizations represent ethnically diverse, multicultural projects embedded in wider societies and ideologies. Fourth, Chapter 9 considers the connections between organizational diversity and sensemaking, in terms of how diversity can give rise to repeating, cyclical social processes of action and interpretation. Fifth, Chapter 10 outlines the importance of place and space as ways of appreciating the geographies of diversity in organizations.

The final part of the book, Part IV, comprises four chapters around the theme of implications for practice and policy in a future of diverse organizations. Again, the chapter structure and contents are not meant to be somehow exhaustive or beyond criticism, but the chosen areas are taken to reflect areas of critical significance to diversity and organization studies as they have been written about to date. First, Chapter 11 argues for the continuing relevance of debates around whether diversity can or should be 'managed' and the problematic aspects of an economically-motivated 'business case' for diversity being emphasized, particularly at the expense of other legal, moral, political or social cases for its engagement. Second, Chapter 12 considers issues of performativity and agency in relation to how critical approaches to diversity and organizations can lead to meaningful, voluntary opportunities for action and change. Third, Chapter 13 discusses utopias, dystopias, and heterotopias in projecting the social and organizational imagination surrounding diversity into the future, with some reference to technology in doing so. Finally, the book concludes with some brief reflections on the importance and ambition of continuing to develop critical perspectives on diversity in organizations, in particular perspectives that are also interdisciplinary and seek to forge new syntheses across research and practice agendas.

The chapters of the book outlined previously do not speak directly to particular types of diversity characteristics (e.g. age, gender, and ethnicity) or critical theoretical school (e.g. feminism, post-structuralism, psychoanalysis). This may lead to some concerns over potential gaps or omissions. However, in spite of the chapter structure, both diversity characteristics and critical theoretical schools appear in multiple places throughout the book. Once again though, the overall aim, purpose, and position of this book is not to be totally exhaustive in range, even if that were possible. Rather, the aim is to engage in pragmatically shining a spotlight on relatively recent, exemplary pieces of social and organizational research, influential thinkers and positions, and real-world examples that focus on different identities, characteristics, and settings.

Beneath the singular topic of diversity and the surface structure of the book's chapters, there are inevitably other dimensions and components to consider in how the topic is broken down and discussed. Certainly one example of this relates to the *international* contexts of diversity management, something that any discerning reader would hope to see a reasonable representation of, and real-world examples and research studies are chosen in later chapters to try to reflect a range of global and international settings. At the very least, there is scope for writing on diversity in organizations to keep moving beyond North America alone, and beyond Western Europe too, to include more of the Global South alongside the North. Diversity management practices do indeed vary widely across the globe, and some may transfer more easily and universally across countries and cultures than others (Syed & Özbilgin, 2009). Another example then for structuring discussions of diversity in organizations is in terms of *practices*, HR and managerial, ranging from basic forms of diversity training through to more controversial practices like using quotas, or even offering to freeze the eggs of career women who don't have time for a baby (Mertes, 2015).

Any discussion of diversity now takes place in the significant shadow cast by the influential concept of identity, a concept of seemingly endless discussion in the social sciences. Considering diversity through the lens of identity means broadly tending towards seeing it in terms of multifaceted, changing symbolic representations of multiple identities – or in terms of Sameness opposed to a contrasting Other, as constructed through various Othering processes (Gabriel, 2012). Yet abstract symbolic representations are far from the only aspect of diverse identities that matter; they also exist in physical, concrete terms as visual, embodied, and material phenomena.

Finally, it seems wrong to talk about diversity without simultaneously considering *similarity*. There are profound questions and views on how we reconcile differences with similarities, how they co-exist, and a lot seems to rest on how we count others as fellow human beings in terms of inclusion, unity, solidarity. Diversity and similarity appear to have something of a dialectical relationship to some extent (Thijssen, 2012), as they collide in our everyday lives and encounters, and we experience them in this existential medium of trying to reconcile them through our behaviors and institutions. Sometimes we may feel emotionally involved in a heated conflict over incompatible values; in other circumstances, the differences of diversity may be totally alien to us, and leave us feeling bemused, or we may manage to hold on to a sense of universal humanism – the reactions to experiencing diversity are, themselves, diverse.

Much of our lived experience of diversity will take place in relation to work, employment, and organizations. Politics, culture, and ethics are unlikely to remain outside the organization. Rather than a unified, eternally committed workforce performing its tasks by neatly pooling its diverse resources, the more critical reality is that organizations will need to keep reconstructing and negotiating their sense of their own understandings of diversity or 'diversities' plural (e.g. Janssens & Zanoni, 2005), against a political economic backdrop of other diverse stakeholders and organizations.

At a more meta-, second-order level, there will always be a diversity of views on diversity, a diversity behind the diversity, signifying it. From the many 'isms', ideologies and subtly diverse modes of thought, right through to the radical humanist universals that we all inalienably share, diversity and similarity are almost never a given – we can never assume them; wherever possible, we must listen, experience, express, discuss our different differences and potential similarities for meaning and value to emerge. Diverse perspectives on diversity will continue to battle these issues out, organizing and reorganizing themselves, only to be challenged by still other perspectives, all the while indicating that they are all just that and nothing more – perspectives. This is because human diversity is itself an ongoing organizational project.

Part I
Diversity in Organizations
An Overview

1   Mainstream Approaches

Before outlining potential critical perspectives on diversity in organizations, this chapter will review what it sees as more 'mainstream' research and theory on organizational diversity and take it as a point of departure for the rest of the book. The chapter does not suggest a particularly damning attack on this work but will argue that its approaches paint a particular picture of diversity in organizational life, one with potential strengths, contributions, weaknesses, and concerning omissions. Mainstream diversity literature is defined broadly here in terms of dominant streams of articles published in top management, psychology and HR journals, often North American in tradition, often taking a quantitative, positivistic methodological approach in attempting to find generalizable, scientific-type findings about workplace diversity and its effects. This is not necessarily a perfect characterization of the literature, and over-generalizations would not be advisable, but it will serve for reviewing significant amounts of work that has taken, and continues to adopt, a particular style or genre in how it pursues and presents diversity research and findings.

When and Why Did We Start Researching Diversity in Organizations?

Ironically, given the tendency to emphasize data and objectivity, much mainstream research on organizational diversity doesn't go very far in considering the history of the topic, its own or otherwise. This will appear more explicitly in other chapters, but here we note that when this type of diversity research does give an account of diversity's history, it tends to be relatively restricted to a few landmarks or broad stages from within a North American perspective (e.g. Anand & Winters, 2008; Nkomo & Hoobler, 2014). While Nkomo and Hoobler (2014) provide much welcome historical and political insight into changing diversity ideologies, North America is still very much the focus.

Overall, two main landmarks stand out in this well-rehearsed, but limited, version of diversity's history. First, there is the Civil Rights era leading up to the 1960s and in particular, the act of 1964, with labor laws aimed at ensuring Equal Opportunities, and outlawing discrimination, across characteristics like race, sex, nationality and religion. Second, there is the *Workforce 2000* report, published in 1987 by the Hudson Institute, an American conservative non-profit think tank, focusing on the need for greater preparations to address the skills and demographics of a changing workforce (Johnston & Packer, 1987, cited in Nkomo & Hoobler, 2014). This second event paved the way for the more practical, corporate, human resource agenda on diversity and the turn from equal opportunities toward 'diversity management' into the 1990s (e.g. Thomas, 1990).

Quantitative research on management and organizational diversity grew alongside and out of these developments, particularly the latter period in the 1980s and 1990s when researchers began to take advantage of access to demographic organizational data. Early work in this stream went by the name 'organizational demography' (Pfeffer, 1985), as researchers investigated the demographic distributions of populations of workers and top management teams, and attempted to relate them to organizational behavior outcomes, such as turnover, innovation, and communication (e.g. Stewman, 1988; Wiersema & Bird, 1993). Instead of looking at distributions in aggregate, there also developed a slightly different, yet related, approach referred to as 'relational demography' (e.g. Tsui, Egan, & O'Reilly, 1992; Tsui & O'Reilly, 1989). Relational demography was more interested in how the demographic (dis)similarity of diverse team members, leaders and followers on single or multiple attributes *relative to one another* affected attitudes, behaviors and performance. Relational demography research has persisted, although debates about how to measure the feelings of relative dissimilarity of individuals-within-groups (e.g. more objectively or perceptually) – and the corresponding inferences that can be drawn from such measures – have continued (Riordan & Wayne, 2008). Mixed findings have persisted, with it remaining unclear how minority and majority individuals may feel about and interpret their relationships and status differences. The only real assertion made, typically via organizational psychology, is that future theory and testing needs to take better account of organizational cultures and individual differences in beliefs, motives and emotional responses (Chattopadhyay, George, & Ng, 2016).

This trajectory arguably reflects a particular instance of a more general, serious limitation of this type of management and organizational behavior research. There appears to be a tendency to lurch between analyzing quantitative demographic data that are relatively easy to collect in large amounts (and considered 'objective' to a significant extent) and generating universalistic diversity theory that tries to extract additional individual psychological variables but struggles to explain in full the many mixed messages of the demographic data. All the data analyzed do not confirm or refine any satisfying theory, and the occasional theory generated still fails to satisfy the data, leading to a cycle of limited, or stumbling, progress in understanding.

One paper did point out this 'black box' problem of the gulf between demographic patterns in organizations and the organizational behavior of teams and employees, about a decade after the body of work had started to accumulate (Lawrence, 1997). Lawrence (1997) noted the theoretical complexity of diversity's effects in organizations and proposed four directions for trying to resolve this in future research – deeper multidimensional explanations, dynamic nonlinear models, identifying factors that lead to demographic distributions, and studying process alongside predictors and outcomes.

Whether or not subsequent research on diversity in organizations has addressed or pursued these four directions, and to what extent, is a very big and uncertain question. Certainly one danger is that quantitative research continues to generate an excessive identification of variables – personality traits, environmental perceptions, contextual conditions – that offer tiny fragments of explanation of what's inside the black box of workplace diversity, fragments that don't add up a coherent bigger picture. How to amass this evidence and make sense of it in a way that might genuinely guide organizational decisions and actions seems vexing and perplexing (Briner, Denyer, & Rousseau, 2009).

Diversity: 'Good' or 'Bad' for Teams and Organizations?

In the 1990s and early 2000s diversity management in developed economies continued to emerge, as organizations considered HR and management practices like diverse teams, diversity training, minority employee resource or affinity groups, mentoring, leadership development, and so on (e.g. Jayne & Dipboye, 2004).

Relatively early on, reviews of management research on diversity and teams acknowledged that diversity had simultaneous mixed effects and could act as a 'double-edged sword' on thoughts, emotions and behaviors affecting performance (Milliken & Martins, 1996). One persistent limitation seemed to be that such research was fairly intent on trying to establish whether diversity was positive or negative, or 'good' or 'bad', in its 'main effects' on various outcomes like performance and well-being, despite such questions inevitably being subject to many caveats (van Knippenberg & Schippers, 2007). Papers worked at the problem by trying to establish 'types' or 'dimensions' of diversity, difference or attribute that might operate differently. One classic dichotomous example of this was to distinguish surface diversity (overt, demographic, and biological) from deep diversity (flexible, attitudinal, and informational) (Harrison, Price, & Bell, 1998). The implication was dressed up in theoretical language but really often boiled down to a sense that organizational actors needed to get past visible categories, demographics, and stereotypes if they were to appreciate the more functional, deeper, meaningful, and useful human attributes underneath.

In tandem with this typing of different differences, quantitative management research, almost always on diverse teams, would try to model moderator and mediator variables to shed further light on diversity's 'good' and/or 'bad' influences. Moderator variables could be included to show when, where, and for whom diversity would operate differently, and mediators could be included to show how/why (e.g. Mohammed & Angell, 2004; Pelled, Eisenhardt & Xin, 1999). Arguably one problem here is that as studies and findings accumulate, a mixed picture and long list of team member variables emerges – such as conflict, time, interdependence, team personality traits, debate and decision norms, information sharing, leadership, beliefs, and more. Associations may feel unreliable, inconsistent or difficult to reconcile to the reader of such research. The implications tend to be of the unwieldy form that diversity types are variously good, bad or neutral in their effects at different times, for different teams, and under different conditions.

Overall, and in review, the 'bad' and 'good' perspectives of this body of team or workgroup diversity research became referred to in theoretical terms as the 'social categorization' perspective of disruptive ingroup/outgroup classifications, and the 'information/decision-making' perspective of creative, valuable expert discussions, respectively (van Knippenberg & Schippers, 2007). In short, diversity was either driving a wedge through teams or leading to useful discussions -but with a tangle of processes in between and a potentially large range of different types of differences and perceptions of them among team members to start with.

In terms of theory, the main theories were mostly social psychological and located behind the negative predictions of the social categorization theory – similarity-attraction theory, social identity theory, self-categorization theory. Furthermore, researchers were potentially misusing the theories by deploying them in a simplistic way to hypothesize that diversity leads to 'us-them' feelings within a team and thus has negative effects as people feel more liking and attraction towards others they deem similar to themselves (van Knippenberg, de Dreu & Homan, 2004). In their categorization-elaboration model (CEM), van Knippenberg et al (2004) reemphasize this point and argue through their model that any attribute of team diversity can lead to positive or negative effects. Ultimately, they argued that the effects of diversity depend on the working context and if team members notice and process such differences in ways that positively help with completion of a task or negatively feed into intergroup biases. To some extent, this appeared to be simply rephrasing the overall problem and urging caution with this type of team diversity research.

Returning to the typing of diversity's different differences (i.e. gender, age, expertise, tenure, personality etc.) – the typologies were inconsistent, proliferating, and not shown to be of consistent or clear explanatory value when findings were reviewed in several meta-analytic papers and reviews, which aggregated findings doing studies of compiled sets of studies. These category or classificatory labels for diversity were seemingly arbitrary, except they tried to make some rough distinctions between background characteristics, in terms of demography, skills, and attitudes/values. For example:

1. In a relatively early meta-analysis, Bowers, Pharmer, and Salas (2000) found a lack of significant effects of ability, personality and gender diversity or similarity on team performance.
2. In another meta-analysis, Webber and Donahue (2001) looked at whether 'highly job-related' or 'less job-related' diversity attributes had clear effects on team cohesion and performance. Results showed that neither type had any appreciable effects.
3. In a third meta-analysis of team demography and outcomes, Horwitz and Horwitz (2007) looked at the effects of 'task-related' and 'bio-demographic' diversity types on social integration and performance. They found a small positive effect of task-related diversity on performance but virtually no support for any other hypotheses or any effects.
4. Joshi and Roh (2009) meta-analyzed the effects of 'relations-oriented' and 'task-oriented' diversity on performance. They found very weak (but statistically significant) effects, negative and positive, for relations and task diversity, respectively. In addition, this was one of the first reviews to explore some significant effects of context – effects varied depending on the industry type, the broader occupational representation, team interdependence, and team type. Yet they note as 'troubling' how they "were also limited in our ability to code contextual variables, as the studies' descriptions of research settings and team tasks were often scanty" (Joshi and Roh, 2009, p.621).
5. Finally, Bell et al. (2011) used Harrison and Klein's (2007) conceptualizations of diversity as 'variety' (categories or ratios), 'separation' (incremental attitudinal differences), and disparity (power and status inequalities) to meta-analyze team diversity and performance. Again, they found some small positive and negative effects for differences in some expertise and demographics but many unrelated findings regardless of diversity conceptualization. They conclude that in team diversity research, "unclear results and mixed conclusions are pervasive... attributed to a consistent oversimplification of diversity... Making statements that suggest diversity is "good," "bad," or unrelated to team performance without specifying the variable of interest and the way in which diversity is conceptualized, is a flawed approach" (Bell et al., 2011, p.730).

It is quite alarming in some ways that such a thriving and ongoing program of research has described its own sense of progress over decades as equivocal, inconclusive, and inconsistent on several, recurrent occasions in top-tier international reviews of world-class management research (Joshi, Liao, & Roh, 2011). Furthermore, Bell et al. (2011), based on their work, seemed to be suggesting that efforts to aggregate diversity into categories of different difference should be scrapped, and researchers should return to where they started – trying to gather data on individual demographic variables and their own particular black boxes.

Variants on this kind of research emerge, as authors try to circle the problem afresh, but often with the same or only slightly modified theories, designs, and statistical tools. For example, Shemla, Meyer, Greer, and Jehn (2016) argue that going forward what matters is perceptions of group diversity, and gaining more clarity and consistency on how people see the (dis)similarities and splits in groups and their effects. In a way, this again reflects a return to the initial 'black box' problem, which presumably demographers had hoped they would be able to skirt around by collecting and analyzing supposedly 'objective' demographic workforce records and relating them to other perceptions and outcomes. There is also the challenging issue of considering diversity in terms of multiple levels of analysis, where the vast majority of this kind of research has focused on the team level (e.g. Nielsen, 2010). One exception to this is the work of Orlando Richard, who has linked diversity to strategies and industry environments at the firm or organization level of analysis (e.g. Richard, Murthi, & Ismail, 2007). However, arguably this work reproduces many of the issues of team-level research but at a higher level of analysis.

In sum, despite an impressive body of work and hypothesis testing in management research over the last few decades, findings on team and organizational diversity haven't stood up well to reviews and the hopes of accumulating reliable and meaningful knowledge about its effects. At best, research seems to circle around addressing ideas of context and conceptualization, repeating that diversity can mean different things to different people in different settings, which future research should keep trying to capture. Moderators and mediators in quantitative analyses give some further insights, but only in a piecemeal way, as they offer up lots of 'ifs and buts' to diversity's effects. We end up only being certain that diversity – of race and gender in teams, for example – can be sometimes good, sometimes bad, depending on a myriad of other factors around measurement, perceptions, context, task, team norms, strategy, time, and industry.

This research leads to a certain kind of progress and understanding but is ultimately only one kind. Other chapters of this book will argue that critical approaches to studying diversity offer various alternatives that can overcome some of the issues around appreciating the context and meaning of diversity in organizations. However, given that a pluralism of diversity research in management is likely to continue, much of it building on the studies mentioned previously but also taking other paths and streams, this chapter concludes by drawing on some other loose ends of quantitative and managerial research that may continue to develop and yield new insights and avenues of inquiry.

The Endurance and Persistence of 'Mainstream' Diversity Research in Organizations

While pointing out some shortcomings of meta-analyses and quantitative self-report surveys on team diversity it would be foolish to ignore the many shades of grey and related forms of diversity management research that complement them, although a single chapter here necessitates a selective analysis rather than an exhaustive one. There is much research that would probably not be classified as being fully critical on the one hand, or fully quantitative or managerial in its approach, on the other – research looking at case studies, or qualitative analyses of HR diversity practices, for example. There is also theoretical and quantitative work on diversity that is continually trying to innovate and move beyond some of the limitations of oversimplified self-report survey conceptualizations and hypothesis testing. What is 'mainstream' versus 'alternative' organizational research will always be in the eye of the beholder to an extent, and always end up being a matter of degree. Although journals, theories, paradigms, institutions and methods do offer some lines of demarcation, even strong ones in some cases, there is no particular monopoly on understanding or ironclad boundary that cannot be crossed for forging insights and aiding in the development of ideas (Oswick et al., 2011).

It is a theme this book will return to – how the interplay of theories, methods, and research styles affects critical representations of organizational diversity (Van Maanen, Sørensen, & Mitchell, 2007). It feels uncomfortable to have to dismiss one approach wholesale and wholly embrace another. The value of 'mainstream' approaches to diversity and its management is likely to continue to prove itself, even if it does so relatively uncritically, unevenly, and only producing a certain kind of knowledge or truth.

Certainly, there are examples of how managerial, quantitative research on workforce diversity continues to refine our understandings of it beyond linear, cross-sectional self-report studies linking predictors and outcomes. Research on diversity *faultlines*, for instance, considers how teams and collectives can split and re-organize according to similarity/ diversity along multiple attributes (e.g. Lau & Murnighan, 1998). In faultline terms, therefore, a team of young Hispanic women performing low-skilled work alongside old White men in professional or managerial roles might exhibit a particularly strong triple 'split' or fracture across age, ethnicity, and gender lines. Research on the faultlines of diverse teams continues to develop, albeit sometimes asserting relatively anodyne conclusions, such as team splits being more likely when team members perceive their diversity as threatening (Spoelma & Ellis, 2017).

Beyond faultlines, *social network analysis* has always offered a different quantitative way of conceptualizing and operationalizing diversity in terms of patterns of tie and social connection, perhaps due in no small part to its interdisciplinary origins (Kilduff & Kelemen, 2001). Social network research on diversity in the workplace continues to emerge, although not particularly frequently, perhaps because of the relatively demanding nature of the methodology. Again, one is tempted to suggest, critically, that many of the questions and conclusions end up being anodyne. For example, one study essentially finds that to build social capital and perform with high creativity, teams of diverse MBA students need to share more knowledge with each other ('bonding'), as well as with others outside the team ('bridging') (Han, Han, & Brass, 2014). Despite the technically proficient execution of the study, the practical implications for managers amount to little more than a paragraph of generic suggestions of training and support for teams around relationships and knowledge of teamwork.

There is a tension or trade-off in that as quantitative methodologies offer more detailed and valuable insights into diversity, they become more complex and challenging to employ, and do not substitute for important, interesting, and imaginative theoretical questions about the nature of difference in working lives (Alvesson & Gabriel, 2013). We need to recognize what we do not know about diversity, what we may never know in any stable sense, and what we can and cannot come to know through a series of statistical associations. Ironically, the only answer may be to maintain an appropriate *diversity* of knowledge production about diversity itself. In that spirit, Michael Zyphur (2009) has suggested switching between multiple 'analytic mindsets' by using more than one type of analysis in a single study or on a particular dataset or setting (although again this does seem demanding in terms of study design and statistical skills). If multiple regression allows us to model relationships between predictor and outcome variables, multilevel models can show us more about nested social and political effects of communities and wider structures, and latent class analysis (LCA) can allow us to classify data into configurational 'types' of phenomena. By triangulating these methods and analyses more carefully, we should inevitably get a fuller picture – although research practices seem to lag behind this level of collaboration and sophistication. Yet once again, large data sets and sophisticated methods are of limited value if the perspective they adopt and the questions they ask still result in anodyne punchlines that reproduce relatively self-evident ideas. These include prominent international journal papers that study hundreds of employees and data points simply to reassert the notion that diverse teams can conflict and split, or that organizations need to reflect the diversity of representation in their local and regional communities (e.g. Leslie, 2017). This work may gradually improve our understanding with hard data – but whether it is relevant and enlightening enough to change organizational diversity in practice is debatable.

There is perhaps an argument that *case studies* of diversity in organizations and teams, even when relatively uncritical in their approach, tend to be more influential because of the richer, more accessible, and more vivid descriptions of practice they tend to provide. One relatively enduring example of this is Ely and Thomas' (2001) study of teams of internationally diverse professionals, which identified three types of approach or 'diversity perspective' that varied in their degree of enthusiasm for integrating cultural diversity into the core work of the firm. The accessibility, simplicity, and parsimony of the three types of diversity perspective and their common sense thematic labels – discrimination-and-fairness, access-and-legitimacy, and integration-and-learning – provide researchers and practitioners with a nice shorthand for describing types of organizational diversity management scenarios or cultures. HR and international HR research also can take a case study approach, which starts to adopt a (slightly) more critical perspective in acknowledging that not all firms readily embrace diversity-based ideals and values, and can experience a range of tensions in trying to implement diversity practices, between the local and the global, for example (e.g. Lauring, 2013).

Nevertheless, most of the criticisms of slavishly mainstream managerial and psychological approaches to understanding diversity management discussed earlier in this chapter still stand. Changes in terminology can reflect slight conceptual advances and co-option of more critical ideas into the mainstream, although the presentation of the ideas often happens in quite simplistic terms. *Inclusion* is now a hugely popular term used alongside or instead of diversity itself but ultimately boils down to a confusing maxim or at least difficult balance of treating people with a sense of equality, while still respecting their individuality at the same time (Shore et al., 2011). The risk here is that we simply reproduce the same issues but with a different word at the helm.

Special issues of journals devoted to diversity, such as the *Journal of Occupational and Organizational Psychology's* 2013 special issue on diversity, still featured an editorial by way of introduction entitled 'getting diversity at work to work: What we know and what we still don't know' (Guillaume et al., 2013). The series of seven articles making up the special issue arguably continue to pursue certain narrow agendas – specific stereotypes and subtle biases shaping inequalities, findings that diversity on specific attributes like age and tenure are only sometimes valuable or functional, and that some cultures are more open and positive towards diversity than others.

Similar to that editorial, and for its own part, HR research continues to wrestle with the problem of describing and identifying diversity *practices*, and not just whether employees perceive them positively or not but how senior managers 'above the line' make decisions about whether or not to implement and invest in these practices, and when (Kulik, 2014). Kulik's (2014) call for more data on diversity practices at all levels and across organizations is hard to disagree with, but she herself acknowledges the significant coordinated efforts needed to achieve it. It also has echoes of earlier calls for 'big science' in HR more generally (Wall & Wood, 2005), as researchers struggle to open the black box of how different organizations respond differently to different socio-economic and socio-political conditions.

Finally, there are voices discussing the numerical and statistical aspects of measuring diversity – its distributions and indices. It is unclear how these will feature in future research agendas at present, and whether researchers and practitioners will heed advice or act on a more principled approach to representing diversity in terms of statistics. Issues such as missing data, the conceptual significance of summary statistics (e.g. means, standard deviations, ranges, and ratios), curvilinear and asymmetrical diversity effects, and the use of bigger, more open data sources such as census data, are all likely to be periodically explored and revisited (e.g. Allen, Stanley, Williams, & Ross, 2007; Dawson, 2012; King, Dawson, Jensen, & Jones, 2017).

Conclusion

This chapter has tried to summarize and criticize the development of a body of 'mainstream' work on diversity in organizations from around the 1980s onwards, spanning psychology, general management, and HR research and theory. The approaches appear to have grown in part from the ease with which interested parties could collect abundant demographic data from organizations and try to relate it to positive and negative outcomes. However, this has ultimately led to a long-standing, confused picture of mixed effects and caveats, highlighting the tensions and fateful conditions residing in the 'black box' of processes between demographic diversity distributions and outcomes for individuals, teams and organizations. Mainstream debates on diversity, its central issues, and framings are likely to persist in media, organizational practices and research, as they try to clearly present 'what works' for and against moral and instrumental ideals like performance, managerialism, inclusion, equality, and creativity.

With the benefit of hindsight, it is perhaps too easy and unfair to simply point out the shortcomings and omissions of such approaches to diversity, which have provided us with plenty to think about. Particularly so as they are not monolithic and continue to develop their frontiers along a variety of conceptual, methodological, and statistical lines. Over time, some diversity research has improved at accounting for all-important features of organizational *context*, for example, and may continue to do so (Johns, 2017). However, progress along these frontiers is arguably quite fragmented and path-dependent. Often the calls to future research, the journal issue editorials, and the cries for progress may be misguided or unheeded, reproduce the same issues in a different guise, and merely reflect a desperate hope that more data, more science, and better statistical pattern identification will provide clearer answers.

As will be outlined in the next chapter, critical approaches to diversity offer some quite different ways of trying to appreciate and accommodate diversity, although they are not a panacea, and any approach will inevitably struggle to escape the trappings of its own partial perspective. The great irony of trying to understand diversity in organizations and societies is the inherent difficulty, if not impossibility, of trying to get fully behind all the multiple, diverse ways of viewing the subject itself, while always being embedded in it and part of it as a subjective inquirer. There is a need for continuing reflections on these challenging themes of how to apply multiple frames and perspectives to diversity, and how researchers and practitioners of diversity might achieve some sense of rapprochement between critical and mainstream perspectives.

2 Taking a Critical Perspective

Defining critical management and organizational research, on diversity or otherwise, is a daunting prospect, and in some ways antithetical to the idea of critique itself. Nevertheless, this chapter will consider common themes among definitions of critical perspectives and approaches to work, employment, diversity, and organizations. The chapter will start at the general level of management and organization theory and then move toward the more specific approach of applying critical perspectives to diversity and diversity management. Some illustrative examples of critical perspectives and research are also provided. Finally, the chapter will conclude with some reflections on the current progress and future prospects of critical diversity research in organizations, in part as a preface to the remaining chapters of the book, which will cover a range of critical possibilities in relation to diversity.

In some ways, we can define critical perspectives on organizations by what they are not; as existing in opposition to, or as the other side of the coin from some of the (largely) quantitative and incremental management and psychology research discussed in the last chapter. Additionally, as mentioned in the introduction to this book, it is also a question of interdisciplinarity; or the different cultures and paradigms associated with pure science outlooks versus the arts and humanities, with critical perspectives embracing more of the latter. Philosopher and cultural critic, Slavoj Žižek (2001), described critical cultural perspectives as recognizing the everyday social and political struggles towards subjective Truth, whereas technical, rational, scientific projects are more concerned with universal and objective knowledge. A key question for the social sciences going forward is (still) thus surely to consider how complementary these two approaches can be, and whether they can respect the need to more deeply appreciate one another's disciplinary skills, rather than dismissing each other as caricatured opponents out of hand.

In discussing the value of literature and popular nonfiction writing genres, one scholar recently described fellow management thinkers as "a motley crew that includes all walks of life committed to various theoretical, methodological, and political convictions and orientations"

(Styhre 2016, p.170). The more mainstream, positivist researchers believe in "maintaining and further refining, a massive theoretical-methodological apparatus, increasingly fine-tuned to produce better predictions and understandings" (p.170). In contrast, the critical thinkers appear to be "engaging in ceaseless investigation in order to understand managerial activities as a form of social and cultural practice, deeply seated in the thick texture of human societies" (p.170). In any case, one conclusion drawn, and perhaps a more critical one given the author in this instance, is that both sides should recognize "a need to keep the mind attentive to the small and fine-grained nuances surrounding us in everyday life" (p.170). Academic communities simply reproduce the characteristics of diversity in the very scholarship they produce that is seeking to engage, capture and reflect it.

This chapter will not present critical approaches as a panacea – indeed, one of the advantages of criticality is always being able to doubt and wrong-foot oneself – but at least a different set of options, alternatives, strengths, and weaknesses in understanding organizational diversity. Like mainstream approaches, and perhaps even more so, the idea of a critical approach is *not monolithic*. Evaluating and understanding a plurality of critical research can be considerably more challenging than reviewing its more mainstream counterparts, and such effort may not always be rewarded in a straightforward fashion. As just noted, one advantage of a critical approach at perhaps its best, although still not particularly straightforward to achieve, is its inherent *criticality* – the reserving of the right to question everything, including itself, as it wrong-foots taken-for-granted assumptions and imagines (diverse) possibilities for social and organizational change.

This chapter will now turn toward trying to offer some more explicit initial definitions of what a critical approach to, and perspective on, diversity in organizations might look like, followed by some more specific cases and examples of diversity in organizations, given that the last chapter was more abstract in presenting some overarching background.

General Critical Perspectives on Management and Organizations

Critical perspectives on management and organizations can be defined in many different ways. Any account must of necessity be fairly selective and impressionistic. The UK Critical Management Studies (CMS) web portal and community resource defines CMS in terms of the following three paragraphs (Critical Management, 2016, n.p.):

> Critical Management Studies (CMS) is a largely left-wing and theoretically informed approach to management and organisation studies. It challenges the prevailing conventional understanding of

management and organisations. CMS provides a platform for debating radical alternatives whilst interrogating the established relations of power, control, domination and ideology as well as the relations among organisations, society and people.

As an umbrella research orientation CMS embraces various theoretical traditions including anarchism, critical theory, feminism, Marxism, post-structuralism, postmodernism, postcolonialism and psychoanalysis, representing a pluralistic, multidisciplinary field. Having been associated mainly with business/management schools in the United Kingdom and Scandinavia earlier, CMS as a research approach has presence all over the world and is not confined to management/business schools. This suggests that CMS is an approach to doing research rather than a school or tradition, and there is no particular 'right' way of doing CMS.

Denaturalisation, non-performativity and reflexivity are the key features of CMS for some, while critical performativity is something other researchers would argue for. Recently there has also been a rise in discussing alternative forms of organising, including alternatives to the growth-driven neoliberal capitalism. Beyond CMS research, the issue of what it means to be a CMS scholar is of particular concern. Challenging the (class/gender/racial) power structures in academic workplaces and the politics of university life (e.g. around journal publishing, corporatisation, precarity), as well as involvement in activism are among the key themes to be reflected on here.

These three paragraphs offer a fairly comprehensive picture of what it means to take critical perspectives in the social sciences and the study of management and organizations. Different origins, disciplines, worldviews, political identities, and projects are all reflected, as well as recent developments and a recognition of the embeddedness of critical communities within higher education and society. Arguably, there is a greater and more unashamedly value-laden commitment here to engaging inequality and diversity more than mainstream, positivistic approaches to organization science and behavior. Perhaps less apparent, but still fairly evident, is a commitment to philosophy, culture, sociology, the arts and humanities, and more literary and ethically focused social scientific influences. In many ways, a critical approach to diversity can be loosely defined as anything or everything a positivistic approach is not.

Another entry point to a critical social scientific approach is to think in terms of a back catalogue of many key texts and thinkers; intellectual 'giants', largely taken from the twentieth century, but also dating back to Karl Marx, and beyond that, thinkers of antiquity (e.g. Sim, 2004). The legacies and works of these thinkers are often gathered together and presented second hand as a series by major publishers, editors, and specialists – in Routledge's *Critical Thinkers* series, for example (Routledge Taylor & Francis Group, 2017), or Reaktion's *Critical Lives* series (Reaktion Books, 2017). Within organization studies, in the late 1980s, Cooper and Burrell (1988) undertook a shorter, focused series around the giant critical thinkers marking the two opposing views or positions of modernism and postmodernism, the former focused on progress and reason, the latter focused on paradox and indeterminacy. This work continued to drive the development of critical approaches to organizations into the 1990s, often in the form of edited book volumes (e.g. Hassard & Parker, 1993; Reed, 1989; Thompson & McHugh, 1990; Willmott, 1992).

The task of a critical scholar of management, work, and organizations then becomes taking stock of the historical, literary, cultural, social, political and economic milieu of these thinkers. The critical perspectives and politics contained in and expressed through their lives, imaginations, uses of language, and theoretical accounts of society are mined for illuminating theoretical concepts and systems that can be applied, critiqued in turn, and extended to address the lived experiences of those working in twenty-first century organizations. Clearly, the scientific paradigm is almost entirely abandoned in favor of developing powerful arguments and critique for raising awareness of, and emancipating readers from, problematic and contradictory aspects of the status quo of organizations and society. One way of thinking about such a critical quality of mind is surely in terms of sociology and the *sociological imagination*, which invites anyone analyzing human and social structures to keep shifting their perspective across social contexts, and to attend to how personal experiences relate to public issues and injustices (Mills, 1959/2000).

The modernist-postmodernist shift or pivot of the early 1990s was one of the major foci of critical representation affecting how to theorize about and challenge the very ideas of organizing and organization, pushing thought beyond the ideas of more scientific or mechanical structures, functions, and systems. Postmodernism and post-structuralism continue to be influential in understanding that organizations are not made up of freely interacting individuals and given objective structures but rather a sense of self rooted in, and shaped by, complex identity relations governed by language and power (e.g. Alvesson, 2010). These post-structuralist approaches have to some extent supplanted the earlier Marxist core of critiques of work and employment dating back to the 1970s. *Labour process theory*, for instance, which essentially argued that societally embedded capitalist priorities and motives based on cost and profit lead to exploitation of employees and degradation of their work in various settings, is a paradigm that some would argue is in need of updating (Adler, 2007).

However, as shown in the CMS web excerpt previously, there are many other, quite distinctive families and trajectories of critical approaches to have emerged from under a broader critical umbrella. These include *feminist* voices urging recognition that organizations in their many structures are pervasively gendered rather than gender-neutral (Acker, 1990). There are also *psychoanalytic* voices urging recognition that organizations are sites of unconscious desires, fantasies, dreams, nightmares, and deeply symbolic role and relational dynamics that cannot easily be managed or controlled (Gabriel, 1995). Perhaps slower to emerge, but with equally long-standing roots in critical theory, are *postcolonial* perspectives critically examining the historical relations between the global East and West, North and South, and other significant international relations legacies (Frenkel & Shenhav, 2006). There are many more strands of critical thinking on organizations, some (but not all) of which can be explored in the current book to some extent, and many others that will continue to split and reconfigure themselves beyond it. Inevitably, most are concerned with refining paradigms and positions around epistemology and ontology (e.g. Fleetwood, 2005); trying to unpick the layers of influence (e.g.g. material, linguistic, symbolic) that affect our sense of social reality, being and knowledge, which necessarily includes our sense of similarity, diversity, and difference.

In sum, critical research on management and organizations is, among other things, *interdisciplinary, politically challenging* to the status quo, and *stands against notions of a positivistic value-free scientific approach* to organizational systems and realities. In one of the most recent and broadest reviews of the field, Adler, Forbes, and Willmott (2007) pull together other common threads and debates, around addressing issues of domination and resistance, the domination of the profit motive (over other ethical and environmental goals), workers and their lived experiences, and varying agendas of reform and activism. It is also important to recognize the problems and weaknesses the field inevitably faces – around its negative and cynical orientation, its internal debates between structural-material approaches and linguistic, abstract post-structuralist approaches, and the inaccessibility and impracticality of its jargon and philosophizing. Finally, there is recognition of the wide-ranging underlying dictionaries of concepts underpinning sociological, philosophical and cultural fields in critical theory applied to power, social relations, and organizations. For instance, in footnotes, Adler and colleagues (2007) take care to highlight definitions of a few key concepts, such as *positivism, capitalism, patriarchy, racism, imperialism,* and *productivism*. Furthermore, these are only the high-level concepts, many more can be presented in a fuller dictionary (e.g. Macey, 2001).

Other reviews and commentaries on critical management and organization have covered similar overarching themes. Fournier and Grey (2000) address some of the political movements on the Left and Right relating to managers and workers across the latter parts of the twentieth century, as well as the ongoing intellectual criticality involved in questioning movements and taken-for-granted assumptions. Grey (2007) reflects on the different types of relationship critical management and education can and should strive for with the mainstream, concluding that some sort of engagement between the two, however challenging, may well be preferable to different camps ignoring one another or seeming to triumph over each other. Klikauer (2015a) takes an almost opposite approach – questioning whether a critical stance towards management and organizations can be as truly committed to human freedom, emancipation, and radical utopia as the critical theory tradition of the Frankfurt School, a cadre of twentieth-century European social theorists building on the works of Hegel and Marx. One tension inherent to any critical work is that of *reflexivity* – how to criticize something in a self-aware fashion, while acknowledging one's own embeddedness within the system one is attempting to criticize – in this case, managerial capitalism. The hope is that these tensions can be productive in some way, rather than diminishing the force of critical work.

As maintained here, critical perspectives inherently produce and position themselves within their own diversity and relations to diversity, rejecting the worldviews associated with a detached scientific perspective on an objective world. However, understanding and addressing the inequalities and unbalanced power relationships across diverse groups and individuals in work and organization is central to the mission of almost all critical organizational projects. Ultimately, by embracing their own diversity, as well as the diversity they are studying, and (re)producing it across a diverse range of approaches, critical management scholars create a considerable number of tensions and viewpoints, some perhaps more productive than others.

The other chapters in this book are therefore dedicated to exploring some of those possibilities, and relating some considerations for advancing a critical interdisciplinary agenda on diversity in organizations. One recurring issue is that if there will always be (organizational) diversity, and it cannot and should not be 'managed' in a conventional way, we need to decide which philosophical and practical stances we can adopt towards forms of irreducible pluralism. One tentative answer is simply to adopt a *pragmatic* perspective of the kind put forward by the liberal philosopher, Richard Rorty (1989). A pragmatist philosophy would be concerned with emphasizing themes of appreciation for *public* suffering, humiliation, and solidarity in diversity but also seeing the more *private irony* in that some differences are not there to be reconciled or subordinated to liberal democracy. We can only ever *contingently redescribe* the latter kinds of differences as webs of meaning and narrative, often by way of the arts and humanities as much as the sciences. Of course, there are no easy answers – and navigating these blurred public and private realms of diversity presupposes no particular respect for workplaces, managers, or organizational boundaries as they express and work through differences, linguistically and materially. With that in mind, we can turn more specifically to critical perspectives on diversity in organizations.

Specific Critical Perspectives on Diversity in Organizations and Diversity Management

If there is now quite a substantial body of work on critical management and organization studies, there is considerably less explicitly focusing on diversity, equality, and inclusion per se. However, as noted previously, diversity and related themes are often implicit in a lot of critical theorizing across various social scientific fields and paradigms and samples.

More specific works will be cited elsewhere in this volume but of the clearest overall places to start is a guest editorial for a 2010 special issue on 'rethinking difference through critical perspectives' in the journal *Organization* (Zanoni et al., 2010). In their editorial, Zanoni et al. (2010) date the root of 'critical diversity studies' to the mid-1990s, which draws on a range of critical theories similar to those outlined earlier to challenge the emergence of 'diversity management' and its potential neglect of 'equal opportunities'. They also note three main targets for diversity critique – a positivistic view that simplifies the concept of identity or identities, a downplaying of the role of diverse organizational contexts, and inadequate theorizations of the forms and levels of power dynamics that shape diversity. Critical approaches address these problems through a greater focus on *discourse*, in terms of the text and talk from which diversity emerges in contexts of social power relations. They also consider the *agency* of minorities in resisting powerful groups and shaping their own identities, the everyday and hierarchical experiences of *inequalities* in particular contexts, and the *intersectionality* where multiple differences combine to shape distinctive experiences. Broadly, the editorial finishes by summarizing the four articles in the special issue, calling for similar and more radical and alternative critical diversity research in organizations that engages closely with emancipation and change in various social contexts. It is worth summarizing here the key aspects of the four studies included in the special issue to give some examples and insights into these 2010 articles deemed symptomatic of a critical approach:

1. Kalonaityte (2010) uses *postcolonial theory* to consider a hierarchy of cultural and ethnic identity constructions in a Swedish school for adults. The paper is critical in accounting for unequal power relations, non-traditional forms of resistance, and distinctive ordering of identity groups in particular national and organizational contexts.

In postcolonial terms, diversity (management) entails an ambivalence about the boundaries and superiority of Europe as a Western power, with language, recruitment, religion and other cultural norms reflecting a space where privileged and disadvantaged identities come into conflict.

2. Boogaard and Roggeband (2010) adopt a *critical intersectional perspective* to look at how gender and ethnicity intersect with organizational identity to shape inequalities and paradoxes, where promoting positive identities and valuable competencies around one type of diversity can reproduce inequalities for other types. Specifically, they conducted an in-depth case study of the Dutch police force. Intersectionality showed how some employees – an ethnic majority woman, for example – can be both advantaged and disadvantaged at the same time. Inadvertently, groups and individuals with various combinations of diverse identity can thwart the opportunities of themselves and others by taking up various unique positions in an organization or playing up to stereotypes. Minorities may be able to use certain skills, preferences, and stereotypical traits to confer small personal advantages in the short-term, while the inequalities in the organization as a whole remain largely unchanged. In sum, their agency (choices) exists in contradictory relationships with the structure (organizational hierarchies and inequalities).

3. Swan (2010) uses the popular *cultural and visual imagery* of a corporate mosaic photograph to highlight how it ironically serves to contain racial diversity within a grid of sameness in its *commodified representation of difference*. The paper is critical in arguing that visual techniques for representing differences are sites of power struggles that privilege certain attitudes towards diversity, often marginalizing more uncomfortable truths behind PowerPoint slides, mass-marketing materials, manuals, and games. This incorporates Marxist notions of commodification and ownership in relation to critiques of capitalism, as well as struggles over misleading and harmful visual channels of communication and symbolic influence. Ultimately, these metaphors reinforce a simplified 'business case' for diversity – exploiting and appropriating difference for commercial gain only. Viewers are placated to some extent by the concession to differences, but difficulties are obscured or assimilated, and the majority only accepts so much difference in consolidating power.

4. Finally, Tomlinson and Schwabenland (2010) look further at the tension between a 'business case' in terms of diversity's financial and instrumental benefits to organizations (e.g. customers, reputation, markets, strategies), and a 'social justice case', valuing moral arguments for equality and human rights irrespective of any economic costs or gains. By interviewing stakeholders of a UK

charity from the voluntary (non-profit) sector, these authors are able to critically investigate in this distinctive context how managers and diversity specialists locally make sense of *ambiguities and contradictions between moral and economic views of diversity.* They find local variation in whether individuals or teams privilege one over the other, or try to inter-relate them both – this sometimes involved dilemmas, at other times reconciliations. A lot depended on resolving tensions between serving diverse staff and diverse customers, but more often than not, moral and business cases (or *discourses*) for communicating about diversity are intertwined – and one cannot simply be abandoned entirely in favor of the other.

Many other scholars within organization studies and across the social sciences have published work that deploys a range of related critical approaches before and after these four pieces from a 2010 journal issue. Space constraints preclude a more comprehensive review in a single chapter or even volume, although the remaining chapters of this volume will try to draw in a wide representation of influential critical diversity scholars and approaches, doing so in relation to a series of specific themes to offer coherence and direction.

Renewed Progress and Prospects for Critical Perspectives on Diversity in Organizations

We can nevertheless finish this chapter on a general survey of critical management studies (and diversity) by considering some of what has happened since 2010. Specifically, this chapter concludes by covering three inter-related areas in this regard. First, there are ongoing debates over how critical approaches can 'make a difference', politically and practically, to the lived experience of managers and those in organizations, and to what extent. Second, there are the recent editorial initiatives at journals that take an explicitly critical stance in welcoming diverse article types. Finally, we can finish with a brief summary of more published examples of critical perspectives on diversity in organizations, as above with the 2010 special issue of *Organization* but drawing on more recent articles post-2010. As might be expected, any selection of such articles must be arbitrary, but the hope is that it can also be illustrative of the ongoing range in progress and prospects of such critical approaches, reflecting on their contributions and challenges.

Taking the 'making a difference' issue first, we can refer to a more recent debate among critical scholars concerning a project of *critical performativity* in how we relate to organizations outside of the main-stream. Indeed, the debate here is about whether or not it is possible or desirable to close the gap between the cynical detachment of critical theory and the influential realm of the social, active, engaged practice of managers and leaders (Gond et al., 2016). There are difficulties across critical approaches in how active they can be – in terms of discursively challenging the language of management and organizations but also trying to address inequalities, injustices, environmental, and other societal harms in more material terms. Inevitably, this is a structure-agency problem – how do you act freely to radically criticize organizations and their practices while simultaneously occupying a structural position within a university or other organization, which may involve conforming to those practices in a self-defeating fashion? The degrees of change and agency theorized about over the last 50 years can make for dismal and confusing reading (Caldwell, 2005), and it is uncomfortable in some ways to be anti-performative – to suggest that certain things should merely be deconstructed, abandoned, or viewed cynically as utterly 'unmanageable' and irrational. Perhaps the best we can hope for, or what we must hope for, is that powerful critical arguments, and the raising of awareness around various perspectives and voices experiencing inequalities in different contexts, are and will continue to be what drives organizational change, even if it does not always seem that way. The managerialist ideas of rational managers that can control and direct organizations in progressive directions are remarkably persistent (Cabantous & Gond, 2011; Klikauer, 2015b). How to make critical perspectives practical and accessible beyond the ivory towers of universities, while retaining a critical spirit within some sort of ivory tower, is likely to continue to shape the very essence of twenty-first-century criticism of organizations and higher education (Parker & Jary, 1995).

The second concluding point here is perhaps a source of optimism, in that academic journals, whether particularly widely read or not, continue to experiment with innovative types of critical article, contribution, 'slot', or 'corner' within the contents. *Organization Studies*, one of the leading critical management journals in Europe (if not globally), has a new essay section called 'X and Organization Studies'. This special critical section allows for critical philosophical and cultural concepts – anger, boredom, color, ruins, irony, theatre – to be more freely explored in terms of how they reveal under-explored aspects of organization (Holt et al. 2016). Another example comes from a more explicitly sociological journal, *Work, Employment and Society*, which has instituted from 2009 a section called 'on the front line' (Taylor et al. 2009). This section emphasizes the importance of an *ethnographic* and *emic* (insider, native or local) tradition to social critique of work and organization and has featured first-hand accounts of experiences from various minority groups and work settings. A third example comes from the journal *Organization*, which has developed a section for 'Acting Up' (alongside another one entitled 'Speaking Out'), where pieces that shun theory in favor of activism and taking action can be valued (Prichard & Benschop, 2018). Similarly, many journals will tend to have 'provocations', 'controversies', and other editorial spaces for dialogue and alternative agendas, albeit often at the margins of a lot of other, less critical research. As with any institution, the world of academic publishing has its own struggles with diversity and inclusion, just like any other organizational setting or organizing problem might face. Many subfields will doubtless continue to discuss and fight for their own critical and contributory turfs within and without organization and management studies (e.g. Hughes, 2018).

Finally, to bring the focus back to diversity more specifically, it seems valuable to share a few more recent (post-2010) general examples of studies with critical perspectives on diversity in organizations before moving on to more specific themes linking critical thought and diversity.

1. Dougherty and Goldstein Hode (2016) use focus groups and interviews in a large public U.S. organization, discussing its sexual harassment policy. Adopting a discursive feminist lens, they show that the way such policies are written and interpreted reveals a 'binary web' of struggles that tended to put men and women in hierarchical subject positions. It is concluded that such policies are far from rational.

2. Varman and Al-Amoudi (2016) conduct a field study in an Indian village, drawing on the work of Judith Butler to show how the organizational practices of a Coca-Cola bottling plant act as a source of violence that renders local farmers and workers highly vulnerable. The workers are 'derealized' (dismissed) and dispossessed, and although they resist through acts of protest, the violence and exploitation against them goes unchecked.

3. Dashtipour and Rumens (2018) use the historical case example of a Swedish anti-racist commercial magazine (*Gringo*), and theoretical concepts from Foucault and Lacan, to show how such acts of entrepreneurship can instigate social change through anxiety, disturbance, and disruption. The ironic content of the magazine allowed its Muslim founders to challenge normal notions of Swedish society and inequality.

4. Friedman et al. (2017) use survey data from the Great British Class Survey and interviews to show the significant underrepresentation of actors from working-class origins in the profession, as well as their occupational struggles even when they have entered it. In the cultural and creative industries (CCI), class inequality is deeply rooted in the various 'capitals' – social, economic and cultural networks and connections – that actors may or may not be able to draw upon.

5. Waites (2017) looks at transnational social movement organizations from across the UK and Commonwealth that form a network of national NGOs striving to decolonize human rights issues traditionally shaped by imperial international relations. The paper's findings trace a

complex political restructuring of the global queer community around various positions on lesbian, gay, bisexual, transgender, and intersex (LGBTI) human rights.

6. Gatrell (2019) undertakes a UK qualitative 'netnographic' study of Internet discussions among employed breastfeeding mothers, drawing on theory from Margaret Shildrick and Julia Kristeva. The study highlights the tensions between being a 'proper', healthy mother and an ideal worker. The lactating body of a breastfeeding mother can be treated with hostility, 'abjection' (disgust/loathing), and exclusion via workplace practices and co-worker behaviors.

Conclusion

This chapter has tried to sketch out what it means to take a critical perspective on organizations, management studies, and diversity in organizations. It seems safe to admit this is not an easy task and is likely to continue to evolve. However, in many ways a critical perspective is perhaps simply everything a so-called 'mainstream' one is not. It is often (but not always) qualitative in method and analysis. It typically eschews scientific and mathematical framings in favor of theory from sociology, philosophy, the arts, and humanities. It digs deeper into the social and international contexts of work and the many different forms that the lived experience of work can take – often calling into question the idea that there are rational, functional, or uniform ways of defining 'managers' and 'organizations' and 'diversity'. It also takes up various political positions and reflects on its own embedded role in shaping and combatting inequalities and representations of difference against a backdrop of capitalism, climate change, patriarchy, postcolonialism, unconscious drives, and other prominent cultural frames of reference. However, any type of critical perspective is far from being a panacea. More often than not, it is likely to revolve around obscure concepts and thinkers, heightened awareness of problems rather than practical solutions, disagreements around the role of language versus more material structures, or vast swathes of fragmented sociology research. Critical scholars tend to be aware of these issues and develop responses to them accordingly, although embracing the idea of diverse subjectivities in this way has limitations of its own.

This book is therefore arguing that critical perspectives on diversity, at the very least, offer to open up engaging re-descriptions of difference, identities, and the need for social change. They accept and reflect the idea that diversity and difference are always in motion in the world of work – how they are experienced, talked about, and represented. Organization studies is surely the more lively and colorful a field for this and would lose a lot if it relied solely on the mainstream perspectives of the previous chapter – ones that try to fix diversity and track elusive universal effects from a standpoint of positivism.

The remaining chapters of this book therefore continue to try to open up some critical angles on diversity in organizations, partly in the hope of winning people over to incorporating them more into future research and practice. It tries to strike a balance between a delimited focus on work most relevant to management and organizations, while remaining open to critical interdisciplinary boundaries and horizons that stretch the way we think about identity and difference. The concern is more with engaging with a variety of critical perspectives or themes, rather than claiming to get too deeply or exhaustively involved in specific debates, where viewpoints inevitably differ, and there is always a risk of mis-representing critical thinkers and schools of thought.

Part II

Defining Aspects of a Critical Perspective on Diversity in Organizations

3 History

Talking about history is not necessarily synonymous with adopting a critical perspective on diversity in organizations, but to get beyond the surface of seeing history as merely 'the facts' or 'the past', it must soon become so. As the American historian Ira Berlin (2015, p.1) puts it at the outset of his book on the history of slavery in the US, "History is not about the past; it is about arguments we have about the past. And because it is about arguments we have, it is about us".

It is perhaps obvious then to say that the very ideas of organization, management, and diversity (management), as well as all related concepts (e.g. Globalization, capitalism), have history – or, more importantly, histories – that we might try to trace or understand from our present. Nevertheless, as with many critical developments in organization studies, there has been a turn, a 'historical turn' discussed and identified in management (Clark & Rowlinson, 2004), going back explicitly only about fifteen years or so, although implicitly much longer, it could be argued. Specialized journals such as *Business History* and *Management & Organizational History* continue to focus explicitly on this relation, with articles continuing to (occasionally) emerge in more general management outlets too.

Related terms such as 'historicism' and 'historiography' start to reflect the critical complexity and urgency of understanding the reality, coherence, patterns, and competing readings and writings of history. If historicism reflects general debates about the influence of history, historiography perhaps reflects more specific critical concerns with the practices of how history is written and interpreted, by whom, and about whom (Iggers, 1995). This is precisely where diversity and inclusion come in – in terms of the diverse people writing history about other diverse people, and which people and stories are included or excluded from dominant accounts or readings of history and social change. Most twentieth-century critical readings of history in terms of business have tended toward some sort of Marxist and/or humanist reading, perhaps increasingly Foucauldian also, around the themes of power, domination, and emancipation in modern capitalist societies and cultures around the globe. As Iggers (2005, p. 476) notes about the new cultural history since the 1960s, "it is generally very critical of the political and social status quo."

In terms of research and practice in organizations, we can adopt some fairly simple starting points for critically considering the importance of history and historiography. A couple that can be presented here come from Zickar (2015) and Suddaby and Foster (2017). Neither article is overtly critical, which in itself is telling in terms of there not being a sharp dividing line between mainstream and critical research. A general point then is that there is something to be said for papers that open up critical ideas that implicate diversity in organizations in more mainstream, accessible ways.

First, Zickar (2015) helpfully outlines four types of historical inquiry: (1) biographical research viewing history through a single individual's life; (2) topical research tracing the history of a topic through time; (3) a historical characterization of a particular time and place; and (4) microhistories that focus in greater detail on a single event. Zickar (2015) also goes on to cover other issues concerning history and organizations – namely, the use of various data sources and methods, including qualitative and quantitative archival, secondary data, as well as ways of evaluating what makes 'good historical research' (spoiler alert: it is honest, critical, and reflexive).

Second, Suddaby and Foster (2017) take a slightly more theoretical, bigger picture view and outline four perspectives on history and organizational change, each of which contains implicit assumptions:

1. *History-as-fact:* Assumes that history makes change very difficult and largely locks us into particular paths for significant periods of time. Probably the most positivist, objective, and least critical, of the four.
2. *History-as-power:* A materialist view, still fairly objective on history and change, but assumes that agency can occur via sudden revolutionary overthrows of dominant power coalitions.
3. *History-as-sensemaking:* Assumes that history and change occur through experience and consciousness – a phenomenological view. History and change are retrospectively 'made sense of' as individuals and groups discover interpretations that seem to fit their identities and sense of reality. This is a flexible view around creating shared interpretations.
4. *History-as-rhetoric:* Assumes that not only is history a matter of interpretation, but that such interpretations can be manipulated for strategic purposes, and such narratives are indeed created to drive change. Emphasizes high degrees of agency and persuasion.

Although such a four-fold scheme is perhaps in some ways an artefact of how articles get written around simple devices, organizations could do a lot worse than use these four perspectives as talking points to reflect on their own history and diversity, and particularly important, to surface and critique assumptions behind them. Of course, in some lively historical case studies, companies such as IBM and Adidas, for example, do go through some version of this type of process, thinking about how the organization was founded, what it stands for, and how it might best reinvent itself (e.g. Ind, Iglesias & Schultz, 2015).

Having given some general overview of a historical perspective, the remainder of this chapter will turn to some more specific ways in which history connects with diversity in organizations, ways which continue to be relevant today. It is perhaps worth mentioning that the aim is not to get drawn into deeper debates about the role of history or time, although we can bear in mind that these will continue to be debated and refined by historians and critical theorists, as per some of the general perspectives outlined previously, among others.

History and Diversity

In chapter one, some of the history of how diversity in organizations became a research topic from the second half of the twentieth century onwards was explored, but we are concerned with something broader here. Linking history to diversity offers vast possibilities – although we might narrow it to some extent by prioritizing themes like slavery, colonial-imperial international relations, and the struggles of many minority groups for equality, rights, and recognition in various organizational contexts. As noted previously, we can read history in many different ways, and diversity in organizations is no exception to that. We might focus on particular ideologies from across the Left and Right of the political spectrum as they have historically evolved and have been related to attitudes toward diversity, equality, and inclusion. Then there are many events, institutions, and figures that might feature more or less strongly in a particular historiography.

In the interests of space and focus – three main types of critical historiography deemed highly relevant to diversity and organizations are highlighted here: slavery, forgotten histories and erasures, and colonialism/post-colonialism.

Slavery

Just the word slavery might conjure up an unusual set of images and associations, not always of relevance to the modern organization. Yet, whether viewed from a critical perspective or not, both the legacy of older forms of slavery, and the continuation of the emergence of forms of so-called modern slavery, do continue to define work and organization in many diverse settings. Crane (2013) puts estimates of slave numbers in today's global workforce at anywhere between twelve million and thirty million people – including workers on Asian fishing trawlers, migrant agricultural workers in Spain, Brazilian charcoal-making camps, Uzbek cotton, West African cocoa, and in most countries, developed or developing. Practices continue across global supply chains and migration patterns, upheld by a complex mixture of institutional arrangements and norms, as well as being relatively opaque and convenient to more remote supply chain partners.

Even notwithstanding these explicit forms of modern slavery, the 'image' or legacy of domination and slavery can be applied to or operating in any organization to varying degrees, viewed from a more critical perspective. One of Gareth Morgan's (1997) images of organization is the *instrument of domination* metaphor – an organization as a physical and/or psychic prison, a place where some sort of aggressive oppression of a group with less power occurs – which could even extend to oppression of animals and the natural environment.

One stand-out paper from critical management studies on slavery is Cooke (2003). The paper argues that American slavery in the antebellum period before the Civil War has been unjustly excluded and denied from accounts of modern management, which tend to focus on railroads, industrialization, and the efficiency principles of scientific management and assembly lines instead. Cooke (2003) makes a strong case that slavery has fundamental relevance to modern management, in terms of its lingering influences of industrial discipline, the very notion of 'a manager' (e.g. on a plantation), and anti-African-American racism. Ruef and Harness (2009) continue to develop this line of thought, going further back to consider the ancient, 'pre-modern' world and Roman republic and empire, alongside the US antebellum South. Again, we see enduring themes of organization and diversity, in terms of elites, hired managers, leadership styles, activism, revolt, land ownership, private enterprise, and unfree labor. Distinctions between 'pre-modern' and 'modern' management discourse are not as clear as some research might have us believe (Ruef & Harness, 2009).

One final, perhaps slightly more positive point about the legacy of slavery, is that it can draw our attention to an opposing, resistant concept of *emancipation*. A stand out critical management studies paper exists on this concept too, a paper by Alvesson and Willmott (1992), who revisit its roots more formally in the Frankfurt School and the Critical Theory tradition. Emancipation is "the process through which individuals and groups become freed from repressive social and ideological conditions, in particular those that place socially unnecessary restrictions upon the development and articulation of human consciousness" (Alvesson & Willmott, 1992, p. 432). It is typically a painful process of resistance, fear, and overcoming restrictions imposed by a powerful majority, although it may vary in terms of its degree and target.

One example linking it to history and diversity is to again look at US slavery on plantations. Jones, Novicevik, Hayek, and Humphries (2012) analyzed the letters of Benjamin Thornton Montgomery from 1865 to 1870. Montgomery was a former slave who became a plantation manager and owner, showing the competence and perseverance at the roots of African American management, emancipating itself from slavery while withstanding ongoing racial attacks and prejudice. The idea that such historical accounts of diversity in organizations can raise awareness, as well as playing a profound remedial and redemptive role of fostering more open discussion of history's great sins and achievements, is surely a powerful one (Jones et al. 2012).

Unsung Heroes, Secret Villains, Forgotten Narratives, and Other Diversity Erasures

An inter-related point on history and diversity in organizations, of which slavery is often a part, is the more general idea that history contains hidden and forgotten stories about majority–minority relations, struggles, crimes, and achievements. Of course, in many cases, from a critical historiographic perspective, minority perspectives may have been structurally excluded or 'written out' of dominant historical narrative accounts, and in the case of preserving powerful interests and privileges, inconvenient truths 'erased' from them too.

As well as research, this sort of critical work is also being done by popular culture and new media – blogs, webpages, book projects, and particularly movies based on true stories. Often work and organization are, of course, implicated. These include biopics of great scientists and mathematicians making professional achievements in the face of staggering adversity and minority status – Stephen Hawking (disability), Alan Turing (homosexuality), and John Nash (mental health). They include stories of class and activism around factories, jobs, communities, and minority ally coalitions - the Ford sewing machinists strike of 1968 in Dagenham that aimed at legislative reform on equal pay for women, and the lesbian and gay activists who raised money to help families affected by the British miners' strike in 1984. Finally, there are true stories historically presented as being in an 'unsung heroes' type of genre, such as the 'hidden figures' of NASA – the African-American female mathematicians who played a crucial role in America's space program – and whose contributions had been hitherto unheralded (Shetterly, 2016). Arguably, there is a lot at stake in these historiographies, addressing critical truth and justice issues facing diversity and organizations today through a retrospective communing with the complexities of the past. In sum, our culture industries are vehicles for many stories of how diversity has been lived out in relation to work and organization, which are much richer than just a narrow conception of equality, inclusion, and management alone might suggest.

Equally, and although we should perhaps resist an absolute dichotomy, we can argue that history has its fair share of *villains,* or at least powerful actors and groups who were able to oppress, exploit, and abuse minorities in various forms of organization and relation, perpetuating injustices and inequalities as they did so. The different times and places and historical conditions where slavery, harassment, and many varied forms of racism were enabled or allowed to flourish invite some analysis as to who enabled or was complicit in them, and how they managed to remain unpunished and unaccountable. The legacies may be long, and crucially, certain traces and residues seem likely to linger on and continue to exert influences in the organizational present. One profound and provocative example is the legacy of ideologies associated with racial purity, social Darwinism and eugenics – as dating back to the Holocaust and Victorian period (Sewell, 2009). Many organizations may have uncomfortable affiliations with prejudicial organizations, political parties and other individuals lurking in their histories. As a subsequent chapter will reiterate, for organizations in longstanding *institutional fields* – the police, the church, celebrity/the media, politics – prejudicial histories can have a strong and persistent hold on the realities of workforce diversity over time, covertly and overtly.

Whether heroes or villains are involved, some histories of minorities in diverse organizations may simply be conveniently excused, forgotten, denied, or even wilfully erased. Some memories are longer than others, and memory can be contracted and distorted. As mentioned previously, such stories are being resurrected and researched in different disciplines and with regard to different aspects of diversity. We can consider the history of autism and Aspergers as one example with implications for the diversity and inclusion of disability. Czech (2018) analyzed a range of previously unexplored archival documents pertaining to the life and work of Hans Asperger, credited with discovering the 'Asperger's syndrome' so influential today. What is troubling in light of this revisiting of the historical evidence, is that Asperger was cooperating with several Nazi-affiliated National Socialist organizations in 1940s Vienna and helped legitimize race hygiene policies, including harsh diagnoses, forced sterilizations, and even child 'euthanasia' programs (Czech, 2018). This 'forgotten narrative' stands in shocking contrast with the more popularly preserved narrative of Asperger as a courageous and principled protector of children against the Nazi regime. We are then forced to ask what it means for us if we are at risk for forgetting or being unaware of the roots of an influential diversity label that is being widely used today to make sense of a minority status, identity, and experience. A related historical point can be made with regard to autism in France, where the population faces serious problems of under-diagnosis and under-developed services, due to the historical prominence of psychoanalysis in French culture, which even promoted sexist ideas that mothers should stay home to care for autistic children (Bates, 2018).

In organization studies more specifically, there is another paper by Bill Cooke (1999), which looks at the erasure or 'writing out' of the political Left and gender from popular or mainstream accounts of the history of the change management field (Hughes, 2010). The article covers the links of key scholars (Kurt Lewin, Edgar Schein) to radical, left-wing and Chinese Communist influences. It is argued that the very existence of management fields and topics is based around processes of historical and political construction, although ultimately, we often end up with mainstream, managerialist accounts that make organizational practices seem like a neutral, technical, white, Western, masculine, and conservative domain. Innovators, settings, struggles, and contributions are denied, along with their richness, nuance, and diversity. Reflexive historiography is encouraged so that we may gain awareness of how theories and ideas become popular in different times and places. Indeed, the phrase 'whitewashing' is now often used to indicate a sense that race and racism are being denied and buried under a privileged white appropriation of a sense of universal progress and status quo (Reitman, 2006).

Colonialism and Post-Colonialism

No discussion of organizational diversity and history would be complete without some consideration of colonial histories spanning decades and centuries, and their post-colonial legacies reflected in workplaces today. The idea looms large in relation to globalization and international business; that organizations and practices are profoundly shaped by a history of international relations with powerful countries establishing colonial regimes and organizations designed to subjugate other populations. This is to view organizations with a newly critical pair of eyes; where a dominant array of imperial powers – Western Europe, the US, the developed world, the Global North, white settlers – exerts a dominant influence over minorities that tend to be deemed 'Other' – slaves, migrants, natives, exotic, foreign, primitive, and so forth.

In ways similar to the critical approach of this book, those writing about international business have critiqued a large, dominant body of 'mainstream' work which takes an *ahistorical* and globalist focus, ignoring postcolonialism in favor of a relatively neutral, technical discussion of the effective and efficient machinations of today's multinational corporations/enterprises (MNCs/MNEs) (Delbridge, Hauptmeier, & Sengupta, 2011; Özkazanç-Pan, 2008).

Postcolonialism can be quite a daunting interdisciplinary area of social and cultural theory, but in organizational terms, one could perhaps do worse than to start with an article by Banu Özkazanç-Pan (2008), that introduces the idea of international diversity in organizations in terms of *'the rest of the world'*. Özkazanç-Pan (2008) acknowledges the complexity and debated nature of the field in terms of multiple potential definitions, but defines postcolonial approaches as a whole in terms of ones that "draw attention to the hegemony of Western epistemology and critique representations about the 'other' in management discourses. In effect, postcolonial scholars demonstrate that, by making claims on behalf of the native, Western management knowledge appropriates the native as unknowledgeable" (p. 965).

Furthermore, Özkazanç-Pan (2008) also helpfully introduces the reader to arguably the three most significant postcolonial thinkers in this critical canon:

1. *Edward Said,* who developed the framework of *Orientalism* to highlight the historical-power relations between European colonial powers and the East, where "colonial discourse represents the East as backward, unable to change, inferior, and feminized, while it represents the West as progressive, advanced, and masculine. These representations produce a fictionalized Orient and are used to suggest there are "real" cultural differences between West and East" (Özkazanç-Pan, 2008, p. 966). A deeper implication of Said's work is that Western academic knowledge is not disinterested and implicated in compounding these (mis)representations.

2. *Gayatri Spivak,* who developed the notion of a *gendered postcolonial subject.* Her work reflects the setting of British-ruled India, and the limitations of Western feminism in depicting the 'double subjugation' of minority women embattled with both Western colonizers and indigenous patriarchy. Spivak also tends to deliberately misapply and deconstruct Western knowledge, to show its limits, and the *epistemic violence* it does where it imposes dominant representations in postcolonial settings. Her modification of the concept of the *subaltern* is often discussed, a term used to describe those unable to speak for themselves, stranded outside the Western and local representations that dominate collective consciousness. In recognizing and wrestling with her own position as an academic in a Western institution, Spivak also deploys a uniquely critical self-awareness or *reflexivity.*

3. *Homi Bhabha,* who builds on Frantz Fanon's psychoanalytic work from French colonies in Algeria and the Caribbean, and reapplies it to examine its operation in British-ruled India. Key concepts here include *hybridity,* as the colonized can choose to occupy an ambivalent space, questioning and resisting the colonizer's knowledge and gaze and way of defining an 'us-and-them' binary relationship. There is also *mimicry,* where the colonized are treated as one undifferentiated *nation,* and encouraged to copy the culture of the colonizer, effacing their diversity.

Frenkel and Shenhav (2006) also give a good overview of what it means to take a 'postcolonial reading' of management and organization. They reinforce points about the dominance of Western texts and practices, and the problem that while we have many fusions and hybrids making up the diversity of our societies, we still have a binary separation that artificially 'purifies' our knowledge of organizations and the world. While the persistent binary exclusion of certain cultures can seem very stubborn, they argue that there lies hope in exposing the true hybridity and fusion across cultures in many of our historical practices and texts (Frenkel & Shenhav, 2006). This sensitivity to the non-Western and to 'let others speak back' is at the heart of the postcolonial project (Jack, Calás, Nkomo, & Peltonen, 2008). This is undoubtedly a difficult cycle to break, because of the powerful legacies and structures of suffering and representation involved. However, this is arguably what a good critical (interdisciplinary) perspective on diversity should do – take the cumulative weight of history and disrupt simplistic understandings of difference, so that we may understand and act upon the present in a more nuanced fashion. If nothing else, we are driven to consider the lexicon (othering, subalterns), and toward recognizing the national and international contexts within which organizations become diverse and try to manage that distinctive diversity.

An exhaustive survey of postcolonial management research would be well beyond the scope of this chapter and volume. However, for example, there is work on postcolonial and 'anticolonial' (resistant) representations of African leadership, and how to rewrite them in ways that are themselves more diverse, striving to help more diverse histories and identities to emerge (Nkomo, 2011). There is also work on the historical legacy of indigenous-colonial relations in New Zealand between the Māori and the white majorities and neoliberal politics governing today's occupations and workplaces that continue to undermine the ideal of a truly bicultural society (Pringle & Ryan, 2015). Global patterns of migration complicate the postcolonial picture further, creating *diaspora* (dispersed networks) of postcolonial ethnic groups around the world that feed into diverse workplaces, while still involving experiences of discrimination and representation that bind minorities and majorities to one another and constrain them from within shared histories. Liu (2017a) observed how Chinese-Australian professionals engaged in strategic self-Orientalism before a majority 'white gaze', which both constrained their lives, but also offered them subtle opportunities to manipulate and re-appropriate the 'mythic' representations of ancient China on their own terms.

From Hong Kong to India, and many other Commonwealth countries and Western echoes of colonizing relationships, there is a need to continue to acknowledge postcolonial contexts, relations, and practices across organizations and at play in their diversity. The Windrush scandal in the UK invokes its Commonwealth history of Jamaican immigration and the Jamaicans' sense of 'un-belonging' compounded by ongoing episodes of inhumane treatment, detention, and deportation (Webster, 2018). At the same time, as well as the backdrops of histories of division and suffering, domination and rule are not always the unalloyed order of the day. There are also spaces where new foregrounded histories can emerge that go beyond a West-Rest dichotomy or opposition and show local agency, cultural fusion, and hybrid forms of cultural organization. For example, Mestyan (2018) has written on the mixed cultural heritage of Cairo's opera in the 1860s, and internationally diverse entertainment in the Eastern Mediterranean region.

Looking Back to Look Forward? What History Can Continue to Tell Us

Before concluding this chapter, we can make three final reinforcing points on diversity, organizations, and history. First, that history continues to change the way we look at the world in the present. This is a point running through this chapter – that history allows us to rediscover organizational roots and stories, and invites us to dig deeper and view history from different, minority perspectives. It may be that history is felt to be repeating itself, or that some relations of difference never change, they merely change form or reproduce themselves differently. We may feel that we can use a language of certain historical phases and ideologies to describe the times we live in and the diverse organizations we work in – others may contest these demarcations. In this sense, related views of temporality and change are important – whether time is experienced as a flow or if it makes sense to talk of the beginnings, middles, and ends of historical phases. 'Histories' plural point toward an inherent diversity – of memories, generations, legacies, and narratives. As this book will repeatedly conclude, diversity and difference are always in motion, and history is a way of giving them a good stir or shake up to reveal new perspectives. It may be that some questions on diversity in organizations may be best posed and answered with a significant degree of history in tow – ancient and/or modern. One key implication is to stop seeing history as mere facts to be aware of and check against but as reflecting a deeper sense of the past that can be more creatively and actively engaged with in terms of diverse connections and stories (Godfrey et al., 2016).

The second related point is simply to acknowledge that it is not easy to combine history and organization studies. It is an interdisciplinary bridge, and we require ways of respectfully traversing it that do justice to both sides; ways that are not necessarily very familiar in wider communities of research and practice. Some thought has been given in this chapter to these critical bridges and decisions about what the object, focus, and historiographic emphases might be when it comes to diversity, but there are undoubtedly more (e.g. legal, aesthetic, economic and geographical histories). We need to frequently question our assumptions about what we think history is, what stories we can tell about it, and how we can creatively engage it to build theory about connections between the past and the present. Not all organizational evidence pertaining to history and diversity will necessarily mention either word explicitly, either. Thinking about history, diversity, and organizations together may also therefore take us into unexpected places. Keith Grint's historical readings of the popularity and emergence of business process reengineering (BPR) as a practice in the 1990s reveal the 'zeitgeist' of wider resonances with social and cultural antecedents. These resonances appear to better explain its meaning and influence than accounts that merely focus on its internal principles and rationality (Grint, 1994). They draw in histories of masculinity, violence, Japanese-American management rivalry, consultancy, and a tradition of aggressive military rhetoric (Grint & Case, 1998).

The third and final point here is to keep engaging and reading business and management history journals to explore ideas, themes, and links with diversity in organizations. Relatively recent examples selected as a fairly random, but relevant, showcase for consideration here include the following:

1. Reed (2017) combines interviews and archival data to present an in-depth case study of the US multinational manufacturer of diesel engines, Cummins Inc. The historical analysis shows that in the 1940s, the management were progressive on promoting LGBT and other minority rights at times when societal and community values were more likely to see them as illegitimate forms of diversity. The influence of the organization, its founder, and its identity underpins a surprisingly long-standing and robust tradition of Corporate Social Responsibility (CSR) and inclusion beyond the societal norms of the time, and progressive even by today's standards.
2. Sanderson, Parsons, Mills, and Mills (2010) draw on archival material to analyze the four-year rise and fall of a women's organization of flight attendants which was established to resist gender discrimination in the US commercial aviation industry – Stewardesses for Women's Rights (SFWR). Although plagued by a lack of funding and political/bureaucratic infighting, the SFWR was nevertheless an important part of the second wave feminism of the time, focusing on improving conditions for women at work, as well as elevating the symbolic value of the work they were doing.
3. Smith (2016) reminds us of the period of decolonialization in the 1960s where discrimination became less acceptable in a globalizing, capitalist world. This prompted the Hongkong and Shanghai Banking Corporation – today we would probably only know of it

as HSBC – to reform its colonialist 'comprador system'. This involved shedding cultural and institutional diversity practices where expatriate British workers dominated executive levels of the organization, and exploited layers of non-British workers in Asian markets in discriminatory ways. The compradors were early Chinese managers that acted as intermediaries between the British and subordinate layers of Asian workers. This evolution from colonial to postcolonial has continued to inform the multicultural, cosmopolitan values of HSBC's global banking operations today.

Conclusion

This chapter has tried to outline various links between history, organizations, and diversity as part of a critical, interdisciplinary perspective that might shape research and practice in important ways. It is perhaps unlikely that everyone will, or undesirable that everyone should, commit to history fully all of the time or on all of their projects, but for many modern diversity topics and practices, historical questions are begging to be asked to better contextualize them. From a postcolonial perspective, or even just a general perspective of inclusion, there is probably still too much management history coming only from the US, about the US, or concerning American or Western European figures and corporations. In many ways, history will continue to be a source of struggle, confrontation, and suffering in public life, although perhaps also of healing and redemption too – whether it is embattled minorities deserving of greater recognition and remembrance, or statues and monuments put up to people who are not believed to deserve the level of esteem afforded them.

If we want to engage today's organizational diversity, then history – and critical readings of histories – present the diverse set of inputs for doing so in a way that matches present diversity with past diversity. The German Jewish philosopher Walter Benjamin is one critical thinker who has hinted that history is not about the way things were, and it is not necessarily about progress or the future. What is more important is looking at the tragedies of the past and trying to grasp and protect a bigger picture, which may contain the seeds of hope and redemption amidst its ruins (Beiner, 1984). Benjamin was speaking from a life lived during the Second World War and the Holocaust. Yet similarly, Hilary Mantel, the historical novelist, speaks today of the value of *historical fiction* in trying to smooth the past into some sort of relatable vicarious experience, even if we can only work with the best available facts (Mantel, 2009). There is therefore the serious importance of considering primary sources and historical contexts in one sense, but in another, more playful sense we are at the same time all already 'doing history' if we are engaging with diverse reflections on the past.

When it comes to diversity in organizations then, there are different ways of reading and writing history to 'make the old new' again (Mantel, 2009). It could be gender history, political history, economic history, imperial history, or any number of critical 'lenses' on the past. It is challenging, but arguably worthwhile, if we can seize upon some of these 'old made new' sources of difference to affect and account for how diverse people organize and represent their diversity today. Many in-depth and lively debates on the critical methodologies and analyses of history within organization studies (and beyond it) are likely to continue – and the interested reader is encouraged to take stock of leading theorists in order to apply their insights further to diversity-related and organizational topics. These include scholars with explicit commitments to management history and historiography, such as Bill Cooke, Stephen Cummings, Todd Bridgman, Michael Rowlinson, Alfred Kieser, Behlül Üsdiken, Matthias Kipping, Albert J. Mills, and Stephanie Decker, among others.

4 Power

This chapter will attempt to outline some of significant themes concerning power as a critical and interdisciplinary perspective on diversity in organizations. Power looms large over any critical perspective on organizations, and indeed over some of the other chapters of this book, in terms of the power residing in institutional fields, language or discourse, and other political and critical representations of difference. Power is an immense topic, and in many ways the principal vehicle through which many *inequalities* are created and maintained. Power isn't always discussed explicitly in relation to diversity, however, which is part of the reason for this chapter. Looking at critical theorists of power we can attempt to tease out a bit more the relationships between power and difference. It seems to make sense to think of the relationship reciprocally. Wherever there is pre-existing power in or beyond an organization, we might expect it to be used in such a way as to inscribe and reinforce differences, in the form of diverse hierarchies, group memberships, and networked cliques. At the same time, any a priori suggestion of difference and diversity in an organization may also be seen as a provocation to build or transform power relations. It is this dynamic, dialectical quality that can make power seem everywhere and nowhere, a great web of forces and structures and tactics, which is probably why it is not always dealt with explicitly.

As with many other topics covered in this volume, a fairly comprehensive review of power in management and organization by Fleming and Spicer (2014) is a good starting point – although as noted earlier, links with diversity are hardly made explicit overall. Instead, a particular focus is given to the *four faces* of power, and *four sites* of power. The faces are labelled coercion, manipulation, domination, and subjectification. In turn, each of the four faces can be related to four sites of power, which are labeled politics 'in', 'over', 'through', and 'against'. We can note the use of the word politics more in association with the latter four sites. Politics is frequently confused or conflated with power, but, following Hannah Arendt, Fleming, and Spicer (2014, p. 239) describe the relationship between the two as being one where

Politics consists of activity that rearranges relations between people and the distribution of goods (broadly defined) through the mobilization of power. In turn, power is the capacity to influence other actors with these political interests in mind. It is a resource to get things done through other people, to achieve certain goals that may be shared or contested.

Crossing Fleming and Spicer's (2014) four faces of power with their four sites of power yields a matrix for classifying *at least sixteen types* of research on power in and across organizations! For the sake of coherence and brevity, they will not be pursued here. The main point about power in relation to a critical perspective is that power has different faces and forms, and some of them run very deep within the fabric of our organizations and societies, not being necessarily located in obvious central people or structures. At their deepest and most diffuse points, faces of power affect our very sense of self, identity, reality, and consciousness. Various individuals and groups may not even be aware of or able to articulate how power affects their influence and status in relation to others – combined with material hardships and discrimination, we might think of minorities in these circumstances as being profoundly powerless. However, power is relational and dynamic and can be described as changing direction, bringing positive or negative effects in different manifestations (Fleming & Spicer, 2014).

This critical awareness of power is a long way from a more mainstream view of those in organizations who have obvious authority and status and control over resources. In mainstream management discourse, Jeffrey Pfeffer (e.g. Pfeffer, 1992) has been an important voice in reminding us that power should not simply be ignored as a taboo or dirty word in organizations, given that in reality it is often a vital aspect of implementing change and leadership. Even though it can mean getting one's hands dirty and is clearly susceptible to abuse, building and wielding power is likely to always be an integral part of getting things done. Yet we can be even more nuanced; here there is also a risk of naturalizing power all over again (naturalization being itself a type of power, over meaning and definition) as merely 'business as usual' or 'doing what's necessary'.

Power is inevitably also interdisciplinary across the social sciences and humanities – in terms of politics, ethics, philosophy, psychology, culture, sociology, history, and so forth. Psychology, for instance, has shown us how merely feeling or thinking we are powerful can change how we behave and see the world as individuals (e.g. Keltner, 2017). This highlights power's paradoxical qualities, and in some senses how power itself can have power over us. Therefore, if we agree there is no such thing as absolute powerfulness or powerlessness, then we can also assert that in some residual way power is relative and subjective, a matter of free will, choice, or agency, as well as a potential awareness and influence over many things, small or large.

However, taking an overly philosophical view of power in this way pushes us to one kind of critical extreme, returning us to an extent to the idea that power is everywhere and nowhere, which isn't especially helpful if we are interested in some of its 'harder' patterns of material disadvantage and inequality as they pertain to diversity and inclusion. Hayward and Lukes (2008) illustrate this postmodern/post-structural problem nicely in terms of exaggerating power structures to the point where agents or agency disappears. We then have to revisit in a puzzled, more careful way who is constraining whom, and who has responsibility over which actions as they affect a chain of many others. They conclude with a scene from the John Steinbeck novel *The Grapes of Wrath*, where a tenant farmer is intent on shooting a man on a tractor bulldozing a shack on his land. Yet it becomes clear that the man on the tractor is merely an agent at the end of a long chain of structures, and if the chain of structures and agencies cannot be traced to a source of power, maybe there will never be 'anyone to shoot' (Hayward & Lukes, 2008). The point to take from this is that we should be aware of this dilemma, resist simplistic attributions, and try to maintain a mindful understanding of the delicate play of structures, freedoms, responsibilities, resources, constraints, choices, and actions when it comes to diversity, inequality, and power.

The French philosopher, historian, and critic Michel Foucault looms large over this problem – being a thinker who has had an immense influence over critical understandings of power in organizations. Foucault's work has involved detailing tirelessly power's systemic and subjective (or 'subjectifying') qualities as they operate to carve up diverse populations and call into question the way we all see ourselves and one another at the deepest levels of organization, that is, around self-definition, knowledge, rationality, and control (e.g. Burrell, 1988; Raffnsøe, Mennicken, & Miller, 2019). If we see everyone and everything as under the influence of some sort of power, however, as noted previously, we run into what has been called a 'Foucaultian trap' where we struggle to meaningfully separate the dominant from the dominated (Dowding, 2006). In their comprehensive survey of the 'Foucault effect' and the many influences on organization studies that constitute it, Raffnsøe and colleagues (2019) suggest we need to move forward from merely recycling dualisms like discipline versus autonomy. Instead, we should move to more positively embrace, and carefully attend to, 'co-produced' possibilities of distributed agency and change.

There are many other excellent critical scholars on the general role of power in organizations, too many to mention here but a few such names are Cynthia Hardy, Stewart Clegg, David Knights, and Hugh Willmott. Yet what is the upshot of all this theorizing of power for diversity and difference in organizations? Simply put, wherever something appears as neutral or disinterested in organizations, we should probably take a closer look to understand the operations of power. Often, if not always, these will run along lines of difference and serve to subordinate, silence, efface, or exclude certain minority groups and identities. The body of this chapter therefore turns to selectively consider some critical perspectives on power and diversity in organizations, starting with Bourdieu and Foucault but also considering the notion of resistance and other themes and topics that have perhaps received less attention.

Power and Diversity: Bourdieu, Foucault, and Resistance Perspectives

Bourdieu

Firstly, there are now many critical studies relating power and diversity in organizations that draw on the concepts and work of Pierre Bourdieu, albeit appearing in some journals and disciplinary conversations more than others. Like Foucault, Bourdieu was a French public intellectual and philosopher, although perhaps with more sociological and anthropological aspects to his work than Foucault.

Like so many critical social and organizational thinkers from the twentieth century onward, Bourdieu is a notoriously difficult and complex figure to draw upon. However, Mustafa Özbilgin and Ahu Tatli (2005) help to bridge the gaps by reviewing his four key texts: *Outline of Theory of Practice*; *The Logic of Practice*; *Practical Reason: On the Theory of Action*; and *An Invitation to Reflexive Sociology*. They emphasize how useful Bourdieu is in helping us to trace power across different *relational* levels of organization and society and also in identifying ways to transcend dualisms around agency and structure, subjectivity and objectivity, and so on. Bourdieu's worldview helps to show us how power and differences emerge in our societies and are maintained – the different practices, tastes, and ways of discriminating between groups are woven into a comprehensive picture, built up from the everyday, to encompass positions, classifications, and fields of influence and violence. With concepts such as *habitus, symbolic violence,* forms of *capital,* and other aspects of the Bourdieusian lexicon, we are provided with rich ways of describing the landscape of diversity and power in organizations and beyond (Özbilgin & Tatli, 2005).

In related work, Tatli and Özbilgin (2012) relate Bourdieu (or a Bourdieusian approach) more explicitly to diversity. They argue and demonstrate that Bourdieu can help us take an *emic* approach to diversity in organizations – one which does not simply assume *etic* or universal categories of diversity a priori but recognizes the need to look at how diversities emerge in very specific local and intersectional ways (see chapter six of this book for more on intersectionality). This approach also allows us to look at the distinctive combinations of difference within an organization made up of multiple categories and not just one majority or minority. Influence and status, as well as disadvantage and subordination, emerge at particular social intersections according to multiple categories of difference. In such a dynamic system, diversity is not fixed to essential categories, it is produced relationally as agents struggle for power and resources, drawing on various sources of Bourdieusian capital, broadly defined – which could be anything social, cultural, and symbolic from language to educational background to upbringing (Tatli & Özbilgin, 2012).

Since then, scholars of diversity in organizations have continued to use Bourdieu sporadically to study elites and the different, relative standing of minority and majority (sub)groups who have different intersections of characteristics that grant them some power, influence, and agency at different relational levels of social structure (e.g. job/role, occupation/profession, industry/sector). However, the appearance of such papers is quite uneven and low-key in some ways, and only indirectly linked to diversity in some cases. It therefore seems likely there is still much untapped potential waiting to be realized in Bourdieusian analyses of diversity in organizations, as well as in exposing more audiences to the strengths of the approaches and making them accessible (e.g. Tatli, Özbilgin, & Karatas-Ozkan, 2015). For instance, the patterns of power, culture, and status emerging across multinationals, transnational professional service structures, migrant populations, and elites in different countries and sectors, all lend themselves well to Bourdieusian analyses and insights (e.g. Erel, 2010; Spence et al., 2016). Finally, Bourdieu can of course be combined with other critical thinkers and perspectives to yield up new insights and explanations for scenarios involving particular dynamics of diversity, power, change, and agency. Nentwich, Özbilgin, and Tatli (2015), for example, analyze the case of getting women the (long overdue) right to vote in the Swiss cantons of Appenzell, finally achieved in 1991. They combine Bourdieu with Judith Butler – another critical philosophical thinker with complementary views on agency – to integrate two ways of transforming gendered power relations. The Bourdieusian route is more concerned with building collective and network power to embed new social structures. The Butlerian route is more about using language and identity to challenge binaries and reinforce new norms. Together, both link power, change, and diversity to organizational structures and relationships.

Foucault

While critical allusions to Foucault and power can be found incredibly widely across organization studies and the social sciences, explicitly

Foucauldian analyses of diversity and diversity management in the workplace are fairly few and far between, representing a specific part of an already specific critical perspective on diversity in organizations.

Perhaps one of the most influential to date is the account presented by Ahonen and colleagues (2014). Their arguments and readings of diversity in organizations are highly critical and difficult to confront, yet arguably very important. They emphasize the hidden and invisible modalities in which power and context inter-relate, asserting that as we internalize the very knowledge and practices underpinning diversity management, we reproduce diversity *as discourse* in ways that maintain power relations, sameness, and difference. Even in relatively critically oriented research, there is a risk that we are still putting into practice a particular diversity discourse that makes assumptions about diversity as an object that separates people. While there are not often easy ways forward from a Foucauldian analysis such as this, the important implication is to recognize that diversity is unmanageable in some sense, but also that in particular contexts, as we attempt to manage and govern it, we fix definitions and obscure as much as we reveal. Breaking the 'biopolitical cycle' means reclaiming difference from diversity (Ahonen et al., 2014), and interrogating the relations of power that produce knowledge about diversity itself.

If this sounds very abstract and impractical, then it is surely because it is such a thoroughgoing critique of the pervasive webs of power coursing through organizations, managerial practices, and relationships where almost any mention of the idea of diversity might be made. It does point to a sort of consciousness-raising around the need to stand back and recognize how power keeps so much of our language and relationships and identities in place, fixing meanings and the boundaries of our sense of reality and self. One reading then is perhaps that truly expressing difference in organization means a rebellious flight from, or at least a vigilant wrestling with, all forms of power, and an attempt to free our mind and reinvent ourselves in more fluid, unmanageable terms. And in another sense, this is one controversial purpose of Foucauldian critique, to always subvert and point out the operations of power. In contrast, to suggest replacing them with anything else would be to manage, to govern, and to miss the point.

Fortunately, there are some papers emerging that start to help us understand and relate this Foucauldian philosophy to more concrete areas of diversity practice in organizations. Van Laer (2018), for instance, adopts a Foucauldian approach to show how the sexual identities of gay and lesbian employees and their co-workers are 'unmanageable' and produced by discursive struggles that are organized loosely around relational power dynamics and governing norms, such as truthfulness, inclusion, and circulation. These processes are controlled, but decentered – no particular employee or organizational entity is *in* control. Brewis

(2019) applies Foucauldian thinking to diversity training in UK organizations, in terms of how diversity practitioners seek to turn employees into 'inclusive subjects' who will subsequently act more inclusively toward others. The training is revealed as a hybrid arena where trainees experience both discipline and freedom as they try to question and adjust their sense of self to the idea of being more inclusive in their practices.

At a more national and even international level, Eräranta and Kantola (2016) link Foucault's work on the 'analytics of government' to the effects of soft Europeanization policy instruments. Specifically, they highlight the role of European Social Fund projects in developing family-friendly arrangements in Finnish workplaces. Such techniques hold the power to change gendered conventions across societies and working populations through managerial and project-based techniques that make it more normal for organizations to get involved in reshaping gender relations and self-regulating family issues traditionally handled by the state (Eräranta & Kantola, 2016). Finally, and working at the boundary of different disciplines, de Jong (2016) highlights the parallels between studies of diversity management in organization studies and migration management in the field of ethnic and migration studies, as well as the benefits of (critically) conjoining the two. From a pan-European perspective, a shared research agenda with Foucauldian points of convergence is outlined – in terms of the power regimes reflected in national histories, political ideologies, government equality legislation, and immigration and economic policy (de Jong, 2016).

In sum, Foucauldian perspectives tend to highlight the intimate, ambivalent, and transformative operations of power through many channels and at many levels of organizing activity and diversity management practice.

Resistance

The work outlined earlier linking Bourdieu and Foucault to diversity in organizations provides some insightful emphasis on both the struggles and transformative dynamics of power in many circumstances. However, if much power in organizations is exerted by certain pre-existing groups with established bases and top-down control 'over' and 'through' the organization, then it is worth giving some more consideration to how minorities can be recognized to exert opposing bottom-up power 'in' and 'against' the organization (Fleming & Spicer, 2014).

This takes us into relatively familiar critical territory and concerns including resistance, emancipation, and social movements. Here, diverse minorities within and outside of organizations may be engaged in struggles to regain power, destabilize it, and/or achieve change through dialectical push–pull relationships with other groups that alter various power bases and relations. The shift in perspective can be useful,

however, for telling us more from the standpoint of the more disadvantaged and powerless, as well as highlighting how even with very
limited power, possibilities for agency, resistance, and change can be
identified.

If a critical perspective sees power within and beyond organizations in
so many places, the same is true of resistance. Power and resistance are
generally held to be closely intertwined, virtually two sides of the same
coin, and in terms of diversity, it may often be a minority or disadvantaged
group held to be doing the resistance. Again, like power, resistance comes
in many forms and varies along many dimensions – private/public, cog-
nitive/behavioral, overt/covert, individual/collective, and so on. Several
authors have suggested that resistance exists in a *dialectical* relationship,
or as part of a duality, with control or power (Fleming & Spicer, 2008;
Mumby, 2005). Essentially, it doesn't make sense to talk about one
without mentioning the other; both make up part of a more general
struggle in everyday organizational life (Fleming & Spicer, 2008). This is
important insofar as resistance can be *productive* in organizations – re-
sistors can achieve a change and transformation in existing power relations (Courpasson, Dany, & Clegg, 2012). Resistance as a legitimate and
distinctive aspect of power relations has been an important recognition,
particularly in change management. In change terms, this means recognising that resistance to change should not be ignored or neglected,
rather embraced for its meaningful value as part of a self-correcting and
adaptive – not to mention democratic – organizational system (Ford, Ford,
& D'Amelio, 2008). A review of the field of organizational resistance over
the last fifteen years covers everything from humor to whistleblowing to
public, collective forms of insurrection, solidarity, protest, and anarchy
(Mumby, Thomas, Martí, & Seidl, 2017).

Critical scholars of organization thus continue to mine the remarkable
and pervasive ways resistance can be understood as part of power in
organizations. For example, Harding, Ford, and Lee (2017) researched
senior managers implementing talent management in the UK in the
National Health Service. Drawing on Judith Butler's and Karen Barad's
theories of performativity, they theorize and show resistance as something happening moment-to-moment as (gendered) bodies, identities,
speech acts, and even objects jostle for recognition and freedom to define
aspects of specific situations. One way of reading performativity then is
in terms of how organizational members both comply and resist at the
same time, resulting in the 'doing' or performing of a particular diverse
identity in situ.

Related work is emerging where the critical links between resistance
and diversity in organizations are being made more explicit. Gagnon and
Collinson's (2017) study of internationally diverse leadership development teams showed how some teams were more successful than others in
their conversations at resisting control practices (e.g. white, western,

masculine leadership norms), and in being able to 'do difference' dif-ferently and practice inclusion of their diversity as a team resource. Fleming (2007) studied a culture change program at an Australian call center organization and found a complex picture of control, empower-ment, and resistance surrounding the sexuality and sexual orientations of the young employees there. Thanem and Wallenberg (2016) studied a group of male-to-female transvestite workers of varying organizational backgrounds working in a North European country, and their struggle of resisting ('underdoing') gender norms in the performing of transgender identities at work. Rather than painfully repressing a transgender iden-tity or consistently trying to pass off as one gender or another, the transvestite workers opted to add, remove, and combine the masculine, feminine, and ungendered in a great and subtle variety of ways.

Resistance has also been reported being used as a tool for opening up value change after the introduction of gender quotas in the Dutch police force (van den Brink & Benschop, 2018). In a more postcolonial setting, resistance from 'subaltern' farming communities in India is shown to be organized and mobilized against the neoliberal and imperial land grabs of powerful corporations and states, centering around ethics, justice, dignity, and shows of (non)violence (Pal, 2016). Israeli combat soldiers use ethnic and gendered practices to resist professional expectations placed upon them, empowering themselves by modifying their uniforms, the aesthetic appearance of their bodies (e.g. not shaving), and per-forming masculinities distinctive to their ethnicities (Kachtan & Wasserman, 2015). Finally, although perhaps not a conventional de-mographic characteristic of diversity, it seems important to recognize the profoundly cross-cutting nature of class power and the resistance oper-ating between workers and employers in a standard asymmetrical em-ployment relationship involving some exploitation of wage labor. Mulholland (2004), in her study of Irish call center workers, for ex-ample, reminds us how concrete and material worker resistance can be, as subordinated individuals come together informally as one 'collective worker' and find ways to resist their employers and managers in labor process conflicts over pay, productivity, and work intensification.

In sum, as these varied examples show, resistance runs along many lines and with different effects in different settings, contingent upon the many diverse identities being performed or in play, and it is rarely as simple in modern organizations as having one 'underdog' to root for and regard with approval (Fleming, 2007).

Ongoing Themes Concerning Power and Diversity in Organizations

Before concluding this chapter, three further critical themes relating power to diversity in organizations seem worth highlighting briefly, particularly in terms of the relations between power, class, race, and gender. These concern (1) privileged *elites*, (2) wide and complex regimes of *inequalities* reproduced by power relations, and (3) feminist struggles to transform *gendered power relations* in organizations.

First, Reed (2012) discusses a reviving interest in understanding organizational and institutional *elites*, in terms of the concentrations of power that spread beyond organizations and across networks and fields to govern, command, and dominate organizations, irrespective of more traditional hierarchical structures that may be in place or not. This involves mapping more carefully combinations of *vertical* and *horizontal* power relationships that grant elites significant power bases over expertise, resource allocations, authority to punish, and authority to regulate societies (Reed, 2012). In terms of diversity in organizations, this starts to blur the lines between majority and minority – a minority of a majority may hold a majority share of power, for example. To some extent this relates back towards notions of class structure and Bourdieu's capitals and sources of influence that enable people to reach the top of organizational systems.

More specifically, in terms of ethnic diversity, and via black feminist and critical race theory, elitism takes us to a critical agenda concerned with assessing *whiteness* and unearned ethnic *privileges* that serve to dominate and exclude non-white ethnic groups in organizations (Al Ariss, Özbilgin, Tatli, & April, 2014). As societies and organizations historically tarnished by racism and colonialism evolve into the twenty-first century, white supremacy is both reproduced and challenged within evolving ethnic and diversity power relations, at times inspiring novel and empowering forms of anti-racist praxis and reflexivity (Liu, 2017b). Privileged notions of leadership and hierarchy are thus challenged from alternative cultural perspectives, namely, ones that are non-Western and non-white. This is a challenge to the power of the status quo, the taken-for-granted nature of whiteness, privilege, and elites – recognising their power as a way to stop change, or simply to not to have to care about the fates, lived experiences, or worldviews of diverse others. That said, privilege should probably not be thought of as a binary property one either has or doesn't have, but rather a question of degree, playing out differently in different contexts and for individuals who reflect certain combinations of *intersecting* differences, such as white women, middle-class black men, and so on (Atewologun & Sealy, 2014). As well as within individuals and groups' particular configurations of differences, elite privileges also continue to endure in professional services and institutions, including those that have diversity management and profess to an inclusive culture, in part due to class-based and educational exclusion (e.g. law firms – see Ashley, 2010).

Second, the results of power dynamics tend to be seen in the *inequalities* that arise in and across organizations and economies, in a sustaining and reproducing relation that clearly runs very deep and is difficult to change, while it lies at the heart of any diversity or social justice project to challenge them. Inequalities are undoubtedly a huge interdisciplinary research topic, but the role they play in organizations has been given a renewed framing by commentaries and movements (e.g. Occupy), popular and academic, on widening global income and economic inequalities. Dunne, Grady, and Weir (2018), for instance, single out economist Thomas Piketty's 2014 book *Capital in the twenty-first Century*. While perhaps not explicitly intended as a manifesto, Piketty's book can certainly be used as a basis to challenge and reorient policies of neoliberal economics, austerity, financialization, taxation, and corporate governance in terms of how they foster widening global inequality and poverty. At the same time, it seems more work may be needed between economists and organizational scholars to connect Piketty's themes to what goes on *within* specific organizations (Dunne et al., 2018), not to mention agendas of diversity and inclusion.

Indeed, against this far-reaching economic and political backdrop of inequality concerns, special issues, and forums of top management and organization, journal articles are appearing on inequality, and in some cases (although arguably not all) there are explicit links to diversity. Hayes, Introna, and Kelly (2017), for example, problematize the institutionalized relationships between donors, NGOs, and Indian farmers in the international development sector. In this context, practices such as impact assessment, viewed in Foucauldian terms, continue to reinforce knowledge and power across diverse boundaries through their governing and calculative influences, ultimately sourced in a market-oriented sector.

In their editorial, Suddaby, Bruton, and Walsh (2018) note the ambiguities when we talk about inequality – whether and how it is getting worse or not, in what ways, the ambivalence of business around helping or hindering matters, and the need to not lose sight of the stubbornly persistent and distressing nature of the related issue of *poverty*. They draw attention to how we read and talk about inequality in ways that sanitize, institutionalize, and internalize it. There is discouragement about its inevitability, and debates about how to define and measure it, but it seems better instead to more directly engage the 'dirty reality' of cheap labor and entrepreneurial struggles in internationally diverse settings (Suddaby et al., 2018). Similarly, Riaz (2015) emphasizes the need to focus on 'inequality footprints', in terms of different stakeholder relations, elites, demographics, global inequality, and debt. Despite some concerns that inequality has been neglected, however, it is important to revisit and revitalize important earlier contributions, such as those made by the late American feminist and sociologist Joan Acker (1924–2016). Acker's concept of *inequality regimes*, among many other contributions, served to highlight how organizations are built on many different power-laden practices and processes that foster different types of inequalities.

Under this view, it is the challenging of these small and invisible inequalities, often purporting to be diversity-neutral, that is so crucial to achieving incremental changes and successes (Sayce, 2019).

Finally, although we have mentioned whiteness as a defining power relation of ethnicity diversity, we should be remiss here to not create some space to explicitly recognize the pervasive role of *gendered* power relations in organizations. The powerfully gendered aspects of so many areas of organizational life have been and continue to be tirelessly and insightfully outlined by feminists and a range of critical scholars, such as, Joan Acker, invariably being mentioned in relation to gender inequality. From a corporate view, there will perhaps always be some attempts to portray organizations as gender-neutral, if only to preserve a status quo. However, such a stance seems hard to defend in the face of overwhelming evidence of gendered disadvantage in organizations (Acker, 1990). These power effects range from persistent patriarchal institutions around childrearing, maternity, and housework through to everyday sexism and misogyny concerning feminine aesthetics, bodies, and sexualities (e.g. Bates, 2016; Broadbridge & Hearn, 2008).

Whole books can of course be given over to the subject of gender and organizations. Here the important critical point is to acknowledge gender as a profound axis of power in organizations, where the gendering of many organizational contents and realities serves to privilege the masculine as normal and desirable. Broadly, the explicit adoption of feminist and gendered lenses on organization seems to have emerged from the early 1990s onwards (e.g. Acker, 1990; Alvesson & Due Billing, 1992). A significant emphasis for power and politics here is the symbolic power of gender as a metaphor, in terms of the various femininities and masculinities shaping conflicts and biases around organizational influence and resources (Alvesson & Due Billing, 1992). Just about any organizational concept, such as rationality, leadership, entrepreneurship, career, hierarchy, and so on, can be read in gendered terms, and often in ways revealing how these concepts have traditionally and persistently valorized masculine norms to some extent (e.g. Billing, 2011; Galloway, Kapasi, & Sang, 2015; Mumby & Putnam, 1992). Furthermore, the classicist historian and feminist Mary Beard has highlighted how, from our history and myths right through to our contemporary realities, we struggle societally and culturally with the very concept of powerful women and women in power, portraying them as threatening and demonic (Beard, 2017).

In some organizational contexts, however, progress can be identified where women are 'undoing' these gendered aspects of organization, by acting as change agents and using their access to executive and managerial power to positively affect levels of representation and inclusion (Stainback, Kleiner, & Skaggs, 2016). This then shifts the emphasis to more agentic, transformational notions of gender and power, which we might more readily refer to in terms of *empowerment*. This empowerment may happen in different, contested ways depending upon the gendered identities and organizational context in question, but it offers glimpses into alternative, radical possibilities of what organizations and practices might look like. For instance, McCarthy (2017) has shown how women managers and farmers in Ghana resisted, in feminist Foucauldian terms, a CSR empowerment program delivered by an international NGO, preferring to define their empowerment and freedom on their own terms, which were different to the economic agenda of the NGO. In contrast, however, a similar study of CSR in the mining sector in Tanzania found that women were silenced by masculine and patriarchal aspects of the CSR discourse (Lauwo, 2018).

In any case, the gendered nature of power struggles remains very real. One troubling way the power dynamics can reproduce themselves is where a dominant perception of equality prevails and overpowers the need to address persistent inequalities. Tokenism, indirect discrimination, or failure to consult and involve women genuinely can all come to make up a 'gender subtext' that reinforces gendered power and conceals its dynamics by hiding behind a semblance of equality (Benschop & Dooreward, 1998). The internationally diverse nuances and context-specifics of organizational and gender relations further reinforce this picture. In over 100 countries, for instance, there are still many laws that prevent women from working in certain types of job (e.g. driving, manufacturing). Equally, campaigns around sexual harassment in work, such as using the #MeToo hashtag to report its prevalence, are also pressing for gender reforms in specific work settings (Arekapudi, 2018).

In reviewing twenty years of critical organization studies on feminist scholarship, Harding, Ford and Fotaki (2013) conclude that while the so-called 'F'-word is perhaps less 'dirty' to organizations than it once was, there is still much unfulfilled potential to be explored by drawing further on work in the disciplines of feminism and gender studies. Going forward, much seems to depend on the power exerted by different framings of feminist perspectives or feminisms, resistance agendas, and the related possibilities of empowerment mentioned above. For some feminist scholars, a crucial moving target of 'postfeminism' has emerged as an object of critical inquiry. Postfeminism is a term that reflects the complicated and controversial sense that feminism has made some sort of progress, but a selective and problematic progress which nevertheless still co-exists with other cultural, economic, and political pressures that affect women differently (Lewis, Benschop, & Simpson, 2017; Liu, 2019a). There is thus a risk that postfeminism dilutes alternative feminist potentials for solidarity, emancipation, and radical change as it becomes entangled with capitalism, individualism, and new femininities and masculinities (Lewis et al., 2017). Similarly, Pullen, Rhodes, and Thanem (2017) propose a renewed emphasis on a special kind of resistance called 'becoming-woman' that recognizes the everyday affective and embodied struggles to break free of gendered organization – in short, an invitation to talk and listen more about how gender makes us feel at work, viscerally, in concrete situations and at events.

Conclusion

By way of a brief conclusion on the vast topic of power and diversity in organizations, we can come full circle and say that power and differences are everywhere in organizations, as well as beyond them. There are no easy answers, but this chapter has sketched out critical perspectives on power and diversity, such as those derived from Foucault, Bourdieu, and resistance theorists. Most critical perspectives urge an intense outward vigilance coupled with an equally intense inward introspection in reflecting on how we engage with contingent relations of power in order that we might resist and transform them, while all the time being caught up in their reproduction (Thomas & Davies, 2005). All differences can be constructed and reproduced as a material and symbolic basis for power relations in organizations, although race and gender, as reflected in critical race/whiteness and feminist work, are surely two of the biggest concerns, both independently and where they intersect. However, similar critical mindsets towards power in organizations do indeed recur by analogy as applied to age, disability, sexual orientation, and other differences under the diversity umbrella too.

A broader overall and formal political and economic backdrop of class, inequality, elites, globalization, poverty and resistance will inevitably frame many critical projects covering diversity in organizations. However, we can also find accounts of positive experiences with power in organizations on an everyday basis, in terms of the working through of emotions, self-awareness, acts of resistance, solidarity and triumph that people can achieve in seizing back power to empower themselves and others and drive positive change in power relations going forward. In terms of symbolism and knowledge, power in organizations is arguably always in motion or being mobilized, and never fully resolved, because anything and everything, as a *subject*, has the potential to become an *object* of contestation and inequality – concepts, selves, practices, ideologies, minds, bodies, souls, and so on. In another sense, this is again a way of fully connecting power to its dynamic *political* aspects in organizations.

In future, where deemed feasible and appropriate to do so, it may be a good idea for critical diversity researchers and practitioners to attempt to join up conceptions of power, politics, diversity, resistance, solidarity, and inequality a bit more explicitly in how they approach their projects and practices. Fleming and Spicer (2014) make some related recommendations about revisiting themes of organizational power in novel ways, often by combining approaches to power that have previously remained unhelpfully separate – such as the formal and the informal aspects, the direct and indirect aspects, and the repressive and the productive aspects. American political scientist Joseph Nye has surveyed how trends and changes will affect the future of power, and draws conclusions about its global shifts away from the West toward the East, and its diffusion via technology and non-state actors (Nye, 2011). More organizationally, Clegg, Geppert, and Hollinshead (2018) present a special issue on political contests and 'circuits of power' flowing through multinational corporations, where international diversity and business shape one another in terms of global headquarters and national subsidiaries, as well as a complex range of other diverse stakeholder relations.

Power will therefore continue to be fundamental to critical perspectives on diversity in organizations because power is *relational* – it flows reciprocally across differentiated relationships – and organizations of all forms are founded on differentiated and interdependent structures and groups. In the twenty-first century context, many settings and trends will continue to shape the organizing of power and difference in ways that require critical inquiry, whether they revolve around social movements and activism, financialization, globalization, government intervention and in more extreme and tragic cases, acts of sadism, terror, and violence.

5 Institutions

Appreciating and adopting an institutional perspective in organization studies is a daunting task. This is not least because of its interdisciplinary roots and evolutionary struggles to define itself in relation to labels like 'institutional economics', and 'old' and 'new' (neo-) competing and overlapping brands of 'institutionalism', as well as various other historical and organizational streams and strands of institutional thought. Thankfully, some authors have taken pains to emphasize that there are some continuities to bear in mind (e.g. Selznick, 1996). DiMaggio and Powell's edited book (1991/2012) remains an essential citation and entry point for most work in an institutional tradition, noting that:

> within organization theory, "institutionalists" vary in their relative emphasis on micro and macro features, in their weightings of cognitive and normative aspects of institutions, and in the importance they attribute to interests and relational networks in the creation and diffusion of institutions. (p.1)

However, we must proceed by asking what institutions are and what taking an institutional perspective means. Crucially, institutions are *not* synonymous with organizations, although organizations may be said to be *institutionalized*. In a clumsy and broad attempt at defining institutions, we might say something along the lines of them being relatively stable and enduring patterns of social, economic and political actions and beliefs. In a recent paper drawing on Friedland and Alford (1991), Mutch (2018, p.244) describes how institutions are:

> Combinations of symbolic constructions and material practices that give meaning to the ways people engage in their social and organizational life. They are few in number, operate at the societal level, and are enduring in character. Society ... consists of a set of institutions, each with its own logics and possessing relative autonomy. Institutions display a logic that gives meaning to the practices organizations and individuals engage in.

An institutional perspective is therefore a very grand and ambitious project concerned with explaining why our societies have institutions as social structures and domains in the way that they do. Institutions are influences that profoundly govern our behaviors in ways that are perceived to be relatively stable, legitimate, and conformist over often very long stretches of historical time. This is a hugely influential way of packaging debates that sociology, history, politics, economics, organization studies, and the social sciences try to contribute to. If this is seen as a strength, it can also be seen as a weakness – where institutional debates arguably become bogged down in jargon-laden descriptions, abstractions, and endless debates about defining aspects of social and economic life.

However, despite criticisms and debates over specific aspects of institutionalist traditions, it seems hard to deny the importance of institutions and their influences on societies, typically mediated by organizational forms. Mutch (2018) helps make this concrete and explicit by outlining nine major enduring institutions in our societies – family, economy, medicine, religion, play, knowledge, politics, military, and law. Although not necessarily exhaustive, such a list allows us to 'bring society back in' to considerations of organizational life. Each underlying institution then gives rise to various logics, and in turn organizations and practices that bear the enduring traces of and beliefs in those logics (Mutch 2018).

Crucially, the current chapter will try to avoid getting bogged down in defining institutional jargon. Although there are many important points of debate for social theory about how institutional logics are made up of historical, cultural, and material symbolism and categorical systems (e.g. see Durand & Thornton, 2018), they are beyond the scope of this chapter and this book. Instead the concern here is to highlight the general value and potential of an institutional perspective as critical, interdisciplinary, and with interesting points of relevance for understanding diversity in organizations. At the same time, it is an important tension for those seeking to adopt an institutional perspective to recognize the need to proceed with caution where definitions and claims need to be made about how societies can be divided into 'fields' or 'orders' of far-reaching and enduring social activities, forms, and domains. This then creates further questions about how institutional logics influence, and are influenced by, organizations, and how we define and deploy further categories and concepts such as practices, habits, routines, and beliefs, all of which may reflect what we might choose to describe as 'institutional' in their manifestations and effects. A potential strength of institutional perspectives is their flexibility and compatibility with other areas of critical inquiry, such as the previous two chapters on history and power. Yet this strength has to be weighed against the need to responsibly reflect on existing institutional terminology and debate.

Therefore, while institutional perspectives have arguably achieved significant traction as interdisciplinary and leading ways of doing management research, it is perhaps curious that not much attention has been given to explicitly questioning how 'mainstream' or 'critical' such approaches are or can be. From all the chapters in the current volume, it is one of the least or most mildly critical perspectives in the organizational genre. It will be argued here that linking it more to diversity is one way to advance and exploit its critical potentials to a greater degree. Exceptionally, *Journal of Management Inquiry* did publish in 2015 a 'dialog', or forum of five short related articles debating whether or not institutional theory can be critical. Munir (2015) raises some concerns that institutional work does not adequately recognize more problematic uses of power. Suddaby (2015) suggests that institutional theory has become more mainstream in management over time but can continue to exist in a productive relationship of tension with more critical perspectives going forward. Hirsch and Loundsbury (2015), while sharing concerns that institutional work can simply equate power with legitimacy rather than domination or oppression, also believe there are currently great opportunities to bridge institutional and critical perspectives. Geppert (2015) proposes that institutional research on organizations can embrace critical issues more by methodologically focusing more on extreme cases, comparative analysis, and asking more challenging questions about politics, agency, and totalitarian tendencies. Finally, Willmott (2015) notes that although institutional theory is critical of orthodox economics, it is still entrenched in a fairly conservative and neo-positivist tradition of social science that is incompatible with critical theory. Provocatively, institutional theory is itself powerful enough – in terms of its knowledge production and academic presence – to be part of the problem with understanding organizations, rather than any supposed 'solution' to their excesses and ills (Willmott 2015).

While this chapter has some sympathy with Willmott's (2015) view, it will continue on the basis of also extending sympathy to the view of the other papers in that forum that tread a more conciliatory path. Indeed, Wilmott (2015) concludes with the challenge that perhaps one should lead with a critical approach to power relations, and then engage with and possibly rework institutional concepts from there. Responding to this challenge requires, in part at least, engaging with what Suddaby (2015) has described as institutional theory's latest stage, one with a new (or renewed) focus on agency and change. What remains is the issue raised by Willmott (2015), which concerns whether it is best to start with some sort of critical perspective on the organization first (e.g. feminism, post-structuralism), or starting with institutionalism, to 'bring back in' the critical emphasis on problematic operations of power.

One obvious way to link critical and institutional perspectives is in their skepticism towards orthodox economic perspectives, although some would surely argue that this line of critique has not been pursued far enough, nor is it likely to be. However, it still seems critically urgent to ask questions about what institutions are, and what institutions we would like to have, or at least try and shape. If institutional theories and studies portray this as an inexorable struggle or a *fait accompli* where the most legitimate logics and forms prevail, then so be it. Critical theories should then be able to complement this by being able to say more about which institutional logics are more problematic socially and economically, and why/how their problematic effects arise. Put another way, institutional theory can *describe* social ontology while critical theory is used alongside to *deconstruct* or *diagnose* certain aspects of that social ontology deemed to be problematic (i.e. exploitative, violent, oppressive, and so on).

Indeed, one area where institutional theory has been forthcoming in organization studies is in openly and explicitly wrestling with agency–structure relations (Hodgson, 2007). Institutional emphasis at its best can caution against giving too much attention solely to individuals or solely to collective structures, and instead direct us toward how both are inter-related through slowly evolving institutional processes of rules, conventions, habits, and other patterns of social conformity, co-evolution, and interaction (Hodgson, 2007). These are very difficult questions central to social ontology, but at least institutions remind us of the importance of these complex webs of cause and effect that create stability and change in human and social behavior.

Institutional theory has come to treat the agentic struggles of individuals and groups to create, disrupt, and maintain institutions as 'institutional work', which typically maps the many ways power and influence are used to affect what is seen as legitimate and taken-for-granted in organizational life (Lawrence, Leca, & Zilber, 2013). While there is much more to be investigated here under this label of institutional work, it represents at the very least a significant bridge with critical theories and approaches, as discussed previously (Lawrence, Suddaby, & Leca, 2011).

Institutions and Diversity

It is important to bring the discussion in this chapter squarely back to diversity in organizations. Diversity is faintly implicit in some aspects of institutional theory, in that organizations can face 'multiple logics' that effectively compete over their structures and activities for attention and legitimacy (Besharov & Smith, 2014). Logics can be read as offering accounts of why organizations exist in the first place, and the fundamental societal purposes they are designed to serve. Although not often explicitly spelled out, multiple logics may be partially aligned with diverse workforce constituencies, and some may be central while others are totally marginalized. Diverse logics may vary according to other features too, such as their degree of consensus, or the time and place of their instantiation. In turn, this also invites a discussion of institutional *complexity*; if there are multiple (plural) logics, and some at least are contradictory or competing, then what can we understand about how these struggles play out and how organizations respond to them? (Greenwood et al., 2011). It seems safe to say that if an institution is facing a significantly intense struggle between competing logics, than the fate of the very organization is probably at stake.

Diverse demographic groups are just as likely as not to be associated with discrete, correspondingly diverse logics to some extent. Alternatively, they may affiliate themselves with different positions when logics collide, or they may be affected differently by the responses and work being done to change those logics over longer periods of time. Pache and Santos (2010) give examples of organizations splitting down the middle due to competing logics, such as consultancy firms disputing whether they should service public or private sector clients, or museums splitting over whether their priority is preserving culture or tapping mass tourism. Finally, it is important to consider the key institutional concept of the *field* in relation to diversity. Fields are mid-level communities of multiple organizations and stakeholders that operate in a commonly recognized area of institutional life, in terms of defining issues, exchange relationships, and other structures, networks, and boundaries (e.g. see Zietsma et al., 2017). Again, these diverse configurations may reflect forms of socio-demographic diversity to the extent that there is a mapping between diverse actors and interests. Furthermore, as ideas of diversity, inclusion, and equality have evolved toward a more raised profile in global and public consciousness, various institutions, such as politics, the media, and the law, have of course played hugely influential roles and yet also been changed by these developments. New, overlapping institutional fields specifically concerned with diversity and equality arguably now exist in considerable number. Examples might include humanitarian and human rights organizations, professional associations, regulatory bodies that represent minorities, global international organizational forms, grass roots campaigns, and informal economies, among others.

If we were to be uncharitable about institutionalism, we could argue that it simply deploys a bewildering array of jargon to re-describe diverse aspects of our social and natural worlds. Yet at the same time, trying to delineate institutional variations helps us grasp the different landscapes diverse organizations with diverse employees are embedded in in a relatively consistent and comprehensive way. In a different, more counterintuitive way, the fact that a good deal of institutional research emphasizes sameness, stability, the difficulty/slowness of change, isomorphism (organizational mimicry), and conformity is a telling provocation for diversity. Harking back to history and power, institutionalism shows us how long deeply ingrained patterns of social behavior take to change, how deep they run in our societies, and along what lines they rise to the surface. Institutions help us trace organizational realities back to the most enduring sources of beliefs and habits and obligations - the powerful sources of social influence that we build upon as we try and maintain or change how we see our natural and social worlds (Mutch, 2018).

It is therefore slightly surprising that there really seems to be a lack of organizational research to review that explicitly links critical theory, diversity, and institutional theory. It may be that greater connections are needed between scholars that have hitherto been working in these areas too separately from one another. While institutional theory is capable of discussing 'diversity and change', it often ends up doing so in terms of a diversity of organizational forms (e.g. Kondra & Hinings, 1998), and therefore not diversity at the level of groups or individuals. It is strategic and economic before it is social, cultural, human, and demographic. These formal types of institutional analyses have little to do with diversity management per se.

In a rare application of institutional theory as a 'lens' on diversity, however, Evans (2014) does apply institutional thinking to understanding why European social funding programs aimed at gender mainstreaming employment in particular sectors often fail to achieve desired outcomes. Institutional forces of funding, legitimacy, power, change agendas, and 'partnership working' arrangements conspired across UK IT sector partner organizations to prevent more radical pro-diversity changes from taking place. Practices became 'isomorphic' and 'mimetic' – diluted into self-serving copycat institutional routines that offered only a superficial appearance of progress rather than the real thing (Evans, 2014). Recommendations then involve taking aim at superficial and self-serving institutional mechanisms, and periodically shaking them up to encourage more genuine change.

Other applications of institutional theory to diversity management or diversity in organizations in any sense have been either indirect or not especially critical in nature, returning us to some of the concerns expressed earlier in this chapter. Yang and Konrad (2011), for example, express an institutional view of diversity management in terms of formalized practices and a resource-based view of the organization that emphasizes legitimacy and competitive advantage. Much critical focus and urgency is obscured by such phrases, particularly 'legitimacy', which seems to risk subordinating the whole exercise of institutional theory to simply pleasing powerful stakeholders in competitive market environments. Zoogah, Peng, and Woldu (2015) do much the same thing in discussing the need to focus on Africa from an institutional perspective. Rather than taking institutions as a critical object affecting lived experiences of practices and inequalities, they are simply read in terms of their market and regulatory opportunities for resources, competition, and organizational effectiveness – a globalized business case for diversity.

The remainder of this chapter will nevertheless try to rescue and strengthen some critical potentials of institutional theory for understanding diversity in organizations. Three ways of taking institutions as a critical object of inquiry are suggested, rather than simply reverting to describing institutions in terms of markets and impersonal competitions for organizational legitimacy, the latter so often self-defeating where diversity is involved. The great irony of institutional perspectives, and perhaps their blessing and their curse, is that the very impersonal, enduring, taken-for-granted, self-reproducing nature of institutions they reveal is both so illuminating and problematic for diversity. They contain the seeds of their own critique of institutions but often without tending to that critique or exploiting it enough.

Below then, *institutional racism*, *institutional sexism*, and *total institutions* are presented as three more critical avenues relating institutionalism to diversity in organizations. The purpose here is not to fully review literature on these issues, which is doubtless fairly vast and diffuse but rather to point briefly beyond the boundaries of organization studies at societal topics that can be brought in and connected with existing areas for fresh insights.

Institutional Racism

To get a proper handle on how the concept of institutional racism emerged in the second half of the twentieth century, typically in US and UK organizational contexts, one has to venture outside of organization and management studies into neighboring social scientific fields like *ethnic and racial studies*. In an early review of definitions and uses of the concept, Williams (1985, p.342) expresses concern that it has been used to "refer to a very wide range of situations, embracing, as it does, ideologies, practices and material forms of dominance. The distinctions between individual actions, group beliefs, wider ideological developments and material forms of inequality already institutionalized in terms of class or gender become blurred."

Thus, using institutional racism and a related stance of 'anti-racism' too simplistically can serve to falsely unify and obscure a multifaceted sense of oppression and struggle, where in reality, many different ideologies and inequalities are at play, varying in how they are legitimated and responded to. Underpinning all of this is not just single institutions but also the complex links between them – jobs, housing, education, welfare, politics, law enforcement, sport, the arts, and so on. Taking institutional racism's complexity seriously means carefully attending to multiple levels of (un-)conscious intention, action, practice, and policy (Williams, 1985). From school textbook contents to police stop-and-search procedures, the implication of an institutional lens on racism is that we can trace the inequalities experienced by racial and ethnic groups back to a complex array of deeply rooted societal practices, artefacts, and assumptions that reproduce them. The discipline of using such a perspective responsibly and insightfully lies in not using it as a vaguely general catch-all term, and to make careful distinctions about levels of intention, means and ends in organizational practices and systems (Williams, 1985).

Institutional racism is doubtless a controversial concept because it is vulnerable to fierce debates about the varying nature of racism and discrimination, and whether it draws attention to some of the more covert, linguistic aspects of racism at the expense of co-existing patterns that involve more explicit and crude bigotry, hate and violence. At the very least, however, it invites reflection on what it means for something or someone to be racist, and the different ways that might occur. An empirical and critical example has been to look at job applications – and the mixture of subtle and not-so-subtle ways in which applications containing names that are ostensibly Black or White in origin reveal striking patterns of discrimination and preferential treatment in favor of Whites (Howitt & Owusu-Bempah, 1990). With examples like these, it seems important to recognize the many manifestations of racism, from the mundane to the more hateful, the linguistic to the material, the unwitting to the collusive. These are not easy things to ascertain in all instances, certainly, and the temptations to invoke essentialized 'new' types of racism and to reduce racism to individual psychology or diffused systemic complacency, should all be resisted. An institutional lens on racism therefore should critically challenge us to keep the focus on complex patterns of action, their characteristics and outcomes – the multiple cracks and formations of organizational life - rather than one-dimensional attributions towards singular types of actor, practice or resource.

From the UK context at least, by far the most prominent, well-known and emblematic case of institutional racism concerns the murder in 1993 of a young black man, Stephen Lawrence, and the associated Macpherson inquiry and report into the police's collective failure as an organization to respond to and investigate the crime fully and competently (Anthias, 1999). Without going into the case in detail here, much was made of the Macpherson report's finding that the police service was institutionally racist. Anthias (1999) analyses and discusses potential problems with the focus of the report on racism as 'unwitting', and the failure to properly separate out various mechanisms of *power* and *accountability* relating to exercises of *judgment* and *agency*. Once again, we see the double-edged nature of an institutional perspective – it draws attention to complex and problematic aspects of racism and discrimination, while also inviting dynamic critiques about what is left out when our organizations and institutions are characterized in a particular narrative account. It brings society back in, and perhaps that is no bad thing if it provokes wider discussions about democracy, citizenship and equality (Anthias, 1999).

Revisiting the Lawrence story twenty-five years on, Bowling (2018) reflects on its status as a 'wake-up call' in British society to the problematic notions of different longstanding patterns of racism (e.g. casual, violent, institutional). While important reforms to law and policing were implemented in its wake, however, serious questions remain about the painstaking journey to rebuild trust and address unsolved, deeply entrenched problems around knife crime and unlawful use of stop and search powers (Bowling, 2018). Organizations thus mediate and refract to a significant extent the institutional hopes and failings of our societies and social contracts, particularly with customers and members of the public. Furthermore, however painstaking, the necessary changes in facing up to cycles of racism, violence and inequality often need to be framed in terms of the institutional shifts and breaks with the historical past that are so urgently required – other reforms and responses risk seeming incomplete or insufficient. This of course goes beyond organizations to invite reflection on wider stakeholder relationships, another potential strength, and critical emphasis of an institutional perspective.

Institutional racism as a concept has helped societies such as the UK to understand how to evolve legal protections and changes to systems that might not otherwise have occurred, such as the formal recognition of forms of indirect discrimination, racial violence, and hate crimes. However, although it can appear obvious after the fact, institutions don't necessarily change and reform themselves in incremental, universally approved directions. They have ironies, as we have seen earlier, in that their 'solutions' are often not systemic enough or inflammatory, lacking nuance and specificity in really getting to grips with the deeply embedded racism central to an institutional perspective, visibly revealed in hundreds of separate places if societies and organizations choose to look closely enough. Yet it is easy to confuse personal and structural forms of racism and focus on one at the expense of another. One is expected to move between the personal, the social, the cultural, the historical, the organizational, and the societal – but it's not clear how this process achieves closure. Bourne (2001, p.20) concludes that the state, in many ways the ultimate organizational and institutional actor, is the culprit, where

...the fight against institutional racism is part of the larger fight against state racism - against asylum laws, against deportations, against stop and search, against deaths in custody, against school exclusions, against miscarriages of justice. You cannot combat popular racism without combating the state racism which gives popular racism its fillip. State racism contaminates civil society.

Imperfect answers about institutional racism then, but answers nonetheless, typically seem to involve movement between different areas of institutional and organizational life, often revolving around the law, the state, general publics, media, and the academy. Murji (2007) argues that concepts such as institutional racism can benefit from a public sociology that renews its engagements with civil society around such difficult concepts, through the media and various other imaginative public channels as yet under-explored.

Sara Ahmed's work (e.g. 2007, 2012) contains some thoughtful, carefully observed accounts of institutional racism and race in higher education institutions or universities. The emphasis is on how changes in documents, legislation, groups, practitioner roles, and other institutional machinery shape understandings of race and its representation. By 'following diversity around' the institution itself, one can trace its effects on racism, albeit effects that are rooted in social action and always unfinished; from one who arrives as a racial 'stranger' to an institution through to many equality projects, tokenistic assignments and other evolutions in relation to other institutions like public relations (Ahmed, 2012). Documents too, for example, have often come to reflect institutional norms of diversity and equal opportunities in higher education and other sectors, yet they can be worked on politically in these organizations, particularly by seeking to show how they conceal and omit forms of racism, and where words and deeds differ from the written documentation itself (Ahmed, 2007).

In their systematic review of British organizational psychology and HR research on ethnicity (sometimes used in place of the scientifically discredited concept of race), Kenny and Briner (2007) note a problematic absence of articles dealing with race or ethnicity theoretically, or in ways that go beyond individual hiring and selection. The very concepts of race and ethnicity themselves thus seem to be institutionally missing from certain fields, journals, communities, and organizational research agendas.

Beyond policing and higher education in the UK and US, research on institutional racism seems uneven and limited, particularly from an international and disciplinary perspective, despite it evidently remaining a distinctive issue and perspective on race and ethnicity. This is understandable if change is demanding and organizations might not want to look too deeply or like what they find. Institutionally, it means looking at racism in highly structural, systemic, and interlocking ways that are nevertheless felt by individuals and perpetrated by collectives. It also means looking out beyond an organization to the wider fabric of organizations in our societies, and questioning the many diversities of experience based on racial identities, perceptions and infrastructures (Tourse, Hamilton-Mason, & Wewiorski, 2018).

Institutional Sexism and Feminist Institutionalism

Institutional racism and institutional sexism have clear and obvious parallels in definitions of how they exclude their respective minorities from many institutional arenas, yet also many particularities relating to the experiences of those with distinct combinations of race and gender identity (Anthony, 1980). We might use the term institutional sexism to distinguish certain gender-based patterns of discrimination, such as those relating to pregnancy or harassment, although these institutional patterns once again admittedly pose legal-definitional problems of responsibility, inclusivity, and intent (Korn, 1995).

In any case, institutional sexism takes us back to the work of Joan Acker, mentioned in the previous chapter in relation to gender and power. It is worth quoting her at length here, to get a clear sense of how institutional sexism arises because of the ways our institutions are gendered in the first place:

> The term "gendered institutions" means that gender is present in the processes, practices, images and ideologies, and distributions of power in the various sectors of social life. Taken as more or less functioning wholes, the institutional structures of the United States and other societies are organized along lines of gender. The law, politics, religion, the academy, the state, and the economy...are institutions historically developed by men, currently dominated by men, and symbolically interpreted from the standpoint of men in leading positions, both in the present and historically. These institutions have been defined by the absence of women. The only institution in which women have had a central, defining, although subordinate, role is the family. In spite of many changes bringing women into all institutions, and the reclaiming of women's history that shows their earlier important participation, males still dominate the central institutions. (Acker, 1992, p.567)

From science to religion to government to professions to the media, gender has been an organizing principle around the world. To critique the differential gender-based organizing of institutions, and the attitudes, behaviors, and inequalities that go with that is therefore, implicitly or explicitly, to raise the issue of institutional sexism. This institutional charging of diversity and gender issues may be a difficult pill for many men and women to swallow – institutions seeming so pervasive, historical, natural, and taken-for-granted; even nigh invisible and inescapable in many instances. This in turn seems to conflate institutions with an absolutely fixed reality – the way things are, the natural order of things, the forces of the market, the decrees of the law. Ironically, this seems to arise from how embedded we all are in our own pre-existing, institutionalized mind sets. There is a nagging sense that things somehow cannot be otherwise. Or that they should or should not be, but there is not much that can be readily done about them. Imagining new, less sexist or gendered institutions is therefore difficult for many, as is changing them from within. Institutional change is threatening to vested interests and ontological security – the status quo underpinning a relatively stable and secure everyday life.

In spite of all this, the spreading of gender-based changes across so-ciety – often politically and culturally surrounding organizations – does occur, and sooner or later, this calls into question the illegitimacy of various sexist and gendered institutional logics and organizational forms, practices and categories. Indeed, a case study by Styhre (2014) is a relatively rare but crucial example of this; a study of how the Church of Sweden has managed to ensure the inclusion of ordained female minis-ters within a widely respected and legitimated professional and institu-tional category, albeit with some residual traces of sexism in some practices. Even in a very old institution, the concept of 'institutional work' shows how socially entrenched beliefs and practices can be con-tested and feminized, in ways that bring the institution in line with the rights and privileges of other areas of a society. Styhre (2014) is quick to remind us that institutional work is ongoing with no end-point and can appear slow, although it also has distributed and cooperative joint as-pects too. Gendered institutional work is arguably very difficult de-pending on the circumstances, yet it needn't be mysterious; it seems to be present anywhere a sexist norm, role or practice is being disrupted, questioned or performed differently by women (or men, if they are po-tential allies to the cause).

Work–life quality and gender equality is another area that is starting to bring organizational and institutional realms more closely together in understanding and ameliorating sexism. Moen (2015) traces the themes of key books on the topic via the state, labor market and social policies, and through to household and individual strategies. Basic wages, pro-tections, working hours, career paths, and salary systems all come to-gether to make gendered experiences of managing work and life something structural to be challenged and changed. These experiences are not solely a matter of private and individual 'balance' – rather they make up a multi-layered *institutional/organizational* situation where jointly exercised agency and capability are aimed at developing more stress-free and egalitarian working lives (Moen, 2015).

Universities have a double-edged quality in this regard, when it comes to the safety to freely discuss problems of sexism and violence against women, versus the danger of institutional norms and gaps that promote and reproduce 'laddism', 'rape culture', and 'everyday sexism' in the same spaces (Lewis, Marine, & Kenney, 2018). Younger generations of US and UK feminist students, activists, and researchers, men and women, are necessary for shaping feminist consciousness and communities that seek to address these contemporary forms of sexism. These more contemporary institutional settings and politics appear to coexist alongside the relatively slowly changing, more traditional corporate ones concerning 'glass ceilings' and various other disputed barriers and mechanisms affecting whether women and other minorities become promoted to top leadership positions or not (e.g. Cook & Glass, 2014).

If deeply entrenched institutional sexism is one part of the gendered organizational diversity puzzle here, then it can be argued that a corresponding *feminist institutionalism* is the correct term for the forces needed to challenge and change it. However, such a label is not explicitly used in much current organizational research at all. Partly it depends on joining the dots between the compatible methodologies and epistemologies of social construction that underpin forms of feminism, economics and institutional analysis (Waller & Jennings, 1990). Ironically, perhaps it is due to the entrenched nature of gendered institutions in the first place that such perspectives seem to not gain as much traction as one might expect.

Once again, it is in a neighboring social scientific field – this time political science – where we find the most relevant work linking feminism to an 'institutional turn' in the discipline's knowledge production. Particular scholars such as Meryl Kenny and Fiona Mackay, among others, have produced a stream of work reflecting on feminist institutionalism. The focus is on political institutions, power struggles, routines, regimes, orders, and other promising institutional concepts placed in dialogue with feminist conceptions of patriarchal structures and legacies (Kenny, 2007). Kenny and Mackay (2009) do express some skepticism about combining feminism and institutionalism along similar lines highlighted earlier in this chapter – that feminism's critical emphasis on gender and power is the important link, rather than (new) institutionalism per se. However, they do note both fields'

> [M]utual interest in temporality, relationality, and contextuality in political developments. Soft concepts of causality that examine the configuration of constellations of elements over time, developed for example in historical institutionalism, appear well equipped to deal with the empirical complexities of gendered institutions and political processes...complexities which often seem to confound approaches using standard variable analysis. (Kenny & Mackay, 2009, pp.272–273)

Related works also note institutionalism's careful balancing of structure and agency in accounting for social structures and behaviors, as well as its focus on both formal and informal 'rules of the game' or 'the ways things are around here' (Mackay, 2011; Mackay, Kenny, & Chappell, 2010). At the same time, Lowndes (2014) makes the cautionary point that institutionalism should not stretch its concepts too far such that they lose all meaning, and should be specific and rigorous in how it investigates phenomena across various timescales, spatial scales, and types and levels of norm and custom.

Nevertheless, Thomson (2018), using the example of abortion legislation in Northern Ireland, returns to the crucial point that feminist institutionalism is a much-needed perspective for pinpointing 'critical actors' and their varying success in changing institutional and political conditions to be more gender-just. The 'critical mass' of institutional work needed to change pivotal societal policies and worldviews via appeals, reformed guidelines, and range of organizations involved arguably come into frame more clearly. The institutional struggles continue and can perhaps seem tedious in their details, but when they have names and actors and a focus such as feminist institutionalism attached, they have the potential to unite more scholars and other stakeholders in achieving critical societal changes. Happily for many women and progressives, at the time of writing, the Republic of Ireland voted decisivelyin favor (66.4% to 33.6%) of overturning its abortion ban, paving the way for further change in Ireland and putting more pressure for change on Northern Ireland going forward (BBC News, 2018). To suggest that institutional feminism is not relevant to scholars of organizational diversity and working lives seems a position hard to defend.

Total Institutions

Total institutions are a third and final under-explored research topic and approach with implications for critical research on diversity in organizations. Total institutions date back to the 1960s and 70s. In particular, in the work of the sociologist Erving Goffman, they are defined as "a place of residence and work where a large number of like-situated individuals cut off from the wider society for an appreciable period of time together lead an enclosed formally administered round of life" (Goffman, 1968 cited in Davies, 1989, p.77).

Perhaps one reaction to total institutions is that they are outdated or only reflect a minority of extreme organizations – the asylums and monasteries of old, for example. Wallace's (1971) edited book volume on the subject, which has gone through several reprints, contains chapters on and studies of psychiatric hospitals, prison systems, women's prisons, public hospitals, college dorms, nursing schools, community mental health organizations, religious communes, and hippie communes.

On the one hand, therefore, total institutions link institutional-type concepts and approaches back to other critical areas of inquiry; namely, history and power, the subjects of the two preceding chapters of this book. On the other hand, they are also ripe for critical refinement and development in terms of recognizing more broadly the *variability* in the extent to which all organizations are 'total' in some of their character-istics – their bureaucracy, their scope, the symbolic strength and trajec-tory of their cultures, and so on (Davies, 1989).

Furthermore, what is valuable critically about total institutions is precisely this relative quality of *totality* as a way of thinking about power and institutions – where great social and societal clusters of power techniques or channels are aligned in a uniform direction. In terms of diversity, this could be a way of keeping a minority group 'unwanted' by society segregated from the majority, as well as an extremely powerful, coercive, and well-organized way of controlling difference and effacing it under rules and techniques that promote high levels of standardization (Wallace, 1971). This returns us fairly firmly to considerations of power. It is therefore no accident that Michel Foucault and other scholars of organizational power have an interest in the most total of institutions.

Indeed, in a self-consciously provocative piece, Stewart Clegg (2006) argues that organization theory has been 'ignorant' of total institutions and the roles they have played in some of the worst crimes of humanity. Re-emphasizing the rich links between scholars such as Goffman, Foucault, and Bauman, he argues how total institutions provide a unique perspective on how deeply troubling practices can become interlocking, routine, efficient, and legitimate under certain organizational conditions (Clegg, 2006). US detention centers Guantanamo Bay and Abu Ghraib are given as more modern examples of total institutions. The broader implication from these more extreme cases is that there is a delicate complicity and interweaving between 'good' organizational functioning and the darker ends it can be put to (Vaughan, 1999).

Since that 2006 article, there has been some limited critical organi-zational scholarship drawing on total institutions. 'Diversity' does not usually appear explicitly, but there are strong implicit themes with wider potential for organization studies. The most obvious diversity theme lies in the differences organizationally reproduced across the demographic lines between those running the total institution and those being in-stitutionalized by it and between other groups outside of the institution relative to those inside it. The latter distinction would encapsulate both prisoners and guards as internal and institutionalized, and blur the lines between the two groups, from a different perspective of society at large.

One paper by Shenkar (1996) compares Chinese state-owned en-terprises to total institutions. The temporal and spatial barriers between sleep, play, and work start to break down under the historically estab-lished authority relations between Chinese officials and workers.

Although there are some differences in terms of the levels of stigmatization, separation, and isolation, there are significant similarities where many workers are treated the same and required to do the same things together in a tightly scheduled and planned manner. These characteristics and partial resemblances to work camps, prisons, and religious orders have obvious repercussions for the organizational behaviors of individuals and groups, such as how they require supervisory approval or the limited flows of information sharing. The important implication of the total institution metaphor lies in the recognition of degrees of totality in all organizations and different dimensions of totality. This also raises critical questions about forms of resistance towards such regimes (e.g. 'playing it cool' by following the minimal amount of rules possible without punishment; Shenkar, 1996), and the ontological nature of various structural or even virtual boundaries between the 'inside' and 'outside' world. In some senses all organizations involve the setting up and adjustment of boundaries and inside/outside distinctions.

Other work on total institutions is often historical, looking at the devastating and tragic effects of regimes of power associated with genocide and communism, in setting such as China and Cambodia (e.g. Clegg, Cunha, & Rego, 2012; Martí & Fernández, 2013). For those willing not to dismiss the Holocaust or communism as anachronisms in relation to the modern business world, these total institutional scenarios shed light on a critical blend of enduring themes relevant to all organizations – mutually reinforcing mechanisms of power, resistance, radical change, ethics, and leadership and followership.

Diversity and contemporary relevance both start to resurface when we consider that organizational practices of separating and marginalizing specific groups from the outside world, often in derogatory ways, have extended far into the twentieth century and are still a concern and reality. Ireland's industrial school system, for example, resembled a total institution in how it took children from society and treated them as repulsively 'abject' entities to be excluded and controlled via dehumanizing institutional mechanisms (Kenny, 2016). Organizations resemble (total) institutions in the regimented ways they take form to police these societal boundaries of exclusion. Once established, total institutions may be difficult to dis-assemble and may be taken-for-granted in their existence until their more harmful aspects are re-exposed to an outside world that may exhibit shock or shame. Other examples, as briefly mentioned previously, include the institutionalized torture of suspected terrorists in detention centers by the Bush Administration and Central Intelligence Agency in the US (Chwastiak, 2015), as well as refugee camps in Africa where Western officials and refugees (primarily Somalian) co-exist in parallel, tightly organized institutional worlds (de la Chaux, Haugh, & Greenwood, 2017). The organizational themes are striking – diversity being managed here by extreme deployments of power that disguise the violent with the mundane using organizational roles, visions, spaces, and practices; manipulating the legal status and societal definitions of minority groups to justify their containment away from the majority.

Conceptual and empirical questions remain around to what extent total institutions and related types of organizational settings hold up a mirror to contemporary forms of organization and diversity management. Yet their persistence and enduring recurrence around the world, as well as their controversial origins and purposes, seem to speak of compelling organizational truths not to be ignored. Total institutions caution us against how easily the morally reprehensible and violent aspects of society can be organized out of sight to mask extreme suffering and injustice. In some critical respects they represent an ultimate act of exclusion, and a negation of the expression of diversity. They imprison and neutralise any minority groups deemed unwanted or undesirable to wider society, yet are often also cultivated and maintained by powerful elites. In other cases, it may well be a question of degree, and some rationales for 'totality' may be more understandable, transparent, and benign. Acts of disruption and resistance by the institutionalized actors may also reshape the more inhumane aspects of total institutions too.

What remains fascinating and debated with some energy and controversy, particularly in psychology, is how easily people can be made to inhabit institutions, identify with them, and play roles accordingly. The classic 1971 Zimbardo Stanford Prison Experiment, for example, is still debated and revisited today, as people weigh up the influences of leadership, the experimental situation, and the conformity and complicity of experimenters and participants in an artificially induced total prison regime (Reicher, Haslam, & Van Bavel, 2018). Totalitarian institutional spaces seem to haunt and trouble us by asking what we, as diverse world citizens, are capable of in oppressive, highly regimented, authoritarian, and conformist situations.

Institutional Theory and Diversity Going Forward

Institutional theory continues to move forward and gain traction in top management journals, and to be combined with various related perspectives on organizations, some more critical than others, and with some risk that it loses coherence and potential if it spreads in too many different directions. Any links with diversity and difference still need to be teased out more explicitly.

The struggle for institutional agency and change continues to be theorized in relation to concepts like institutional entrepreneurship and institutional work. These perspectives paint a picture of embattled actors strategically vying for allies, communicative airtime, and network influence from within the enduring structures they seek to change (Battilana, Leca, & Boxenbaum, 2009). To the extent that diversity involves change agents, minorities and coalitions seeking to change existing orders, these perspectives would seem to be relevant to diversity. Vacarro and Palazzo (2014) studied the case of an activist group in Sicilian society that set out to challenge the persistence of practices where business owners would still pay protection money to the Mafia. By working in carefully coordinated stakeholder groups and spaces and securing commitment to focal values such as dignity, legality, and solidarity, they managed to achieve institutional change in a highly change-resistant context.

Slowly but surely then, aspects of institutional theory seem to be connecting up with slightly more critical concerns, although the extent of this remains disputed. Vince (2019), for instance, proposes connecting perspectives on psychoanalysis, systems psychodynamics, and the unconscious aspects of organizations with institutional approaches. Instead of institutional logics, we can acknowledge a parallel concept of institutional 'illogics', highlighting the more emotional and irrational fantasies and social defence mechanisms that might be underpinning institutional influences. The idea that organizational groups and collectives are not always rational and instrumental when it comes to something as emotive as diversity and inclusion seems a worthwhile avenue to pursue, given that it might uncover various fantasies and anxieties about institutionalized identities and intergroup relations. Similarly, Moisander, Hirsto, and Fahy (2016) have argued and shown how *emotions* such as shame, pride, and pathos are managed and constructed in institutional terms relating to power, communication, and legitimacy, using changes in the Finnish government's relationship with the European Union (EU) as an example.

Radoynovska (2018) takes an institutional perspective on the 'micropractices' surrounding inequality in a French social service organization. Specifically, the study focuses on the discretionary manipulation of institutional rules and boundaries in the daily work of frontline workers, in terms of variations as to when they insist on equal treatment and when they make exceptions in deciding to allocate/withhold benefits. Such studies raise questions about the tricky institutional balances between rules, procedures, and discretionary adaptations in everyday work on diversity in organizations.

What is always at stake in institutional theory is the relationship between structure and action. Delbridge and Edwards (2013) argue that adoption of a *critical realist* perspective can help us embrace the complexity of this relationship as historically grounded and occurring at multiple levels of analysis. Diverse actors vary in their reflexivity and capacity to spot and pursue opportunities for action and change. Actions are conditioned by institutional logics but more needs to be understood about the nature and variation of such 'conditioning' rather than simply assuming action is determined or agentic (Delbridge & Edwards, 2013).

Another moderately critical perspective on institutional change applicable to diversity in organizations going forward is to adopt a *process view* or ontology of institutions. Zundel, Holt and Cornelissen (2013) use a study of the US TV series *The Wire* to show how features of structure and agency can be combined over time by thinking of institutions less as stable objects, things, or entities, and more as unfolding relationships between interactions and events. Institutional work involves exploring flexibility and expending limited energy across various patterns and processes of behavior change as subsystems of drug dealers, gang members, police officers, and other stakeholders interact (Zundel et al., 2013). Institutional dynamics are portrayed as more fragile and restless under this view.

Two other perspectives that try to marry up or reinvigorate institutional theory with related approaches relevant to diversity concerns are (1) morality and (2) comparative institutionalism. First, Moore and Grandy (2017) argue that institutional theory can bring morality back into its core concerns by drawing on the work of Alasdair MacIntyre. Institutional concerns such as logics and legitimacy all have a moral dimension, in terms of the driving purpose of organizations, their core practices, and discrepancies between the moral value, virtues, and forms of goodness inherent to the organization and its means-ends relations with wider society. Second, Hotho and Saka-Helmhout (2017) argue for the benefits of comparative institutionalism and the ways different societal institutions contribute to shaping the collective organizing of work. Comparative institutionalism emphasizes the institutional differences between and within countries, in terms of domains such as labor relations, corporate governance, market capitalism, and educational systems. Such perspectives help us to explain how organizations face challenges as they expand internationally across different institutional settings and societal diversity.

We can round off this section and its series of theoretical perspectives with a final further array of more concrete settings and examples of studies that take an institutional lens to diversity in organizations.

- Monro (2007) considers the institutional field in the UK focused on sexualities equalities partnerships and inter-agency local government work arrangements. The study draws attention to rituals, symbols, templates, networks, isomorphic imitation, and hybridization or fusion across different organizations engaged with lesbian, gay and bisexual community safety issues.
- Creed, DeJordy, and Lok (2010) show how gay, lesbian, bisexual, and transgender (GLBT) ministers in U.S. Protestant denomination churches resolve the institutional contradictions between being a diverse but marginalized group and embedded in an institution they would like to see changed. GLBT ministers engaged in challenging forms of 'identity work' to reconcile and claim institutional roles and

practices (Bible studies, prayer) as compatible resources for change in embodying an inclusive, healing and accepting church.

- Nwonka and Malik (2018) trace how UK politics and public funding have undergone institutional changes related to the 1999 Macpherson Report and its concerns over institutional racism in UK organizations. The UK film/cinema sector is specifically shown to be pursuing a complex multicultural and commercial institutional agenda in getting black films made at a historical moment when racial pressures and tensions were running high. Ultimately such films are portrayed as institutionally problematic – they are made for thin and conformist instrumental reasons, which leave underlying issues of inclusion, access and inequality unaddressed.

- Doldor, Sealy, and Vinnicombe (2016) gathered data from the institutional field of UK executive selection and attempts to promote greater gender diversity and women on FTSE100 company boards. They draw particular attention to core interviews with a group of specialized headhunters; finding them to be opportunistic and precarious diversity agents in their marginal institutional work, rather than heroic entrepreneurs or genuine, intentional radicals. As 'accidental activists' (AAs), they were instead partly reactive to external pressures and allowed themselves to be shaped by distributed actors and logics in their motivations and strategies for institutional change, with some success. The implication is that there may be different kinds of actors or allies in an institutional field, and even the seemingly marginal ones are engaged in valuable micro-processes of institutional diversity change agency.

- Altermark (2017) focuses on diversity in the form of the institutional history of intellectual disability politics. He argues that while intellectually disabled persons are generally no longer kept in state institutions (resembling total institutions – see above, this chapter), the de-institutionalization process and transition to greater integration and citizenship is only partially complete. In ways similar to postcolonial 'decolonization', different national contexts are experiencing a 'post-institutional' era, which still struggles to avoid defining intellectual disabilities in terms of deficiency and paternalism, rather than empowerment and more equal knowledge production. Attempts to integrate those with disabilities are still characterized by forms of control and marginalization to the extent that majority policies and theories dominate and articulate what an 'ideal citizen' is held to be.

Conclusion

This chapter has wrestled with the connections between institutional theory and diversity in organizations. This has been particularly challenging given that institutional links with diversity are often implicit rather than explicit and vary in the degree to which they are viewed as truly 'critical', as opposed to being deemed more rational, instrumental, value-neutral, descriptive, or similar. Therefore, some may dispute its inclusion in this book's structure as a 'defining aspect' of a critical approach. However, this chapter would re-assert that institutionalism is a very far-reaching and pervasive backdrop to most studies of organizations and work, as well as being conceptually rich, influential, and flexible in its ability to connect with other critical and theoretical camps. Whether scholars of organization and diversity choose to acknowledge it or not, institutionalism frequently connects with themes of power and history. Furthermore, institutional sexism and racism, feminist institutionalism, and total institutions all offer critically resourceful ways of linking highly organized and conditioned patterns of social action, inequality, inclusion/exclusion and diversity.

That said, much research and theory, in organization and management at least, does tend to arise from UK and US institutional settings, with less of a comparative, international, or cross-cultural emphasis to date. Therefore, there is more to be done concerning diverse institutions that many Western scholars and practitioners are less familiar with. This may necessitate drawing on other disciplines, such as anthropology and studies of the Middle East, Africa, and Asia, where organizations encounter and operate in different historical, religious, and political societal conditions (e.g. Al-Rasheed, 2013). Institutions represent diverse ways of life in and of themselves, a diversity that runs very deep.

Institutional theory thus seems valuable to understanding organizations to the extent that it brings societal contexts back into focus. It is a reminder of the diversity of organizational forms, environments beyond organizations and across them, and of tensions between small-scale action and large-scale structure. It challenges notions of undiluted individual freedom and intentional agency, often showing instead a more distributed, slower, and uneven struggle for change, with shades of grey and longer timeframes.

Total integration and acceptance as a critical perspective by many working in organization studies may not be feasible or desirable, but there are certainly some promising bridges and points of engagement. These run in both directions. Specifically, while institutional theories may draw our attention to certain conditioning aspects of diverse societal contexts, customs, norms, and rules, perhaps critical theories for their part can also help disrupt the taken-for-granted legitimacy of aspects of our institutions, logics, and practices. Debates about overlap, symbiosis, and encroachment between critical theory and institutional theory seem set to continue (Lok, 2019; Willmott, 2018). Institutional theory may need to cede more ground to critical theory's radical and emancipatory emphasis on political and social change. Alvesson and

Spicer (2018) go as far as to suggest that (neo-) institutional theory is now in the throes of a midlife crisis, but that it can address its relationship to organization studies by sharpening its focus and reflecting more precisely about how its assumptions relate to other areas of research. The hope here is that diversity, inclusion, and equality provide some fruitful stimuli for achieving this.

Part III

Elaborating on Critical Themes Concerning Diversity in Organizations

6 Intersectionality

Intersectionality has become a fairly well-known, far-reaching inter-disciplinary concept for understanding diversity in the social sciences. More specifically, it reflects a simple but profound recognition that the form and content of *multiple differences* can be represented in terms of how they simultaneously and distinctively combine, interact, and *intersect*. Very much like a cross-roads, when differences come together in config-urations or multiples, they can be thought of as forming a unique spot or intersection. However, the criticality or controversy of intersectionality lies in how to proceed from this more basic recognition. If black women's experiences are different from white women's experiences, and older white women's experiences overlap more with older white men's than they do young black women's, for example, then we end up with a sort of mathematical complexity or messiness that comes with multiple differ-ences. Intersectionality arguably has its greatest critical value in en-gendering this uneasy sensation of recognizing diversity as many possible permutations, overlaps, and uniquely distinguished identity combinations. The rest of this chapter will therefore review and explore some of the critical potential and contentiousness of intersectionality as a critical 'lens' or way of looking at diversity in organizations.

The origins of how intersectionality became explicit in social scientific literature have been frequently told, and they invariably lead back to critical race theory, black feminism, and the work of Kimberlé Williams Crenshaw. Crenshaw, a law professor, was searching for an everyday metaphor for capturing how anti-discrimination laws can fail to make visible the interaction of more than one dimension of diversity associated with power and oppression (Adewunmi, 2014). For Crenshaw, race, gender, and the neglected experiences of black women were a very salient example (Crenshaw, 1989, 1991). This multidimensionality can be threatening and difficult to accept for other groups who feel it as a sort of splitting or rivalry within what had been perceived as a single overall category. Yet for precisely this reason intersectionality is an immensely powerful argument that diversity needs to be organized along *multi-dimensional* lines. The implications from this are that coalitions need to be built more carefully in this regard, and that one group cannot necessarily speak of the experience of another that lies in part along a different dimension of difference.

In articles on management and organization, and on the back of these developments, intersectionality has become subject to emerging, ongoing discussion, often from critical perspectives. Styhre and Eriksson-Zetterquist (2008) have described it as similar to other critical theories and concepts that aim to encourage 'thinking the multiple' – thinking more fluidly in terms of how multiple dimensions dynamically overlap, clash, and shift in their emphasis, rather than just being fixed, stable categories. In psychology too, intersectionality has in recent years encouraged a more critical series of questions to be asked by researchers of categories, identities, and inequalities, affecting potentially the whole research process, from how literatures are reviewed through to interpretations and conclusions (Cole, 2009). Furthermore, and unlike some critical perspectives, intersectionality does not necessarily distance itself from quantitative methods, which can be used to sample, measure, and test interactions between multiple dimensions (Cole, 2009), although far less of this research seems to have emerged to date (Allison & Bannerjee, 2014; Ramarajan, 2014).

Holvino (2010) proposes that intersectionality opens up theoretical and methodological avenues for disentangling the simultaneous influences of gender, race, and class in organizations. Accordingly, intersectionality is often presented as a critique of a dominant white liberal feminist perspective that serves to marginalize other intersections based on race and class, where socialism and white privilege are key critical concerns that risk being overlooked. In international business, Zander, Zander, Gaffney, and Olsson (2010) have argued that an intersectional view on diversity can be fruitfully applied to understanding the intersectional design of a multinational corporation (MNC), with its headquarters, subunits, and overlapping structures. It stands to reason that larger, more international organizations are likely to contain and manage more possible social and demographic intersections, although whether their HR practices and career and talent management frameworks reflect the complexity of individuals' diversity is another matter (Zander et al., 2010).

However, beyond its obvious value in acknowledging the messy but rich complexity of our social world, intersectionality has become mainstreamed into much feminism, and it is not always clear how it is being developed in a deep, coherent way to stay true to some of its roots in critical race theory and black feminism (Carasthasis, 2014). In management and organization studies too, it sits within a broader interdisciplinary discussion around 'multiple identities', and the messy networks and multiple ties, memberships and layers of power that divide and connect diverse groups and individuals along multiple lines

(Ramarajan, 2014). Intersectionality does seem to provide something slightly distinctive in terms of its critical, feminist emphasis, as well as the idea that certain identity combinations are seriously repressed and displaced through power and privilege. However, while there is a lot of theoretical engagement with deconstructing binaries and recognizing multidimensional patterning of differences, beyond that many questions remain, and there is a risk that intersectionality itself becomes too burdensome and fragmented in how it is used and applied.

Much thinking in organizations and institutions, on diversity or just more generally, is still arguably very reductionist and categorical (e.g. Alvesson & Spicer, 2012) – for the sake of enforcing control, ensuring simplicity, or both – and changing this in intersectional, multidimensional directions appears to be an uncertain work in progress. In their review and quantitative content analysis of intersectionality in organization studies covering 1990–2009, Allison and Banerjee (2014) found evidence for an intersectional approach in less than 1% of articles in several leading journals. It seems reasonable to assume that its adoption has grown since 2009 to some extent – and this chapter will aim at reviewing some of that growth – but intersectionality nevertheless seems vulnerable to uneven, partial, and limited use in research and practice (Carasthasis, 2014). This is surprising in one sense, given that intersectionality speaks to the multiple differences that exist within each and every one of us, and in another sense it is perhaps markedly unsurprising, simply mirroring, and serving to reproduce wider patterns of power, privilege, and inequality where false unities or binaries prevail.

In sum, there is perhaps some self-fulfilling irony here worth revisiting, common to other critical perspectives on organizations, in that intersectionality typically seeks to secure justice for marginalized identity combinations, and yet as a perspective on diversity remains itself relatively marginalized, in some domains at least. It is therefore important to consider what the risks and opportunities are in relation to whether intersectionality remains a challenging perspective on the margins or if it becomes co-opted in various ways to more mainstream organizational research. In the latter case in particular, further questions also arise around how it should retain a vital critical and political edge.

Intersectionality and Diversity

The body of this chapter proceeds by considering more closely some of the strengths, limitations, and applications of intersectionality to diversity in organizations. The chapter then concludes with some further thoughts on its future utility and validity, and the types of social and organizational settings where it is only beginning to be applied and debated.

Strengths

One strong argument in favor of intersectionality is that it gives researchers, managers, and others a raised consciousness and sensitivity to more internationally and economically diverse experiences in their workforce (Holvino, 2010). Carastathis (2014) summarizes four main 'analytic benefits' to intersectionality – simultaneity, complexity, irreducibility, and inclusivity. All are inter-related and tend to amount to a consciousness-raising and deeper consideration of multiple differences without simply adding one on top of another or trying to reduce or isolate them in more singular, superficial ways. It's interesting to reflect on how these purported advantages would translate as useful to managers and employees in organizations. If leveraged effectively, they might help create deeper inter-connections between diverse employee support groups and networks. Instead of separate enclaves, groups of employees could dynamically meet in more cross-cutting, overlapping ways as part of an intersectional 'caucusing' process. Ideally, overlapping identities would be more sensitively discussed and solidarities between subgroups facilitated and mediated via more intersectional organizing activities (e.g. Haslam, Eggins, & Reynolds, 2003).

At times, intersectionality can be expressed as a slightly unlikely critical and practical combination of feminism and psychology. Warner (2008), for example, attempts to outline a 'best practices' approach to incorporating intersectionality into research on identities and behavior. She notes in particular, three main issues that need to be managed. First, there is a need to transparently and thoughtfully use decision rules to choose which intersections to focus on and which to collapse. Second, the need to explicitly make sense of how overall 'master' categories such as gender or race relate to nested 'emergent' categories of multiple intersecting identities. Finally, the importance of placing the individual and interpersonal experiences of intersecting identities in their wider social structural context. Together, these three suggestions do seem to provide some ways of capitalizing on the strengths of an intersectionality perspective while avoiding or minimizing most of its weaknesses.

Garry (2011) argues that we should not demand too much of intersectionality, and that its greatest strength might be as a family of helpful approaches and standards that unite feminisms rather than fragment them. Intersectionality is not in and of itself a theory for specifically explaining issues of power, agency, oppression, and identity. Nevertheless, it can be mobilized to understand simultaneous oppressions and privileges that vary across particular societal and workplace issues as to who is affected and how. Garry (2011) insists on the necessity and value of messy visual metaphors and imagery as something intersectionality has to offer. These are typically distinct from images of supposed purity, splitting, and separation, and closer to images that are more intermeshed, dynamic, and indicative of family resemblances between different 'genders' or intersections.

Another potential strength of intersectionality (although not unique to it) is simply its influence and ability to evolve across times, disciplines, and to attract global engagement. Carbado, Crenshaw, Mays, and Tomlinson (2014) introduce a special issue on this idea – that intersectionality is already doing good work we may not be aware of and is also suggestive of further developments. In short, intersectionality is never done or exhausted and can be seen in fact as very much a work-in-progress. Example include applying it to building or understanding new potential forms or sources of solidarity and social movements, enriching social explanations of phenomena such as marriage, family and genetics, and further variations in the experiences of subgroups of black men and women (Carbado et al., 2014). Rather than debating what intersectionality is, to discover its strengths we should look to what it shows, what it does, and how it could be used.

In fields concerned directly with work, employment, and organization, it has been argued that intersectionality has not yet been significantly engaged with (McBride, Hebson, & Holgate, 2015). What can be separated out are the general implications from the specific. Generally, it is important for *all* workplace researchers to be sensitive and aware to intersectionality in contextualizing their research and not over-generalizing. Specifically, smaller groups of researchers may want to develop intersectionality more explicitly as a framework and method. A general sensitivity can help identify where diversity and inclusion data are missing and guide future, cumulative research-building efforts that give voice to different experiences of work. A more specific, specialist use of intersectionality is also valuable for studying workplaces, in terms of looking more deeply at the operations of power and knowledge between and within categories of difference (McBride et al., 2015). However, more ways of 'doing' intersectionality in organizations could still be explored and engaged with.

From more of an activism and social change perspective, intersectionality has the distinct strength of urging researchers to promote social justice and equity in ways that might not otherwise be realized (Rosenthal, 2016). Areas such as psychology, education, and HR have agendas on well-being, inequality, inclusion, stigma, ethics, and social responsibility that could draw on intersectionality to enrich these agendas with communitarian, collaborative, and critical/resistant attitudes (Rosenthal, 2016). For social movements, there are practical implications for building intersectional solidarities, particularly globally, where intersectionality can raise a collective consciousness of shared identities, interests, and political opportunity structures (Tormos, 2017). Far-reaching problems associated with globalization, such as regional trading, supply chain practices, human rights, migration, and unionism may all cut across national lines and reveal intersectional groups that are affected.

Limitations

As is often the case, some of intersectionality's purported strengths can be problematized and flipped to be viewed and argued as limitations instead. It is a framework inherently vulnerable to charges of being confusing and fragmented. It is not always clearly defined in terms of its core theoretical and methodological aspects and projects. Its detractors may also be tempted into arguing that it fragments identity groups by being too politically divisive and creating competing claims for victimhood status. Equally, some of its advocates may feel it suffers from the opposite problem of being not political enough, and risks losing some of its political urgency and critique where it is applied in neutralizing ways that obscure or marginalize inequalities and differences all over again. Finally, it forces difficult decisions and conversations in research, education, and practice that many may be unwilling or feel ill-equipped to engage in.

Davis (2008), while noting the success and potential success of intersectionality as a 'good' feminist theory, also expresses ambivalence about the uncertainty and confusion this 'buzzword' creates. McCall's (2005) work, much-cited, tries to separate out different ways of applying intersectionality, *anti-categorical, intra-categorical,* and *inter-categorical.* However, complexities always seem to remain, slightly out of reach, and bound up with the interdisciplinary evolution of various strands of feminism (McCall, 2005). Collins (2015) seems to argue that intersectionality is to some extent a victim of its own success, and that while it has gained acceptance and popularity, its definitional dilemmas have not necessarily gone away. A key tension lies in balancing competing demands between rigor, creativity, application and critique.

Another issue is that arguably most writers on intersectionality are inherently sympathetic – being presumably quite critical and reflexive by nature to engage with it in the first place. Similar themes of challenge recur, and the research could be accused of being somewhat inward-looking, but then again, it is not clear how intersectionality should be 'mainstreamed', or if it should be popularized at all. Dhamoon (2011) integrates concerns around terminology, complexity, decisions, principles, and choices of accompanying models in using intersectionality. One could perhaps be forgiven for becoming exasperated with all the introspection and aesthetically pleasing visual representations with lists of differences and repeated exhortations to embrace 'complexity'. A lot is at stake in terms of how it is explained and applied.

Intersectionality can be used rhetorically and politically in ways that erase and undermine the very subjectivities of the black women and feminists that it was developed to liberate and empower in the first place. Similar questions reappear in slightly different forms; around who can and should be using intersectionality, and how. As Alexander-Floyd

(2012, p. 11) argues, "[T]he issue is one of subjugation, not complexity." In this reading, it is easy for black women to be rhetorically pushed aside by uses of intersectionality that still universalize and focus on the suffering of other groups. Ultimately, Alexander-Floyd (2012) urges that black women's voices and narratives are kept center-stage in intersectional epistemology; otherwise, as noted previously, they are simply obscured and re-subjugated all over again. If intersectionality is everywhere, then it is not where it needs to be, the argument might go.

Patil (2013) argues that intersectionality has unresolved issues with patriarchy, in terms of the move from monolithic oppression to a more nuanced view of multiple intersecting oppressions. One area where further development is needed in this regard is in terms of *transnational feminisms*, where intersectionality is held in greater connection with cross-border and postcolonial issues, with geographical and historical constructions of oppression. It need not be wilfully complex to critically read intersectionality itself as reproduced from within the intersection of multiple discourses of "nation-state, industrial capitalism, and the burgeoning social and biological sciences—in the time and space of colonial modernity" (Patil, 2013, p. 862). The local, the national, the global, and the historical are all junctures that intersectionality may need to consider more thoroughly in future.

These limitations of intersectionality may seem very abstract and far-removed from the practical realities of organizations and diversity. However, if we choose to view organizations as sites of intersectional organizing and oppressions, then it stands to reason that the intersectional identities of their workforces and stakeholders are socially and politically significant, not to mention dynamic. The main challenge yet to be overcome seems to involve ensuring that intersectionality doesn't fragment and confuse majorities, or re-subjugate minorities, with misguided connotations of division, inclusion (of whom?) and endless differences (Carastathis, 2014). These are fundamentally problems of organization – of axes, multiplicities, and interdependencies.

Finally, in reviewing the latest slew of books on intersectionality, Jennifer Nash (2017) talks about the discontents and anxieties that continue to be associated with it. Intersectionality, she concludes, "occupies a curious position…both celebrated and reviled" (Nash, 2017, p. 127). In sum, intersectionality probably does not always need to be defended or scrutinized in minute detail; however, it does need to be applied in combination with institutional and transnational critiques of its own epistemologies, and retain firm ties to its roots in black feminism.

Applications

Even within studies of work and organization, it is challenging to do justice to the many great scholars doing work informing and informed by intersectionality, explicitly or implicitly. Therefore, illustrative examples have to suffice. Intersectional papers in organizational journals do appear to have grown in the last decade to some extent, although not necessarily in all of the most influential outlets. Their influence and prevalence are also likely to be underestimated to the extent that there is significant work going on that is relevant to an intersectionality agenda but does not use the word itself, perhaps even deliberately so to avoid some of the above difficulties. This relates back to the ongoing reflections in this chapter about how to make intersectionality applications and topics more explicit, accessible, and visible, while also trying to determine whether genuine intersectional analysis is going on, and how it is being presented.

Özbilgin, Beauregard, Tatli, and Bell (2011) apply intersectionality (and diversity) as a 'lens' to work–life issues, as researched from the 1990 onwards. Here, they deploy intersectionality to reveal blind spots in the way many researchers – both positivist and critical in orientation – are likely to treat work–life issues as a topic of organizational interest. These blind spots include focusing on gender over other strands of diversity, focusing on how individuals choose to manage work and life under wider social and historical forces and focusing on work and the domesticity of a nuclear family over a wider range of life domains and family contexts (Özbilgin et al., 2011). These contributions of intersectionality are important for remaining sensitive to shared but pluralized experiences that may get obscured by some idea of an ideal or prototypical 'work–life balancer', which is in reality only a dominant intersection that resides alongside many others.

Intersectionality can also be applied to understanding the career and professional experiences of disadvantaged groups, such as in Sang, Al-Dajani and Özbilgin's (2013) study of migrant women academics in UK higher education. Crucially, however, they applied intersectionality to challenge views proposing straightforward 'double disadvantage' when two strands of diversity (gender and ethnicity) act in combination. Rather, the academics studied, while in a minority and disadvantaged, were also found to show significant levels of agency, connection. and entrepreneurship not explained in terms of double disadvantage (Sang et al., 2013).

Rather than gender and ethnicity, Wasserman and Frenkel (2015) applied intersectionality to gender and class, in relation to how workspaces are used by various groups, using the case of a new headquarters constructed for the Israeli Ministry of Foreign Affairs. The intersections of gender and social class gave rise to distinct forms of 'spatial work' for women of different social groups. From senior diplomats to junior administrators, the building was found to be layered with an enacted intersectional hierarchy of diverse expectations and challenges around office design, communication, dress codes, and the movement of gendered and class-defined bodies through space (Wasserman & Frenkel, 2015).

Riach, Rumens, and Tyler (2014) investigated the threefold intersection of age, gender, and sexuality in LGBT employees aged 40 years or more, using an 'anti-narrative' methodology derived from Judith Butler's work on performativity. This Butlerian application of intersectionality to employees' lived experiences highlights how employees can use their unique intersectional differences to 'make trouble' and perform their identities in disruptive ways. Organizational settings are replete with norms and encounters underpinned by the perceived viability and linearity of heteronormative and 'chrononormative' (ageing and life-stage) working identities, where age and sexuality take on stereotypical profiles for workers. However, these same stereotyped abstractions also provide opportunities for diverse minority employees to negotiate, play around with how they are made visible, desired, and recognized by others (Riach et al., 2014).

When applied to organizations, intersectionality therefore reveals how people draw on unique knowledge about themselves to challenge partial organizational knowledge about what is visible, credible, legitimate, professional, neutral, and so on. Intersectionality appears uniquely in situated, concrete, and embodied work encounters, performed to challenge the idealized and naturalized imagery of an abstract majority ideal. Adamson and Johansson (2016) show this to be the case in the work of Russian counselling professionals performing their work, for example. Similarly, Harris (2017) shows how the intersectional standpoints of ethnic and gender minorities on US university campuses reflect their unique knowledge in relation to sexual violence on campus, and the associated practices endorsed by those in power.

Intersectional knowledge, experiences, visibility, and credibility also continue to be identified where actors occupy positions of uneven disadvantage and struggle in various emerging fields of practice and event. These include applied intersectional work on gender, race, and class as signaled online and offline for digital entrepreneurs (Dy, Marlow, & Martin, 2017), or as informing the shifting collective mobilizations and attitudes of diverse Toronto hotel workers during a strike and lock-out in a 2007 industrial relations case study (Soni-Sinha, 2013).

Understandings of context-specific organizational settings and ways of describing inequalities grow in tandem with a growth in intersectional research. Accounting and professional services employees in a Mexico branch of a Big Four firm were found to experience their career paths and work as raced, gendered, and classed in terms of 'inequality markers' and 'cultural scripts' (Ruiz Castro & Holvino, 2016). While these concepts appear to cover a large range of complex and variegated social signals and group-specific ways of talking and being that wink in and out of focus across situations in ways difficult to track – they should certainly give pause for thought. They take us a long way away from comfortable majority notions of uniform, linear, meritocratic career paths and inclusive, cooperative working. As with many critical perspectives, there is a need to combine intersectionality with other critical lenses to develop insights further. Carrim and Nkomo (2016) make this point well and see it through empirically by wedding intersectional understandings of identities and categories to the wider institutional, political, and societal practices that shape South African women managers' life and work histories. Their findings speak particularly to larger external state and historical influences – such as the segregated and marginalized status of Indian women entering corporate South African settings with legacies of patriarchy and apartheid. More structural and systemic intersectional analyses may help to more forcefully reveal the bigger societal pictures of a tapestry of historically intersectional groups. These groups enter organizations and bear witness to the degrees and forms of negotiation and resistance involved in redefining work, careers, practices, and professions away from a privileged norm of some kind.

In sum, applications of intersectionality in critical organizational research continue to grow empirically, and the tensions of the approach are borne out as researchers emphasize their readings of chosen empirical settings, intersections, and voices of their participants. Intersectionality invites a certain messiness in having to go through the many possible combinations and permutations of at least two or three axes of difference, and trusts that readers will go along with an academic sense of 'contribution' and prioritization of certain aspects of participants' 'lived experience'.

It's not clear whether intersectionality can or should be 'mainstreamed' in some corporate, pragmatic sense. In any case, where it is perhaps redeemed in its applications is in the profound ways it reveals the local, embodied knowledge and subject positions of organizational actors. These reflect delicate webs of differences that people experience differently in different situations, to their relative advantage and disadvantage. That people experience their diversity in terms of complex, multiple, shifting identifications in combination seems beyond doubt. These intersections typically contain knowledge of value and dignity but come up against the operations of power unless mutually recognized in organizational encounters between ethical subjects. Can intersectionality be managed? Probably not, but it is giving empirical accounts of itself and the 'identity work' of disadvantaged intersectional groups. The political issue then becomes who in organizations is truly listening or not listening to which intersections, and why.

The Future of Intersectionality and Diversity in Organizations

It is perhaps unfair to challenge intersectional approaches to diversity as to what the end game might be. However, it seems important to pay attention to how such scholarship will continue to highlight the distinctive intersections of identities in organizations, and whether it can renew its legacies and roots in feminisms and critical race theory to emerge as something greater than the sum of its parts.

Simply put, between the 1960s and today, intersectionality is still about combining gender with race and class – and presumably any other identities that might be relevant to a specific context – to understand the inequality regimes woven into organizational status, job opportunities, representation, and advancement (Acker, 2012). Chang and Culp (2002) argue that intersectionality now borders on common sense but will require further conflict, risk, sacrifice, and courage to put it into practice in tackling subordination and acknowledging privilege. One option is to go straight up a hierarchy of privilege with forms of wealth, whiteness and maleness at its apex and to try and understand the intersections there in more detail. Indeed, we might expect to see more organizational research taking this approach going forward, in tandem with a focus on relative inequalities and disadvantages (Al Ariss et al., 2014).

A 2018 special issue of the critical organizational open-access journal *ephemera* probed the tensions of intersectionality and the limits of what it can 'do' in terms of theory, method, and politics, with reference to democracy and emancipation. In their editorial, Villesèche, Muhr, and Śliwa (2018) highlight the risks where intersectionality gets co-opted by capitalist and post-feminist forces to reproduce the very positions of privilege it was originally designed to challenge. Intersectionality may need 'reclaiming' and 're-radicalizing' in this regard – by diverse actors, their voices, biographies and histories (Liu, 2018b).

In another special forum on intersectionality in *Gender, Work and Organization* journal, Rodriguez, Holvino, Fletcher, and Nkomo (2016) note how some intersectionality research focuses on subjectivities, while a lesser portion focuses on more systemic power relations. Importance is therefore placed on linking the subjective and the structural in crafting intersectional research. They also constructively elaborate upon the need to push intersectionality forward through methodological innovations – participatory, visual, longitudinal, transnational, and the like, as well as explicitly linking it to the practicalities of change activism and curriculum design (Rodriguez et al., 2016). One useful methodological avenue is provided by Mooney (2016) in the form of 'nimble intersectionality'. This nimbleness involves asking questions about focus, boundaries, and framing at the outset of a study to determine how to proceed in a clear, pragmatic fashion, while remaining true to core principles of the approach, balancing critical complexity with accessibility. Campbell (2016) links intersectionality to policy-oriented research, using healthcare and institutional ethnography as examples of how to shine a light on 'what actually happens' as organizations apply categories and rules to ways of knowing and doing in relation to diverse groups. Under this view, intersectional participants are more likely to be made visible as knowing subjects rather than ruled objects of inquiry, and stakeholders can tailor policy initiatives more democratically and coordinate actions for change more effectively (Campbell, 2016).

Finally, it seems like there is something to be said for the future of intersectionality research in organizations in terms of straightforward, empirically driven approaches that render it alive and persuasive to diverse audiences and readerships in future, which will help its fields of application to mature and grain traction. This seems to be what Marfelt (2016) is arguing for in an empirically grounded approach to intersectionality, one that remains open to organizational activities and changes, as well as open to both privilege and oppression, concerned with different 'entry points' rather than trying to fix complex identity relations a priori. While hierarchies are important, intersectionality may also show how they give way to more nuanced, shifting networks of diverse actions and organizing. There is also the tension of continuing to deal with intersectional sameness alongside difference and building up diverse coalitions based on an acceptable level of solidarity and unity. This can be thought of as 'same difference', with commonalities across women of color and other minority groups, as well as 'difference-within-sameness' that avoids marginalizing more distinctive lived experiences within gender and ethnicity collectives (Luna, 2016).

As empirical intersectionality research continues to emerge on novel forms of collective organizing, this issue of negotiating inclusion and pulling together for a common good moves center-stage. To name just a couple of examples in closing this chapter, a study by Peretz (2017) looks at diverse men's groups' engagements with women's rights and anti-violence movements, where 'gay/queer' and black Muslim men show distinct intersectional engagements as women's allies, adding extra dimensions and pathways to positive contact and motivations across differences. Similarly, Tapia and Alberti (2019) link trade unions with the need to recognize 'migrant intersectionalities' at multiple macro/meso/micro levels of analysis, unpicking the contested category of migrant to better understand complex relations between trade unions and migrant workers.

Conclusion

This chapter has endeavored to review and reflect on the growing critical literature on intersectionality and diversity in relation to work and organization. In many ways, intersectionality has everything you might hope for from a critical perspective – it generates powerful empirical framings of distinct participant voices and lived experiences, as well as generating further debates and reflections on its own emergence. It hovers around the edges of mainstream research agendas and disciplinary boundaries and is not necessarily a word circulated positively in relation to media and public consumption. The organizations and organizing involved are often by definition marginal and vulnerable to misunderstanding and fragmentation. Yet where it continues to be applied and innovated with, it shows great promise for activism, visibility, and coalition-building – all forces for organizational change and inclusion that could arguably not be achieved elsewhere or by other means.

Intersectionality is continuous in many readings and does not seek obvious end-states or outcomes, instead generally going after renewed relations of collaboration, visibility, literacy, and understanding of diversity's nuances (Cho, Crenshaw, & McCall, 2013). Most critical theorists would urge that it not depart too far from its roots in critical race theory and plural feminisms inflected by race and ethnicity. Many might feel that on its own intersectionality is not quite theory or method and so needs to be combined with other organizational foci and tensions (institutions, inequalities, practices, histories, hierarchies, structures, movements, and so on) to reinforce its contributions toward the complex and messy layers of diversity's realism it signifies (Walby, Armstrong, & Strid, 2012).

Ultimately, intersectional reflections tend to revolve around mapping it to theory, method, practice, and inequalities – quite daunting in some respects for researchers, let alone organizations. There are also many points of entry to intersectionality – categories, groups, processes, relational power dynamics – and many intersectional audiences to convince about the demonstration that multiplying points of intersection are indeed working as theorized, open-ended even after race, gender, and class have been considered (Choo & Ferree, 2010). Intersectionality thus demands a certain perseverance and acceptance of incompleteness, which may be a price well worth paying in exchange for insights into the complexity of diversity's multiples. This messy, expansive set of interacting (intersecting) variables residing in minority voices and experiences puts intersectionality at odds with scientism and proponents of a more scientific method, inviting a proliferation of political subjectivities and clashes.

We must conclude that the study of intersectionality in organizations will continue to face cross-roads and intersections of its own as it is practised in diverse ways. Healy et al. (2018) revisit a set of studies in the light of Joan Acker's legacy of inequality regimes and intersectionality. Intersectionality can be held to carry empirical flexibility with it, and to draw attention to distinct inequalities otherwise masked by capitalist systems purporting to be meritocratic or diversity-neutral. There are even possibilities of some degree of quantitative reconciliation, where intersectionality findings can be presented to more mainstream audiences as numerical patterns, in the form of latent statistical clusters, classes, profiles, stratifications, and/or networked linkages (Lawrence & Zyphur, 2011; Tomlinson et al., 2018). It will be interesting to see how more visual and quantitative representations of intersectionality emerge alongside more subjectivist, political, and structural critiques. Intersectionality should perhaps not be thought of as a panacea. However, while intersectional knowledge production is inherently a struggle to varying extents (Rodriguez et al., 2016), there is equally much to be hopeful about in terms of consciousness-raising and a maturing pluralism of intersectionality as an approach to diversity.

7 Discourses

Language, talk, text, and communications are foundational and critical aspects of organizing and diversity. Paradigmatically, critical views of communication and meaning can of course vary dramatically. Under postmodernism or poststructuralism, language involves games with indeterminate outcomes, where power over meaning and order is playful, elusive, and fragile. Here, difference itself (or the *différance* of Jacques Derrida) is built into constantly shifting flows and inter-referential patterns of language (e.g. Parker, 1993). In contrast, more stable and instrumental views of language and communication might be more likely to emphasize competing rhetorical and metaphorical framings of diversity, inclusion, and diversity management practices in organizations. In some senses, language is inescapable. It shapes our world and we shape it even as we reproduce it, having a powerful organizing influence on our sense of organizational reality, knowledge, and grasp of diversity in research and practice.

This chapter will therefore take some steps to review critical aspects of these issues in relation to critical views of communication and diversity in organizations. Although difficult to summarize, a useful umbrella for understanding these areas is as subsumed under the rapid expansion of *organizational discourse* research over the last two to three decades. Phillips and Oswick (2012) have reviewed this domain or 'linguistic turn' in how we think of organizations, with reference to a family of methods and levels of analysis. Fundamentally, considerations of discourse start from a position that the power of text and talk lies not in simply describing reality but in actively producing, ordering, mediating, and organizing it.

The discursive perspective or approach supplements and expands the more modest critical proposition that organizations are 'socially constructed', via three dimensions in terms of "pieces of talk or text, the collection of texts that gives them meaning, and the social context in which they occur" (Phillips & Oswick, 2012, p. 433). In turn, forms of discourse include various media – text, speech, objects, pictures, symbols – and how they make organizational realities socially meaningful. These may be realities marked by strategy, change, power/domination, identities, histories, or any other significant objects or topics of communication and expression. In addition, the methodological and analytical scale of approaches to organizational discourse can vary ("small d" versus "big D" discourse), from close observations of specific conversations and interactions through to connections with more sweeping historical and societal bodies of communicative practices and institutions (Phillips & Oswick, 2012).

Ultimately, Phillips and Oswick (2012) conclude in the thoughtful manner of many diligent reviewers of large bodies of literature. They urge greater consolidation and connection of organizational discourse research; first *within* the domain of discursive approaches to communication itself but also *beyond* the discursive domain of abstract linguistic phenomena to incorporate more of the non-discursive and material aspects of organization (i.e. matter, physicality, and activities). Indeed, these are critical points of future connection and engagement that can be returned to briefly in relation to diversity more specifically towards the end of this chapter.

Critical linguistic and sociolinguistic approaches to discourse and discourse analysis have their key thinkers and practitioners and extend beyond studies of management and organization. We can note some of them here in passing – Norman Fairclough, Ruth Wodak, Teun van Dijk, among many others. Reviewing them needs to be foregone here, however, for disciplinary and space reasons. Nevertheless, it is their bodies of work that can be mined for greater appreciation of how some of the linguistic concepts surrounding discourse can be used for subsequent application and development in relation to organizations and diversity. Van Dijk's (2015) critical discourse studies, for example, draws extensive and triangular linkages between discourse, cognition, and society. These can be used to make sense of speech acts, implied meanings, propaganda, ideology, genres, attitudes, and other influential building blocks of some of our most 'muscular' or powerfully interlocking forms of discourse, such as those supporting forms of racism and anti-racism (van Dijk, 2015).

Discourse and Organizations

Before turning to diversity and discourse more specifically, it does make sense to acknowledge some of the more general reflections on discourse in relation to organizations and management, as this reflects how discourse has come to occupy a place in these disciplinary fields of inquiry. In a relatively early 1994 article, David Boje linked the notion of historical struggles and dialogues between premodern, modern, and postmodern discourses to how organizations tell and pursue various stories defining their engagements with learning, diversity, and capitalism (Boje, 1994).

More traditional, nostalgic discourses vie for attention and disciplinary influence with modern discourses of efficiency and postmodern ones seeking explosions of diversity and fragmentation. Critical recognition of these multiple narratives and some of the tensions and blind-spots between them (e.g. progress, political correctness, hypocrisy, community, masculinity) is one way to embrace diversity more deeply and democratize organizational change and learning (Boje, 1994).

Although worthwhile, discourse in organizations can be challenging to research, not least because discourse is inherently ongoing, conflict-laden, incomplete, and in talking and writing about it we are never free of the influence and co-production of discourses ourselves – we are implicated in discursive power relations. Tracking down texts and capturing naturally occurring conversational talk are labor-intensive and expansive tasks for discourse research. However, if done reflexively and pragmatically (reciprocally linking texts and contexts), discourse analysis can help to creatively 'unpack' how organizational struggles to define meaning have powerful effects and are grounded in wider structures and contexts (Hardy, 2001).

Special issues, collections of articles and books on organizations and critical approaches to discourse have continued to emerge over time. Grant, Keenoy, and Oswick (2001) again note the three-dimensional 'intertextual' framework of critical discourse analysis (text, interaction/ discursive practice, and social practice/wider context), as well as communicative organizational themes such as metaphor, stories, language games, rhetoric, drama, rituals, dialogue, identity, and sensemaking. One ongoing area of contention for proponents is working through concerns over too much of an obsession with talk and the need to not downplay agency or the close relationships between talking and the 'doing' of organization. Ultimately, however, it is hard to imagine understanding the 'action' of organizations and diversity without language, and particularly the critical limits of such language under wider social and political conditions of capitalism and diversity, where some powerful discourses may dominate over more marginalized ones. Boje, Oswick, and Ford (2004, p. 576) answer the 'so what?' question of discourse in organizations accordingly: "there are a few official discourses and many marginalized discourses in every organization. The theory and research challenge is to ascertain and trace the dialogue across fragmented discourses from the local into the situated social, historical, and economic contexts."

Ainsworth and Hardy (2004) go a step further, asking 'why bother?' with critical discourse analysis (CDA), using the example of the identity of 'the older worker' to compare its offerings with other theories, fields, and approaches, such as economics, labor markets, and gerontology. One conclusion is that CDA offers a unique way of questioning and understanding worker identity/identities. It involves more directly engaging the neglected *processes* whereby influential versions of a diverse identity emerge from struggles to linguistically and categorically define it, and in turn how this accounts for *material effects* of disadvantage and discrimination, where a dominant identity discourse is represented and enacted in organizational practices and contexts (Ainswoth & Hardy, 2004). Whatever the shortcomings of critical discourse approaches, it would seem hard to argue with the potential value of investigating – in the case of 'older worker' discourse, for example – how we talk, write, and represent age identity in relation to linguistic framings of pensions, retirement, redundancy, and so on.

Perhaps the biggest hindrance to making discourse more accessible in understanding organizations is the ontological question – how language, practices, and actions come together to discursively construct organizations as 'real' and ordered. The organizing of organization is 'under construction' in some way, but there are different schools of thought around how enduring it is, how contested, and how it is composed of, and emerges from, actions, structures, and objects (Fairhurst & Putnam, 2004). Fairclough (2005) urges organizational discourse to resist views associated with extreme postmodernism and social constructivism and to adopt *critical realism* as a social ontology instead. A critical realist approach to CDA can help by simply asserting that there are mediating layers of reality that explain how processes and events are caused and experienced as more or less durable and stable. This in turn arguably helps to situate discourse, to contextualize it, and make its symbolic influences more concrete (Fairclough, 2005).

We need not be detained too much here by the finer points of discourse and ontology, except to note that they have some important implications for linking theoretical assumptions about talk and text to methodology and context. Some useful protocols and starting-points have emerged in organization and management studies in this regard. In their review, Leitch and Palmer (2010) summarize five treatments of discursive context, as *space, time, practice, change,* and *frame,* with many subcategories for each. From this follows an equally rigorous methodological protocol comprising nine critical issues or decisions around concepts and data in a discourse study (Leitch & Palmer, 2010). In a short responding piece, Chouliaraki and Fairclough (2010) argue that this may be too strictly reductionist and rigorous, and propose an alternative approach that preserves more relational, dialectic, 'integrationist', and openly trans-disciplinary values. Ultimately, both pieces complement one another quite well and highlight the hope that organizational discourse research can balance some measure of rigor in systematically gathering evidence with the equally pressing need to remain critically open to power relations and theoretical nuance or novelty.

Alvesson and Kärreman (2000) note the many theoretical and methodological varieties of discourse, including those linked with Michel

Foucault – the *archaeology* of the history of discourse formation, and the *genealogy* of the forces and relations uniting discourse. They caution against moving too quickly toward grandiose, deterministic claims beyond the initial encounters with specific text, suggesting continuous reflection may help uncover more nuanced meanings and readings. Remarkably, the same authors return with a follow-up commentary eleven years later, concluding that discourse is still generally used in ways that are too vague and all-embracing, suggesting a need for counterbalancing concepts that cultivate a more precise and delimited view of language's effects on meaning (Alvesson & Kärreman, 2011). As with other critical perspectives, some of this intense academic and philosophical introspection may be off-putting to other interested parties. This would be a shame as the underlying principle of discourse seems profoundly valuable – an imperative to play close attention to language use in organizations and its embedded role in shaping meaning (in conjunction with other critical and contextual forces).

Language use and discourse need not stitch up and critically enfold everything about organizations, yet it clearly has a powerful ordering influence. One way to get out of some of the difficulty is to think of discourse organizing as a part of an ongoing process, in tension with other discursive and non-discursive forces, and empirically this sets possibilities for courses of meaning and action in organizations (Leclercq-Vandelannoitte, 2011). However, there does seems to be a perpetual risk that discourse loses what it has to say about language and dissolves into vaguer discussions about knowledge, power and politics, particularly in its Foucauldian variants.

Taking yet another different tack, Cederström and Spicer (2014) pursue a 'post-foundational' approach to discourse that links it with psychoanalytic and affective conceptions of 'the Real' – an element of reality that can never be captured by discourse. A 'post-foundational' view thus also sees language and discursive meaning-making as in flux and as a process – but one impossible to finally resolve. There may only be 'nodal points' of temporary connection and affective drives organizing discourse by trying to capture precisely what cannot ever be fully captured by language or desire. This perspective surely has some novelty and nuance in acknowledging how language can make us disoriented, driven, and confused, although it needs further development and application in organizations (Cederström & Spicer, 2014).

Bearing some of these ontological puzzles surrounding discourse in mind, it is apposite to take diversity in organizations as a subject and object of discourse more specifically and to channel some of the abstract debate into more concrete examples and claims. Indeed, diversity is itself an intense, vibrant topic of linguistic and discursive debate and representation, full of shifting 'isms' and diverse ways of talking about diversity, identities, and intergroup relations, in our societies and workplaces (e.g. Blommaert & Verschueren, 2002).

Diversity Discourses

There are several key articles from the 1990s and turn of the century looking back and assessing some of the main different ways in which diversity has been talked about and discursively framed. A short comment from Taylor Cox (1994) noted the need for consistency in use of the word diversity for ensuring conceptual clarity and clear research progression. While not a deeply discursive point, important examples of what diversity does *not* mean are highlighted – it is neither shorthand for gender and ethnic minorities alone, nor for a very small number of equality practices. In short, diversity is vulnerable to being trivialized, used inconsistently, and reduced to single dimensions or levels (Cox, 1994).

Litvin (1997) traces the origins of contemporary workforce diversity discourse and how they are reproduced in a sample of organizational behavior textbooks. In the western tradition, prior to management, diversity has roots in natural science, biology, and philosophy. One critical issue with the enduring path this discourse has taken is how it *essentializes* conceptions of diversity. Essentialist assumptions in diversity discourse in management textbooks and other organizational texts and practices retain subtle and problematic links to environmental biodiversity, genetics, and Darwinian evolution. This discourse connotes virtually all human diversity as obvious, fixed, innate, discretely categorical, manageable, and divorced from time and context (Litvin, 1997). These observations lead us back to some of the 'mainstream' diversity tendencies in organizational research – as opposed to more critical ones – outlined earlier in this volume.

Across the late twentieth century, Lorbiecki and Jack (2000) identify four additional, overlapping 'critical turns' in the discursive evolution of diversity management. Diversity has been expressed in terms of demographic statistics (1980s–), political correctness (late 1980s–early 1990s), economic value/business cases (early-mid 1990s), and critical responses to diversity management implementation (mid-late 1990s on). These discursive shifts in emphasis mirror to some extent wider interdisciplinary shifts across other areas of humanities and social sciences, and now pose serious dilemmas for the twenty-first century in acknowledging persistent problems of discrimination and inequality. However, we now have the benefit of hindsight at least, and some awareness for critical dialogues going forward of how diversity can be undermined through essentialist, dualist, and binary assumptions about its management (Lorbiecki & Jack, 2000).

For their part, different organizations and communities can and do (re)produce their own distinct discourses of diversity. Janssens and Zanoni (2005) studied service companies and assert from their findings that these companies produce organization-specific understandings of diversity or 'diversities', products of power relations and work organization rather than a priori sociodemographic characteristics or categories. Discursive understandings are shown to emerge more dynamically as groups and communities interact around their work – policies, customers, teams, friendships, practices, and so on. Janssens and Zanoni (2005) find that a hospital, a call center, a technical drawing company, and a logistics company think about diversity differently according to how customer service is delivered and how professional standards are set. These discourses can be enabling of agency and diversity, but they can also constrain diversity's expression if it exists in tension with organizational aims, skills/HR frameworks, or customer interactions.

Along similar lines, within the community of an MBA course, Tomlinson and Egan (2002) find that putting a 'valuing diversity' discourse into practice can be limited, problematic, and lead to occasional breakdowns in group friendships and interactions. More macro discourses of globalization and cross-cultural management are enacted through more micro group contact, shared interactions, and understandings, sometimes reframed or learned over time. Here there are inevitable nuances and stresses as to how similarities and differences are uncovered, celebrated, and exploited interpersonally – be it via humor, work styles, personalities, group norms, and other distinctive micro-discursive interactions (Tomlinson & Egan, 2002). Multinational organizational forms channel these more local and national diversity discourses back up to the macro level of globalization discourse, trying to reconcile and integrate multilingual employee communities around a higher-order functional language associated with the corporate headquarters or parental unit of the firm (Luo & Shenkar, 2006).

Beyond cultural diversity discourse, gendered discourse in organization and management theory has taken decades to emerge in the form of research topics such as work–family conflict and women in management, and then in ways that often privilege masculinity and problematize femininity (Runté & Mills, 2006). Historically, these academic diversity discourses can be traced to a connective tissue of other, related but fragmented discourses, including war-time employment, suburbanization, and economic and political anxieties such as anti-communist sentiment in the US. In sum, "gender organizes discourse, discourse (dis)organizes gender, organizing (en)genders discourse, and discourse (en)genders organization" (Runté & Mills, 2006, p. 716).

If diversity's struggles in history and organization are carried through fragments of discourse, then this raises questions about how further processes, outcomes, critical dialogues, and counter-discourses are engendered over time. Raelin (2008) considers the potential of discourses of emancipation and liberation to bring about change in diversity relations through dialogue, empowerment, and enlightenment. George Herbert Mead and Jurgen Habermas can be invoked to appreciate the need for public reflection and recognition between diverse groups, but this raises questions about whether simply trading discourses is radical enough for truly revolutionary change within existing organizational power structures. Christiansen and Just (2012) argue that much diversity discourse is constraining – using Danish diversity discourse as an example – due to its 'regularities'. Namely, it asserts that diversity can be managed for mutual benefit between minorities and organizations – and so diversity (or a minority) is *addressed* as a problem to be solved, *categorized* as a series of dimensions deemed organizationally lacking, and *invited* for remedial action and resolution (Christiansen & Just, 2012). In this form, diversity discourse is itself not very diverse with imaginative possibilities and merely (re)constitutes diverse subjects in constrained positions not much different than before. Simply phrased, the language serves to put diverse workers back in their place.

Diversity as anti-discrimination discourse analyzed over forty years (1970–2010) shows rhetorical cycles involving the words 'equality', 'diversity', and 'inclusion' co-evolving and giving way to one another partially over time (Oswick & Noon, 2014). These discursive trends around diversity (still the most prominent term of the three overall) do not clearly signal any material changes in diversity practice in organizations and show some problematic characteristics of management fashions. However, academics, practitioners, and consultants might now be better discursively equipped as a result of this hindsight – to engage with breaking free of any further rhetorical cycles and working with a more eclectic and substantive repertoire of approaches (Oswick & Noon, 2014).

In a similar study of macro/societal discourses of equality and diversity across three decades in Canada (newspaper articles 1986–2014), Cukier et al. (2017) also find overlaps, trade-offs, and competition between discourses emphasizing aspects of diversity management, such as voluntary initiatives versus regulatory compliance. Channeling Habermas' discourse ethics and theory of communicative action, operationalized through quantitative and qualitative lexical analysis, their findings reveal complex patterns of stakeholders negotiating legitimacy, truth, and sincerity in relation to making valid claims based on evidence about what courses of action may be appropriate (Cukier et al., 2017).

At a general societal and organizational level then, diversity discourse remains a shifting configuration of assumptions, actors, and interconnected issues, often revolving around different domains and dimensions of diversity, alongside tensions between business, legal, and political interests, unfolding from a complex metaphorical, rhetorical, and historical base.

Discursive Framings of Diversity in Organizations

Beyond more general diversity discourse, we can also critically consider and analyze more specific *framings* of diversity in organizations. Like discourse, organizational framings can occur at multiple levels of analysis; as joint cognitive representations and knowledge structures guiding interpretation, communication, and action (Cornelissen & Werner, 2014). It does remain slightly unclear, however, whether framings are distinct from discourse or the two can be collapsed in certain respects. What we can say here is that they combine in specific ways to guide and delimit perspectives and meanings constructed as salient in various organizational situations, while also always remaining partially open to change or revision.

In the case of diversity, and an array of differences, contexts, and roles, the potential discursive framings are vast and various. Nevertheless, salient examples from existing organizational literature can be highlighted, and the framings do, as studied empirically, seem to bind or coalesce their forms and contents around certain influential meanings in the social-organizational lifeworlds where diversity is discussed and represented. Often it is indeed certain actors in certain roles who are poised to deploy or challenge discourse locally from within the power relations within which they are embedded.

Zanoni and Janssens (2004) studied Flemish HR officers as rhetorical 'makers' of diversity discourse with the right to speak, argue, and persuade workforces about the nature of diverse groups, individual differences, value-added aspects, performance problems, and different practices and intergroup initiatives. In a later study, the same authors studied multiple diversity discourses as distinct by *occupation* in the Belgian branch of an international automobile company (Zanoni & Janssens, 2015). Occupations such as supervisor, worker, HR, trade union member, and medical staff deployed different patterns of interlocking discourses of diversity in relation to corresponding issues of production, relations/relationality, fairness, bureaucracy, and medicine/health. In this critical analysis, co-existing diversity discourses are deployed, defended, and played off against one another like symbolic currency to reinforce status and position, by those with the voice and social practices afforded them to do so. Diversity is de-centered (no one has a monopoly on its meaning) and de-essentialized (understood in a lively plurality of ways).

In a related and similar way but concerning UK police officers' gender and diversity management practices, Dick and Cassell (2002, 2004) show how minority and majority subjects construct their own sense of discrimination and inclusion from within existing role and power relations. These officers appear to do so through a complex mixture of resistance and consent, in relation to the workforce politics of promotions, cultural 'banter', and occupational identities within wider society. It appears difficult to shift or destabilize diversity conversations to challenge the exclusionary power of existing practices –whether minority or majority – while inevitably juggling other discourses accepted as unproblematic about one's occupation and role. In any case, critical discourse analyses usefully highlight these complex tensions. Trade union equality officers are therefore also found to be understandably wary of upbeat and individualistic diversity discourse deployed by top management if it deflects attention from the discourse of group-based inequalities of discrimination and disadvantage, even while they can accept that it also allows for some potential critical engagement (Kirton & Greene, 2006).

Studies on internationally and culturally diverse project teams, often pan-European, again show how diversity discourse is constrained by the composition, contingencies, and lifecycle of the project members and activities (Ahonen & Tienari, 2009; Barinaga, 2007). (Inter)national discourses around culture, but also the organizing traditions of the project work being performed, have disciplinary and normalizing influences on how diversity can be enacted and mobilized. However, members can still draw on these discursive resources to try to challenge and reshape the ways they account for their diversity in relation to group life, interactions, and purposes. This is arguably more illuminating than more positivist, mainstream approaches that fix diversity into patterns for explaining positive/negative group outcomes, which inevitably tends to reproduce mixed findings (Barinaga, 2007).

Large organizations for their part will exist in wider institutional and discursive fields, where various practitioners and stakeholders will be staging conversations and initiatives around diversity. In a study of Canadian petroleum and insurance organizations, Prasad, Prasad, and Mir (2011) critically highlight how consultants and experts can weave diversity changes and initiatives into generic discourses of 'fashion', generating issues of employee cynicism, meaningless imitation, and a superficial lack of attention to local conditions. At the same time, these powerful discursive influences can always potentially be 'spoken back to' with counter-discourse, using their very popularity to repurpose then to some extent. Yet the idea of diversity programs and workshops being new, trendy, real, branded, and a bandwagon remains a frustrating corporate paradox. It enables rent extraction, with corporations taking out more of equality's benefits than they put back in – putting some of the right content in some of the wrong form, or cloaking diversity in a forced, antithetical unity of fashion-setting, virtue-signaling, and conformity (Elfer, 2018).

A series of studies involving Ahu Tatli has probed diversity discourses and framings further as they exist across organizations in the UK and Europe. Sociological concepts from Pierre Bourdieu are invoked to understand how the professional field of diversity and equality operates in part like a game, with its own inside rules and entry fees, with actors pouncing on new layers of terminology, practices, and pieces of legislation to shore up credibility in the absence of wider standards (Tatli, 2011). Özbilgin and Tatli (2011) empirically map out some of these multi-layered discursive tensions in the UK in terms of the dimensions of *individualism-collectivism* and *regulation-voluntarism*. These multi-actor and contested framings across a range of industry and sector contexts show slow, uneven change, inertia, and symbolic struggle. Organizational and stakeholder framings exist along a loosely defined continuum, with trade unions favoring collectivist-regulation solutions, while private sector and professional groups favor individualist-voluntarist solutions to thinking and talking about workforce diversity. This is nested within a wider socio-political context of neoliberalist policies and discourse, with stakeholders swept up in problematic tides of deregulation and questioning the role of the state in framing diversity issues (Özbilgin & Tatli, 2011).

Bringing in France and Germany alongside the UK, the discursive politics of diversity is molded and reshaped over time by distinct, path-dependent, national, and regulatory contexts (Tatli, Vassilopoulu, Al Ariss & Özbilgin, 2012). Diversity framings are redefined as they cross national and regional borders. Countries evidently have their own laws, bodies, movements, and cases of national interest. If France has often been concerned with framing diversity as the integration/assimilation of immigrants to its Republican values, Germany's discourse is affected by national guilt relating to the Holocaust, with some limited discourse of integration but marred by silence, hesitance, and lingering ethnocentrism. Many countries and their organizations cannot therefore simply adopt US or some other 'ready-made' diversity discourse but must instead wrestle with their own taboos and frames – fixing, bending, shrinking, and stretching political, and public discourse to address matters arising (Tatli et al., 2012).

There is surely a welter of other examples of discursive framings pertaining to roles, worldviews, and characteristics surrounding workforce diversity. They are too many to review in full here but selectively presenting a few more seems worthwhile to reinforce an awareness of the variety and granularity of ways of debating diversity in relation to different forms of language and modes of representation:

- Benschop, van den Brink, Doorewaard, and Leenders (2013) identify *discourses of ambition* that are organized around gender and part-time work from Dutch men and women's focus group discussions in healthcare and financial services. Individual development, task mastery, and upward career mobility are discursively associated with hegemonic masculine ideals of working full-time and/or being a man.

- Adamson (2014) explores *competing discourses of masculinity* in the female-dominated profession of counselling psychology in Russia. Gendered discourses can be *contradictory* – affording praise and criticism to masculine and feminine ideals in equal measure. Women counsellors are shown to talk about men and masculinity in different, contradictory ways – as biological sex, as social construct, or in terms of roles and relationships. Levels of scrutiny, reflection and self-awareness can vary.
- Śliwa and Johansson (2014) show how foreign women academics working in UK business schools, as minorities, contest and/or reproduce the *discourse of meritocracy*. Critically, definitions and applications of merit tend to remain largely unchanged as challenges are limited, and power-laden performance pressures and biased evaluations still believed in by minorities hoping for recognition, achievement, and progression come what may.
- Toyoki and Brown (2014) studied men in a Helsinki prison and found discourse can be used to manage *stigmatized identities*. By referring to other, non-stigmatized aspects of their identities, actors can appropriate and pursue more coveted self-images of themselves as certain kinds of prisoners and 'good' persons. The implication being that minority organizational selves are fragile but can be talked about in manageable ways to some extent, even under very contradictory and challenging circumstances.
- Disabled employees need to engage with *ableist discourse* that defines them in terms of lower productivity and what they are unable to do yet still expected to do. Jammaers, Zanoni, and Hardonk (2016) interview disabled Belgian employees and find that they sustain positive identities by enacting discursive practices that challenge ideas of lower productivity, redefine productivity, and by refusing individual responsibility for lower productivity. As is often the case with discourse, these practices can simultaneously challenge and reproduce the discourse they engage.

While these examples are very diverse, certain discursive themes of diversity do come through consistently at times. If organizations are generally trying to talk about diverse groups, diversity management, performance/productivity, and valuing of diversity, then this is often occurring while minority actors discursively speak back to challenge and reproduce their identities accordingly. European studies of public and political organizations show that there is more to diversity discourse than market or instrumental business framings, with some more nuanced space given to social justice, inequalities, and hypocritical contradictions between talk, decisions and actions (Dobusch, 2017a; Markard & Dähnke, 2017). Studies of how managers and consultants in various countries and sectors navigate and contribute to discursive framings of diversity continue to appear (e.g. Knights & Omanović, 2016; Knoppers, Claringbould & Dortants, 2015; Mease, 2016).

Perhaps unsurprisingly, agents of global and managerial capitalism often struggle to discursively frame diversity in any terms beyond present business value and ahistorical group categories that exploit the sameness of differences in support of generic notions of ideal workers. However, as contradictory discourses go into motion and are enacted in practice, there are arguably more positive spaces for realizing change as minorities voice and draw attention to discursive contradictions and shift the focus to alternative specificities of difference, inequality, and responsibility for change.

Diversity and Communication

It is easy for discussions of discourse to move quickly towards abstract (albeit important) discussions of identity, power, and overall framings of the diversity situation. Yet other related studies go more directly to specific forms of *communication*, topics, and applications of diversity language and ways of talking. This is where research becomes a bit more scattered, niche, interdisciplinary, and adjacent to critical organizational research, but with important things to say from perspectives of applied communication.

For instance, in the case of gender, organizations can be described as having a 'meta-communication' aspect (Mills & Chiaramonte, 1991). Addressing gendered inequalities and discriminations goes beyond just engaging communications *within* organizations and management ranks, to encompass the cultural and masculine status of many organizations themselves as entities. Historically and contextually, a variety of gendered positions are communicated about in organizational settings as part of public life and diverse representations of self. Being 'hard', 'soft', 'rational', 'emotional', 'controlling', a 'bitch', 'slut', or a 'dick' at work all have obvious gendered and sexualized connotations in situ and in communicative acts (Mills & Chiaramonte, 1991). Invisibly, but pervasively, men and dominant forms of masculinity (i.e. 'hegemonic') are often the default communicative reference point in organizations, representing ideological nodes for communicating about divisions of labor, domesticity, and other differences such as race and class (Mumby, 1998).

The question for applied and critical communication research then becomes how men and women alike might construct ('do', 'perform', 'talk about') gender and masculinity differently. On the one hand, 'doing machismo' is often part of a socially legitimizing order or 'male standard' in certain cultures and industries (e.g. automotive) governing the selection into male-dominated workforces (Stobbe, 2005). On the other hand, 'feminist practice' enriches organizational communications in other directions and settings (e.g. organizations with feminist missions), typically through critiques of impersonal bureaucracy portrayed as objective and neutral. In fact, organizations are permeated by alternative conversations and dilemmas around the gendering of professional norms, emotions, and relationships (Ashcraft, 2000). Ultimately, gender, masculinity, and feminism are rooted in everyday discourse and communicative acts, concerning the politicization and organizational responses to many topics, including family, private–public boundaries, health, and subgroups or 'types' of men and women (Buzzannell, Meisenbach, Remke, Sterk, & Turner, 2009).

Similar issues apply to communicating in organizations about race, ethnicity, and culture (indeed – just consider the use of these three terms themselves). Postcolonialism emerges again here as a critical concern, where nations are talked about in ways resembling Benedict Anderson's *imagined communities*. Discourses rooted in Euro-American intellectual traditions afford them privilege as rational while neglecting dialogue with more indigenous worldviews, voices, and systems of meaning (Broadfoot & Munshi, 2007). Namely, there is a need to communicate in ways that recognize and empower cultural knowledge local to Asia, Pacific-Asian regions, Africa, and South America. Furthermore, this runs in parallel to how much Western scholarship and (diversity) management practice is communicated from a standpoint and epistemology of *whiteness*. Subtle (but also in some cases, more blatant) forms of racism can be 'unmasked' or 're-centered' by interrogating how diversity management is being communicated about in ways palatable and nonthreatening to the majority and the status quo (e.g. Grimes, 2002). This may involve purportedly benevolent denials of aspects of racism or celebrating progress from a white majority supremacist perspective that trivializes minority struggles, for instance.

Organizational communication in scholarship and practice has racial foundations and subtexts, and in key textbooks and discussions race is often glossed over as a special interest issue to be managed, not as a more systemic and historical one with many contextual variations (Ashcraft & Allen, 2003). Such communicative positions become increasingly entrenched and conflict-laden amidst crises of globalization around immigration and religious freedoms, across Europe for instance, and organizational diversity is framed by media discourses of nationalism, liberalism, and multiculturalism (Scalvini, 2016; also see next chapter of this volume). Global voices continue to be raised and silenced, subject to the constraints of translation and community participation (Broadfoot et al., 2008). It would seem prudent and reasonable for organizations and managers to listen to the stories of cultures and countries residing in a diverse workforce, particularly non-white and non-Western ones, and to resist any temptation to write them off as irrelevantly 'other', which risks closing off any hope of dialogue and more pluralist visions of what the organization could be.

A final point about diversity and communication here concerns the form of the communication beyond its context – the medium as message, the types of metaphors, vocabularies, and pragmatic set-up of dialogues and pluralistic conversation situations. Bendl and Schmidt (2010) note the ongoing usefulness of 'glass ceiling' and 'firewall' metaphors for discrimination, for example. Metaphors open further discussion while containing many discursive assumptions and analogies for communicating what something might feel like in terms of what something else is like, as re-constituted from another domain (e.g. architecture, technology, finance). Donald Trump's controversial proposal of building a new US border wall to control immigration is potentially a good example of diversity as literal, material, and metaphorical all at once. Once again, and a running critical theme of this chapter and volume, the default metaphorical way of talking about diversity is often managerial and financial – something to be 'managed' so it can contribute to the 'bottom line'. This can act as a powerful suppressor of alternative metaphors, marginalizing more human experiences and ethical engagements with diversity as process and outcome, and perpetuating a world of quick fixes and competitive advantages accrued to a presiding majority with vested economic interests (Kirby & Harter, 2003). As policies and legislative measures shift alongside societal views, organizations hang in the balance offering a communicative situation of 'mixed messages' – Compton (2016) finds this to be the case for US employees with minority sexual orientations, where policies, cultures, and workplace relationships still demand navigation.

Communicative forms become more complex in their organization according to the diversity that underpins them. One such communication-centered way to think of diversity then is in terms of Mikhail Bakhtin's 'polyphony', or an array of voices articulated and mediated by each other, shot through with a range of individual opinions and societal discourses (Trittin & Schoeneborn, 2017). Under this view, the very organization itself emerges from a diversity of voices interrelating, and to the extent that they are not marginalized, they can be recognized and allowed to connect and reorganize differences through communication. Open and varied discussions of organizational practices are important here in sustaining polyphonic dialogue (Trittin & Schoeneborn, 2017).

If a decision is being made about a diversity management practice, then communication will reflect decision-making talk, along with competing social accounts and vocabularies associated with different intelligible positions. These serve to manage and resolve acceptable meanings on what diversity is, what policy measures might look like, and what goals and responsibilities might be involved (Castor, 2005). A dialogic theory or lens is often crucial to critically linking communication and diversity in organizations – to recognize the stakeholders and groups collaborating, negotiating, and problem-solving as they take turns and exchange views ('the communication situation') (Heath, 2007). Moments of more authentic dialogue or dialogic interaction are more likely to occur when something unexpected by the parties involved takes place, such as a creative or democratic framing of mutual interests or the generation of new understandings (Heath, 2007). However, the critique of diversity in organizations here is that it occurs in and through communication, but wherever it becomes pragmatically fixed in language it is also inevitably compromised. Diversity gets abstracted from time and place as something articulated, measurable, and manageable, but this is a flawed and temporary resolution, brought continually back into dialogue by contexts and experiences of inequality and conflict (Urciuoli, 2016). The implication – keep talking and keep listening for a diversity breakthrough – may itself feel unnatural, effortful, and frustrating to pragmatically minded organizational actors, particularly those who favor singular meanings and easy consensus.

Discursive Constructions of Difference Going Forward: Diversity, Language, and Communication in Organizations

Communication and diversity are a fascinating and vital pair of ideas for organizations to keep meditating upon, and research and practice around this linkage are likely to continue to bear fruit on several fronts. This includes, perhaps especially so, more critical, radical views that assert the inherent limitations and abuses of language as communications flow through various power relations and influential discourses that constrain – and occasionally liberate – forms of meaning and expression.

Management scholars are continuing to question whether discourse is just the 'words, words, words' (to invoke Shakespeare's Hamlet) of incessant talk and text, or whether we can relate it back to more *material* aspects of our social world also – the "technologies, objects, sites, and bodies...through which we experience reality" (Trittin & Schoeneborn, 2017, p. 318). Debates therefore continue; on how best to engage the close discourse–materiality relationships surrounding talk, spaces, bodies, objects, and practices, the mutually constituting and organizing qualities often leading us back to Foucault and related views on how these are all ontologically and dialectically tangled together (e.g. Ashcraft, Kuhn, & Cooren, 2009; Hardy & Thomas, 2015; Putnam, 2015). These weighty discussions could perhaps crudely be summed up as considering how language closely intersects and interacts with 'other stuff' in organizations. Regarding diversity, it is perhaps best to consider empirical examples where the symbolic and material are in motion and giving rise to specific expressions of organizational identities. For example, McCabe and Knights' (2015) study of corporate videos and masculine leadership in a UK building society, or Godfrey, Lillis, and Brewis' (2012) study of the movie *Jarhead* in terms of the discursive and material production of masculine military bodies. Future research on communication and diversity can probably learn a lot from these non-verbal, verbal, and visual integrations for studying power structures, diverse identities, and discourse in practice.

It also seems instructive to consider what communication about diversity simply *cannot* do – various metaphors and dialectics of communication mean we are always playing catch-up, something is always being left out of our representations, or pulling our emphasis toward one aspect of meaning and away from another (Schwabenland, 2012). From a psychoanalytic perspective – the 'lack' of Jacques Lacan – it is precisely this imperfect, unfinished quality that drives us to communicate across difference, impelled by the fantasy and titillating anxiety of an impossible ideal groped after in language (Christensen & Muhr, 2018). It is hard to imagine what a totally 'diverse' organization would look like, or one that always carries out totally effective 'diversity management', but this needn't be too troubling if it can be used as a catalyst for reflection and change. Indeed, the emerging perspective on *communication-as-constitutive of organization* argues that organizations emerge from communication and not the other way around – in many senses, ongoing patterns of joint communication is *all that organizations are*, ontologically speaking (Cooren, Kuhn, Cornelissen & Clark, 2011). Future research on diversity in organizations might do well then to really consider diversity as emerging dynamically from flows of communicative organizing activities and events – never quite fully organized and subject to backlash, breakthrough, and reconstitution by diverse parties.

At a more practical level, some diversity-related research on organizations and management is becoming more *language-sensitive*. Karhunen, Kankaanranta, Louhiala-Salminen, and Piekkari (2018) review twenty years of international management research on language use in multinational corporations. They conclude that the most fruitful way for looking at language is in relation to social practices and joint interactions, as embedded in multi-layered contexts where globalization and technology give rise to highly customized, situation-specific forms of communication. Diverse employees are likely to mix and adjust language use in interaction, but with reference to it as a shared resource or 'lingua franca' (Karhunen et al., 2018). In addition, a study of an ethnically diverse Danish supermarket and traffic department found both linguistic barriers (misunderstanding, language competence levels) and bridges ('small talk', collaborations) played a role in hindering and helping social relations, respectively (Thuesen, 2017).

Returning to the idea of discourse or discourses in reflecting communicative organizations of shared meaning, identities, and power relations, we can expect new diverse and diversity discourses to continue to emerge and exert influence. Irving and Helin (2018) show how the sustainable development discourse of a World Business Council's vision for 2050 is problematic from an *ecofeminist* perspective, in that it reproduces unequal dualisms and hierarchies around how gender and nature are represented. Certain ways of knowing and being are still treated as inferior and needing a boost in value, often through market reforms, to 'bring them up' to the level of the globally superior forms of diversity. More local initiatives come to represent counterforces to these types of claims. Spedale (2019) uses *deconstruction analysis* to show how the language of an ageing comprehensive school teacher at the end of his career is full of contradictions, interruptions, and hesitations. The retiring teacher cannot decide whether his age renders him entirely valuable or unproductive, and casts himself as both victim and perpetrator of ageism in discussing family, health, death, and being experienced versus enterprising at work.

Within many critical views of communication, language, and discourse there resides a lingering sense of unease around how strains of capitalism and neoliberal discourse continue to underpin ideas of diversity, difference, affect, and work. Mumby (2016) adopts a concept of 'communicative capitalism' to illustrate how *branding* pervasively mediates and produces our identities. Hiding in plain sight, branding campaigns are poised to stir up, commodify, and tear down diversity issues and images of diverse employees and consumers in politically and culturally charged spaces. In everyday interactions, diverse majorities and minorities are often referencing – with varying subtlety and awareness – their business communications to wider neoliberal issues. These include government policies, market forces, political affiliations, and contested notions of contributing to a developed economy populated by various privileged and vulnerable groups (Shrikant & Musselwhite, 2019).

Conclusion

This chapter has sought to selectively review critical perspectives on communication, diversity, and organization. As such it has been necessarily broad, and only scratched the surface of the many communication concepts, issues, and opportunities for rethinking how we think, write, talk about, and represent difference. It could be said that our societies and workplaces have perhaps too much communication – are saturated with it – or at least communication that is often of the wrong sort, shot through with power and contradictory discourses struggling to represent minority interests and experiences. Like many critical areas of inquiry, communication is inescapable, we are all implicated and must at times turn the lens quite painfully on ourselves to admit the privileges and limits of modes of representation. In that realization, there are ethical and political responsibilities for majorities to listen, give voice to, and take up intercultural dialogues that maximize an inclusive and shared sense of reality (Isotalus & Kakkuri-Knuutilla, 2018). Beyond the hegemony of English, organizational scholarship itself has the potential to become more reflexive about multilingual translation and imaginatively different expressions across other languages (Steyaert & Janssens, 2012).

Methodologically, identifying organizational discourses remains challenging, because of the sheer richness of the meaning systems permeating the use of talk and text. Integrating possible meanings across micro and macro levels seems likely to help develop more thorough understandings of discourse (Fairhurst & Putnam, 2019). There can be no doubt that communications about diversity frequently involve overt and covert struggles over meanings. Often powerful narratives hold sway or are appropriated and parroted, in the manner of a ventriloquist, to suit certain business interests – being mindful of this and demonstrating how discourse functions continues to be an important critical task (Caidor & Cooren, 2018). As a Special Issue of *Management Learning* convincingly showcases, 'writing differently' taps an inherent diversity for learning and change that is neglected if we seek to write only according to restrictive norms pretending to scientific objectivity and neutrality all the time (Gilmore, Harding, Helin, & Pullen, 2019).

A critical perspective means being wary of diversity *rhetoric* in organizational communication. There appear to be many forms of communication that are deployed as rhetorically persuasive and unchallenged in their assumptions about diversity's value, manageability, and remit. New media and messages throw up further challenges and opportunities for communicative exchanges about diversity. Chief among these are social media platforms, which allow for more multi-directional communications but also formidably novel and turbulent dynamics around ideology, authorship, data, design, imagery, and technological systems (e.g. Bouvier & Machin, 2018). In addition, and finally, an organizational politics of 'post-truth' and 'alternative facts' appears to now surround today's multimodal and informationally abundant communications (Knight & Tsoukas, 2018). Freedom of speech, hate speech, and charges of political correctness will clamor in spaces of diverse communications. This should mean more diversity than ever in all communications to some extent. However, from a pragmatic perspective, this does not negate the need to be mindful of all the alternative organizational realities expressed – seeking them out, engaging them in dialogue, and deconstructing them by critically making sense of what is said and not said.

8 Multiculturalism

Multiculturalism can seem like a fearsome term, often marked out by opening-line disclaimers observing fundamental disagreements over its meaning, utility, and failings. Like other concepts and perspectives in this volume, we are free to question how 'critical' it is in reflecting a critical view of diversity, management, and organization. This chapter will argue that it can indeed be considered a critical perspective, and that it has interdisciplinary and international value that is perhaps a bit neglected in this regard.

To get up to speed on multiculturalism and significant views on the topic, introductory texts and encyclopedic entries are invaluable (Modood, 2007; Rattansi, 2011). In his *Very Short Introduction*, Ali Rattansi (2011, p.12) notes the elusiveness of a single definition, but suggests multiculturalism can be thought of as usually referring to "policies by central states and local authorities that have been put in place to manage and govern the new multiethnicity created by non-white immigrant populations, after the end of the Second World War." This hints at a grand societal project of achieving equality and pluralism in a celebration of cultural diversity overseen by the modern nation-state. However, this version of multiculturalism starts to seem increasingly problematic as it connects with topics like immigration, rights, religious practices, education, identity, community, racism, feminism, liberalism, and many other jostling 'isms' and tricky verbs-become-nouns like 'integration' and 'assimilation' (Rattansi, 2011).

This is delicate territory, and in many quarters, the word itself has fallen into disuse or is used in limiting descriptive or derogatory ways. However, none of this should lead us to be too dismissive of multiculturalism – much has been achieved and doubtless much tragedy and suffering have been experienced in relation to the ideal. Either way, more so than ever we still live in a globalizing, transnational world of multiple, interpenetrating, and co-evolving cultures. This is where critical thinking comes in, in terms of what we can learn from multicultural traditions and scholarship, to develop a greater appreciation of its nuances, and where more renewed language and sophisticated understandings may be possible from intra- and intercultural dialogues. Multiculturalism may seem a far cry from narrowly-focused corporate and economic concerns, and yet it is worth another look because it is a fundamental way of thinking about our societies. The policies it implies are inextricably linked to an affecting and affected web of organizing, organizations, and organizational stakeholders.

Early management papers from the 1980s and 1990s have used the word 'multicultural,' but typically in a non-critical fashion, dropping the 'ism' and having it serve as a mere descriptor for recognizing a growth in culturally diverse workforces, markets, and economies (Adler, 1983; Cox, 1991). This recognition from that point in time seems important, insofar as it concerns the integration and pluralism of ethnic minority cultural diversity within the wider organizational culture. However, it seems ill-equipped to acknowledge the more serious issues of racism, justice, and inequality associated with the sharper end of multiculturalism. This more critical emphasis gets lost under a welter of majority-driven diversity management practices, with risks of cultural imperialism or ethnocentricity and limiting aims of minimizing conflict. Similarly, but more recently, Stacey Fitzsimmons' work uses the adjective 'multicultural' to describe the background of individual employees and leaders (e.g. Fitzsimmons, 2013). Again, the work is surely valuable for recognizing the multiculturalism residing *within individuals* having experience of multiple cultures as part of their complex demographic backgrounds. However, such approaches are still developed in quite an individualistic, value-neutral way; presenting (multi)cultural identities as neatly bounded materials to be juggled and managed for positive outcomes, only vaguely moderated by ideology and other social conditions.

Nemetz and Christensen's (1996) paper seems more of an exception to this rule of non-critical multicultural management research. It deploys a stronger critical tenor in considering the 'isms' of belief systems driving politicized reactions to formal diversity-training programs associated with multiculturalism. Majority backlash, polarization, and charges of 'political correctness' are acknowledged as possible reactions, depending on individuals' belief systems regarding how much cultural and moral diversity is tolerable, feasible, and desirable in societies and workplaces. Unfortunately, these more political and ideological distinctions do not seem to have been built upon in a focused, critical way by subsequent diversity research. While there may not be easy answers here, there is huge potential in revisiting Nemetz and Christensen's (1996) work for the sake of more realistic, open, and ongoing dialogue about the limitations of formal cultural diversity training programs and unpacking the less-than-positive reactions to them.

Multiculturalism: Earlier Debates

More critical work on multicultural diversity in organizations will be considered in subsequent sections below, but before doing so, it seems worth briefly acknowledging some of the more interdisciplinary political and philosophical treatments of multiculturalism that might help enrich critical organizational research on cultural diversity. There is a litany of potential names and figures here, and only an illustrative sample can be given, but interested readers would do well to consult introductory works and bibliographies on the topic of multiculturalism (e.g. Rattansi, 2011).

Perhaps the most useful critical aspect of more political and philosophical perspectives overall is that they tend to ask more searching 'why' and 'how' questions of multiculturalism, as opposed to, or in addition to, the 'what,' 'where,' 'when,' and 'who' of more descriptive managerial accounts. The 1990s is where the wealth and growth of most of the reflection on multiculturalism lie, considering the tangle of interlocking and contradictory ideologies and worldviews underpinning various accounts of its existence.

An article by Seyla Benhabib (1999) is typical and instructive by way of taking stock of the turn-of-the-century developments. Its commentary notes the increasingly fierce contests and controversies around the political nature of cultural diversity, including culture 'wars' and 'identity politics' in modern liberal societies. Culturally diverse groups vie for political legitimacy, organizing and seeking organized forms of recognition and redistribution. This multicultural legacy is characterized by four dogmas in relation to the contradictory ideals of a liberal imagination (Benhabib, 1999): (1) cultural holism; (2) the overly socialized self; (3) the prison house of perspectives; and (4) the distrust of the universal. The dogmas differ in how they commit culturally, philosophically, and politically to the idea of multiculturalism. However, they allow us to ask important questions about individual freedoms, socialization into collective cultures, and the dynamic openness to finding common ground for respect across cultural perspectives. In short, sustaining multicultural democracy with a virtuous liberal imagination is a delicate business. It involves "[f]lexibility, openness to the new and to the unknown; tolerance in the face of what seems strange; respect for fallibilism, faith in the capacity of individuals and collectivities to learn from their mistakes; acceptance of contingency" (Benhabib, 1999, p.412).

More politically, the 1990s has seen growing awareness of the complex relationships between multiculturalism and views of justice and nationhood, often referring to left-leaning public intellectuals and liberal philosophers such as Richard Rorty and John Rawls. This then has a contrasting relationship across the political spectrum to right-wing populism, where multiculturalism can forcefully be presented as a threat to national unity and majority freedoms and ideals. What becomes clear is how difficult it is for thinkers to sustain a postmodern and pragmatic orientation to multicultural democracy without trying to assimilate and integrate cultures to a reductively unrepresentative view that begets further tensions. Giroux (1995, p.56) concludes such a discussion by viewing the task thus:

> [I]f national identity is not to be used in the service of demagogues, it must be addressed pedagogically and politically to unravel how cultural differences have been constructed within the unequal distribution of resources, how such differences need to be understood around issues of power and struggle, and how national identity must be taken up in ways that challenge economic and cultural inequality.

If one is not in agreement with the previous quote, then engaging further with multiculturalism is likely to prove a difficult or unappealing prospect. Yet organizations, leaders, and their cultural diversity continue to reflect microcosms of these extensive interdisciplinary debates that have emerged principally from the 1990s onwards. Bluntly, employees and managers do not leave their views of multiculturalism, pluralism, liberalism, and nationalism at the door of organizations.

As with intersectionality, multiculturalism has enough force as a diversity-related word and a project to attract some overlapping, recurrent interest from psychologists. Fowers and Richardson (1996) argue that multiculturalism can be a force for good in shining a light on the moral traditions and ideals of European and American civilizations, and the tensions around how they are practiced in fields like psychology. They conclude by emphasizing *hermeneutics* – the need to understand how cultures emerge in context, via their practices, traditions, and self-understandings. This also implies profound two-way openness and dialogue between cultures, even – or perhaps especially – when they find one another's values in conflict and morally abhorrent and incomprehensible (Fowers & Richardson, 1996).

Less in psychology and more in political philosophy and sociology, Steven Lukes has revisited the example of cannibalism (Lukes, 2003); a practice likely abhorrent to liberals, but one that should be reasoned about in a self-critical relation to the liberal observer's own culture. Multiculturalism means interrogating the universal against the particular, not being too quick to assume that cultures are uniform and neatly-bounded entities, and appreciating that moral diversity can co-exist with moral similarity as we sort through our cultural practices and identities (Joppke & Lukes, 1999). Somewhere between cultural relativism ('anything goes') and cultural universalism ('my way is the best way') there is scope for making the familiar strange, the strange familiar, and mutually adjusting our identities in dialogue with cultural diversity.

Difficult, related concepts of *pluralism* and *toleration/tolerance* also lie at the heart of the 1990s multiculturalist discourses (Sartori, 1997). A spontaneous order emerges in multicultural settings where there are communities with consensus and dissensus on certain cultural issues. However, pluralism represents the dynamic reasoning and challenges inherent to teasing out a higher-order consensus of co-existence from a universal standpoint, if such standpoints can be said to exist. As Sartori (1997, p.65) puts it, "The bottom line thus appears to be that the on-going vitality of pluralism rests on the tension between conviction and toleration, not on the still waters of indifference or relativism." Karl Popper's *paradox of tolerance* similarly states that we should not 'tolerate the intolerant' in a democracy, but then who decides how tolerant or intolerant any given cultural encounter or claim is held to be? (Freeman, 1975). Ultimately, multiculturalism tests the limits of liberal democracy through these notions of pluralism and toleration. The broadly liberal need to prioritize more material rights, interests, (in) justice, and equality based on ethnic exclusion and disadvantage remains in tension with other forms of 'recognition' of a more complex array of identities and practices (Lukes, 1997). In another sense, multiculturalism provides a critical description or outlook on how a social system (nation, organization, community) is faring in terms of inclusion, equality, and integration of its cultural diversity – something historical, challenging, and ongoing, and far from a linear progression with a clear end state (Glazer, 1998).

All of this is further complicated by the unlikely prospect of neatly defining cultures as enduring, bounded entities and clearly differentiated groups. There is also the issue of how likely or possible cultural integration of groups and values appears to be. Politically and ethically, multiculturalism becomes a particularly intense problem where claims and standards for justice conflict to the extent that they are highly incompatible and/or incommensurable (Gutmann, 1993). This really takes diversity down to the 'nitty-gritty' level of apparently stark, group-level disagreements about gender, marriage, family, education, the state, citizenship, and many other issues.

Much rests in multiculturalism therefore on bringing together those who radically disagree to respectfully deliberate on their moral diversity, and the reasonable and justifiable policy decisions that might support some more acceptable form of conflict resolution (Gutmann, 1993). Cultures have to come together to reconcile moral and political differences by directly representing and stating their claims, on behalf of whom they are being made, and with what justification and evidence they are based upon. However, cultural groups also have *intragroup differences* – not least as regards gender and the need for feminist voices within and across cultures (Okin, 1998a, 1998b). Cultural gender diversity highlights the delicate relationships between feminism and multiculturalism. For instance, Okin (1998b) summarizes how women threatened by human rights violations from within their cultures report needing three things: (1) to be listened to and deliberated with, (2) financial support for women's organizations resisting cultural practices, and (3) political support from the West and the international community that does not assault the non-harmful aspects of their culture. Indeed, pitting feminism against multiculturalism is problematic for gender equality insofar as it obscures common forces of patriarchy across cultures and risks reinforcing postcolonial assumptions around the inherent cultural superiority of Western liberal feminism (Volpp, 2001).

At their most accessible, common themes of multicultural theorists from the 1990s seem to involve a careful sensitization to the dignity, suffering, and well-being of minority cultural individuals. Crucially, this sensitization involves acknowledging and deliberating upon the socio-historical influences of both home and host cultures, and the claims for justice, equality, and recognition flowing from these relations. As implied earlier, the dangers and opportunities are many, and these remarkable multicultural debates have evolved and continued unabated into the twenty-first century. Certainly, they feel quite different in tone from standard corporate narratives of diversity management and inclusion, and with some additional perspectives for complementing and challenging the latter.

Multiculturalism: Later Debates

In the year 2000, *The Future of Multi-Ethnic Britain* or Parekh Report was published and was subsequently described as containing 'muddles' of multiculturalism, or inconsistent public policy recommendations around anti-discrimination measures for cultural diversity in various sectors of the economy and polity (Barry, 2001). There remain an extraordinary difficulty and lack of clarity at the national and public level in mediating between liberal and universal ideals on the one hand, and particular local values, customs, and practices on the other. However, Schubert (2002) defends multiculturalism on the grounds of Pierre Bourdieu's 'symbolic violence' – it enables both the dominated and the oppressed to examine and question the cultural practices they take part in.

At this point, the main political theorists of multiculturalism include Brian Barry, Will Kymlicka, Jacob Levy, and Bhikhu Parekh (Yack, 2002). The use of the power of the state to reinforce cultural diversity remains controversial, as do different emphases on cultural border-guarding versus cultural border-crossing. Frameworks of rights, justice, and citizenship play a role, alongside being able to know when to question the principles underlying cultural values while knowing when not to exaggerate their harms to the majority (Yack, 2002).

Perhaps the important point here for organizations is that like societies, they can be viewed as multicultural environments with populations that have various limits to the liberalism and pluralism they can politically and culturally accept and enact. Much rests on how organizational actors react to cultural diversity and the political and ethical traits they cultivate to engage with its pluralism (Curtis, 2007). Presumably, many will continue to want diverse workforces to also be liberal political communities with practices capable of supporting robust and equal dialogue between plural cultural worldviews. These 'odysseys' or twenty-first journeys and experiments away from assimilation toward greater multiculturalist policies have an international character, reflected in strivings for liberal democratic consensus over the norms and discourses of accommodating cultural diversity and minority rights (Kymlicka, 2007). Diffusing liberal multiculturalism around the globe successfully is a fragile project, to say the least. However, this also makes it no less urgent to consider what the minimal standards for organizations in different countries should be for the protection and autonomy of cultural minorities. Furthermore, minorities in different parts of the world can be 'old' indigenous peoples or 'nationalities,' or 'new' immigrant minorities (Kymlicka, 2007).

To the extent that organizations have intercultural engagement across their workforces, they could be described as moving toward multicultural integration and social solidarity (Berry, 2011), in ways that reflect positively on the social and cross-cultural psychology of the employees and managers. Under this view, multiculturalism is an ongoing problem of social representation that could equally be summed up by the term *inclusion*, where an integration strategy means maximizing both preservation of cultural heritages while also maximizing intercultural contact, exchange, and participation in the larger society (Berry, 2011). Empirically, Bloemraad and Wright (2014) note both the difficulty and importance of assessing the evidence for effects of multicultural policies across immigrant-receiving democratic nations, while political rhetoric runs high around its 'doom' and 'utter failure' across much of Europe. In national survey data across European and Anglo countries, they find modest positive effects for immigrant minorities' socio-political integration, while urging more research into the variable levels of majority backlash and efforts to recast and reimagine national identities (Bloemraad & Wright, 2014).

In ways analogous to multiculturalism's challenges to the nation-state and notions of citizenship, it challenges organizations' dominant cultural understanding of themselves and who gets the status, rights, and belonging afforded to full organizational citizens (Bloemraad, 2008). The most recent work on multiculturalism does seem to suggest, though, that a change in language might be needed to reflect emerging twenty-first century realities. For instance, Vertovec (2010) deploys 'post-multiculturalism' and 'super-diversity' to reflect more dynamic transnational patterns of global migration and polyvalent modes of immigrant belonging. This recommends more recognition of greater multiplicity and complexity, not less.

Despite ambivalence about explicit use of the 'M-word' and serious evidence of racism, decades of multiculturalism have driven ethnic diversity gains in organizations and workplaces in the broadest possible sense. Ideas of cosmopolitanism and valuing of ethnic diversity are therefore ultimately likely to continue to evolve (Vertovec, 2010). For Werbner (2013), daily interactions in the twenty-first century in Britain involving more recent generations of immigrants can proceed smoothly and respectfully – on the surface at least – as part of 'everyday multiculturalism' and the discussion of multiple identities (e.g. around the London 2012 Olympics). Beneath the surface, however, this can still be deconstructed to reveal lingering tensions around racism, nationalism, and unresolved postcolonial melancholia. The point is to recognize both: "Although far less prevalent and pervasive than in the immediate postwar period, everyday racism and institutional racism may co-exist in some places and contexts with everyday multiculturalism" (Werbner, 2013, p.415). Werbner (2005) also distinguishes between multiculturalism 'as usual,' where we are able to celebrate cultural differences in public life, and 'in history,' where more longstanding and incommensurable cultural conflicts define a multicultural controversy, such as Islamic blasphemy versus freedom of speech.

Whatever the ways in which multiculturalism is defined – thinly or thickly, politically or philosophically, in the past or in the present, from the top down or the bottom up – it is these tensions in its histories and trajectories that remain compelling and bring it forcefully into the present fabric of daily interactions in organizations. At its most distressing and fraught, this is where multiculturalism reaches limits in conflicts of tolerance and (in)equality around violence, religion, and gender (Haque, 2010). At its most hopeful and advocated, multiculturalism is sometimes now expressed through the complementary, overlapping notion of 'interculturalism': "encouraging communication, recognizing dynamic identities, promoting unity and critiquing illiberal cultural practices" (Meer & Modood, 2012, p.175).

Characteristically, perhaps, these distinctions still remain subtle and difficult to grasp, but speak to the persistent and evolving concerns around the encounters between cultural identities. The fact that racism, racial abuse, and racialized inequalities clearly remain, and can periodically strengthen, sits uncomfortably with multiculturalism at times, giving it a 'zombie' status in countries like Britain and cities like London, as the sheer complexity of society erupts suddenly in public and virtual spaces (Gilroy, 2012). Ironically, leaving racism out of discussions of multiculturalism and diversity risks perpetuating new forms of modern racism, by seeing 'racisms' as just part of cultural diversity in a 'post-racial' milieu, rather than something more serious and political (Lentin, 2014).

In these thorny debates, it is hard to reduce multiculturalism to a straightforward set of propositions without exhibiting and reproducing some sort of bias or historical oversight. It is probably not entirely fair to expect individuals to act as fully equipped, educationally and ethically, to behave as model multicultural citizens. Nevertheless, in terms of workplace interactions, hopefully some version of liberal multiculturalism can still be used to shape common ground in sensitively and seriously discussing accommodation of cultural diversity in organizations. As Terri Murray (2014, n.p.) put it in a philosophy article on judging Islamic culture, the issue is not:

> [T]hat we have to choose between one form of bigotry and another. Western liberals need not remain in a deadlock over whether or not tolerance and respect for religious minorities trumps respect for women. After all, religious women fall into both categories. Instead, *liberal multiculturalism* offers a framework within which all people can live their faith, be prevented from coercing others into doing so, and remain free to offend, and be offended by, others in an open, dynamic, sometimes uncomfortable (but genuine) dialogue.

Nothing is simple in the interdisciplinary and critical world of multiculturalism as it survives today. However, having laid some of this interdisciplinary groundwork, the remainder of this chapter can consider organizations more directly, as well as relevant critical organizational research on multiculturalism more specifically, to the extent that it exists.

Multicultural Diversity and Organizations

Clearly, multiculturalism is relevant to organizations, but the literature and use of the word are scattered and scrambled by the far greater attention to 'diversity management' more generally. Miller and Rowney (1999) actually link both – multicultural societies and organizational diversity management – and study Canada as an example of where relatively recent multicultural policies prompted mixed reactions from organizations and a need to consider diversity management more explicitly. Canada is frequently used as an example because of how its official multicultural policies and values penetrate everyday (and organizational) life, particularly French versus English language-usage in a French-majority city like Quebec. Intercultural conflicts, leadership, democracy, language policies, and other practices then become ethical issues at the organizational level (Pasquero, 1997).

Regardless of the country to an extent, multiculturalism can be connected to other contexts, discourses, and phenomena as they affect particular organizations, although these tend to be few and far between, and outside the organization studies discipline. Pieterse (1997), for example, considers *museums* from a multicultural perspective – organizations inherently involved in representing national cultural heritages but in an evolving context of globalization, where culturally diverse visitors, staff and exhibits frame multicultural issues. In an ethnographic study of a multicultural sorority chapter at a predominantly white US university, McCabe (2011, p.521) notes that despite "the many references to multiculturalism in academic works and media accounts, we know little about what it is like in practice." She found that 'doing multiculturalism' took place to some extent through supportive relationships across cultural differences, but was ultimately constrained by the overall culture of the university and the 'Greek system' of sororities.

Banerjee and Linstead (2001) do refer to multiculturalism in organization studies, but conceptualize it in highly broad and critical terms as a rhetorical fiction serving to assimilate minority cultures to a dominant ideology of global capitalism. This critique of globalization has broad resonances, and suggests that organizations too often neglect 'the local' knowledge and identities of cultures, particularly in the Third World. The 'differences' shaped here are more economic than cultural, more based on consumption than alternative values of community and nature - multiculturalism itself merely part of this homogenizing twenty-first century influence (Banerjee & Linstead, 2001). In a similar critical essay, Hoobler (2005) expresses concern with the apparently superficial, ideological 'lip service' approach of organizations to embracing multiculturalism. Drawing on Foucault's notion of 'docile bodies,' she emphasizes how 'true' multiculturalism seems improbable where imperatives for authority and efficiency are fundamentally opposed to dealing with difficult issues of race, gender, and class politics. The organizational order of the day remains avoiding discrimination lawsuits and throwing limited resources after faddish diversity management practices (Hoobler, 2005).

The general critical organizational perspective is therefore damning. However, while clear in some respects, there are arguably still many contexts and concepts related to multiculturalism that resurface for worthwhile examination if we allow ourselves to break free from the unsatisfactory hymns of globalization and diversity management best practices.

In a 2015 issue of *American Behavioral Scientist* entitled 'Multiculturalism During Challenging Times,' Ng and Bloemraad (2015) present a suite of six articles spanning Canada, Europe, Mauritius, and South Korea. The accompanying SWOT (strengths, weaknesses, opportunities, threats) analysis reveals configurations of positive and negative potentials and influences operating within and across national environments. One conclusion might be that multiculturalism is clearly the positive 'right thing to do' in many instances, but it is very difficult to 'do it right' in terms of implementation of policy amidst competing political ideologies. Organizations have a clear role to play here as they are often at the heart of the cultural and economic experiences characterizing multiculturalism in a given national context. Depending on the policies in place in particular host countries, organizations in nations such as Australia and Canada may be able to positively embrace multiculturalism as a strategic form of competitive nation-building and international alliance-building with the home nations of immigrants (Ng & Metz, 2015).

A positive way of viewing multiculturalism's influence on organizations is how it can expose US-centric and Western views of diversity management to alternate, non-Western histories and cultures. Syed (2011) argues this in relation to the example of Jalaluddin Muhammad Akbar, a Muslim ruler of the sixteenth-century who developed threefold principles of absolute peace (Sulh-i-Kul), the path of reason (Rah-i-Aql), and the maintenance of livelihood (Rawa-i-Rozi). Indeed, these forms of leadership and role modeling represent principled ways of taking a refreshed look at changing limited diversity management discourses in novel socio-political ways, promoting wider authentic dialogue and tolerance.

Multicultural and Cross-national Organizing

To critically engage an organization as something culturally plural and multicultural means to critically engage conceptions and visions of what nation and culture might mean. This offers a way of reinvigorating connections between organizational culture, national culture, and diversity management, topics that surprisingly do not often get brought together in research and practice. Even without the term 'multiculturalism,' this is where management and organizational research have more foundations to build upon. Culture and nation can be viewed critically and reflexively through various methods and paradigms in organizational studies, from the functionalism of Hofstede's dimensions through to more constructivist and interpretive views of culture as local, improvised, and jointly negotiated (Williamson, 2002). Robert Halsall's critical work on conceptions of nation and culture in (global) business and management discourse powerfully dissects the illusions and ideals of a capitalism that is neither truly cosmopolitan nor deeply sensitive to cultural diversity (Halsall, 2008, 2009). Instead, multicultural discourses (and similar) serve as a neoliberal branding tool that abdicates corporate and state responsibility in pursuit of a universally convergent approach; transnational and flexible in serving the interests of capital across managed locations, while only paying lip service to cultural attachments and values.

Whether this grim globally corporatized vision is accepted wholesale or not, we should probably also consider the complex adaptations and struggles of forms of culture co-existing alongside it in oppression, indifference, or resistance. Debates then move into areas of *hybridity*, and to what extent cultures can be legitimately combined, and the political and economic significance of such mixing (Pieterse, 2001). Research such as that of Shimoni and Bergmann (2006) highlights the autonomous cultural hybridity of local managers of global corporations – in Israel, Thailand, and Mexico, for example, with headquarters in European countries. These combinations are highly improvised and customized, and not readily reflected in straightforward multicultural acknowledgements of global and local roles. Questions remain about these critical hybridities, their power to harness diversity, and whether managers can turn multiculturalism into positive forms of organized and inclusive cosmopolitanism (Beck, 2008). If traditional corporations and the state have ceased to shape diverse and inclusive cultures, identifying influential bases for their organization becomes central.

Some critical organizational research appears to move in this direction of looking at distinctive global and cultural organizational forms and approaches, many of which have explicit relations to multiculturalism, albeit not always positive ones. For example, Moufahim, Reedy, and Humphries (2015) studied an extreme right political organization, the *Vlaams Belang*, highlighting how it uses powerful rhetorical frames and strategies to persuade followers to identify with its Flemish nationalist aims and values. Part of the organization's position rests on undermining postwar European politics of multiculturalism and cosmopolitanism, invoking separatism and assimilationism regarding minorities. Similarly, Bell (2002) considers the 'force field' of global jihad in facilitating the global organization of Islamic terror, with its own particular organizational strengths and vulnerabilities rooted in cultural discontent and revolutionary commitments. The absence of sustained cultural and organizational values of decency, vigilance, patience, and respect for the denied arguably help cultivate these violent and alarming forms of organization (Bell, 2002). Less destructively but still under difficult circumstances, organizations and organizing work between diverse cultures appear in relation to refugee camps and services. While De La Chaux, Haugh, and Greenwood (2018) have looked at how Western camp officials and Somali refugees communicate and co-exist in a Kenyan refugee camp, other scholars have looked at how employee service providers for UK refugees – particularly refugee women – strive to empower and include them in ways that don't perpetuate an outsider status (Tomlinson, 2010; Tomlinson & Egan, 2002b).

As with local managers, transnational managers need autonomy and skills to navigate and blend national cultures under a 'one-company approach' in very different subsidiaries (subcultures), although such multicultural work may face limits and not be prevalent at all levels of the organization (Ailon & Kunda, 2009). Going further, Witte (2011) makes a case for the 'post-national' cultural analysis of organizations, given that many forms – NGOs, professional associations, public agencies – aggregate in ways that do not correspond neatly to national cultures and locations. This would offer opportunities for novel insights but entail downplaying national analysis in favor of greater emphasis on media representations, stakeholder encounters, and non-managerial exchanges and conventions.

Perhaps the most radical and challenging critical perspective on multicultural organizing is one that considers it a fantasy of denial or wishful thinking, one related to achieving a robustly open liberal democracy or reformed capitalism that can work for and include all diversity (De Cock & Böhm, 2007). From this follows that more radical change is needed, and existing agitations and debates are too cautious and may even be an unconscious way of denying or closing off the need for more radical possibilities and public normative visions. Certainly, this challenge to the multicultural and organizational imagination is relevant to the changing 'idea of Europe' as a complex set of nations, communities, and multi-ethnic belongings (Amin, 2004). National models of multicultural citizenship and integration are subject to various changes and interpretations, and close analysis in relation to organizational actors can yield insights, particularly from migrant workers and communities and those who work most closely with them (Bertossi, 2011).

Reviving multiculturalism for organization studies, if indeed that is desirable and feasible, seems to mean making a renewed case for engaging questions of racial, ethnic, cultural, and religious belonging within and across workers and workplaces (Pathak, 2008). One threat to this agenda lies in terms of multiculturalism being obscured by a global spectacle of Western culture versus Other (e.g. Islamophobia) – a crude but seductive way of seeing cultural difference that risks precluding the use of art and critical vision to interrupt dehumanizing closure and invite more authentic integration (Kersten & Abbott, 2012).

Political and organizational leaders engaged in social movements and diversity issues remain ambivalent to multiculturalism and can feel pressured to resolve that ambivalence in public debates and positions by moving closer to one extreme or another (Bygnes, 2012). However, the challenge is not to resolve ambivalence, but to embrace it, live with it, and to organize with the necessary flexibility and engagement to deliver positive outcomes from it, such as creativity, trust, and adaptation (Rothman, Pratt, Rees & Vogus, 2017). Perhaps part of this ambivalence needs to be directed at multiculturalism itself, as but one part of a wider history of perspectives on diversity, and one that should not detract from issues of 'race' and inequality (Collins, 2011).

Multiculturalism and its Future in Relation to Organizational Diversity

The earlier sections of this chapter raise a few lines of thought pertaining to possible futures for multiculturalism and critical views of organizational diversity, and it seems worth briefly reinforcing these here before concluding on the topic.

The first concerns ongoing conceptualizations of multiculturalism and the key issues of its organization that either play around with the word and idea itself, or perhaps employ different concepts that seem indirectly related. Colombo (2015) gives a critical overview of the 'multiculturalisms' and multiple, polysemic meanings of the word in today's Western societies. The term can be used normatively, ideologically, or descriptively, and although subject to backlash and policy retreat, there is some increased interest in 'everyday multiculturalism' regarding urban interactions and social practices.

Vertovec (2018) has noted that "Rightly or wrongly, the term has become associated with socially disintegrative effects" (p.174), and the backlash toward discourse and policies "has largely been based on a misreading of their purposes and effects" (p.177). What we are left with is a state of 'post-multiculturalism,' where public and private sector organizations are still seeking greater voice and embedding of a diversity that is based on "a strong common identity and values coupled with the recognition of cultural differences (alongside differences based on gender, sexuality, age, and disability)" (Vertovec, 2018, p.175). After all, the fundamental historical problem remains the same; that of "questions of multi-group governance and negotiation surrounding everyday practices and interactions...in populations composed of linguistically, culturally and religiously heterogeneous groups" (Vertovec, 2018, p.168). De Waal (2018) argues for a complementary mixture of multiculturalism and 'interculturalism,' where multiculturalism considers the role of the state in negotiating questions of power sharing and inclusion, while interculturalism focuses more on civil society and how to cultivate citizens with intercultural attitudes and capabilities (see also Boucher & Maclure, 2018).

For Kymlicka (2015), the key social issue is to engage an 'inclusive solidarity' where multiculturalism is not linked to neoliberalism or welfare chauvinism, but more deeply participative forms of nation-building and social membership. One conclusion from this is that organizations have a clear and crucial role to play in building such bases of inclusive solidarity and multicultural national identity. We should probably give management research some credit in some quarters for starting to encourage greater connection and translation between Western and Eastern practices, institutions, and geographies (Filatotchev et al., 2020). In terms of the poorer global South and the colonized nations or 'victims of globalization,' *Organization* journal credits itself with being an early champion of enabling colonial voices to speak back critically against Eurocentric organizational assumptions (Mir & Mir, 2013). East and South are crucial to acknowledge, but micro aspects of cross-cultural contact and dialogue need to be combined with a macro focus on political contexts and power relations. It is at this juncture that the 'zombie' of multiculturalism lurches on, inviting searches for new 'ways of being' in a world of cultural differences, encounters, oppressions, and emancipations (Sealy, 2018).

A second way for critical research on organizational diversity and multiculturalism to advance in the future is by continuing to study national and global contexts and relations that seem to be affecting organizations in ways relevant to multicultural debates. This could be where cultures are in dense, plural and close contact organizationally, or where issues that disproportionately affect cultural minorities and organizations' multicultural relations are the subject of investigation. For example, Pio and Syed (2018) use a novel 'poetics' approach to reflect on Islam and inclusion versus exclusion of an expanded Muslim workforce in the West. Poetics approaches encourage a more open and imaginative dialogue with the positive and heterogeneous aspects of cultures, allowing an organizational, human, and relational understanding of Islam and Muslims that is less linear and stigmatizing (Pio & Syed, 2018). Another example is a study of race relations and multiculturalism among prisoners in West Canadian prisons (Tetrault, Bucerius, & Haggerty, 2020). The authors find a mixed picture of liberal multiculturalism as a lived political philosophy in this population. Beliefs about Canada's national mythology shaped racially color-blind perceptions that supported inter-group relations, but they also served to downplay structural racism, individualizing racism, and even declaring it had been overcome (Tetrault et al., 2020).

Future research on multiculturalism can walk a tricky line between a media discourse of 'failed spaces' and findings that contain grounds for both pessimism and optimism. Thomas and colleagues' (2018) study of low-income White working class Yorkshire communities' attitudes toward diversity found negative perceptions and ambivalence toward inter-ethnic relations, but also some appetite for more inter-ethnic contact and a relative absence of organized anti-minority politics – in brief, 'hopes and fears.' Where it is in evidence, terrorism offers a challenge for organizational theorizing as it arises in different geographical and ideological contexts, but it has been described as variously adopting elements of a formal organization, a network, and a social movement (Comas, Shrivastava, & Martin, 2015).

Furthermore, it is not just that organizations shape and enact multiculturalism, but also that exogenous multicultural crises and events shape and enact organizations. The relationship is reciprocal. The nongovernmental organization and 'citizen start-up' *Train of Hope* was found to play an outstanding role in addressing how the 2015 refugee crisis was handled in the city of Vienna (Kornberger, Leixnering, Meyer, & Höllerer, 2018). The organization used technological, economic, and social movement mechanisms to balance and reshape the necessary economic and moral dimensions of the organization of sharing (Kornberger et al., 2018). Also on the continuing multicultural and organizational themes of refugees, immigration and nationalism, and a topic of much concern to critical management scholars working in the UK and Europe is that of Brexit. Bristow and Robinson (2018) argue that Brexit represents a 'phenomenon-in-the-making' for management academics to take a more public and performative critical stance toward in helping to shape post-Brexit organizations where populism, xenophobia, and post-truth politics pose significant challenges, not least within academia's own ranks. Similarly, Grey (2018) argues that Brexit marks a significant break or turning point in the heritage of British critical management studies, where the liberal-left pro-European orientation of its scholars leaves them stranded in a complex and ironic position between establishment elites and polarized voters. Elusive national and cultural alliances must be sought to uphold projects of political and critical import.

However, a third way for critical organizational scholars to investigate multiculturalism in the future is to make contributions at a more micro level; to understanding organizational interactions, mindsets, and behaviors between multicultural co-workers, be they deemed enlightened and progressive, or reactionary and problematic. After all, these can potentially be conceived of as micro 'foundations' underpinning more macro, aggregate dynamics surrounding multiculturalism. A case in point is work by Amanda Wise and colleagues on humor and conviviality in everyday multicultural work interactions in countries like Australia and Singapore (Wise, 2016; Wise & Velayutham, 2014, 2020). Humor can evidently have both positive and negative effects for workplace encounters between diverse individuals. In general, however, it is a way of negotiating and mediating cultural frames of reference and group memberships across shared spaces and relationships. Making humor and playful connections positive and comfortable for all is, ironically, a serious matter requiring labor and understanding to render it a productive and transactional resource (Wise & Velayutham, 2014). Cosmopolitanism is a related concept here, where professionals, expatriates, and locally diverse communities consider the multicultural features of their identities and environments, accomplishing some level of belonging between global openness and anti-cosmopolitan nationalism (Skovgaard-Smith & Poulfelt, 2018). Yet another multicultural concept and practice concernstolerance, although seeking a culture of *respect* for diversity beyond what is being tolerated can be seen as more ethically meaningful and inclusive (Lozano & Escrich, 2017). Indeed, tolerance and respect constitute neglected features of diversity training that could help boost its acceptance and impact (Gebert, Buengeler, & Heinitz, 2017).

As noted above to some extent, multicultural workplace interactions are likely to contain varying attitudes toward populism, immigration, political parties, religion, and other ideologies that cannot be disregarded as non-work-related or issues exclusive to the Global North West (Masood & Nisar, 2020). Migrant integration policy officials and professionals wrestle with restrictive bureaucracy, political interference, and personal convictions in their work (Swinkels & Van Meijl, 2020). Anti-Muslim discrimination and Islamophobia cases show that workplace legislation is not enough, moral development and learning need to be more strongly encouraged by managers (Sekerka & Yacobian, 2018). Workplace accommodation of Muslim religious practices emerges as a particular issue, often resolved dispassionately and privately in organizations, away from the media and political arenas, according to three 'i's' – instrumentally, informally, internally (Adam & Rea, 2018). These shifting workplace orientations to national and global cultural diversities surely bear further discussion, research, and interventions along these lines.

Finally, a critical organizational future for multiculturalism should consider engagement with some psychology and international business perspectives on the psychology of global employees, albeit while taking into account that they are not strictly critical in the first instance. What some of these works do well is maintain a focus on the individual level sometimes missing from other accounts. Typically, this involves viewing multiculturalism from a *cognitive* perspective that emphasizes individuals' internal representations of multiple cultural meaning systems and the processing of task-relevant, distributed connections and patterns between them (Lücke, Kostova, & Roth, 2014). Multiculturalism resides *within individuals* to the extent that their knowledge, identities, and internalizations draw on more than one culture (Vora et al., 2019). Moving between individual and group psychology also highlights *paradoxes* of multiculturalism that are important to acknowledge; regarding how to practice inclusion across other values of individualism, self-expression, openness, and group belonging (Ferdman, 2017). The psychology of a *worldview* is valuable for looking at how many component views are subtly embedded in cultural belief systems – views to do with human nature, relationships, the planet, truth, and a life well-lived (Koltko-Rivera, 2004). If critical organizational perspectives can engage with some of these latter points, they can fulfill more of their obligation to viewing multiculturalism in a more systematic, interdisciplinary fashion.

Conclusion

This chapter has explored the potential of multiculturalism as a critical concept of value intertwined in interdisciplinary ways with organizations and diversity. Points of connection between disciplines, critical and mainstream views, and organizational and work contexts have been suggested. Despite being a concept defined in part by fierce contestation and declared failures, the overall conclusion drawn here is that multiculturalism presents significant opportunities in opening up a neglected lexicon for critical work on diversity, management, and organization. Multiculturalism enables scholars to move more readily between notions of politics, nation, state, and cultural ways of life, weaving them into organizational mediations and concerns. If multiculturalism is contested, it is also flexible, and has interdisciplinary, reflexive, and evolving foundations that can be drawn upon.

Multiculturalism resides just as much in organizations as it does in societies, and continuing to use the term to frame critical inquiries of diversity and inclusion seems valuable because of the distinct focus and emphasis it brings on cultural identities and encounters. Critical multiculturalism recognizes minority struggles for equal recognition and can be combined with intercultural dialogue to bring minorities into spaces where identities and interests can be further negotiated within the shared values of a larger society (Stokke & Lybaek, 2018). In this way, multiculturalism can also be used to enrich the thirty years of research into the 'many faces' of organizational culture that continues to evolve and incorporate many theories (Giorgi, Lockwood, & Glynn, 2015).

Multiculturalism often encourages a more attentive *comparative* perspective that compares and contrasts organizational issues in multiple countries and specific policy areas (Ghosh, 2018). It retains a *psychological* perspective when it considers attitudes and behaviors toward immigration and integration and social justice at the individual and group levels of analysis (Ward, Gale, Staerkle, & Stuart, 2018). It has its own leading theorists and thinkers in Britain making up the influential *'Bristol School'* – Tariq Modood, Bhikhu Parekh, Nasar Meer, and Varun Uberoi – that continue to defend multiculturalism in strong social and political terms as a national project (Brahm Levey, 2019). Furthermore, other social and cultural theorists continue to consider the puzzles of coexistence, solidarity, unity, antagonism, multiplicity, and the diplomatic working through of plural interests that symbolize multicultural connections and configurations (Conway, 2020).

However, relationships between multiculturalism, 'race,' and diversity are likely to remain uncertain for some time into the twenty-first century. Cultures can cut across other forms of diversity in positive and negative ways, but 'race' can cut across cultures to highlight long-standing, problematic issues to do with skin color and prejudice toward ethnic minorities. The rising threat of the political right in many parts of the world in recent years has lent support to a view of diversity and multiculturalism as in decline, under threat, and struggling for survival as a progressive political force for supporting justice, integration, and citizenship (Tremblay, 2018).

Resolving the political deadlock of how 'race' and 'white privilege' are engaged within public discourse is a significant challenge here. Books by Bhopal (2018) and Eddo-Lodge (2018), for instance, both highlight the persistence of structural racism in many areas of public and organizational life. In many quarters, these messages are met with fierce white denial, backlash, and resistance. What seems most urgently needed, however, is much more humility, generosity, patient challenging of ignorance, listening, and learning shown by white researchers and practitioners (Swan, 2017). In particular, *critical race theory* offers some of the most promising resources and traditions for organizational researchers seeking to critically engage with how our (multi)cultures are racialized. Critical race theory foregrounds the racialized structures within which multiculturalism and diversity efforts are embedded, mapping the changing manifestations of whiteness and color-blindness, and tirelessly drawing attention to the historical continuity of racial inequalities (Christian, Seamster, & Ray, 2019).

9 Sensemaking

This chapter will argue that a *sensemaking* perspective allows us to critically elaborate on how diversity is experienced in organizations – through its focus on *the ongoing social and cognitive processes of interpretation supporting the accomplishment (or failure) of shared meanings*. This statement risks sounding quite abstract, uncritical, and not even necessarily related to diversity or organizations, but this chapter will try to show otherwise. At a fundamental level, people are held together in organizations by the shared interpretations that 'make sense' to them in explaining their environments at any given time. However, this 'sense' is constantly open to changes and reworkings – as surprising and unexpected stimuli are encountered that demand fresh interpretation and reorganizing work. Diverse individuals and groups, and their negotiation of issues to do with coordinating work and organizing among themselves, seen in this way, can therefore be argued to be highly demanding of revised sensemaking interpretations and narratives.

As with other chapters in this book, the 'criticality' of the approach can be called into question, or be seen as a question of degree. Certain kinds of sensemaking processes and perspectives could be considered politically disengaged and exclusionary, neglecting to address social problems. At the same time, sensemaking can offer surprising insights and explanations for how and why the world is organized and enacted in the way that it is. Sensemaking can be problematized as much as it can be endorsed, and its openness and versatility is probably both a strength and a liability. In any case, the sensemaking perspective remains influential, both within areas of management and organization studies, and with interdisciplinary linkages beyond them. It is methodologically and theoretically inclusive beyond standard quantitative methods and managerial prescriptions, and although diversity – treated critically or otherwise – does not feature much in sensemaking publications to date, this chapter will emphasize that there is great potential for it to do so more in the future.

Perhaps therefore this is one of the least explicitly critical chapters of the current volume, although we can return to the idea that sensemaking might be made more critical, or that it has latent critical potentials, and we should think about how to realize them. The debates over whether institutional theory is 'critical' or not are relevant again here, with valid points on both sides. For Munir (2019), a critical theory is one with an emancipatory agenda, a recognition of hegemonic and dominant power bases, and a self-critical awareness of the need to address complicity with such power bases through critical reflexivity. More flexibly perhaps, Drori (2019) asserts that a critical theory is any approach equipped to deal with power, change, inequality, and diversity in social relations.

It may be that sensemaking in organizations is in some cases taking steps in several or many of these directions. Regardless, sensemaking offers distinct emphasis on social construction and how organizations are accomplished through the organizing activities of actors acting, noticing, and interpreting ongoing flows of events and information. Meaning is generally held to be fragile, elusive, ambiguous, performative, and enacted, a view that is many things at once – philosophical, existential, pragmatic, critical, and psychological.

Sensemaking Perspectives on Organizations and Difference

It is hard to overstate the fundamental importance and influence of *Karl Weick* in doing more than any other figure to establish a sensemaking perspective as informing organizational theory and research. Indeed, Rowlinson (2004) classes sensemaking – along with contingency theories, institutional theories, and cultural theories – as one of four essential foundations of organization theory. Weick's (1995) book *Sensemaking in Organizations* is probably the most crucial introductory text for understanding what a sensemaking perspective entails. However, the book covers a challenging array of concepts; relating actions, beliefs, and interpretations within an overarching, open-ended process of discovery in our actions and experiences, shared with those around us. More concretely, Weick (1995) proposed seven principles of sensemaking at the heart of his book. It seems surprising that they have not been applied more to diversity in organizations, but we can attempt to do so here:

1   *Identity* – we think about who we are in a particular context and use that as a basis for action and interpretation in making sense of unfolding situations and events. Similarly with diversity, identity acts as a foundational concept of social construction regarding our sense of self, and its similarities and differences with diverse others.
2   *Retrospection* – a temporal focus of our attention and interruptions that make us continually notice and consider 'what just happened?' or 'what did that mean?' as an opportunity for sensemaking. Encountering diversity and diverse others would seem to be just

such a series of opportunities to notice, recall and reflect on our speech, actions, and interactions.

3   *Enactment* – recognition of the idea that we shape our environments through our own actions and stories, as we seek to impose, refine, and organize meaning in the face of uncertainty and complexity. Enactment may lead to a restricted focus on the possible meanings of diversity if we act too quickly or decisively in how we understand it, risking conflict escalation, errors and misunderstandings.

4   *Social* – sensemaking involves sharing and inter-relating our sense of meaning with that of others, whether physically present, imagined, or implied. Similarly, diversity involves sharing and inter-relating in evolving conversations and activities organized around social and demographic differences between ourselves and others.

5   *Ongoing* – sensemaking never explicitly starts or finishes, as we are constantly and simultaneously acting and reacting to the feedback of our actions, seeking to accomplish a sense of order and meaning from ceaseless flows of information. Diversity could also be seen as a constant flow of encounters and exchanges with difference, demanding we update and revisit our own sense of being implicated in the meanings of differences.

6   *Cue extraction* – recognition of the processes whereby we focus on integrating similar and more familiar pieces of information ('cues') in our environments to get a larger sense of what is happening and what we might do. In the case of diversity, people will use different sets of cues to focus on differences in different ways, finding some ideas and associations more relevant, meaningful, and acceptable than others.

7   *Plausibility over accuracy* – in complex and ambiguous events and contexts, accuracy may not seem necessary, possible or practical. More engaging, actionable, and coherent accounts are preferable when things are changing anyway. When interacting with diversity, we may prefer what is easy to understand and reasonable rather than insisting on absolute accuracy and truth regarding the details of differences.

Note that these seven principles are descriptive – they could both help and hinder more normative goals of equality or inclusion. 'Sense' is relative – noble or abhorrent, it makes sense to those enacting it, temporarily at least. However, a better understanding of sensemaking principles provides a thorough description of the social and cognitive processing that surrounds diversity and how interpretations of its essence are organized, offering implications for how more normative engagements might be attempted.

It should also be noted that Weick rarely mentions diversity at all, although toward the end of his 1995 book he cites the Mexican writer

Carlos Fuentes. This citation hints that working with difference is what organization and sensemaking are all about – "how to accept the diversity and mutation of the world while retaining the mind's power of analogy and unity so that this changing world shall not become meaningless" (Fuentes, 1990, cited in Weick, 1995, p.171). In other words, a world with too much diversity or too little diversity would make little sense, at a human or an organizational level.

This earlier foundational work by Weick has set the tone for the majority of research considering sensemaking in organizations ever since, whether authored by Weick himself, or by many others. In this way, sensemaking has been extended and related to modes of organizing and understanding in many directions; organizing activities that are institutionalized, distributed, emotional, power-laden, embodied, and narrated (Weick, 2012; Weick, Sutcliffe, & Obstfeld, 2005). Weick's concepts and style have inspired other critical theorists of organization such as Czarniawska (2005), who find enduring wisdom in the reflections on ever-present themes of uncertainty and change. Sensemaking is not in fact interpretation of preexisting frames and meanings, but the *imaginative creation* of frames through belief and/or action, in order to assemble new cues and connections in meaningful ways that were not apparent before (Czarniawska, 2005). Similarly, in 2006, *Organization Studies* published a Special Issue in honor of Karl Weick and making sense of organizing, comprising seven papers plus a rejoinder from Weick himself (Sutcliffe, Brown, & Putnam, 2006). The papers develop themes of metaphor, process/verbs, the formalization of interorganizational collaboration, institutional contexts, and many other connections and influences, but still there is no mention of diversity, (in)equality, inclusion, or difference.

Difference and diversity again remain under-explored in an account of 'interpersonal sensemaking,' despite this theory asserting that 'others' or co-workers are a crucial source of motivation and meaning for understanding one's job, role and self (Wrzesniewski, Dutton, & Debebe, 2003). However, the three storytelling themes presented from hospital cleaners – that others in the hospital either affirmed, disaffirmed, or expressed ambivalence in relating to them – seem to resonate equally well if taken as ways of reacting to or making sense of diversity (Wrzesniewski et al., 2003). Theories of sensemaking and emotions could also be applied much more to diversity and difference, because encountering difference can trigger emotions, which, depending on their valence and intensity, will in turn affect further cycles of feeling and attempts to make sense of difference (Maitlis, Vogus, & Lawrence, 2013).

When we turn to recurrent definitions and frameworks of sensemaking, it is almost as if the stages of the process and the social-contextual levels or ecological influences of its scope remain too abstracted (e.g. Jeong & Brower, 2008). Here, diversity and difference could integrate well as the content 'filling in' the abstractions with concrete details and substance. Two of the largest and most recent reviews on sensemaking in organizations barely mention diversity (Maitlis & Christianson, 2014; Sandberg & Tsoukas, 2015), but do offer updated definitions and arguably inch closer to a critical diversity agenda by identifying power, emotions, distributed information and the body as topics for future research. On the one hand, Sandberg and Tsoukas (2015) argue that sensemaking resists a single definition, seeming to suggest that future work should continue to critique and develop definitional aspects of sensemaking, and here diversity should surely play a role. On the other hand, however, Maitlis and Christianson (2014) do attempt an integrated definition of sensemaking as:

> a process, prompted by violated expectations, that involves attending to and bracketing cues in the environment, creating intersubjective meaning through cycles of interpretation and action, and thereby enacting a more ordered environment from which further cues can be drawn (p.67)

In terms of critical understandings of diversity, definitions of sensemaking seem important because they suggest that differences in our social environments can surprise and disrupt our sense of meaning, but equally, a lot rests on how we work to interpret, act on and adjust our beliefs regarding such changes on an ongoing basis. Like sensemaking in general, making sense of diversity means working to accomplish a sense of order and understanding with others. However, without critical, reflexive and other imaginative, pragmatic or political frames of reference, such sensemaking 'accomplishments' could nevertheless involve escalating conflict, polarizations, miscomprehensions, and ideologies hostile to difference.

This apolitical, versatile aspect of sensemaking may help explain why scholars keep revisiting it, over and over again. Holt and Cornelissen (2014) pick away at philosophical and existential aspects of sensemaking as traditionally conceived, suggesting greater attention should be given to the possible influences of non-instrumentality, moods toward the world around us and openness to the unknown rather than retrospective assessment. Brown, Colville, and Pye (2015) present another overview that continues the work of linking sensemaking to critical themes, giving five this time – discourse, power/ politics, micro/macro concerns, identities and, decision making/change. In closing, they do note a need for more critical appraisal of the 'blind spots' in sensemaking and what it serves to 'obscure, marginalize, and ignore' (Brown et al., 2015, p.273). It is on this basis where such topics as equality, diversity, and inclusion could be strongly argued to need to be brought back into sensemaking inquiries.

Because Weick has always been interested in cognition and information processing and coordinated human performance rather than diversity per se (Starbuck, 2015), it may be that sensemaking research needs to depart more from Weick as a thought leader to connect more with the 'social' part of social cognition with respect to differences and diversity. The provocation here from Weick's somewhat unusual and distinctive legacy is how to critically map its views of organizing cognition onto critical views of organizing for diversity. Characteristically, Weick continues to insist on how constrained and partial comprehension of organizing activity is, including his own, which involves following 'hunches' and continued struggles to connect perceptions with conceptions (Weick, 2015a, 2016). In that spirit, the remainder of this chapter will aim to dig a bit deeper on a few more specific links between critical perceptions and conceptions of diversity, on the one hand, and critical perceptions and conceptions of sensemaking activity, on the other.

Sensemaking and Diversity

Outside of the mainstream of sensemaking introduced previously, there is some research linking sensemaking and diversity, and it can be reviewed here.

The first point to observe is that organizational actors are often trying to make sense of diversity and difference as they try to make sense of a good deal of related actions, changes, concepts, meanings, and discourses. Often the puzzle to be interpreted or figured out takes the form of how to value diversity in the middle of complex and noisy organizational interactions. For example, Tomlinson and Egan (2002a) have shown how culturally diverse groups on an MBA programme made sense of the limits of enacting a 'valuing diversity' discourse. The sensemaking activity revolving around cultural diversity and connecting perceived similarities and differences to friendships, conflicts, and learning. Ultimately, culturally diverse managers working together have to decide what experiencing diversity means to them, and how to attribute positive and negative experiences via narratives and rationalizations. Relationships and shared experiences vary in how they are enacted and retrospectively reflected upon in sensemaking terms – some disappointment and disillusionment appear to be inevitable. However, contradicting a straightforward 'valuing diversity' discourse or moving beyond it can be achieved by:

> coordinating actions and interactions, anticipating each other's cues and making mutual adjustments to accommodate differing perspectives and expectations...the transgressing of boundaries and the challenging of assumptions...facilitating further opportunities for interaction...ongoing activities of reframing and reconstructing experience to accommodate the 'other' as both like and unlike, as both similar and different, as both a person like oneself but linked to separate systems of meaning and identity (Tomlinson & Egan, 2002a, pp.95–96).

In contrast with this openness to making sense of cultural diversity, Pratt (2000) studied the more closed system of spiritual and religious sensemaking occurring at a direct selling organization, Amway. The fundamental, all-encompassing values and beliefs of its distributors – tied to Christian principles – served as a strong ideological fortress that encapsulated them in their views of the world, rendering their community protected and impervious to attack. This form of sensemaking involves a strong commitment to a common culture of order and predictability, but also risks being controlling and exclusionary in its relation to the outside world. One hesitates to use the word 'cult' too readily, but in any case, sensemaking highlights the need of organizations to create strong shared meanings that justify their existence based on some principles of similarity, even if that means ideologically distorting their sense of reality to some extent.

As organizational contexts shift – demographically, culturally, politically – adaptive sensemaking means finding ways of engaging diverse ideologies, deconstructing them in dialogue and interaction, and forging new pathways to inclusion based on meaningful actions and beliefs. This is an enormous challenge, not least because of the social and technological complexity and diversity of today's organizational environments. One such diversity framing that has been proposed in sensemaking terms is 'all-inclusive multiculturalism' (AIM), striving to transcend colorblind and multicultural sensemaking to emphasize positive social capital and relationship-building between both minorities and nonminorities as part of diversity initiatives (Stevens, Plaut, & Sanchez-Burks, 2008). Too often, diversity panels, task forces and leadership fail to actively involve both minority and nonminority cooperation and accountability, a key ingredient for supporting inclusive sensemaking across diversity. Another way of putting this is that the success of the organization becomes the sensemaking frame, and the diversity initiatives help assemble a diverse set of cues – diverse experiences, contributions – as fitting together acceptably within that frame (Stevens et al., 2008).

(In)justice and (in)equity are another area that often accompany diversity in organizations, and both require some interpretive work to make sense of. Helms Mills and Mills (2009) develop a conception of critical sensemaking by linking it to rules, power and gender as a more holistic set of influences for making sense of discriminatory outcomes in organizations. Making sense of inequities through rules means recovering some agency for apprehending where such rules originated and whether by masquerading as knowledge they mask deeper conflicts of interest and patterns of domination – such as explaining women's exclusion from various occupations for decades during the twentieth century (Helms Mills & Mills, 2009).

When discrepant rules are questioned or noticed or disrupted, sensemaking is likely to be triggered, and different parties may be asking themselves what has been happening, and whether or not it is fair. Accordingly, Roberson and Stevens (2006) asked hundreds of employees in low-skilled roles at a large US newspaper organization to provide accounts of positive and negative gender or racial incidents at work within the last two years. Analyzing the natural language of accounts of such events – discrimination, representation, treatment, relationships, respect, climate – they found that language varied by group membership in how abstract it was or likely to mention justice concerns. Perhaps the general point on the value of linking sensemaking and diversity here is that sensemaking shows how contextual diversity-related information and incidents get filtered in various ways by organizational actors, and more often than not, distorted to provide certain accomplishments of meaning.

More specific representations of diversity and identities may get made sense of in particular ways, and those sensemaking representations will prove influential sources of meaning, order and, organization for many of those implicated. Diverse individuals and groups in diverse contexts may experience changing demands in the form of sensemaking concerns around questions of who they are, who they are perceived to be, what kind of person they can choose to be, what kind of people other persons appear to be in relation to themselves. In short, organizing which differences are most meaningful in work, and what they represent. Most work to date appears to tackle this in terms of gender, perhaps because notions of masculinity and femininity are such powerful sensemaking frames for representing gender diversity and organizational life itself.

An analysis of the changing images and texts of company reports from a US utility company between 1972 and 2001 revealed the gendered aspects of certain job roles and seniority levels, echoing sensemaking junctures and external shocks of strategic change in the company's history (Helms Mills, 2005). Returning to paid work following maternity leave, women managers have to make sense of conflicting work and family choices which may establish their worth as a 'good mother' or a 'good working mother' in the eyes of diverse others (Buzzannell et al., 2005). Indeed, sensemaking about gender tends to be dialectical – based on conflicting schemata or mental models that compete for our attention (Foldy, 2006). Committing to understanding inconsistent views on the stereotypical skill sets or task preferences of men and women and whether they are more similar or different in particular ways and circumstances can help to push sensemaking through superficial biases toward more cognitively complex representations of gender and other differences (Foldy, 2006). Teams in meetings deploy sensemaking to enact gendered forms of leadership in these situations, driven by labels for team activities, the composition of the team, and other gendered power and decision-making dynamics (Grisoni & Beeby, 2007).

Another area where sensemaking and diversity intersect to some extent is workplace bullying, and explaining how perpetrators, victims, and bystanders construct the stories and identities of bullying situations. Vickers (2007) uses auto-ethnography as an act of sensemaking applied to her own experiences as a disabled woman being bullied by a senior colleague who was a man. She reports how her experiences shifted her identity in lasting ways toward someone who was less trusting at work and more cautious and defensive, as a result of sorting through emotions, memories, and events pertaining to diversity-related bullying.

Another bullying study has shown how sensemaking sustains initial hostile interactions between actors and targets and can fuel escalations between them, drawing on the collective biographies of academics' bullying experiences recounted in a small group storytelling workshop (Zabrodska, Ellwood, Zaeemdar, & Mudrak, 2016). Sensemaking is driven by shifting power and roles, judgments by both perpetrator and target and failures to gauge how to repair or reset the situation. Perversely, bully-victim interactions can be ambiguous and precarious but follow a sort of 'sense' as actors lay claim to particular meanings over the events or even unwittingly commit to them and feed into them (Zabrodska et al., 2016). This also applies to bystanders, who have recently been theorized in sensemaking terms as continuing or worsening the progression of bullying through appraisals of severity, victim deservingness, and their efficacy to intervene that rationalize and justify a moral disengagement with bullying (Ng, Niven, & Hoel, 2019).

A challenge for sensemaking when it comes to diversity and social change is that some interpretations can descend more powerfully on organizational situations than others, and exert a stronger organizing hold over the ordering of majorities and minorities' interactions, proving difficult to shift. Actors are always caught up in a flow of powerful interpretations rooted in the past, with certain reinforcing justifications in ready supply, offering comfortable rationalizations for those seeking to impose order at the expense of ambiguity (and minority views) (Weick, 2015b). This reinforces how auto-ethnographic methodology is valuable, allowing writers to pursue their own sensemaking as 'self-investigation' and 'self-implication,' examining past, present, and future, as well as the influence of intersections of race, gender, and class and changing opportunities for fresh interpretations and actions (Sobre-Denton, 2012).

To understand the sensemaking of diverse groups and individuals in organizational lives and settings is to take a closer critical look at the shifting cognitive structures of their schemas, interpretations, and stories in relation to our own. On the one hand, relatively privileged elite professional identities and careers are justified by sensemaking storytelling that legitimizes their positions, their journeys, and the circumstances that led them to particular changes and successes in life (Maclean, Harvey, & Chia, 2012). On the other hand, ethnic minorities and blue-collar workers arguably face additional sensemaking challenges in terms of how to make sense of disadvantage and discrimination, questioning how to work well with diverse others in diverse spaces (Mills, 2002; Shenoy-Packer, 2015).

Sensemaking, therefore, has the potential to unite some aspects of experiences of diversity, but also to create divergent narratives and accounts that can become self-reinforcing and self-fulfilling. This also applies to how diversity management practices are enacted and interpreted. Mikkelson and Wåhlin (2020) look at this issue in their case study of a diversity-conscious Danish retail branch, and identify three levels of diversity management sensemaking, infused with emotions, power and politics, and taken up by different actors in different situations. The *dominant* layer stresses unproblematic performance and people improvements, the *hidden* layer stresses tensions and performance reductions, and the *forbidden* layer stresses a hierarchy of difference with foreign-born employees occupying the lowest position. Similarly, in a study of six Swiss organizations, diversity management was constructed in terms of four different interpretative sensemaking repertoires – as a *luxury,* as an *emergency,* as addressing special *interests,* and as *inclusion* (Ostendorp & Steyaert, 2009). To truly address inclusion, organizations struggle with the sensemaking frame of the 'ideal worker' and accepting a more hybrid, plural organizational form as a result of diversity.

Studies on sensemaking and diversity (management) have been relatively limited to date, but they continue to emerge intermittently, most recently showing a deepening concern with challenging (and rewarding) interactions, power, politics, and emotions. The implications are clear – people on all sides are engaged in continuing struggles to interpret diversity and the efforts of the organization to manage it, variously taking actions and telling stories that may shape very different environments and experiences. It is important that organizations are able to allow critical airings of competing narratives and to cultivate the expression and reworking of sense between diverse actors with diverse frames of reference and interpretations, showing engagement with the ambiguity and discrepancy of narratives.

Diversity, Crisis, and Change

There is a strong tradition in sensemaking research of emphasizing and researching crisis and change in and around organizations, because these conditions tend to reveal most powerfully the impact that shared meanings and emotions can have in making sense of the situation, with positive or negative results, depending on the processes involved. The most adaptive and effective sensemaking is proposed to be cognitively flexible, in terms of capacities for *updating* and *doubting* multiple accounts of events; and emotionally moderate, in terms of capacities for *experiencing positive and negative emotions at a moderate intensity* with awareness of changing bodily states (Maitlis & Sonenshein, 2010).

To the extent that diversity, crisis, and change are implicated in each other, sensemaking can help to critically engage these issues. This section seeks to integrate some of the work that exists at this fairly neglected intersection and encourage that links be made more explicit in future. This is important given the scope for diversity to cause distinct types of scandal or crisis for organizations that draw nuanced responses and calls for change from a variety of internal and external stakeholders – discrimination and harassment lawsuits being one obvious example (James & Wooten, 2006).

During crisis or change, organizational actors face unexpected people and environments that cannot be readily interpreted by standard frames of reference, requiring searching and acting across distributed complexity to rework the sense of the situation (Weick, 2005). Unexpected issues and processes constitute powerful sources of organizational *surprise* through losses of meaning, and space for new interpretations needs to be managed and permitted to match the incomprehensible aspects of the situation (Cunha, Clegg, & Kamoche, 2006).

Diversity can feature in crisis and sensemaking where actors in various roles are diverse and cues about what is happening can be surprising and become salient with regards to diversity between actors. For example, flight attendants perform a gendered and feminized sensemaking role aboard aircraft during in-flight emergencies, communicating with passengers and crew to make sense of emerging and conflicting cues around service, safety, emotions, accommodations, and reassurances (Murphy, 2001).

Transport and terrorism are often where diversity, crisis, and sensemaking collide with tragic consequences. The mistaken 2005 shooting by police of Jean Charles de Menezes as a terrorist suspect in London's Stockwell tube station was in part due to an emotional build up of commitment and communication under pressure that made sense of his ethnicity matching that of the target and therefore his being the only possible target (Cornelissen, Mantere, & Vaara, 2014). Counter-terrorism involves making judgments across ethnic diversity associated with risk and dynamic complexity, where the limits of existing organizing frames and routines to cope with diversity are exposed (Colville, Pye, & Carter, 2013). In the wake of such incidents, *inquiry sensemaking* also involves the second-order sorting through of diverse stakeholder perspectives on such crisis events (Brown, 2004). Under sensemaking pressures to depoliticize events, legitimize the continuation of established institutions and restore a sense of authority and control, a majority view may prevail that obscures more diverse perspectives (Brown, 2004). A study of the British 'Arms to Iraq Affair' public inquiry identified self-deception, hypocrisy, and scapegoating in sensemaking accounts of military and defence trading between Britain and Iraq (Brown & Jones, 2000).

Admittedly, diversity and equality are rarely fully teased out of these studies, but they show how the mechanisms of crisis management and inquiry reporting involve organizations, policies and sensemaking processes that stand to disadvantage minority targets, victims, and subordinates. This area of research is under-developed, but scandals and crises concerning immigration, sexual abuse and harassment, and mistreatment of other diverse groups (e.g. those living in poverty and/or with disabilities) suggest further diversity, crisis, and sensemaking links.

Media organizations narrate and frame public debates on diversity like immigration policy, producing narratives that affect the sensemaking of majority and minority stakeholders, at times undermining rationality about diversity and equality issues, and creating 'moral panics' and backlash (Balch & Balabanova, 2011). At the same time, however, the media can help to 'sensegive' and 'sensebreak' in lending coherence to more moral and politically progressive narratives that expose figures' abuses of power over vulnerable groups, such as the child sex abuse scandal surrounding US university football coach Joe Paterno (Bishop, Treviño, Gioia, & Kreiner, 2019). Beyond the media, organizational cultures of sexual harassment suggest sensemaking communications that complicate formal policies of complaint and remedial action. Ripples of discovery, humor, anger, heroism, victimhood, and contestation extended beyond the original event, perpetrator and victims of sexual harassment at a large US university (Dougherty & Smythe, 2004).

Whether crises are sudden or gradually deepening, political and ethical sensemaking processes are instrumental in renegotiating majority-minority relations across organizations and groups implicated in the crisis. Industrial agriculture and food banking organizations in the US have, to varying degrees, been triggered to engage in ethical sensemaking to address growing hunger and food-related illnesses, participating in trying to solve social problems and morally imagining better worlds (Elmes, Mendoza-Abarca, & Hersh, 2016). Where established institutions and systems put those they are meant to serve in a state of crisis, understanding how these inequalities and injustices do and don't mobilize sensemaking and social innovations to address the crises seems an invaluable avenue for similar research. If organizations aren't making renewed efforts to make a more inclusive sense of a crisis with diversity and (in)equality dimensions (and most crises have these), they are nowhere near resolving it, and may be part of the problem rather than the solution.

Although all crises involve change, not all changes need to be a crisis. Change and changes – individual and organizational – can still involve diversity and sensemaking in their own right. One example is a sensemaking and critical race study of how school leaders made sense of racial demographic change in terms of a growing African American population, with leaders' change management approaches enabled and constrained by their identities and ideologies relative to those of their stakeholders (Evans, 2007). In terms of critical change communications between non-managerial and managerial employees, Tourish and Robson (2006) have theorized these as having sensemaking qualities that distort and demonize minority outgroups and contrary value systems. Indeed, an over-commitment to sensemaking in top-down, self-serving communications from management can escalate conflict and crisis in a self-reinforcing and amplifying feedback loop, exacerbating the very change management issues they are trying to address (Tourish & Robson, 2006). Thus effective change management in sensemaking terms means remaining open to critically varying flows of local and minority communications. This bottom-up change sensemaking among diverse groups is reflected empirically in Bird's (2007) action research ethnographic case study with a women's group, looking at how they used their networks, storytelling, and shared resources to make sense of restructuring changes at a global IT corporation. The conclusion is that minority and inclusive sensemaking can lead to emotional and economic benefits during organizational change, via support, advice, and problem-solving.

Other research on sensemaking, diversity, and change has addressed career changes. A study of women executives in the technology industry showed women's sensemaking of career barriers as shaping their decisions over whether to voice concerns, exit the company or rationalize the circumstances based on other organizational conditions (Hamel, 2009). Careers are ripe for sensemaking analysis because they involve framing immersive ongoing flows of work activities, punctuated by changes and events open to various interpretations.

Careers often cross paths with diversity when it comes to age and gender. Vough, Bataille, Noh, and Lee (2015) theorized and studied how sensemaking relates to retirement decision-making as individuals follow particular trajectories, experience situational constraints, and engage with end-of-career scripts or narratives regarding identity threats and opportunities. Their study showed how retired Canadian managers of the 'Baby Boomer' generation (born 1946–1964) need to make sense of career changes and events in relation to work versus non-work aspects, timing and agency in retiring, as well as how to follow or deviate from institutionalized career norms and relationships (Vough et al., 2015). Sensemaking has also been used to study professional and managerial women's transitions from workers to stay-at-home mothers, particularly how they experience a sense of loss when exiting the workplace, but cope by addressing their constrained 'choice' and enacting positive change narratives across work-home-community boundaries (Kanji & Cahusac, 2015). Sensemaking and identity theories are often coupled in these types of studies – they have also been applied to dual-earner couples and the experience of 'work-life shock events,' such as promotions, pregnancies, relocations, and illnesses (Crawford, Thompson, & Ashforth, 2019).

Together, and relationally, couples must strive to make sense of these changes by renegotiating their sense of their respective roles and future selves, investing resources in the relationship to do so (Crawford et al., 2019).

Other changes experienced as sensemaking processes and challenges by diverse individuals and groups in and around organizations might include the culture shock of entrepreneurs and employees staying and working overseas. For example, expatriates face sensemaking adjustments associated with expressing one's identity and role in co-creation with diverse others in culturally diverse national environments (Lowe, Hwang, & Moore, 2011).

While in many cases crisis and change sensemaking studies remain quite psychological, individualistic, and uncritical, there is arguably great potential in developing them in more critical directions regarding diversity. In particular, exploring how sensemaking is bound up in minorities' experiences of crisis and change in and around organizations, typically in terms of struggles to make positive meaning from stressful life events (Park, 2010).

Diversity and Learning

In ways not too distant from crisis and change, *learning* also presents opportunities to link sensemaking and diversity in organizations. However, what's important about learning is that it exists to some degree in tension with sensemaking and in ways incompatible with it – where sensemaking involves fixing and organizing variety, learning often involves opening up to and embracing moments of disorganization (Weick & Westley, 1996). Nevertheless, learning and sensemaking can be conceived of as intertwined, where sensemaking is more than mere interpretation, and learning renders sensemaking more open and attentive as a process, with learners and organizations becoming something different from before (Colville, Pye, & Brown, 2016).

There is a relative lack of organizational work explicitly linking learning and sensemaking with diversity. This is regrettable because clearly our encounters with diverse others raise exciting possibilities, as well as obstacles, for learning to reorganize our perceptions and conceptions of organizations and social relations in more inclusive ways. When managers integrate learning with sensemaking, they are better able to reflect on how their actions and judgments create meaning, and this may allow for greater change and appreciation around diverse perspectives, even by managers simply seeing themselves as learners, reflectors, and sensemakers in the first instance (Schwandt, 2005). This makes management more of an art than a science, and workarts or arts-based initiatives in organizations can support sensemaking by generating a state of mindfulness in perceiving and experiencing artistic experimentation – becoming more aware of different ways of seeing and noticing (Barry & Meisiek, 2010). Even with forms of scientific knowledge, a sensemaking perspective allows learning to be viewed more inclusively – as continuous with everyday experiences of learning where diverse communities talk and interact in trying to build shared understandings of complex concepts (Warren et al., 2001).

Newcomers to organizations must 'learn the ropes,' typically through socialization processes, and diverse minority newcomers will deploy sensemaking to reconcile their expectations with any surprises they encounter in relation to incongruities involving the job and organization (Louis, 1980). In a job, cultural minorities and majorities will use sensemaking in encounters to inform their identity development as they decide how to process unfamiliar and uncertain situations, ideally achieving some measure of integration and self-awareness (Ojha, 2005). In teams, 'resourceful sensemaking' has been articulated through a study of diverse interdisciplinary product development teams, linking Weick to Habermas in describing to what degrees teams can use events as 'shocks' to communicate cooperatively and broaden their horizons beyond narrow strategic managerial concerns (Wright, Manning, Farmer, & Gilbreath, 2000).

Learning from diverse cultures and intercultural exchanges has obvious sensemaking resonances. Employees may undergo training and work with certain cross-cultural classification or stereotyping schemes, but continue to encounter cultural paradoxes and trade-offs between values that require further sensemaking to revise schemas in light of cultural diversity (Osland & Bird, 2000). Training and developing these intercultural sensemaking capabilities and experiences is arguably crucial as countries around the world continue to receive students and expatriates, who face challenges in how they perceive, identify with and adapt to a range of culture-specific structures and practices (Chiang, 2015).

The tension between sensemaking and learning unfolds as we are exposed to diverse worldviews and environments, and we may inevitably both like and dislike aspects of what we learn about ourselves and others, placing a strain on how to make sense of what we learn amid diversity. The example of generational diversity is illuminating because it has only more recently emerged as a topic of workplace research and practice. Categories like 'millennial' are useful but fuzzy sensemaking devices, ultimately constructions where sensemaking means sorting the myths from the truth, the stereotypes from the prototypes (Campbell, Twenge, & Campbell, 2017; Lyons, Urick, Kuron, & Schweitzer, 2015; Williams, 2020).

Stimulating the exchange of actions and beliefs between diverse parties offers up productive tensions that stimulate sensemaking and learning – shocking us into activities of questioning and change that induce us to confront our priorities and commitments, and most importantly, to try to *learn together as a system*. This is likely to offer much-needed insights into solving complex moral and cooperative problems involving diverse views. For instance, organizing activities around service learning and joint learning through multi-stakeholder dialogues encourage diverse parties to make sense of their commitments to social justice issues and take pluralistic views of social responsibility challenges in communities and societies (Calton & Payne, 2003; Mitchell, 2014).

Fostering More Critical Approaches to Sensemaking

In relation to diversity, but also more generally, there is perhaps an open question about how critical – and self-critical – the sensemaking approach has been, is currently, or might be in relation to organization studies. As shown earlier, critical links between sensemaking and diversity remain fairly scant and under-developed overall, despite promising connections with understanding issues like cross-cultural interaction, conflicting interpretations, crisis, change, and learning.

To foster more critical approaches to sensemaking is likely to involve recognizing how sensemaking is 'decentred' – distributed across a diverse world of humans, objects, animals, and natural environments. Sensemaking is a rich process with many authors and influences over meaning, not just a few focal actors who step in occasionally to succeed/ fail in comprehending a singular episode.

One potential supporting step is to keep developing and applying the vocabulary associated with 'sensemaking' to diversity – in their review, Maitlis and Christianson (2014) define and tabulate twelve specific forms of sensemaking (e.g. intercultural, environmental, political) and six related constructs (e.g. sensegiving, sensehiding, sense-exchanging). However, there is of course a risk here that sensemaking becomes overstretched and superficial with its use of too many different terms. This leads to another critically reflexive point about sensemaking, and a very ironic one – that sensemaking research is inherently paradoxical because at times it tries to be 'objective' about what is inherently 'subjective.' In trying to make sense of sensemaking in organizations, we are ourselves inevitably constrained by our own processes of sensemaking. Methodologically, Allard-Poesi (2005) suggests two possible solutions in the form of *postmodern deconstruction* approaches that uncover an interplay of contested meanings, and *participatory action* approaches that pragmatically invite and recognize a range of socially constructed positions from organizational members.

Albert and Jean Helm Mills and colleagues have explicitly developed a critical approach to sensemaking that remains relatively under-utilized (Mills, 2008; Mills, Thurlow, & Mills, 2010). This is regrettable because it further develops a welcome emphasis on how contexts of power relationships, identities, and social change are produced in terms of psychological processes underlying social structures. In contrast, and perhaps less constructively, Basbøll (2010) focuses his critique directly on Karl Weick's writings, arguing that they lack rigor and discipline, and are evasive and dubious in some of their details, a reading unsurprisingly not shared by Weick himself (Weick, 2010). Nevertheless, it seems appropriate to at least question the limits of Weick's legacy and influence in some respects.

Another potential way to develop sensemaking more critically is to simply focus more deeply on the *process* – how it is experienced in an embodied way over time by different entities passing through different states. For Colville, Brown, and Pye (2012), 'simplexity' or the balance between complex thought and simple action reflects the dynamic story-telling realities of sensemaking in the twenty-first century. The flow of experience and narration in sensemaking processes is also *embodied* through our felt bodily and emotional states that attune to situations, be they a sports team of athletes on tour (Cunliffe & Coupland, 2012), or a researcher rowing down the Amazon (de Rond, Holeman, & Howard-Grenville, 2019). For Introna (2019), the sensemaking process is fundamentally *decentred* – a 'meshwork' of more loosely connected, sometimes ineffable, more-than-human, and always-already-in-motion experiences, as opposed to discrete episodes deliberated upon by central human subjects. These views are perhaps more philosophical than political in their critical tenor, but they offer avenues of connection with diversity just the same. They suggest a sensitivity to the diversity of experience according to bodies, stories, and emotions – albeit one that currently falls short of applying it to specific aspects of organizational diversity, such as gender or disability, for instance. The relative lack of uptake and bridging with certain fields and disciplines, such as feminism and women's studies, remains curious (e.g. Shields & Dervin, 1993).

In addition to 'zooming in' on critical sensemaking processes, sense-making can also be rendered more critical by 'zooming out' to consider it in relation to wider organizational structures and systems of ethical and social change. Sensemaking can be linked with institutional perspectives on diversity (covered in chapter five of this book), in terms of how larger social and historical contexts provide types of roles, scripts, and frames that act as substantial cues, feedback, and puzzles for priming, editing and triggering sensemaking, respectively (Weber & Glynn, 2006). 'Epistemes' (after Foucault) are another type of structure informing sensemaking and diversity, in terms of forms of knowledge tied to particular historical and cultural eras, such as traditional, classical and modern influences for legitimating knowledge, order and social convention in business (O'Leary & Chia, 2007).

In ethics, sensemaking has some potential to critique rationalist approaches, supporting alternative explanations of how individuals experience ethical issues in organizations. Under a sensemaking view, ethical decision-making involves more uncertain, spontaneous, and intuitive processing of the issue(s), relating judgments and justifications to social contexts and constructions in situ and post-hoc (Sonenshein, 2007). In the case of international stakeholder groups setting minimum prices for fair trading standards, Reinecke and Ansari (2015) found that sensemaking played a crucial role in managing ethical complexity and forging truces among conflicting interests, mainly by mediating between moral universals and particulars. In these ways, sensemaking opens up the social and cognitive aspects of ethical reasoning to include the challenging processes diverse individuals and groups experience in terms of emotions and reflexivity as they contemplate ethical issues and decisions (Diochon & Nizet, 2019).

The same is true for CSR, as managers and stakeholders think, discuss, and act around social issues – a multidimensional sensemaking process that is an intrinsic part of how an organization relates to the world at large (Basu & Palazzo, 2008). One problem here is that much of this work remains at a fairly general conceptual level, describing a sense-making process but not necessarily relating and refining it empirically to situations of crisis and inequality more concretely.

It is tempting here to encourage a return to Weick's traditional approach of looking at case study examples of crisis and change to illuminate sensemaking, but with a renewed critical focus on diversity and inequality instead. One exceptional and partial example of what this might look like is a critical sensemaking study of the 2000 Walkerton crisis, involving a water contamination situation in Ontario, Canada (Mullen, Vladi, & Mills, 2006). The authors blend in a more critical focus through Foucault and Sartre to draw greater attention to how power in wider social structures creates knowledge via discourse, which exerts organizational pressures in tension with the existential responsibility of individual sensemaking agents (Mullen et al., 2006). Neither context nor individuals are entirely to blame, but rather a better understanding of the dynamics of power and responsibility that pass between the two as part of sensemaking processes is needed. Diversity and inequality are still not explicitly considered here, but they are more strongly implied in terms of the critical theories and power structures taken into consideration alongside sensemaking.

Indeed, increasing recognition of power (chapter four, this book) and politics in relation to a sensemaking perspective is perhaps the final frontier to enhancing its critical value in relation to diversity, as discussed here. In their discussion of collective sensemaking and the politics of interpretation, Marshall and Rollinson (2008) link sensemaking to a need to better understand how power/knowledge dynamics shift in specific episodes where specific practices are enacted or disrupted (e.g. diversity management practices). Essentially, this brings Weick into productive contact with Foucault, Bourdieu, and other critical theorists of knowledge and power regarding organizational maneuvers associated with authority, expertise, practices, and communications. Similarly, other theorists and researchers have been led to link sensemaking to Bourdieu; chiefly in terms of actors' social positions in relation to the logics and practices of organizational change and how such positions can be used to influence and resist sensemaking relationships (Lockett et al., 2014; Strike & Rerup, 2016; van Hilten, 2019). Most recently, Schildt, Mantere, and Cornelissen (2020) have systematically bridged power and sensemaking by elaborating on how systemic and episodic forms of power shape different forms of information processing, from the automatic to the more reflective. Diversity is only present at a very theoretical level here, yet practically it is revealed as a sensemaking force for creativity and insight, bringing threatening uncertainty and doubt along with it.

Conclusion

This chapter has considered sensemaking both as a critical perspective on organizations and as a perspective with things to say about diversity in organizations. Sensemaking arguably has strengths and weaknesses on both counts. If used in a reflexive, open-ended, and (self-) critical way it shows how diversity is a struggle for interpretation and meaning in light of our actions and beliefs. Empirical research and theory linking it directly to diversity are infrequent and under-developed – although this chapter has reviewed what there is and suggested some themes and links for further development. Perhaps it should be viewed as desirable that sensemaking can help maintain an explanatory layer of social psychology, agency, and process in conjunction with more traditional critical concerns over oppressive structures.

What it might sometimes lack in political and critical energy and commitment, sensemaking can compensate for in other respects, such as its versatility and powerful philosophical foundations. Undoubtedly it has changed the way many look at and think about organizations – even unsettling the noun by suggesting 'organizing' as a verb to be more reflective of processes and transformations (Bakken & Hernes, 2006). In a very detailed and careful way, sensemaking shows us how, at our best, we can *work with differences* through participatory relations, dialogues, and everyday anticipations of how our knowledge is socially transformed through encounters with diverse others (Cunliffe & Locke, 2019; Cunliffe & Scaratti, 2017; De Jaegher & Di Paolo, 2007).

Scholars continue to reconsider and elaborate sensemaking on critical and philosophical grounds (e.g. existential phenomenology – see Sandberg & Tsoukas, 2020), urging greater application to a range of emotional and ethical issues, including diversity and diversity management (Aromaa et al., 2019). Ultimately, sensemaking links the social and the symbolic as we interact and pursue common meanings and understandings that can often remain elusive (Weick, 2020). Diversity, however, deserves a more prominent place in these understandings of organization – for differences are surely a huge catalyst and site for the social-symbolic work of (re)producing common meanings and understandings. Experiences of difference give rise to our sense of diversity.

10 Place, Space, and Geography

This chapter reflects on how place, space, and geography capture an extra layer of critical insight for understanding diversity in organizations. The critical credentials associated with these perspectives are straightforward at a basic level – they generally assert that inequalities reproduce themselves across places and spaces as diverse parties use and experience them in diverse ways, shaped by various structural and discursive forces inherent to power relations.

Schools and figures of critical theory can be connected in interdisciplinary ways with the spatial imagination or a 'spatial turn' in the social sciences. An edited volume by human geographers Hubbard, Kitchin, and Valentine (2004) on 'key thinkers on space and place' contains no less than 52 entries, each devoted to the work of a key critical thinker and their spatial contributions. These entries include some critical thinkers more specifically associated with spatial and geographic themes throughout their works (e.g. Henri Lefebvre, Doreen Massey) and others whose bodies of critical work are perhaps more general but have spatial implications that can be teased out nonetheless (e.g. Bourdieu, Foucault).

Some more specific books and edited volumes have appeared in the twenty-first century that address space in organizations. An edited volume by Clegg and Kornberger (2006) entitled *Space, Organizations and Management Theory* presents a collection of chapters rediscovering space as a way of thinking about organizations past, present, and future. Topics include power, diversity management, identity regulation, bodies, connections, virtual technology, architecture, built spaces, transport, cities, and other processes of managing and organizing in and through space. Another text by Dale and Burrell (2008), *The Spaces of Organisation and the Organisation of Space* focuses on the triad of power, identity, and materiality. Here, the history of organizations and modern thought can be read in terms of the organizing of political, economic, and symbolic spaces and places around us giving rise to embodied experiences – spaces that "construct us as we construct them" (Dale & Burrell, 2008, p.1). A third and final exemplar is a book edited by Van Marrewijk and Yanow (2010), *Organizational Spaces: Rematerializing the Workaday World*, with a further series of chapters on community ideals, creativity, virtual worlds, embodied experiences, filmic representations, and work building practices, designs and uses.

These examples indicate to some degree the vastly different ways of conceptualizing organizational space, as well as related concepts like place, community, and geography. Often space is conceived of in terms of its embodied and material aspects (i.e. people physically located in buildings and other areas), but it can also include more abstract symbolic, virtual, and even conceptual forms. Chanlat (2006) summarizes organizational space as "simultaneously divided, controlled, imposed and hierarchical, productive, personalized, symbolic, and social" (pp.17–18).

Relating Place and Space to Organizations and Diversity

Concepts like space, place, and community are closely related, although as physical geometric space becomes infused with social meanings and attachments and participations, it arguably becomes transformed into a 'sense of' place and community (Calvard, 2015). Organizations as *places of work* inevitably reflect a key influence on our psychology and identity – with workers spending considerable time physically or virtually co-located in a place or set of places (Calvard, 2015). The way organizational actors talk about places and spaces is culturally significant and *metonymic* – sites and locations are used in organizational speech and sentence structures to transmit symbolic framing power through the social order, affecting the meanings of other objects and actions (Musson & Tietze, 2004).

The question of spatial and geographic *scale* becomes relevant when we couple organizations and globalization – as organizations move or expand across globally diverse spaces, their institutional logics or views of what is legitimate and reasonable also diversify (Spicer, 2006). Rescaling the internal and external spaces of organizations involves geographical contests over capital accumulation, regulatory controls, and discursive articulation, where organizations are embedded in multiple spatial scales (Spicer, 2006). Critical diversity research can thus become more 'space sensitive' – not only by considering multiple spatial levels or scales, but also through threefold distinctions of space as distance, material power, and experience; or as practised, planned and imagined (Taylor & Spicer, 2007). These latter distinctions reflect the hugely influential legacy of the Marxist philosopher, Henri Lefebvre, and his theoretical 'triad' for accounting for the social production of space – space as *conceived, perceived,* and *lived* (Lefebvre, 1991). Other perspectives on work, employment, and organization from the last twenty years have echoed calls for greater sensitivity to space in future research, emphasizing political economic struggles over space, and the reciprocal relations between space, social relations, and communications (Herod, Rainnie, & McGrath-Champ, 2007; Ward, 2007; Wilhoit, 2018).

From an office stationery cupboard all the way through to a sprawling national region then, we might feel there is value in critically considering the complex mutual relations between space and organization. A logical starting point is to think about how place informs a sense of individual and group identities in organizations, for better or for worse. For example, Brown and Humphreys (2006) studied a merged UK College of Further Education, finding that senior managers and different groups drew on place as a discursive resource for authoring contrasting accounts of personal and organizational identity. Discourses of place formed part of ongoing and unstable struggles to define the spaces involved and to 'emplace' identities, some constructions being infused with nostalgia and fantasy (Brown & Humphreys, 2006).

Grey and O'Toole (2018) revisit these issues in their study of RNLI volunteer lifeboat workers, whose sense of identity and place are symbiotically related in a 'place-identity,' encompassing unique conjunctures of danger, history, family, and community in and around their work. Overall, Wasserman and Frenkel (2011) argue that place mediates between diverse identity hierarchies outside organizations (nationality, gender, ethnicity) and how they are culturally expressed through the internal aesthetics of an organization; its control system and opportunities for 'jamming,' or resistance and improvisation. Organizational spaces and places, experienced through relocations to old, new or award-winning buildings, for example, provide actors with sensory maps; intuitive cues about organizational values and ideals (Wasserman & Frenkel, 2011).

A critical 'socio-spatial' perspective on organizations can be thought of in terms of everyday, slow motion 'spacing,' as diverse bodies act and react to each other and their environment in situated movements suggestive of organizing (Beyes & Steyaert, 2012). Under this view, organizations become worlds of choreography, rhythms, and distances; always defying closed representation through an excess of flowing interruptions, emotions, and encounters (Beyes & Steyaert, 2012). Organizational spaces can seem familiar and taken-for-granted, but artistic and theatrical interventions can help make them strange again through 'unsiting' processes that expose and undermine our assumptions about them by encouraging us to witness and interact with them differently (Beyes & Steyaert, 2013).

Organizational spaces are therefore populated with potential human and aesthetic diversity – diverse ways of using them and bringing them into being. However, they are also political in terms of conflicts and negotiations around who gets to use them and how. For example, an ethnographic study of street artists at the Edinburgh Fringe festival showed how they used various tactics to carve out hybrid workspace within public spaces, selecting spaces for 'pitching' their work to passersby as audiences in the street, and taking ownership of 'smooth space' for open engagement with a new purpose (Munro & Jordan, 2013). In this regard and others, space is *territorial*, and it can be de- and re-territorialized as people exit and enter, appropriating it for different purposes. Organizational members are likely to exhibit territorial feelings and behaviors around many spaces and possessions, with consequences for commitment, conflict distraction, and isolation (Brown, Lawrence & Robinson, 2005). More broadly and critically, the study of territoriality in and around organizations can be considered an interdisciplinary field in its own right, addressing the symbolic power, boundaries, and defence dynamics inherent to maps, roots, and navigations at various levels of analysis (Maréchal, Linstead, & Munro, 2013).

Diverse organizations and actors have a hand in (re)producing space and making places. Social entrepreneurs and innovators, understood in terms of geography and anthropology, travel to places in the Global South, for example, and embed their project activities and learning in 'place-making' processes as they experience social and environmental problems in different ways in different locales (Elmes et al., 2012). A multinational corporation can be thought of in postcolonial and geopolitical terms as a 'third space,' as knowledge 'transfer' between western first world colonizer countries and third world colonized countries is interpreted and contested (Frenkel, 2008). Organizational research on sustainability also continues to increase its engagement with cultural and human geography, where incorporating a sense of place helps to root organizational endeavors more comprehensively and transformatively within ecosystems of social and natural life. As Guthey, Whiteman, and Elmes (2014) note, "place calls attention to the diversity of actors involved in its creation" (p.261), including animal and plant species.

The critical perspective again flows from this in terms of the power relations and struggle for domination and legitimacy over how organizations negotiate a sense of place with diverse stakeholders (Guthey et al., 2014). Workers have been found to seek refuge from dominant organizational spaces, turning liminal 'in-between' spaces into 'transitory dwelling places' – for example, hairdressers seeking out corners, rooms, and stairways across the spatial boundaries of a salon to address different human needs (Shortt, 2015). *Liminality* is an important concept here, individually and collectively; referring to a process of transition, carving out a particular position between other positions, and/or places where traditional scenes are suspended and renegotiated (Söderlund & Borg, 2018).

Ultimately, the organizing of diverse places by diverse parties gives rise to geographies of organization and the labor process – literally where work 'takes place,' in different parts of the world and across changing networks and regions of technology, production, and communities of workers with agency (Ellem, 2016). Industries, professions, and organizations can also have institutional histories attached to places and spaces that can stabilize and legitimize them – 'putting people in their place' – according to certain established interests, exerting a powerful awe-inducing influence (Siebert, Wilson, & Hamilton, 2017). The legacies of spaces in organizations call out for engagement with their claims to legitimacy, where the walls are 'speaking,' and "diverse organizational stakeholders may perceive a space differently and associate it with more or less persuasive legitimacy claims" (De Vaujany & Vaast, 2014, p.728).

The remainder of this chapter, building on these broader links between place, space, and organization, delves more deeply into critical views of diversity and organizational space along three main lines of inquiry – how minorities organize in space, how a sense of place can foster inclusion, and how wider geographies surrounding organizations reproduce patterns of diversity and inequality.

Space and Minority Organizing

One key aspect of public and organizational spaces is how minorities make use of spaces and places for practices relevant to sexual identities and socializing – such as bathhouses, clubs, restrooms, and dungeons (Green, Follert, Osterlund, & Paquin, 2010). Gendered and sexual organizational minorities like lesbians and gay men experience space and place differently, in ways that are under-researched. In a study of a UK government department, for example, lesbians and gay men reported experiences of silence and 'absent presence' in 'negative space,' as private lives and identities outside of work collided with social events and majority discourse inside of work (Ward & Winstanley, 2003).

Space and place in organizations therefore create tensions for minority voice, identity, self-expression, and participation in relation to majorities. This is why British trade unions are concerned with creating and maintaining separate 'safe spaces' for lesbian and gay members, and although separate organizing isn't without its complications, safe spaces help mobilize and confer recognition on minorities by representing them more effectively within wider movements (Bairstow, 2007). Safe spaces pose organizing tensions where they threaten splits in intra-group diversity, but they allow, geographically and emotionally, minority groups to "discuss their identities, interests, and requirements independently of privileged elites" (Bairstow, 2007, p.395).

At the same time, safe spaces for LGBT, gender, and racial minorities can also be argued to obscure intersectional diversity, inhibit coalition-building and create a premature and false sense of intimacy juxtaposed with a 'dangerous' outside (Fox & Ore, 2010). Nevertheless, spaces in various institutional and organizational contexts – sports, for example – continue to privilege heterosexual masculinity and exclude LGBT groups, necessitating minority campaigns and initiatives to penetrate deeper into the lived spaces of stadia, training grounds, and locker rooms (Lawley, 2019).

Where management and majorities try to 'colonize' work space, questions of gender, emotions and private/public differentials become open to resistance and renegotiation. This was found to be the case in a study of night nurses, who enacted a feminized form of emotion work by making a special care baby unit into a differential space for resisting dominant masculine authority over emotion management, replacing professionalized formality with a more friendly, generous atmosphere (Lewis, 2008). Using the example of women working in diverse roles in a university setting, Tyler and Cohen (2010) have shown that spaces 'matter' in terms of materializing the organization, and spaces are performative through the medium of the body and masculine, hetero-sexual constraints. Women intricately negotiate their identities and 'otherness' – *in* organizations but not *of* them – by hiding and appro-priating, changing their layouts, routines, displays, and networks as embodied by them and encountered by others in space (Tyler & Cohen, 2010). To give a further example of masculinity and race, Gallo and Scrinzi (2019) have explored the gendered racialization of the migrant masculinities of Asian porters working in affluent households in Rome, Italy on tasks of cleaning and caring (feminized), and maintenance and security (masculinized). The study shows the complex patterns and di-visions around how migrant minorities access work and space in terms of particularized niches and global hierarchies of reproductive household labor, further shaped by employer concerns over religious differences and public security (Gallo & Scrinzi, 2019).

Research on minorities organizing in their work according to the lived experience and global geographies of space is almost by definition fragmented and limited to those working directly and self-consciously with particular socio-spatial samples and settings. However, this re-search serves to embed organization studies literature surrounding di-versity more concretely in space. Agar and Manolchev (2020) make this form of contribution in their study of migrant labor in the UK agri-food industry, drawing on interviews with migrants from a range of EU and non-EU countries, as well as the authors' personal experiences with the sector. The authors draw on Lefebvrian 'rhythmanalysis' to chart dy-namic and precarious flows between the opening and closing of spaces. Migrants have to navigate challenging rhythms of subordination and survival, opportunity and adjustment, as they enter the country and es-tablish where they are to work and how to get to and from the work (Agar & Manolchev, 2020). Attending to these rhythms can offer insights into how to regulate the social ordering of migrant experiences more fairly and humanely. Beyond migrant workers, other examples of spatial minority research include studies of how young people (aged 15–24) in deprived urban areas develop employment aspirations about where they are willing and able to work (White & Green, 2015), and how Indigenous workers on ancestral territories and construction sites in Canada remain marginalized in neocolonial terms (Guimond & Desmeules, 2018).

Clearly, space and minority organizing involve a significant measure of struggle, with minorities' organizational agency limited by complex matrices of power relations inscribed onto pre-existing spaces and places. However, there is equally something fundamental to the spatial layer of organizing and organization that keeps it entangled with social diversity, and therefore available to some extent for resistance and re-appropriation by minorities. This also can be taken to include re-imaginings of space, particularly from a political perspective, where spaces are occupied and expressed to promote alternative visions of diversity, inclusion, and minority identity.

Solidarity initiatives are one example of this, often involving re-imaginings and transformations of space that make new forms of minority resistance and representation possible. Groups of grassroots organizations in Greece have come together in solidarity initiatives to resist harsh government austerity measures, using local space for general assembly meetings and resistance laboratories, and opening up existing spaces for nurturing and expanding diverse connections and relationships (Daskalaki & Kokkinidis, 2017). The Alternative, a radical political party in Denmark, develops policies by practicing 'open-source politics,' where oscillations between the use of physical and digital spaces correspond to managing tensions between openness and closure, imagination and affirmation, universalism and particularism (Husted & Plesner, 2017). There appears to be an argument here that to achieve more authentic forms of diversity, equality, and inclusion, more radical departures from formal organizational space are needed, and although they may be ambiguous and unstable to an extent, such spaces invite alternative values to capitalism to be lived and endorsed.

At the same time, it is important to acknowledge the relative organizing failures of minority activism in spaces of political fantasy and imagination, themselves engendering further spaces for working through emotions and reflections. This was the case for Callahan and Elliott (2020), two critical scholars and academic activists involved in an event designed in response to the populism of Donald Trump in America and his election victory. Contentious political landscapes generate searching collective responses from the diverse groups affected, who reach out to one another to work through emotions, fantasies, vulnerabilities, and hopes for effecting change. However, the energy and momentum needed to establish new spaces are fragile, and can easily fall prey to erasure, division, silence, short-lived enthusiasms, and misguided assumptions, derailed by the more traditional and neoliberal professional and academic spaces that reassert themselves (Callahan & Elliott, 2020).

Minorities may feel a sense of relative success or failure in how they try to reorganize spaces and places. Perhaps equally important is the idea that spaces and places *produce* organization; themselves *organizing us* to a significant extent along demographic, cultural, geographic, and institutional lines (Peretz, 2019). Intersectional social movement groups based on distinct patternings of shared gender, race, sexual and religious identities therefore need to consider how their organizing is constrained and enabled by these precursors of space and place against which their activism is taking place (Peretz, 2019).

Sense of Place and Inclusion

As considered earlier, minorities typically have to struggle and organize to inhabit and challenge spaces as part of work and organizational life. A slightly different way of approaching this problem is to inquire as to how far spaces are invested with meaning and a sense of inclusion, to the point where we might describe a 'sense of place' as conveying attachment, belonging and community because of or in spite of diversity.

In general, finding and making spaces that provide a sense of place is closely related to accommodating forms of diversity by providing a sense of inclusion. This can be done in ways both familiar and surprising, if we consider how places are created and maintained to include a sense of meaningful difference in historical, spiritual, and moral terms. In a recent study of an Australian emergency department disrupted by the threat of the Ebola virus in 2014, doctors and nurses were shown to act as custodians maintaining a place of social inclusion through a process of carefully protecting and safeguarding finite resources and vulnerable patients (Wright, Meyer, Reay, & Staggs, 2020). The authors suggest that "the nature of human needs and the depth of association with, and accomplishment of, values of social inclusion involving equality, dignity, and human rights vary across different public places" (Wright et al., 2020, p.4). In emergency and crisis situations, key places and workers can strive to provide inclusion for marginalized groups and universal access to human services.

In terms of inclusive places fulfilling universal human needs, many people continue to create spiritual space in their everyday lives for God and worship at home, at work, and for leisure, arguably a form of religious and spiritual inclusion (Williams, 2010). Historically, spaces can also be used to commemorate organizational identities and events more inclusively, seeking to socially and materially address trauma, injustice, and conflict. In postcolonial Cuba, commemorative spaces link inclusive memories and symbolic connections to different figures and ideologies, although it should also be noted that the contested politics and hegemonic associations with such sites may remain problematic and limit inclusion as well (Alonso González, 2016). As organizations, various museums around the world built on sites of trauma and genocide wrestle with these issues, trying to design places where victims and their testimonies can be faithfully included in our post-conflict memories and experiences (Violi, 2012). In the present day, there is living history and diversity in the form of *four* generations of workers sharing space in organizations, and including them means adapting places of work to include a greater variety and flexibility of spaces for collaboration and mobility (e.g. Bennett, Pitt & Price, 2012; Joy & Haynes, 2011).

As diverse people enter and move around in spaces and places, they experience themselves and others as diverse bodies orienting in diverse spaces that may or may not fulfill particular needs for inclusion. Employees working across multiple cultures and engaged in international travel encounter generic, bland, and Westernized 'non-places' such as airports and hotel rooms, which nevertheless provide some important familiarity and similarity for belonging and identity work when juxtaposed with places more demanding, new and strange (Muhr, 2012). In service environments like bars, employees and customers of different gender and sexual orientation negotiate 'bodyspace,' where spaces create certain expectations and afford certain possibilities as parts of the workplace and its objects form a contingently acceptable and accommodating 'background' to diverse bodies and intentions (Riach & Wilson, 2014).

Other diverse bodies may face greater challenges regarding workplace inclusion in space(s), but at the same time constitute catalysts for rethinking space to provide a better sense of place. For instance, working mothers who lactate and breastfeed face general stigmatization and exclusion to the boundaries of many workplaces (Gatrell, 2019). However, the inclusion politics of working mothers and their bodies is an ongoing conversation that can be taken up by organizations seeking to be more progressive family-friendly institutions, ones concerned with expanding spaces for lactation, childcare, and parental flexibility in line with expanded possible work identities (Porter & Oliver, 2016). The same is true for organizations and disabled employees. A study of Australian community arts and sports organizations highlighted the value of groups with common interests coming together at accessible locations for creating 'boundaryless' inclusion between disabled and non-disabled groups of stakeholders, via a holistic set of social and environmental practices (Fujimoto et al., 2014). Although funding cuts and market discipline across many private, public and non-profit organizations can limit prospects for 'socio-spatial inclusion' of disabled employees, some evidence shows that minor, cost-effective modifications to work environments can readily "create enabling workplace geographies" (Wilton & Schuer, 2006, p.193).

In terms of gender, Nash (2018) adopted the spatial urban practice of the *flâneur* (stroller, loiterer) as a woman walking the city of London, observing and interacting with men and women as they navigated organizational life in terms of materiality and masculinity – phallic buildings and homogeneous masculine groupings. Although women working in London reported experiences of 'otherness' and invisibility, the innovative practice of gendered *flânerie* at least serves to reveal how spatial patterns of oppression and belonging are performed, rendering them more visible and open to the recovery of gender inclusion by occupation (Nash, 2018).

It's important to acknowledge that there are centuries of patriarchy literally built into organizational places and environments. That history, however, can also be a resource for a renewed sense of gender inclusion, as Liu and Grey (2017) have shown in their archival study of the Royal Holloway, University of London (RHUL) Founder's Building, opened in 1886 as a college for women. The historical legacy of gendered segregation lingers into the organizational identity of the present, but can also be cast as a resource for changing and questioning the gendered nature of 'space in history' and how spaces accumulate and signal social meanings regarding minorities and practices (Liu & Grey, 2017). Alternatively, in physical spaces where men come together to organize themselves, such as rugby players on and off the playing field, they are influenced by codes of masculinity, and must adhere to them to secure a sense of belonging and inclusion (Giazitzoglu, 2020). These hyper-masculine, hegemonic codes include shows of toughness, aggressiveness, hierarchy, and competitiveness, as well as appropriate emotional displays and rituals, mediated by the language of spaces and bodies, motivated by the pride and status that comes with a feeling of belonging to something meaningful (Giazitzoglu, 2020).

Interpreting diversity and inclusion in space most broadly can even be taken beyond the human, toward the importance of considering the placement of nonhuman animals and other features of the natural environment coexistent with human organization. This emphasis challenges the 'anthropocentrism' of place and diversity, and also engages novel theoretical perspectives such as actor-network theory that show how humans are more often than not entangled in networks of nonhuman forces and actions in space and time. In their study of a UK and a Scandinavian construction project, Sage and colleagues (2016) found that concepts of exclusion, invitation, and disturbance were important for understanding how organizational actors negotiate roles and boundaries across time and space in conjunction with the agencies of animals, such as the seasonality of their behaviors and their habitats. Jansen and Sandström (2019) also emphasize the spatial openness and pluralism of a modified actor-network theory in their ethnographic study of the organizing of state-owned underground mine operations in Sweden. Their analysis is anchored in tensions around coexistence and difference, exclusion, and inclusion. Organizing is embedded in rocks, reindeer, indigenous culture, dams, and towns, as well as the core strategy and workforce of the organization in question, just further nodes in a network (Jansen & Sandström, 2019). A final example of nonhuman diversity, place, and inclusion is reflected in a study of the work done in community gardens in cities. Work across various communal Glasgow gardens was shown to bring together new collectives to work more progressively toward social and community goals, such as local ownership and various minority outreach activities associated with food, housing, and poverty reduction (Cumbers, Shaw, Crossan, & McMaster, 2018).

In sum, places themselves generate a variety of possibilities for inclusion and exclusion, as diversity is encountered and demanding of organization in space. Human individuals and collectives, animals and the built and natural environment come together in combination to generate these possibilities, which are at risk for being overlooked in non-spatial perspectives, which tend to foreground a core organization, its strategy and disembedded, disembodied human actors.

Geographies of Diversity and Inequality in Organizations

The two preceding sections have taken a critical but relatively positive look at how spaces and places are implicated in minority organizing and a sense of possible inclusion. However, it is important here to also acknowledge a third, more problematizing lens focusing on how power and inequalities are reproduced across various geographies of space in relation to a variety of diversity and organizational dimensions. In addition to minorities and specific places, this perspective represents spatial implications at their broadest, concerning structural inequalities that can seem difficult or slow to change, and resurface in different cultures, economies, and societies.

As is evident from the existence of the subdiscipline of feminist geography, spatial divisions and inequalities can be gendered in terms of distinct activities and experiences of place and organization. Feminist post-colonial and transnational critiques show at the broadest level how globalization and 'geographies of power' affect the gendering of spaces and places, and how intersectional gender categories are read and performed, such that "gendered geographies of place reveal uneven patterns of development and opportunities, and shape individual subject identity positions" (Metcalfe & Woodhams, 2012, p.134). While western, and to some extent Asian, geographies are relatively well-represented in research, the same cannot be said of Africa, Latin America, and the Middle East (Metcalfe & Woodhams, 2012).

The hope and aspiration seem to be for greater feminist and intersectional diversity research more attuned to layers and relations of power and geography and how they are interwoven with globalization and transnational territories. Bryant and Jaworski's (2011) study of skills shortages in the Australian mining and food and beverage industries shows how politicized assumptions about the gender and class of workers' bodies feed into gendered inequality regimes and HR practices based around place and site location. Skills shortages and a lack of diversity persisted because of a lack of inclusive engagement with various regional, rural, and remote locales. For women working as managers in South Korean organizations, a feminist geography perspective reveals a gendered lack of access to business trips, training, and positions amenable to promotions (Gress & Paek, 2014). However, growing numbers of women in these organizations, anti-discrimination policies, and non-Korean firms increasingly produce new 'differential spaces' to challenge the prevailing discriminatory atmospheres (Gress & Paek, 2014).

Women doctors working in Pakistan also face spatialized inequality regimes through patriarchal practices of *purdah* that aim to ensure women's modesty is shielded from the world of men, taking in religion, class, and race in persistently excluding and segregating women from the ownership of organizational space (Masood, 2019). However, in marked contrast to this, a study in Uppsala University in Sweden used a performance artist to redesign the organizational space of a unisex toilet into an all-gender or 'hir-toilet,' critiquing notions of gender binaries in space using inauguration, new signage, and captured online communications to map the transformation and range of reactions elicited (Skoglund & Holt, 2020).

Beyond geographies of gender in space, from traditional separations to futuristic visions of boundaryless inclusion, other minority identities, such as race, age, and disabilities, have to some extent been linked to space and organization. Race in North America, for example, contains its own geographies of power and of experience as regards places of work, of research, of education (Delaney, 2002). Race can be geographically scaled and spatialized, and space can be racialized, through the mapping of identities and inequalities in these terms:

> The geographies of race we inhabit also include the gated community, the boardroom and the faculty lounge, the dish room, the locker room, the stitching room, the classroom, the prison, the convenience store, the cafeteria, public spaces, and—perhaps especially—home. But there is no outside to a wholly racialized world. And where the Africanist presence may be recessive, the Latin, Asian, or Native-Americanist presences may be more prominent. In most cases, these presences enter into the processes that maintain or challenge the spatial conditions for the construction of whiteness. (Delaney, 2002, pp.6–7)

Furthermore, organizational spaces continue to be influenced by colonial history in ways that often go unnoticed but resurface emotionally from the unconscious as ambivalence and subversion. This tends to occur when individuals discuss experiences of working under conditions of racial and geographic diversity from a postcolonial perspective (Ulus, 2014). While formal colonial relations between white and non-white geographies and actors may have ended, they live on in unconscious emotional experiences and postcolonial spaces of global work, characterized by mixtures of oppression and subversion as histories are redefined (Ulus, 2014).

The spatial human geography of ageing requires thinking through how organizations treat workers' ageing bodies, socially and physiologically, as well as time and 'spatiotemporal' transitions across an extended lifecourse (Schwanen, Hardill & Lucas, 2012). Disabilities too are spatialized by organizational geographies where the spaces are designed in an ableist way expressive of power relations with non-disabled employees, experienced as disabling by disabled employees with underlying impairments (Van Laer, Jammaers, & Hoeven, 2020). Indeed, it is organizational spaces and the way they are conceived and represented and inhabited for practices that are 'disabling' for anyone with an 'impairment.' Rather than an employee being disabled per se, they have to be disabled (or enabled) 'by' something. Too often the way spaces are designed in organizations for productivity, inclusion, independence, comfort, and safety is based on something supposedly 'normal' or 'ideal,' which in reality seriously disadvantages and excludes those with a variety of impairments in a variety of ways that might be more readily accommodated (Van Laer et al., 2020).

As fashionable modes of work organization and co-working change, as well as the types of labor performed, difficult questions need to be asked with renewed urgency about whether organizational geographies and spaces can be rendered more supportive and inclusive, or are instead serving to exacerbate inequalities. Spatial organization of inequalities is likely to be ongoing and difficult to manage, but traditional, masculine, middle-class aesthetics and designs may be bureaucratic and outdated when it comes to inclusion of a diverse workforce. Wasserman and Frenkel's (2015) intersectional study of a new Israeli government building shows how actors with different gender and class backgrounds enact inequality regimes through 'spatial work,' with social hierarchies defined by architects, managers, and employees relating to segregations and evolutions in spatial areas of the organization.

As well as organizational buildings, the aesthetic nature of work and the bodies performing it in space matter too. Men working as massage therapists, in sex shops and as Santa Claus performers, for example, all work in spaces where they have to carefully balance intimacy, proximity, and propriety in embodied interactions with diverse customers

(Hancock, Sullivan, & Tyler, 2015). A growth in remote working has led to coworking movements and shared spaces being taken up among diverse independent workers, who then try to co-construct a sense of community by endorsing the space, building on encounters there, and engaging in activities and routines there (Garrett, Spreitzer & Bacevice, 2017). It is perhaps debatable how widespread and inclusive such spaces really are at this point, but in any case, changing spaces for senior professionals such as hospital doctors can also be subject to deterioration and loss, disconnecting and isolating them from ways of working meaningfully and effectively (Siebert, Bushfield, Martin, & Howieson, 2018). The erosion of elite status as signified by spatial distinctions needs to be balanced against the performance of organizations and the need for spaces that nevertheless bring diverse stakeholders together in distinct, meaningful, and egalitarian ways.

Around organizations rather than within them, we can also consider broader lenses on urban versus rural environments as telling us about the need to address spatial geographies of inequality. In the UK and other countries, it is relatively common for organizations to spatially evolve such that they have a high-status strategic center in the form of a modern urban office building, juxtaposed with important but devalued units relegated to 'edgeland' peripheries between town and country (Hirst & Humphreys, 2013). This points out the power of relational, co-dependent spaces in organizations and organizing, where inequality is built into a geographical landscape connecting the human with the nonhuman, one that continues to send powerful signals concerning segregations signifying difference.

However, just as being rooted in a spatial location can seem discriminatory, mobility can also be problematic. Highly mobile elite management consultants can still experience feelings of ambiguity, stuckness, friction, disorientation, and loss as they bounce between the sterile non-places of everywhere and nowhere (Costas, 2013). Spaces and places mean different things to different people, but to some extent they need critical questioning and action because they typically reproduce inequalities and may not work well for anyone, even elites.

In stark contrast with mobile or modern elites, we still require institutional places that serve to provide homes for the homeless, chronic or terminally ill, and the elderly, where workers strive to organize and support the most vulnerable in our societies, and those with the most complex needs. In their study of such settings in Canada, Lawrence & Dover (2015) conclude that "places have been significantly overlooked in organizational research despite their potentially profound consequences for organizational life...places affect how organizational actors understand problems, marshal resources, employ routines, and construct connections between concepts" (p.398). If we do not critically question how places do these things, we leave environmental influences on our motivations and emotions unexamined, and important aesthetic, embodied and geographical dimensions of inequality unaddressed.

Conclusion

This chapter has developed and reviewed critical arguments and evidence linking organizations and diversity to spaces, places, and geography, reflective of a so-called 'spatial turn' in organization studies, relative to similar sentiments across other disciplines and fields of inquiry. It seems that organizational research in general is either explicitly spatial in outlook or doesn't concern itself with space or place much at all. Even when research is explicitly spatial, connections with diversity, equality, and inclusion may still be left implicit. This chapter has sought to make these connections more explicit in and around relevant work that already does so to varying extents, offering some modest avenues for better future integration, such as through inquiries into how minorities organize in space, how spaces can provide places of inclusion, and how spaces mark out geographies of inequality.

Reviews and conceptualizations of the relations between organizations and space continue to emerge, although research remains fragmented, both generally and in relation to diversity. A recent review proposed organizing inquiries more consistently around key spatial concepts of boundaries, distance, movement, distribution, isolation, differentiation, and intersection (Weinfurtner & Seidl, 2019). Rather than fixed, physical workplaces there is a growing emphasis on spatial movements and dynamic processes (Stephenson, Kuismin, Putnam, & Sivunen, 2020), with spaces subject to change from multiple human and nonhuman influences that are continuously coconstituting and reconstituting it in mutual communications (Wilhoit, 2018). Related spatial challenges facing organizational practitioners and researchers concern paying attention to neglected large-scale and small-scale issues in time and space, such as climate change or local poverty (Bansal, Kim, & Wood, 2018), and the relationships between manmade and natural spatial environments (Bansal & Knox-Hayes, 2013). Paying greater attention to spatial topology also means a focus on how various objects and actors continually adjust and deform organizational space, making size, scale, and shape achievements against a background of disorganization where micro-macro and inside-outside distinctions can be called into question (Ratner, 2019).

Equally, it is hard to do justice to the sheer diversity of empirical settings and media in which organizational space may mediate, produce, and manifest itself. Three features ripe for greater relation to diversity might be global, virtual, and distributed working space. Global teams working in virtual distributed conditions increasingly need to conceive of and create new rhythms, spaces, and scripts for building positive, playful relationships and interactions online across international diversity; spaces that resemble, or perhaps even surpass, the spacing of the offline world (Lee, Mazmanian, & Perlow, 2020; Maznevski & Chudoba, 2000; Whitty & Carr, 2003).

More materially, politically, and symbolically, the worlds of art and cultural production can also be used to stage institutional struggles in space, where diverse stakeholders seek to disrupt or defend local and global ideologies and interests in relation to museums, galleries, state buildings, fairs and other venues (Rodner, Roulet, Kerrigan, & Von Lehm, 2019). As well as innate human desires to use space to create and share in art, biophilic work and office design propose that humans can reap energizing benefits from having more multisensory contact with nature on the job throughout the workday, making space more outdoors than indoors (Klotz & Bolino, 2020). From a perspective of diversity and ethics, Lacerda, Meira, and Brulon (2020) suggest that a spatial ethics must be applied to better understand ethics and organization in various global spaces – such as Brazilian favelas – in ways that avoid abstract North-South classifications.

Finally, the methods and tools used to critically investigate diversity, space and organization warrant further reflection. The majority of studies to date tend to adopt and develop perspectives and methods based on the work of Henri Lefebvre. Lefebvre's triad of conceived, perceived and lived spatial relations, and his rhythmanalysis method of bodily movements and sensing through time and space, are both likely to remain influential and valuable to organizational inquiry (e.g. Nash, 2020). Furthermore, broader extensions and elaborations of Lefebvre and organization have been explored in a recently edited book volume (Dale, Kingma, & Wasserman, 2018). However, as Petani (2019) has reflected, many other forms of personal and heartfelt writing about space represent tools for engaging organizations and diversity with a welcome affective sensitivity and accessibility for change and activism:

> [O]ur spaces and work are populated by jargon-littered, dead (uncited and/or unread) texts. If we wrote about different spaces and places in more lively and affective ways, this would not only help us to turn our writing into activism...it might also stand a better chance of boring us less as readers (p.969).

Part IV

Implications of Critical Perspectives in a Future of Diverse Organizations

11 Beyond Diversity Management and the Business Case

As one of the chapters making up the final part of this book, by addressing the issues of diversity management and the business case we come, to an extent, full circle with where the book started out. There is plenty of mainstream work on diversity management in organizations, and a great deal of it is not critical in the terms defined in this book. While this work will not be reviewed in this chapter, what will be reviewed are the critical perspectives with implications for challenging mainstream views of diversity management and the business case for diversity in organizations. This has inevitably been touched upon in other chapters because it is at the heart of much mainstream versus critical theorizing; that is, whether diversity can or should be managed and how, and whether this can be shown to be beneficial for individuals, groups, and organizations or not. However, this chapter endeavors to look more explicitly and specifically at the concepts of diversity management and the business case for diversity, as well as alternative 'cases for/against' arguments when it comes to diversity and organization.

Diversity Management and the Business Case for Diversity

Diversity management and the business case for diversity evolved in closely related ways in developed countries in the latter decades of the twentieth century. The legal and political developments of Civil Rights and Equal Opportunities in the 1960s and 1970s gave way, in part at least, to a commercial rationality in the 1980s and 1990s asserting that 'value-in-diversity' could and must be treated as an asset, inviting a strategic response to demographic changes in markets (Nkomo & Hoobler, 2014). For addressing the range of demographic groups identified, diversity management was defined as "the policies and programs employers used to attract, hire, and retain these groups" (Nkomo & Hoobler, 2014, p.251). However, the business case has not been established and remained problematic, because of the positivist difficulty of showing any decisively positive relationship between diversity and performance, or the bottom line (Nkomo & Hoobler, 2014). As a point of departure, one can question whether or not this is such an important aim after all, and whether or not it should be the only or most important aim.

If we consider businesses that address or manage diversity beyond legal compliance as assuming a specific kind of social responsibility, then even in the 1970s there were a whole host of cases both for and against such activities, concerning which business outcomes would be improved and how, and what the costs and risks might be (Davis, 1973). In any case, amid rhetoric and multiple discourses, various cases for diversity blur together and are not necessarily mutually exclusive. Legal compliance and ethically positive values have not ceased to be relevant, and can be reaffirmed in tandem with economic value and a whole host of practices with different philosophies and objectives.

Diversity as management does raise useful questions and reflections for organizations willing to engage with them, but taken seriously they are very challenging. There are questions around how to truly value difference inside the organization, how to balance treating people similarly and differently in different respects to support equality and justice, and how well existing organizational means and ends can be used to pursue diversity in conjunction with other goals (Weber, 1993). Much rests on 'how,' 'why' and 'relative to what' questions in terms of managing relations between majorities and minorities. Many further interpretations of managing diversity and positively valuing differences can be elaborated and questioned.

For instance, critical insights can be found by considering the legacy and overlapping co-existence of Equal Opportunities initiatives alongside diversity and diversity management initiatives. Typically the distinction has been that equality and equal opportunities are focused more on government, law, reactive measures, assimilation, discrimination, and collectives, whereas diversity is focused more on voluntary measures, proactivity, individuals, internal culture, integration, and performance (Weber, 1993). Yet considering both agendas together highlights the nuanced relationships between the two; how efforts to treat people the same or differently risk being either too simplistic or liable to lead to an oscillating confusion, in terms of rhetoric, goals, conflicts, and prevailing views. Critical perspectives demand more radical, dynamic organizational efforts to rethink the status quo of how work is organized and the various ways it disadvantages a range of groups in light of contradictions and challenges, pointing to "opportunities for progress rather than to faultless solutions" (Liff & Wajcman, 1996, p.92). Equality and diversity are not straightforwardly synonymous with sameness and difference, respectively, and thus need to be deliberated on interdependently and practically, in connection with economic, policy, and legal implications.

This tension between equality and diversity in context is further reinforced by findings from an analysis of the 1998 Workplace Employee

Relations Survey (WERS98) of 2,191 UK workplaces, showing that adoption of Equal Opportunity policies was highly uneven and far from comprehensive. Even workplaces with policies often reflected 'empty shells,' failing to offer supporting practices and access to them (Hoque & Noon, 2004). Two important implications are surely that (1) honoring of equality and diversity in practice varies according to a range of organizational factors, such as unionization, size, sector, structure and ownership, and (2) emphasizing diversity without the precursor of equality policies is at best premature and at worst harmful and deceptive.

Nevertheless, in the 1990s an important part of managing diversity was generally held to be the building of a tangible, predictable business case populated with a host of customer and employee savings and revenues, in order to win leadership support and resources (Robinson & Dechant, 1997). As a 'new organizational paradigm,' diversity management represented a popular way for businesses to talk about diversity in commercial terms, replete with case studies, models, and frameworks, but also taking focus away from preceding narratives (e.g. affirmative/positive action) to an extent (Gilbert, Stead, & Invancevich, 1999). Gilbert and colleagues (1999) noted how this pro-diversity case has been "heavy on rhetoric and light on empirical findings" (p.71).

In a relatively early and unusual paper, Barry and Bateman (1996) theorized that diversity management initiatives and decisions could be perceived by managers as 'social traps' or dilemmas, and only be solved if majorities are made to see long-term, collective benefits of pro-diversity actions. In various ways, discussions of how to best manage diversity became tied up in strategic discussions akin to those on how to best manage anything (e.g. people, change), resting on assertions like 'it depends' and 'there is no single best way' (Dass & Parker, 1999). Organizations would be seen as either resisting diversity or embracing and learning from it, or somewhere in-between, depending on a whole host of other clustered conditions and variables.

Into the twenty-first century, changing views on diversity management continued to evolve, with some progress in the sense of greater levels of genuine learning of the potential business benefits arising from diversity, but still suffering from a failure to recognize social and political dimensions of difference (Lorbiecki, 2001). Conflict and unrest regarding racism and discrimination, for instance, remained absent from considerations, and the dynamics of majority and minority resistance to diversity not confronted in terms of power and identity, classification and valuation (Lorbiecki, 2001). What anyone learning about diversity management is left with is a broadly accumulated strategic HR framework of many possible practices and initiatives for organizations to try and implement – everything from legal compliance to recruitment, training, diversity networks and councils, and more (Jayne & Dipboye, 2004; Shen, Chanda, d'Netto, & Monga, 2009). At the same time, critical and empirical questions remain about how these practices work or fail to work and why, and how decisions are made and enacted about them down the line in organizations (Kulik, 2014).

Critical Elaborations of Diversity Management and the Business Case

A general critique of diversity management and the business case rests on accepting that it acts as an ideological device to suppress true public inclusion and critical dialogue on issues like race and gender, by reducing diversity to a series of more private corporate decisions (Kersten, 2000). The 'shadow side' of diversity management is revealed in damning terms:

> diversity programs have not proven to be effective in eliminating workplace discrimination; there is no serious scholarly study of the impact of diversity management; the diversity literature ignores the reality of white rage and the white male backlash; organizational monoculturalism and the related issue of institutional resistance to diversity remain unaddressed and/or are underestimated; the litera- ture fails to deal with the rising resistance to acculturation; and finally, diversity is commodified (Prasad & Mills, 1997, cited in Kertsen, 2000, p.243).

These sorts of critical acknowledgments then lead the way to further critical readings of diversity management and its practices – the power and the rules – and insights into how they can involve political effects, such as questioning, refusal, and exploitation (Jones, 2004). Mainstream diversity work acknowledges this only up to a point, typically by de- scribing how diversity management can have 'unintended negative ef- fects,' where it is designed and delivered poorly or insensitively (Von Bergen, Soper, & Foster, 2002). However, this does not probe deeper into employee perceptions of the institutional racism and sexism un- derlying the implementation, or the rhetoric-reality gap between equality policies and diversity practice. However, in a study of racial and gen- dered minority employees' perceptions of a race equality plan in a local council in the UK public sector, multiple concerns were sustained about whether minority interests were being meaningfully related to deeper discrimination culture, leadership performance, ownership, and effica- cious results (Creegan, Colgan, Charlesworth, & Robinson, 2003).

In an important summary of critical elaborations, Wrench (2005) outlines how diversity management can be decidedly 'bad' for many stakeholders, because while it is "[a]ttractive to employers, it can be a means of evading hard choices about equality and justice at work" (p.73). This is particularly so where it becomes wielded as a soft option comprised of limited, diluted, individualistic measures that gloss over long-standing moral and political struggles for equality and recognition, pretending to a benign, market-driven view of all differences that may well reverse or exacerbate anti-discrimination and equality gains (Wrench, 2005).

Perceptions of the authenticity and sincerity of diversity management are also critically tested where they do not adequately or legitimately deal with specific group differences and perspectives. Much diversity management literature and practice can appear utterly generic, declaring an engagement with all differences and yet connecting with none to any real depth. Disability is one example, where disabled employees make up a heterogeneous group with complex needs and barriers to inclusion, and reflect differences not easily addressed in terms of a general commitment to diversity, equality, or a business case (Woodhams & Danieli, 2000). Similarly, when it comes to race, much diversity management text and talk does not directly interrogate whiteness, but instead acts to 'recenter' or 'mask' it as an invisible, benevolent, and systemic norm that continues to be reinforced and to dominate diversity proceedings (Grimes, 2002).

Critical elaborations of managing 'diversity' continue in terms of needing to track in organizations what diversity management might imply for terminology, activities, and its complex relationship with work to address social justice and inequalities (Ahmed & Swan, 2006). As Noon (2007) sees it, diversity and the business case has 'fatal flaws' for ethnic and other minorities where it is prone to short-termism, blinkered business views, dangerous arguments based on rational cost-benefit analyses, and its flawed assumptions that markets and managers will always work to value diversity. Diversity management discourse can treat identity as something essentialist and heteronormative – based on a set of categories, binaries, and boundaries – which fails to reveal the power and politics of hierarchy, division, and fluidity that would be highlighted by alternative queer theory and poststructuralist views of diversity management (Bendl, Fleischmann, & Walenta, 2008).

On both sides of the Atlantic in Europe and the United States, critical concerns have continued to emerge about whether diversity management is a step in the right direction for social justice in specific international contexts where marginalized groups continue to be hidden and devalued (Holvino & Kamp, 2009). A critical and realistic assessment of diversity management needs to be both international and relational, taking into account power and potential for change across levels of structures and areas of public policy, from history, culture, and laws down to distinct trajectories of individual experience (Syed & Özbilgin, 2009).

For its part, the business case also has continued to receive critical scrutiny in the last decade. Beyond diversity, the more general business case for corporate social responsibility typically refers to a 'narrow view' of clear links with financial performance, where a more appropriate 'broader view' stretches to an appreciation of more complex direct and indirect relationships between diversity, performance, and society (Carroll & Shabana, 2010). Solely emphasizing business arguments at the expense of justice and sustainability is risky and problematic, because both the concept of diversity and the outcomes it produces are likely to raise contextual issues, but ones left unaddressed by business logic alone (Bleijenbergh, Peters, & Poutsma, 2010). Companies can come to employ minorities for a variety of reasons with sound strategic and business logic, but still be all the more deeply discriminatory and unequal for it, where tokenistic symbolism, cheap labor, and other forms of exploitation predominate (Ortlieb & Sieben, 2013).

In many ways, a critical view of diversity management and the business case is a starting point for showing how organizations formally, selectively, and problematically address difference and inequality. In contrast, more authentic political and ethical engagements with these issues are far more likely to come from activism and protests, such as #MeToo or #BlackLivesMatter (Vachhani, 2020).

Problematic Diversity Management Practices

Beyond general critiques of diversity management and the business case, the practices and experiences themselves also become more specific objects of critical inquiry in terms of their design and implementation.

Diversity recruitment practices aimed at minority job applicants will backfire and result in increased turnover if they paint a misleading picture of the organizational culture as more supportive and favorable than it is really experienced to be (McKay & Avery, 2005). In Australia, private sector managers have to report on affirmative action programmes to address gender representation and discrimination. However, managers in the hospitality sector, as studied over a fourteen-year period (1990–2004), deployed rhetoric to deny the importance of gender issues and to shift responsibility in accounting for a lack of progress (Ainsworth, Knox, & O'Flynn, 2010).

Practices for selecting qualified employees such as assessment centers (ACs) also have competing rationalities and political conflicts around how diversity fits into their design, management, and implementation as formal interventions in context. In a study of such selection processes used to achieve diversity among judges of the UK judiciary, Healy, Kirton, Özbilgin, and Oikelome (2010) found that their effectiveness for addressing diversity was partial and contradictory, at times driven by the self-interested political need to be doing something visible with an overall feel of fairness. Similarly, the fashion of unconscious bias training has been criticized in sociological terms as 'pointless' – unlikely to eliminate racism because of the multiple forms prejudice can take, the structural constraints preventing real behavioral change, and psychologists overstating the agency of individual trainees (Noon, 2018). Even diversity networks aimed at informing majorities and supporting minority employees with similar social identities are flawed due to their being based on single category structures and individual and group needs for career and community, rather than intersectional and systemic patterns of privilege and disadvantage (Dennissen, Benschop, & van den Brink, 2019, 2020).

The specific efforts and relative lack of progress in many contexts concerning gender and diversity practices indicate that diversity management reaches ultimate limits in how far it can really challenge notions of difference. As the British Army shifted from a language of equal opportunities to one of diversity management, this merely served to reinforce certain aspects of institutional sexism, such as continuing to exclude women from direct combat roles, differentiating itself from civilian society in its special war-fighting role (Woodward & Winter, 2006). In the Swedish forest and mining industry also, diversity management's business case language was found to enable engagement with gender equality only up to a point, while other interests (male norms) and power relations were left unaddressed, amid marketing and skill utilization discussions (Johansson & Ringblom, 2017).

Indeed, gender *inequality* can be perceived as good for business where women are essentialized as offering a different alternative to the male norm, but placed in feminine roles with less power and resources. For organizations and public agencies in general, diversity management and public policy diversity strategies like 'gender mainstreaming' often introduce technologies of control or governmentality in a Foucauldian sense, controlling people's conduct in neoliberal and bureaucratic ways as they are urged to make difference productive and compliant (Prügl, 2011).

As feminism and business cases for gender equality are exported around the world, they are filtered through the interests and instrumental motives of various actors, and often feminist agendas are coopted into neoliberal projects, with limited structural change in access to governance and power (Cullen & Murphy, 2018). The same is true of multinational headquarters exporting 'business feminism' out to hubs in different countries; there is a depoliticized emphasis on empowering corporate leadership and individual career responsibility, and the potential for women to change their organizations remains limited, cut off from any wider civil movement or nonwestern political economy (Fodor, Glass, & Nagy, 2019).

Various diversity management practices can fall afoul of the nuances of gender inclusion in organizations in various ways. A study of diversity management practices in a variety of Austrian organizations revealed both inclusion and exclusion at the intersection of gender and disability, with disability inclusion being more fragile and subject to individual negotiation and organizational prioritizations (Dobusch, 2017b). Work-life balance initiatives can be thought of as a struggle for structural and cultural changes in organizations, with mixed effects concerning who benefits from them and whether they really change the mainstream at the core of employment systems (Kossek, Lewis, & Hammer, 2010). Flexible working policies can sow complex tensions between support and resentment across women colleagues with or without children, depending also on their life course stages and other aspects of workload and scheduling in organizations (Teasdale, 2013). Practices and policies as just 'quick fixes' left for workers to manage among themselves is an all too common theme (Teasdale, 2013). Women's recruitment and retention policies in Australian engineering firms have also been found to fail to acknowledge and challenge the male-dominated sexual politics, something deeper and more systemic in sustaining gender discrimination (Sharp, Franzway, Mills, & Gill, 2012).

Beyond gender, similar findings arise regarding diversity management practices in relation to other minority groups and contexts. Lesbian, gay and bisexual workers in UK workplaces, despite reporting the positive step of sexual orientation equality regulations passed into law in 2003, also reported a policy-practice implementation gap, underpinned by a lack of proactive leadership and a feeling of being the 'poor relation' within organizations' diversity and equality efforts more broadly (Colgan, Creegan, McKearney, & Wright, 2007). Hill (2009) shows how and why LGBTQ sexual minorities can face majority resistance to supportive diversity initiatives in many organizations – so-called 'backlash' or 'blowback' – because of majorities feeling their entitlements are threatened, resenting changes in language, and citing political and contextual sources of conflict, fear, and intolerance. Ultimately, without genuine safety and openness, minorities may need to find their own sources of courage and agency elsewhere, in more complex and contradictory positions distinguished from formal diversity management (see Chapter 12, this volume).

Another area of diversity management practice with legal protections but arguably not taken seriously by the mainstream is religion, with organizational researchers and practitioners remaining wary of its sociopolitical associations as not sitting easily with expressions of company culture (King, 2008). However, this does not negate the influences of religion and culture or render such obstacles insurmountable. Getting past diversity management rhetoric in cultural settings like the Middle East, for example, means understanding how to articulate and implement practices locally in relation to religious and cultural differences of interpretation that may make their reception seem otherwise paradoxical (Jamali, Abdallah, & Hmaidan, 2010).

It's not hard to point out how diversity management practices fall short of the fine-grained engagements needed to connect with the dynamic nuances of specific protected characteristics of diversity, but it seems important to do so nonetheless. Age has become a huge priority with ageing populations and workforces around the globe, with diversity managers and HR still gradually coming to terms with the deeply in-grained social norms and discourses surrounding ageism (Riach, 2009). Diversity management risks becoming outdated, and a poor match to designing age-positive jobs and HR structures and reversing popular myths to encourage mature workers to keep working (Murray & Syed, 2005).

The general experience of diversity management practices by mino-rities as 'recipients' of these changes has not been positive in critical studies of their implementation. Ultimately, the relative presence or ab-sence of diversity management can manifest as a series of control tech-niques that minorities struggle to comply with or resist, in terms of expressing their identities and engaging in bureaucratic procedures (Zanoni & Janssens, 2007). In this respect, diversity management does not differ much from management controls more generally. Other stra-tegies and practices may simply crowd diversity management out in re-producing underlying class relations of capital and labor. In a Belgian branch of an American car manufacturer supposedly renowned for its diversity, the 'dark' reality was that lean production, restructuring, and outsourcing reduced gender, age, and disability minorities to actors fa-cing unequal power relations rooted in class disputes about productivity and exploitation (Zanoni, 2011).

The techniques of control and rationality for governing diversity, difference, and sameness in ways that suit the organizational status quo are striking. A boxing gym chain in the Netherlands was shown to have used a series of ambiguous and interlocking rationalities about sport, gender, violence, fitness, and competitiveness to condition bodies through a range of masculine tactics and practices (Dortants & Knoppers, 2016). Perhaps the essential point is that diversity is 'man-aged,' but through practices of power and control. While equality and inclusion are publicly and formally affirmed, the real diversity manage-ment happens in the informal interactions surrounding a host of other practices and relationships. In a study of diversity practitioners in the UK voluntary sector, diversity management was surrounded by disengage-ment, reluctance, resistance, anxiety and fear, and a gothic metaphor of 'phantasmagoria' proposed to capture its "invisible, unacknowledged or shadowy aspects" (Schwabenland & Tomlinson, 2015, p. 1914). Diversity management as a modern gothic tale means that "its practice causes difficulties; people behave in difficult and unpredictable ways, benign actions produce malevolent results, things we try to make quantifiable escape from the efforts to control and bind them" (Schwabenland & Tomlinson, 2015, p. 1930).

The important and uncomfortable critical conclusion may be to admit that diversity is unmanageable to a significant degree, and at the very least not to fetishize quick fixes and hymns of good/best practice. However, rather than abandon diversity management, the task perhaps becomes one of sorting through all the problematic and critical aspects of its implementation. One key aspect is acknowledging the political game-playing to try to understand how diversity is being resisted and appropriated for different ends (Swan & Fox, 2010). A related point is to accept the need to manage ongoing paradoxical tensions, as inclusion raises new and simultaneous questions about exclusion, for instance (Solebello, Tschirhart, & Leiter, 2016). Another is how diversity management 'translates' from its origins (often American) to its destinations in the hands of majorities and hierarchies elsewhere, through many other competing norms and logics, such as welfare, redistribution, recognition, talent, CSR, solidarity, merit, and so on (e.g. Holck & Muhr, 2017).

One irony is that critical diversity research has become so effective at these sorts of critiques that some scholars have suggested its use as an educational tool for learning to appreciate the microlevel complexity (boundaries, emotions, politics) of trying to implement *any* strategy supposed to be good for a business (Lindsay, Jack, & Ambrosini, 2018).

Legal Cases for Diversity

A full consideration of diversity and equality law and public policy is beyond the scope of this chapter or book, and difficult to readily incorporate because of distinct terminology, source materials, ongoing updates, and contextual variations. However, some books have useful chapters considering the foundations of legal equality duties and forms of discrimination in organizations (e.g. Kirton & Greene, 2010), and the general argument here is for renewed and greater engagement with the legal case for diversity and equality in and around organizations. A legal case for diversity has more history and reasoning behind it than the business case, and legal 'cases' provide a constant source of distinct insights into how minority employees are hired, managed, and fired under contentious but relevant circumstances. Furthermore, many areas of corporate and employment law interrelate in ways that might be able to shed new interdisciplinary light on organizational diversity through a legal perspective, similar to other perspectives suggested by chapters of this book. The issue here is perhaps one of considering greater education and cross-fertilization across the relevant academic and professional communities, legal and organizational.

While not a straightforward panacea, evolving legal concepts and decisions nevertheless draw our attention to many aspirational ideas, issues, and rationales that the business case does not (and may deliberately seek to avoid, exploit and evade). Relevant laws and areas of public policy can cover specific types of differences, protections, discriminatory experiences, rights, duties, obligations, conflicts, interests, values, boundaries of responsibility and perhaps most importantly, problems that need the force of the law to uphold a sense of fairness and justice. For their part, various policies may vary in how voluntary they are in particular sectors and how much influence they have in relation to the law, but they too can influence distinct activities and framings of diversity such as transparent reporting, targets, and values to be concretely realized in programmes of organizational action. From quotas to reasonable accommodations of disabilities and equal pay reporting, the landscape is continuously evolving around the world. Several areas are considered in brief here to underscore the general importance of legal cases for diversity, particularly around employee discrimination, protection, and trying to change the organizational and societal status quo.

Probably the number one area here concerns discrimination and discrimination lawsuits. Much rests on how organizations learn from discrimination lawsuits, and the ways in which they do so, or the barriers encountered where they fail to do so, despite existing attempts to manage diversity. Wooten and James (2004) consider how various organizations have handled racial discrimination lawsuits in the United States. They argue that companies like Georgia Power and Denny's restaurant chain were better able to learn from, resolve and prevent discrimination lawsuits because they showed more signs of swift, concerned, and reflective leadership responses, although Denny's had to work more reactively with regulators to help change routines and beliefs (Wooten & James, 2004). Defensiveness, denial, and slowness to respond risk the mishandling of complaints and even generating a crisis. The link back to the business case should be relatively obvious in terms of how costly lawsuits can be for organizations, both directly and indirectly in terms of their reputations.

The same issues are true for women and sexual harassment on Wall Street. Despite strict policies and family-friendly diversity measures, sexual harassment charges and costly discrimination lawsuits have continued, change being slow because of underlying cultural issues with workaholism and beliefs in competitive markets and rewarding masculine behaviors (Roth, 2007). Where the legal case interacts with the business case lies in terms of changing strategies - in an ideal world, organizations would proactively collaborate with regulators and even innovate in legislation, but an equally common response is simply to block or stall regulators and reduce liabilities in the short term (Marcus, 1987).

A critical question is whether and how government policies can challenge institutional forms of discrimination. Drawing on the example of Indigenous policy strategy in Australia, Eveline, Bacchi, and Binns (2009) argue that there is a politics of methodology and implementation in translating laws and policies into action in the mainstream. An implication is that if the policy is implemented with institutional care and minority participation, it can achieve more genuine framings of diversity that avoid simple categorical distinctions and embrace experiences of intersectionality (Eveline et al., 2009). Gender diversity in the board-room and in corporate governance is another area where a lack of progress has reintroduced a case for stronger regulations, although doing so too suddenly and coercively can negatively impact corporate perfor-mance in the short run (Labelle, Francoeur, & Lakhal, 2015). Nuanced debates are likely to continue across countries regarding a continuum of soft-hard regulatory measures based on principles of 'comply or explain,' optimal board structures, supply and demand and public interest (Labelle et al., 2015).

A different target for law and policy lies in the case for eliminating and reversing biases at the heart of longstanding forms of discrimination. Mike Noon has argued persuasively for positive discrimination policies to be used in hiring and selection decisions, which would make more genuine progress via fairer 'threshold' and 'tie break' decision mechan-isms, relating to an organization's diversity goals in more transparent and unbiased ways (Noon, 2010, 2012). Essentially, we need to go further to eliminate biased decisions by having stronger mechanisms for ensuring minority representation, but this need not automatically involve quotas, just different levels and stages of decision-making that in-corporate diversity more explicitly and irrefutably. Biases and forms of discrimination evolve in complex ways in conjunction with ethical the-ories and societal norms. Civil rights and other equality legislation may protect many characteristics from discrimination under some circum-stances, but areas like appearance and (un)attractiveness – with potential for 'lookism' or 'lookphobia' – cut across these in ways that necessitate other deliberations, depending on what can be proven or defended through analysis of the particulars (Cavico, Muffler, & Mujtaba, 2013). Where legal systems reach their limits, there is still a case for employers and managers to try to write policies that explore the legality and morality of their practices as an ongoing process (Cavico et al., 2013).

In other areas of management practice, the role and reception of di-versity management laws and policies can become especially relevant regardless of the business case. Two examples are downsizing and the international transfer of diversity policies. In pre-downsizing re-structuring decisions, a social regulation strategy involves establishing stakeholder involvement and voice mechanisms, making it less easy to ignore or neglect disproportionate impacts on minorities (Campion, Guerrero, & Posthuma, 2011; Greene & Kirton, 2011). Similarly, in transferring equality policies internationally from western to Muslim majority countries, attending to the host country's institutional and contextual relations is likely to be more effective than simply seeking to transpose the essential character of a law or policy originating from elsewhere (Özbilgin, Syed, Ali, & Torunoglu, 2012).

In sum, where there is a relative lack of firm evidence for a business case for diversity, the legal case remains a powerful corrective normative influence, mandating changes in attitudes and behaviors by changing the substance of moral judgments, breaking down bias in non-instrumental ways (Williams, 2017). Collaborative and context-sensitive approaches to diversity laws, policies, and regulations can be persuasive, educational, legitimizing, and strategically enabling – they should therefore not be eclipsed by the business case.

Moral and Ethical Cases for Diversity

As with the legal case for engaging organizational diversity, moral and ethical cases can be made in terms that complement, supplement, or mount critiques against the more commercial, instrumental focus of a business case. In contrast perhaps to both a business case and a legal case, moral and ethical cases allow for more expansive philosophical reimaginings of diversity to an extent, and although only a few areas can be highlighted here, bear further and more systematic consideration.

One ethical case for diversity lies in recognizing that it can evoke a variety of emotional and stress-related responses, and how these emotions are addressed and reflected upon involves moral considerations as well. Diversity stress can be thought of as a type of morality stress, where competing moral principles can give rise to stressful situations and a sense of inadequate coping resources, particularly where organizations do not provide corresponding guidance and support (André, 1995). Emotions themselves are often overlooked as a constituent part of moral reasoning and diversity practice, but the ways in which emotions like anger, guilt, or compassion are mobilized have implications – for whether social justice is pursued because human flourishing is a valuable end in itself or whether it is merely a means to business ends (Brewis, 2017). Even well-intentioned efforts made with positive emotions by HR professionals in exemplary organizations to address discrimination can be morally problematic by way of 'benevolent discrimination' – actions framed as helping inferior minorities in need of help, perpetuating structural subordination and discrimination as a result (Romani, Holck, & Risberg, 2019).

As well as helping us understand the emotional experiences and framing of diversity efforts, moral and ethical cases for diversity also help us appreciate the role of diversity in underpinning robust organizational cultures and values. At its most obvious, diversity tends to bring a diversity of *values* associated with lifestyles and upbringings, the understanding of which can be extremely useful for an organization looking to accommodate group interests, conflicts, and decisions (Eastman & Santoro, 2003). Value diversity is often used vaguely or rhetorically to uphold a business case for diversity in terms of better decision-making and creativity, but this seems a long way removed from more genuine engagement with the balancing and corrective influences of values in terms of changing decisions and practices (Eastman & Santoro, 2003). A truly inclusive culture is one that engages with values and norms for more than just strategic reasons, embarking on more reflection and transformation of an organization's principles, processes, and practices – dismantling hierarchies and dogma that lack an inclusive moral basis, for example (Pless & Maak, 2004). In this light, many of the shortcomings and problems with the business case for diversity become better understood in terms of an inadequate or self-serving moral basis for diversity being the underlying, unchanging issue.

While actions and initiatives may appear morally 'good' (or evil) in terms of seeking equality (or not), this does not address the moral case for other activities and intentions accompanying them. This is a point made by Köllen (2016), drawing on Schopenhauer, arguing that a business case argument may be necessary for wider legitimacy and functionality purposes, but what really determines moral worth is if the individual actors initiating and supporting diversity in organizations are motivated exclusively by genuine compassion. More generally, the use of terms like 'equality' and 'justice' in relation to diversity initiatives needs to be subjected to more careful moral reflection and legitimization, as the words can be used vaguely or to reference very different frameworks, intentions, and outcomes (Köllen, Kakkuri-Knuuttila, & Bendl, 2018).

Specific practices and policies can also be scrutinized in terms of the nature of their moral and ethical foundations with regard to diversity. A study of five mining companies in Australia considered how HR programs have been aimed at involving Indigenous communities following Native Title legislation in the early 1990s (a legal case), but finds that most of this activity falls short of genuine power sharing and ethical cross-cultural engagement (Crawley & Sinclair, 2003). As well as power sharing, the ethical governance of diversity management in organizations can also be linked indirectly back to the business case in terms of high-quality financial reporting, which can develop a corporation morally by avoiding opportunistic earnings management behaviors that privilege shareholders and threaten genuine value creation (Labelle, Gargouri, & Francoeur, 2010).

Moral cases can also appeal to the urgency and concern over moral issues that have not been adequately addressed. For example, Bell, Connerley, and Cocchiara (2009) have argued for mandatory diversity courses, education, and training, justified by persistent discrimination and inequality, an obligation to prepare people for diverse environments, and the need to go beyond the business case to shape more formalized standards and behaviors. There is also a moral case that by diversity management becoming more 'socially responsible,' it can better achieve both business and justice outcomes through a broader, longer-term, more context-sensitive set of approaches at multiple levels (Syed & Kramar, 2009).

Finally, a moral case implies a certain way of putting a diversity philosophy into practice as an ethical way of living and applying theories and values, including where one really stands, ethically and politically, in relation to an organization and its business case. A special issue and set of articles in this area on critical diversity philosophy and praxis emphasize creating new spaces and ways of living and organizing difference, by decolonizing exclusionary forms of knowledge and understanding postcolonial and anti-racist praxis in diversity management contexts (Pullen, Vachhani, Gagnon, & Cornelius, 2017). For instance, Rhodes (2017) draws on Emmanuel Levinas, Judith Butler and the example of LGBT activism to argue that rather than artificially separating and opposing business and ethical cases for diversity, "the business case can be strategically used to pursue ethically informed justice, without succumbing to its self-oriented logic" (p. 541). Along similar lines, we can go further and make a case for an 'embodied' feminist ethics of diversity, where organizational inclusion is critically reimagined based on diverse individuals actively assembling and recognizing their inter-relationships and vulnerabilities, taking responsibility apart from the controls and limited tolerance of the business case (Tyler, 2019). An embodied approach to disability within diversity management also readily problematizes the business case in social and ethical terms, shining a light on how people's real experiences – not general rhetoric or abstractions – are defined by coping with physical, social, and material difficulties in organizations (Thanem, 2008).

The Future of Diversity Management and 'Cases for' Diversity

Having seen that the business, legal, and moral and ethical 'cases' for (or against) diversity management and its various practices overlap, coalesce and contradict one another in various ways, we might well ask what the future holds for how these 'cases' for diversity are framed and carried out in organizations.

First, it seems likely that generic and under-specified cases for diversity, defaulting to a general business case or win-win variation, will continue to be subjected to critical problematization. A newly radical starting point might be to think explicitly of diversity (management) as an ideology, or as comprising several ideologies, that contribute to gaps between principles and policies and allow majorities to retain power while professing good intentions (Smith & Mayorga-Gallo, 2017). Less critically and in a more benign framing, mainstream diversity management perspectives are also recognizing these issues. The issues are described in terms of 'unintended consequences,' some of which might be positive, but generally haphazard in whether they actually engage minorities, reduce discrimination, and/or hold people accountable for deep, lasting changes (Leslie, 2019). Pivoting back to a critical perspective again, the same is true for well-intentioned practices *other than* diversity management, such as the health and well-being at work agenda, which can focus excessively on resilience and HR controls, while displacing disabilities and minority experiences, employee rights and health and safety concerns (Calvard & Sang, 2017; Foster, 2017).

Second, any critical discussions of the 'cases' framing and justifying diversity management in the future will likely benefit from considering how various dimensions of context shape the particular initiatives being addressed. In other words, getting specific about what initiatives or practices are being proposed, the specific forms of diversity involved and affected (or excluded), and the legal, economic and moral reality of the industry and sector. Elite professional settings such as leading law firms in London are on long uncertain journeys to tackle class exclusion, and ambiguities around entrenched image and knowledge considerations mean business cases and government policies fall short when it comes to tackling social mobility and a will to collectively engage inequalities (Ashley & Empson, 2013). Private sector organizations more generally face an increasing need to work with both business cases and social justice cases, together rather than apart, against broader horizons and visions of activism and corporate social responsibility worldwide (Colgan, 2011).

At the other end of an organizational size/structure/ownership continuum, there is the need to factor differences like ethnic minority identity into discussions of small business ownership and self-employment, where these organizational contexts come with their own distinct business case and regulatory challenges (Jones & Ram, 2007). Outside of the corporate mainstream, the real diversity management may be less like management per se, and more like diversity participation through self-organizing – such as in community filmmaking practices, where cultural diversity organizes in a bottom-up way from independent networks at the margins (Malik, Chapain, & Comunian, 2017). Conversely, in large traditional organizations, such as the French manufacturing outfit studied by Yang and Bacouel-Jentjens (2018), we find indifferent and selective reactions from minorities to the organization's attempts to respond to institutional pressures to legitimately address diversity. In context, diversity policies and practices trickle down to minorities, who exhibit a corresponding diversity of reactions in terms of their own identity construction processes and concerns (Yang & Bacouel-Jentjens, 2018). This is also true of the perceptions of diversity management practices held by first- and second-generation migrant workers in France, where second-generation workers report greater discrimination and injustice concerns, and stronger expectations to be treated as an insider, in line with their identities (Hennekam, Bacouel-Jentjens, & Yang, 2019).

Third, the future of diversity management 'cases' is likely to rest on the further evolutions of distinct approaches and methods when it comes to research and practice. Various approaches may be helpful for bringing out more critical and experiential aspects of diversity management. Participative aesthetic inquiry workshops involve finding room for artistic expression and learning in a liminal, transitional space – exploring tacit, unspoken meanings that dream and reimagine how fairness and equality might be transformed and brought about in practice (Page, Grisoni, & Turner, 2013). Proactive organizational approaches to diversity will give more explicit consideration to a 'diversity identity' – both in terms of the organization as a whole, and its connections with other internal and external identity groupings, while neither excessively nor inadequately managing the process (Cole & Salimath, 2013). Greater critical connections between diversity and identity management literatures might help clarify how diversity management is experienced by people in terms of relational 'selves' and 'others,' and what is at stake for people on an everyday basis in terms of choices, meanings, and controls (Holck, Muhr, & Villeseche, 2016).

Emerging critical approaches to diversity management tend to also be more context-sensitive and connect a general/business approach to where it converges with other, more specific concerns. For example, De Jong (2016) outlines connections between diversity management and migration management in plural societies, where both fields face similar critical issues around how they seek to control and structure ethnic minorities' labor market participation. Others argue organizations need to move from 'classical' diversity management to 'alternative' diversity management, addressing ethnic equality by consciously refusing to imitate institutionalized patterns of inequality, broadening definitions, norms, and competencies to cover expressions of multiple identities (Janssens & Zanoni, 2014). A 'multi-level' case for approaching diversity management stresses the need to incorporate macro (national), meso (occupational) and micro (individual) influences and the relationships between them (Pringle & Ryan, 2015).

A 'historical' case for diversity (management) has been suggested, which rests on historical empathy for Eastern legacies and teachings as valuable for reconstructing the present of contemporary organizations, where Europe and North America today are not the 'one best way' to frame values, activism, and legislation (Pio & Syed, 2020; see also chapter three of this book). Finally, a 'practice-based' approach to diversity management focuses on the ongoing accomplishment of practices themselves, through bodies, tools, activities, relationships, and connected situations unfolding over time and space, be it career mentoring or coordinated performances from diverse groups (Janssens & Steyaert, 2019a, 2019b).

Most of these points shift the emphasis of the 'what' of diversity management toward greater critical engagements with the 'how,' the 'why' and the 'when/where/whom.' The critical future of diversity management is shot through with ambivalence and dissent around how it addresses dimensions of difference and legitimizes its activities and practices, not diminishing in importance or popularity, but rendered contested and fragile in conjunction with other demographic and political forces of change (Köllen, 2019). Two main challenges remain. One concerns going beyond the business case because it is not socially and morally forceful enough to create meaningful change on its own (Kaplan, 2020). The other concerns harnessing a better critical understanding of how diversity initiatives give rise to a formidable array of mixed signals, complacent assumptions, and unintended consequences in the form of minorities' and majorities' views on fairness, inclusion, and competence (Dover, Kaiser, & Major, 2020).

Conclusion

As noted earlier, this chapter brings us cycling back toward the beginning of this book, considering mainstream versus critical views of whether diversity can be scientifically studied and controlled in organizations to yield various effects and outcomes. Indeed, more mainstream views of diversity management, particularly with diverse teams as central objects of analysis, continue to try to carve up how different types of diversity, task, process, practice, and level of social unit might interact in complex formulae to improve predictions of effectiveness and performance (Nishii, Khattab, Shemla, & Paluch, 2018; Roberson, Holmes, & Perry, 2017; Tasheva & Hillman, 2019).

These approaches are formidably detailed and all-encompassing in their abstract conceptualizations, but arguably do not yield accessible, context-sensitive knowledge. Another way of describing this is by saying that as theories, these approaches perhaps follow too much logic of scientific rationality rather than practical rationality. Practical rationality would entail paying closer attention to the relevant aspects of actually trying to practice diversity management in concrete conditions and situations – using specific tools, people, and activities and seeing what unfolds in practice (Sandberg & Tsoukas, 2011).

In any case, most researchers agree new approaches are needed to understand the management of diversity in organizations and its effects on organizational outcomes. Diversity is not only a 'complex phenomenon' at a 'critical juncture' in management, but an area where the business case may well have held back progress in understanding sociopolitical struggles and discrimination that never went away, but reverted, worsened, or reappeared in new forms (Nkomo et al., 2019). We may expect some creative interdisciplinary and practice-based approaches to diversity management to continue to emerge, such as 'The Theory of Generative Interactions,' which emphasizes the need for meaningful intergroup interaction conditions to equip organizations to overcome exclusionary dynamics (Bernstein, Bulger, Salipante, & Weisinger, 2019). Among other disciplines, this approach draws on knowledge from "health care, disability, gender in STEM fields, and global virtual engineering teams" (Bernstein et al., 2019, p. 13).

There is also a considerable disillusionment with the business case for diversity to be reckoned with, and the many problems with the practices associated with it. It is important that we continue to try to listen and learn from the lived experiences of embattled and cynical workers who do not feel their organization is anywhere near inclusive, despite corporate initiatives and reputation, as well as the smaller or less prominent organizations doing more authentic moral, legal, and political work with diversity (Calvard, O'Toole, & Hardwick, 2020). Furthermore, organizations are complicit in actively creating and designing new types of diversity to be managed – today's young adult 'Millennial' employee generation, for example (Williams, 2020)–and may be able to conveniently and collectively 'forget' where they have failed to manage diversity responsibly in the past (Mena, Rintamäki, Fleming, & Spicer, 2016).

Ethically, we can challenge partial 'cases' on diversity by invoking a 'common good' perspective and principle, one which lifts up a sense of basic happiness and dignity in line with human and societal needs through a common commitment to rights, duties, and solidarity (Frémeaux, 2020). However, another critical starting point for understanding diversity management is to adopt a paradox perspective, where the management of diversity is determined by how actors navigate competing demands – either acknowledging manifold inconsistencies or choosing one path over another, but with the latter tactic bringing only temporary relief (Nadiv & Kuna, 2020). Simply pursuing equity and fairer organizations for all, for instance, risks ignoring how valuable knowledge is paradoxically entangled with minorities' experiences and burdens of inequality (Steel & Bolduc, 2020).

Perhaps the most significant indictment of diversity management research is how the majority of it from 1991–2018 has come from the USA and a particular concentration of journals, with indications that the production of such articles has peaked, remaining limited in focus and failing to capture diversity in its full breadth and depth (Yadav & Lenka, 2020). If diversity management is to survive, in research and practice, it may need to reinvent itself as more diverse, and take some of its own advice, because there appears to be a 'case' for more diverse diversity management research.

12 Critical Performativity and Agency

This chapter pushes a critical perspective on diversity further in terms of its implications and elaborations for those who might be eager to focus on the need to take the right sorts of action to produce the right sorts of change in organizations. This idea is implicit throughout much of this book – that organizational minorities and actors are engaged in struggles to exert their wills, express themselves, and wrestle with rules and systems of control that they might resist or reshape.

This chapter makes this aspect of critical organizational theory and diversity in organizations more explicit. In critical terms, struggles to take action or make change happen can involve terms such as performativity, agency, and praxis, as well as notions of 'doing' and 'undoing' when it comes to normative understandings. Finally, there are various forms of individual and collective role enactment and organizing that are particularly concerned with shaping conditions for organizational change. One further aim of this chapter is therefore to bring together critical understandings of diversity in organizations and change in organizations, as arguably diversity management and change management have tended to form independent conversations in research and practice, rather than being usefully thought through in conjunction with one another.

Praxis, Performativity, and Critical Agency

In discussing praxis in relation to organizational ethics, Nielsen (1993) notes how praxis "focuses on theories and methods of acting appropriately in engaging with concrete ethics issues and developing ethical organizations in interpersonal organizational situations" (p. 132). Praxis is often relatively neglected compared to other major dimensions of organizational inquiry, such as epistemological knowing or learning, ontological being or existing, and theoretical understanding or explaining (Nielsen, 1993). Praxis and theory can inform one another, but praxis opens organizations up to a vocabulary of doing, acting, becoming, accomplishing, and performing.

The word praxis is not always used – but related debates and discourses about agency and change in organizations appear to touch upon similar issues. Caldwell (2005) argues that fifty years of agency in organizational theory makes for "dismal reading" (p. 83), in part because weighty, competing discourses have emerged that make for fragmentation and complexity around how freely and rationally people in organizations can ever take action and produce change. Are we masters of our destinies or mere puppets? At one extreme, you might have a managerial rationalist viewing planned interventions as producing measurable changes in a very autonomous and centered way, while at the other extreme you might have a poststructuralist arguing that change is very decentered from any clear action or intention, buried under chaotic webs of discourse and power. Caldwell (2005) understandably concludes by emphasizing how vital it is that we "affirm the possibility of a positive middle way...*the hope that we can make a difference*" (p. 111).

A problematic twist to this middle way is the lingering concern that all praxis or attempts to 'do things well' in organizations are *performative* – certain theories, actors, tools, and activities come together to produce persistent social realities, which more often than not have a rational, technical, and objective character (Cabantous & Gond, 2011). In a review of the field of performativity, Gond, Cabantous, Harding, and Learmonth (2016) outline five foundational perspectives: doing things with words; searching for efficiency; constituting the self; bringing theory into being; and socio-material mattering in technological practices.

However, a further twist is that critical organizational researchers are still debating how different perspectives on performativity might be best mobilized and reconciled. On the one hand, a 'critical performativity' could represent a way to avoid armchair critique by more actively working with organizations to explore progressive possibilities for change in practice (Spicer, Alvesson, & Kärreman, 2009). On the other hand, to properly retain the theoretical value of performativity, we need to take care to retain a sense of the material and political struggles that lie behind more substantive efforts to change organizational conditions and discourses (Cabantous, Gond, Harding, & Learmonth, 2016). Ultimately, many researchers, particularly institutional ones, for example, might be content to agree that structure and agency in organizations involve 'embedded agency' at the general level. In other words, everyone works to change their contexts from within while 'embedded' in various constraints and opportunities surrounding their ability to act legitimately and effectively, and what matters are the specifications of those actors and contexts, as well as the constructions of their struggles, successes, and failures (e.g. Shadnam, Crane, & Lawrence, 2020).

In research terms, these issues speak to why 'action research' methodologies have yet to reach their full potential in organizational inquiry. There is a longstanding detachment of scientific knowing from practical knowing, and various logistical difficulties of collaboratively solving problems by moving between theory and practice while taking actions and reflecting on them all the while (Coghlan, 2011). Overcoming these barriers and difficulties toward greater collaborative activities and problem-solving would seem to be a worthy goal, not least in management education and business schools, and other public bodies and spheres. From the perspective of theorists such as Bourdieu and Foucault, it can be argued that global power networks conspire to reproduce particular beliefs, values, and practices that limit diversity, autonomy, and choices around how to act and enact change in global society (Vaara & Faÿ, 2012). These struggles for action and change in the face of dominance help to explain more specific examples. For instance, how Baroness Meral Hussein-Ece and Lord Simon Woolley lost their positions in 2012 as the only Muslim and black commissioners, respectively, at the UK's Equalities and Human Rights Commission, the country's equalities watchdog, for being 'too loud and vocal' about issues of race (Mahmood, 2020).

Relating this back to critical stances on diversity, equality, and inclusion in business schools, new questioning approaches to inequality are needed. Fotaki and Prasad (2015) suggest management educators take neoliberal capitalism more to task for its role in producing economic inequality. First, by emphasizing the 'answerability' to moral communities for acts that affect the societal flourishing of others, and second, through the 'relationality' of recognizing how our survival and ethical relations depend on caring for others we may not know and have never met (Fotaki & Prasad, 2015). In part these need to be supported and recognized as ethical dilemmas for critical management educators; their own partial positionality being set against the diversity of their students, while they are trying to teach practical skills without losing critical intent (Fenwick, 2005).

These ideas aren't new, but they nonetheless reflect urgent, renewed calls for reshaping the topics, perspectives, and experiences addressed in business schools. Business classrooms are globalized and have a hand in shaping the future of organizations. Yet they remain dominated by functionalist approaches focused on effective industrialization and multinationals, with far less space given over to postcolonial and non-Western histories, identities and practices (Joy & Poonamallee, 2013). In turn, this should lead to critical questions about the 'impact' of management research; how, when, and whom it changes and influences in its activities and dialogues, and whether those involved are truly open and reflexive when it comes to critically self-questioning their own perspectives on action and change (MacIntosh et al., 2017).

Common elements when it comes to critically acting and shaping change with diversity tend to include staying faithful and close to the voices and experiences of those most vulnerable or with most at stake, engaging self-critical reflexivity through exposure to diversity, and crafting a dialogue that leads to mutual and responsive actions and changes. Transformational change is bound up with shared experiences of inquiry and consciousness across differences. For instance, 'becoming a feminist' cannot be achieved or enacted according to a straightforward plan or singular transition but rather flowers through a consciousness-raising cultivated over an organizational life of narratives, identities, encounters, feelings, influences, revelations, and insights (Segal, 1996). Some of this transformation of self and/with others may therefore be informed by certain spiritual aspects as well (not to be conflated with religion), in terms of perceptions of ecological interconnectedness, and organizing foundations and aims that go beyond purely material goals (Steingard, 2005).

Critical interventions on behalf of oppressed differences in organizations are often described as moment-to-moment interruptions and disruptions, with verbs signifying forms of ethico-political praxis, guided by anti-racist and feminist precepts. Thus, in terms of addressing post-colonial issues in management, corresponding change action involves 'decolonizing' management knowledge of western/American/Eurocentric models and reintroducing alternative cross-cultural bodies of knowledge, histories, and philosophies (Jaya, 2001). If organizational thoughts for change and action stem from knowledge, then it matters where knowledge comes from and what constitutes its diverse origins (Jaya, 2001). At the same time, organizational interactions between people located differently in hierarchies of race, class, and gender involve significant emotion work, depending on the work context and the difficult and emotional silences where privilege, oppression, and the need for caring, understanding relationships come to the fore (Mirchandani, 2003). Riach, Rumens, and Tyler (2016) go further and take Judith Butler's theoretical performativity precepts, working them up into an anti-narrative methodology, where participants in a research process are themselves addressing the continual (un)/doing struggles between organizational and individual subjectivities. Here, action and change are recognized as continuous, contingent, precarious within lived experiences, and recurrently 'done' and 'undone' in relation to matrices of rules and norms in organizations which try to pin people down to fixed categories and linear narratives (Riach et al., 2016).

In sum, forms of critical praxis, performativity, and agency are hard work, cognitively and emotionally, and admitting this is important so that the work can be shared and understood, in order to feel, think, and change organizations in alternative directions. Ashcraft (2018) has drawn on affect theory to suggest, provocatively, that as critical researchers move from 'home' (e.g. academia) to 'field' (other workplaces) and back, they could be better change agents if they contended more directly with their own vulnerabilities and feelings to do with power, difference, relationships, and complicity. Otherwise, certain popular corporate calls to action, such as Sheryl Sandberg's *Lean In* book and mantra, prove influential but are also critiqued to an extent. This leaves us in a state where we "still do not know about how and why women leaders succeed, and, most important, what can be done to help them succeed in the future" (Chrobot-Mason, Hoobler, & Burno, 2019, p. 125). Academic literature and corporate rhetoric remain locked in an arms-length relationship, constantly reappraising one another while more diverse change dialogues and experiences are happening elsewhere, charged with politics and emotion. The remainder of this chapter will try to survey some more of the 'elsewhere' referred to in this regard.

Queer Theory and 'Queering'

Queer theory and the critical activity of 'queering' a concept or practice are difficult to define and fully address here, but they have far-reaching associations to do with resisting and subverting fixed norms and categories that unify and universalize differences and concepts across hierarchies and matrices of power relations. Since its emergence in the early 1990s, queer theory is often associated with sexualities, genders, bodies, and appearances but can also be applied to how we think about capitalism, globalization, management, and organization more generally (Gibson-Graham, 1996; Parker, 2002a). Any identity, knowledge, or practice that claims assimilation to a fixed binary or series of categories can have these conventional representations continually destabilized and deconstructed by critical 'queering' activities, the latter calling them into question and performing possible alternatives. Although grounded in the field of communication studies, West (2018) offers a comprehensive overview of the origins, terminology, people, representations, politics, and bibliographic sources associated with queer perspectives.

As Parker (2016) notes, queer theory has been and still is relatively popular across the arts, humanities, and social sciences, but preferences for adopting this level of radical critique and doubt vary, particularly in management. Its future may depend on how people use the term and perceptions of its fashionability as a way of thinking differently and thinking politically about identities and the fluidity of differences. As such, 'queer' itself can be subject to 'queering' (Parker, 2016). It fits this chapter well as an ongoing, unfinished mode of action and critique, mobilized for interrogating sexual politics and organizational (diversity) practices, and engaging in activism and discourse around the visibility and rights of marginalized groups, voices, and subjectivities. Queer theories and stances still have a lot of unfulfilled potential in management and organization studies, in terms of engaging more with the politics and lived experiences of LGBT groups in business and at work but also any tensions between individual and organizational self that might call for ethical and political action and articulation (Pullen, Thanem, Tyler, & Wallenberg, 2016).

By way of a definition in organization studies, queer theory

> aims to unsettle the persistent and harmful binaries (e.g. hetero-sexual/homosexual, male/female and masculine/feminine) that are discursively (re)produced within and through organizations and modes of organizing...to analyse and problematize heteronorma-tivity, focusing on the discursive construction of 'minority' sub-jects...typically those coded as lesbian, gay, bisexual or transgender, or LGBT – within heteronormative relations of power, and funda-mentally questioning this constitutive process. (Rumens, de Souza, & Brewis, 2019, p. 594)

Importantly, this includes heterosexuality, the coercive aspects of which can affect everyone and can also be performed in non-normative ways, such as non-hetero or non-white masculinities, acting like a 'tomboy', or simply by resisting the assumptions and labels imposed by relations and institutions as 'normal' in a particular time and place (Rumens et al., 2019). Heterosexuality is not the target of critique, however; rather it is hetero-normativity – the power and force of the idea that certain forms of human association are coded by gender and sexual relations as normal, natural, and the only legitimate basis of society and organization (Rumens et al., 2019).

More context-specific research is needed on how queer relationships, experiences, and activism operate in and around today's organizations (Calvard et al., 2020). However, educational settings and business and management schools are one site where critical diversity studies and commentaries have emerged. In a study of LGB school leaders in England, Courtney (2014) finds that while the leaders perceived their sexual identities as relatively fixed and essential, they engaged in 'inad-vertently queer' leadership practices to "increase the visibility of non-heterosexual identities and life-styles in the curriculum, policies and by promoting inclusive cultures" (p. 394). Similarly, Ozturk and Rumens (2014) studied gay male academics, finding that they negotiated and challenged heteronormativity in their teaching and research activities.

One way of understanding queering a business school is in terms of finding ways to foreground LGBT perspectives and issues, through vis-ibility, knowledge production and allies, problematizing and trans-cending heteronormativity, and organizing to promote education and safety around LGBT inclusion (Rumens, 2016). In developmental and educational terms, queering involves undermining and interrupting norms and categories to question their power, and the work of Judith Butler can help to underscore the idea that there are always possibilities for reinventing and modifying how you present yourself, but these may not always be recognized or understood by others (Rumens, 2017).

A good example of how UK gay and bisexual men challenge hetero-sexist norms is by constructing cross-sex workplace friendships with heterosexual women, although these processes can be challenging if they reproduce other heterosexist norms that limit our understandings of attachment and gender (Rumens, 2012). This can make it difficult to evaluate the goals and strategies of LGBTQ activist organizations. Ghosh's (2015) study of such organizations in India, also from a post-colonial perspective, shows how they creatively mix forms of knowledge and social movement activity to interweave the 'respectable' (conforming to normalizing patterns) with the 'queer' (challenging normalizing patterns), rendering themselves 'respectably queer' to an extent. Platforms for influence, diversity politics, and various stakeholder interests and issues still have to be navigated to achieve queer goals (Ghosh, 2015). The same is true of institutional allyship for LGBT equality – a study of a mainstream US Methodist church's shift from an anti-LGBT stance to a supportive one showed the problematic prejudices and motives involved in some majority ally activity, with more genuine socio-political support for disadvantaged groups only coming at a later stage (Russell & Bohan, 2016). Organizations describing themselves as 'LGBT-friendly' can end up with this twisted back through their cultures as a form of control. Financial and economic imperatives render diverse gender/sexual sub-jects as sources of tokenistic value to be exploited and discarded, such as an employee constructed as the 'right kind of gay guy', or an LGBT employee failing to fit in or improve the organization as envisaged (Burchiellaro, 2020).

More fine-grained understandings of LGBTQ minorities and calls for recognition and organizational change are starting to emerge, such as those concerning the bisexual 'B' (Calvard et al., 2020), but also the transgender 'T'. Biphobia can signal an aversion toward bisexual people, a denial of bisexuality as a genuine sexual orientation, and/or negative stereotypes regarding bisexual people. In relation to transgenderism, *cisnormativity* constitutes an unawareness or denial of the existence of transgender people and experiences, an insistence that gender assignment is compulsory, binary and naturally unchanging into adulthood (Robinson, Van Esch, & Bilimoria, 2017). Management educators have a responsibility to make students aware of transgender issues affecting millions of people and workplaces worldwide, to address transphobia and cultivate respect and understanding of trans issues around health-care, gender-neutral language, training, and physical space (Robinson et al., 2017).

Despite a growing interest in and awareness of transgender narratives and lives in popular culture and organizational research, trans identities are often conflated with queerness or as further instantiating binaries, putting trans people in a particularly vulnerable and frequently 'unlive-able' position (O'Shea, 2018). Furthermore, societal obsessions with and pressures toward normalizing bodies can exacerbate the abuse and issues facing trans persons and non-binary bodies, such as forms of gender/ bodily dysphoria (unease, distress) and mutilation stigma associated with people changing their bodies (O'Shea, 2019). Instead, we might do better to think *with* trans people to produce new practices of freedom in organizations and transformed relationships with ourselves and each other, as also reflected in the enduring histories of non-binary gender cultures worldwide (de Souza & Parker, 2020).

There are a lot of complex horizons still to be charted, and a lot of change needed, when it comes to gender and sexualities in organizations and LGBT inclusion. Queer theory has provided some sense of critical perspective and energy, but the LGBTQ lens is also broadening and evolving to include other important voices, contexts, intersections, and calls to action (Aydin & Colgan, 2020).

Diversity Officers and Change Agents

With some notable exceptions, there is often a lot of general discussion of diversity management and inclusion in organizations, but less attention is paid to the actual people whose roles and responsibilities involve developing these agendas, and how they shape and are shaped by their experiences in their roles as change agents. There is also some ambiguity around whether these staff are present in the organization, and how formally their work is valued and supported in its interfaces with more established strategic, operational and human resources functions. In short, we still know relatively little in research terms about the experiences of diversity, equality and inclusion officers and professionals in organizations.

A study of British diversity professionals' work in a variety of private and public organizations showed that these roles have evolved in recent decades and agents enact and experience their work with varying degrees of isolation, co-optation, and the juggling of liberal (more formal) versus radical (more political) strategies for reform (Kirton, Greene, & Dean, 2007). Their difficult change agent work reflects efforts at reconciling tensions between a passion for social justice and a commitment to a business case for diversity (see chapter 11 of this book). Their approach is often explained in terms of them adopting the stance of 'tempered radicals'. Tempered radicals bring their 'radical' identification with a value, belief, or cause originating beyond the organization into the environment inside the organization, where the status quo may involve ambivalent conservative constituencies, necessitating a tempered, tailored approach to change (Meyerson & Scully, 1995).

This dual, political work increasingly involves costs and opportunities, having gained to some degree in respect and legitimacy, and involving a diversity of specialist and part-time actors across many organizations, but with experiences still being contingent on associations with seniority and the broader political climate (Kirton & Greene, 2009). A study of UK equality and diversity officers in higher education institutions found that extra-organizational bodies (e.g. funding sources, national policies) can also provide support and influence in these change agent roles, as the officers manage relationships, goals, resources, and sectoral context in their praxis and amid the political processes of change (Tatli et al., 2015). External diversity and inclusion (D&I) consultants in the UK must repeatedly assess relationships with clients and how to manage and resolve conflicts between societal and organizational discourses by changing language, values, and ways of thinking – the discursive strategies necessary to 'tell and sell' diversity change to HR functions and senior managers (Kirton & Greene, 2019).

Diversity professionals then come in a wide variety of forms (academics, consultants, and HR professionals) and hail from a wide variety of sectoral backgrounds. The deeper critical problem is that, where their work involves 'selling' diversity to white male workforces, that work is in itself a racial and gendered performance that involves economic and market managerial capitalist logics and amoral detachment, reproducing whiteness and impeding structural change (Carrillo Arciniega, 2020). Diversity change agents are thus involved in a wider reckoning with their economic, discursive, and moral contexts, a struggle that itself plays out as embedded in systemic inequalities. In this sense, resistance to diversity change can be both active and deeply institutionalized in the very idea of management; rooted in repression, denial, and inaction that need to be named, analyzed, and mobilized against if systemic discrimination against the powerless and disadvantaged is to change more genuinely (Agócs, 1997).

Rather than think of change as happening through organizations and discrete agents and entities, it might be more productive to think of networks of social and material relations. This view is in line with actor network theory, where diversity-related change is more difficult to pin down but present in more heterogeneous possibilities and relationships, human and nonhuman, including documents, ideas, and communities shifting and oscillating in and around organizations (Hunter & Swan, 2007). Change agents for diversity and equality are rendered more like 'secret' or 'double' agents, caught between multiple discourses inside and outside organizations, only able to affect partial change from their own particular discursive locations (Jones, 2007).

Despite decreases in trade union density in recent decades, trade union representatives and evolving forms of unionism and union response on behalf of diverse membership and causes represent another source of change agency when it comes to diversity and equality. Trade unions tie together notions of ethics, equality, activism, and HRM through an emphasis on employee voice, employment rights, representation, participation, and evolving areas of employment regulation, such as immigration (Cornelius et al., 2010). However, a study of equalities officers in unions in Scotland reminds us that unions themselves are still developing their approaches to structural inequalities, in their recruitment, their internal positions, and their collective bargaining (Lindsay, Munro, & Wise, 2007).

Indeed, across Europe, the union movement has been slow and inconsistent to lead change and act on equality due to a crowded bargaining agenda, slow legal machinations, national/sectoral/local variations, and a distrust of managerial diversity discourse (Milner, 2017). That said, this in no way precludes unions playing an important diversity change role in relation to specific issues and contexts, making a positive difference to working lives and employment relationships. Regarding ageing workforces in the UK and Germany, for example, unions are developing responses to protect retirement benefits and pensions, while also supporting longer working lives, although the patterning and scope of their negotiation strategies depends to an extent on the pre-existing national capitalistic context (Flynn, Upchurch, Muller-Camen, & Schroder, 2013). Regarding disabled employees in the UK as another example, Richards and Sang (2016) showed how a transport union used a learning fund project to represent and support employment for neurologically impaired employees.

Beyond varieties of diversity, equality, and trade union officers, an overlapping source of change agency resides with minority employees themselves, in dedicated roles or otherwise, and those working closely with them. Any encounter where a minority identity is made self-consciously and intentionally visible in an organization represents a deployment and mobilization of that identity, making a statement that can advocate and educate in effecting change, and perhaps a story that can have symbolic significance beyond the initial encounter (Creed & Scully, 2000). This is not to deny that speaking up or remaining silent in organizations about an invisible, oppressed identity represents a dilemma, and these moments can accumulate and spiral and have serious consequences for organizational relations (Bowen & Blackmon, 2003).

However, minority identities can be strategically deployed where agency is available. A study of professional migrant Indian women working in New Zealand found that when faced with labor market exclusion and job discrimination, such women found ways of drawing on a kind of transnational feminism to shift perceptions of their otherness in how they spoke, dressed and accounted for their success (Pio & Essers, 2013). The conditions of possibility for minority (change) agency can be political, ethical, corporeal, and temporal, making them surprising, personal, fragile, and contingent. In a study of women working at Australian universities, experiences of menopause at work were described in terms of gendered agency bound up with experiences of time and the ageing body (Jack, Riach, & Bariola, 2019).

Although ethnic and gender identities generally present an agency of struggle full of tensions and contradictions, it is a form of change agency nonetheless. In everyday experience and actions, ethnic minority professionals discursively construct available positions within relations of power, juggling ways to comply and resist, and make difficult trade-offs in changing how they focus on their identities, careers, and attempts to influence social change (Van Laer & Janssens, 2017). Some top women managers in Mexico act as change agents by engaging in 'strategic essentialism' – deliberately performing, training, and mentoring at work in ways that play off of accepted notions of 'machista' and 'marianista' work culture, or masculine and feminine, respectively (Barragan, Paludi, & Mills, 2017).

This emphasis on individual agency, however, does tend to take us away from structural issues and carries the risk of over-emphasizing individual responsibility and resilience at the expense of wider socio- and ethico-political support. It takes us back into the exclusive province of the business case for diversity, and minority individuals' leveraging and mobilizing of their identities to achieve instrumental goals, while the reproduction of inequalities and stereotypes remains largely unaddressed (Cha & Roberts, 2019). This is very micro-level change and soon requires building up through relationships and values if it is to be harmonious and generative over time.

A transformational change toward organizational equality is far more likely to necessitate participative groups of researchers and practitioners coming together as change agents and recipients to reflect on experiences of resistance and empowerment and ways to keep the changes going (Bleijenbergh, 2018). Finally, White allyship is also a crucial part of a transformational diversity change puzzle, to the extent that it is anti-racist, feminist, intersectional, and prosocial in orientation, avoids the pitfalls of privileged benevolence, and ensures that would-be allies are supported and cultivated by the wider organization (Erskine & Bilimoria, 2019). When it comes to transformational change agency, it is likely that many actors will need to be involved. There are unlikely to be shortcuts to change, and responsibility will need to be shared in a genuine, continuous, and reflective manner (Erskine & Bilimoria, 2019).

Diverse Entrepreneurship and Leadership

Leadership and entrepreneurship are two vast and established fields of inquiry in their own right, but it is worth giving them some selective consideration here as they relate to critical concerns over diversity and change agency. Minorities and diverse actors starting up and growing diverse kinds of organization, and diverse leaders leading more established organizations in diverse ways both constitute obvious, influential, and interrelated sources of change agency.

The need for critical perspectives on entrepreneurship is framed in terms of questioning how certain types of entrepreneurial figure are idealized as a purely market-based phenomenon, concealing the ideological aspects of entrepreneurialism and privileging the white male entrepreneur as the archetype of venture creation (Tedmanson, Verduyn, Essers, & Gartner, 2012). Consequently less consideration is given to economic crises, feminist concerns, entrepreneurs from marginalized groups and contexts, and the possibilities of more communal public entrepreneurialism (Tedmanson et al., 2012).

For example, gender and entrepreneurship are both culturally produced and reproduced in social and situated practices, such that 'doing' gender and entrepreneurship in changing, alternative ways means wrestling with how the two are intertwined – entrepreneurship being generally equated with masculinity and economic rationality (Bruni, Gherardi, & Poggio, 2004). Small enterprises in Italy run by minorities present more 'anti-heroic' and 'private' accounts of entrepreneurship than the hegemonic masculine versions concerned with growth and triumphing in the marketplace (Bruni et al., 2004).

Leadership is perhaps a more mature field than entrepreneurship to a degree, but both fields are having to reckon with how the way their focal concepts are interpreted in research belies the changing diversity of the real business world and alternative interpretations (Galloway et al., 2015). Performativity, as developed in feminist theory, helps to correct these interpretations in critical terms, restoring meanings of 'entrepreneurial leadership' that include fuller treatments of the roles of emotions, resistance to masculine norms, and inclusive relationships beyond individuals (Galloway et al., 2015). One striking example is starting a business in a dangerous region of the world; women entrepreneurs working in Afghanistan actually perceived war zones as less dangerous than men because they were more concerned with dangers closer to home, relating to their families and having the courage to be a woman business owner in the first place (Bullough & Renko, 2017). Another example is CSR – part of which is comprised of initiatives around the globe aimed at increasing women's entrepreneurship, but which would benefit further from attending to feminist economics critiques, which challenge the separation of production from reproduction, or 'work' from family and unpaid care (Johnstone-Louis, 2017).

Changing and diversifying leadership from within and without is an ongoing agenda. In changing MBA management training and leadership development, 'women-only' approaches – in addition to, not instead of, general practices – can help create symbolic space and learning experiences for supporting a new generation of talented and diverse leaders without reproducing masculine career norms (Vinnicombe & Singh,

2002). Constructions of desirable leadership styles, such as 'authentic' leaders, are not essential and unchanging, but rather gendered and performed in context, as illustrated by media representations of a male and female Australian banking CEO during the global financial crisis (Liu, Cutcher, & Grant, 2015). Leaders in the same sectors facing the same contexts must nevertheless contend with different constructions of how they perform authentically or inauthentically, in line with context-specific, embodied gender norms and stereotypes (Liu et al., 2015).

However, a feminist leadership ethics perspective reminds us that women's leadership needs to be understood on its own terms and not just as feminized ideals that are 'other' to and merely complement male leadership (Pullen & Vachhani, 2020). The Prime Minister of New Zealand, Jacinda Ardern, despite being an exemplary, caring and compassionate leader, is still caught up in gendered expectations from a global public that differentiate her as a feminine leader. However, via Luce Irigaray and feminist ethics, her leadership can be read in more transformational political and relational terms, such as when she wears headscarves and cloaks in solidarity with Muslims and Maoris, her leadership challenging "the individualism, universality, difference, and rationalism found in leadership ethics" (Pullen & Vachhani, 2020, p. 8).

Similarly, women's leadership in India differs from the Western perspective, where women harness power via collective support from marginalized groups and communities, mobilize their status as victims of injustice and tragedy and stand up "against the patriarchal mindset...to act in cases such as sexual harassment, inheritance and family laws, or developmental works" (Saifuddin, 2017, p. 286). Away from corporate contexts, ethnically diverse British and American women union leaders blend different combinations of masculine and feminist leadership talk, drawing on complex, multiple, and contradictory discourses about good leaders and women's leadership (Kirton & Healy, 2012). Critical views of diversity and leadership show that alternative organizational performances and changes are possible, but difficult, and often require pointing out the problematic influences of competing discourses and 'othering' constructions. In this regard, a relatively neglected area would seem to be changes in constructions of masculinities and men's responses to feminist leadership challenges in organizations, be they intersectional, profeminist, or otherwise (Hearn, 1989, 2014a). Another would be the increasingly large global business of leadership development for youth, with its own particular discourses of leadership suspension, separation, smallness, self-leading and semi-leading (Carroll & Firth, 2020).

In today's organizations, where white women and people of color do manage to occupy elite leadership positions, they tend to be seen as 'nontraditional' leaders, having to make continual 'performative contortions' to obtain and sustain their positions, itself indicative of continuing failures to ensure leadership equality and inclusion (Glass & Cook,

2020). Celebrated as 'atypical' individuals, they may nevertheless delegitimize diversity management as well as legitimize it, depending on how the dual tensions of who they are, what they say, and what they do are presented in organizations as leadership opportunities and constraints (Samdanis & Özbilgin, 2019). They remain highly dualistic in the sense of potentially being constructed as both insiders and outsiders, influencers and conformers, normalized and marginalized, encouraged and discouraged.

As with so many critical tasks to do with diversity in organizations, a key project is in terms of how we collectively reimagine leadership. Surrounded by and saturated with images and identities of leaders in a culturally diverse global economy, truly inclusive leadership represents a moral, embodied and expansive challenge, having more to do with differences and relationships than any one individual or group (Fisher & Fowler, 1995). Far from being an intellectual exercise, much corporate leadership is persistently saturated with masculine bodies and verbal and visual cues (Liu, 2017c), and laudable concepts like 'servant leadership' ironically reproduce who gets to be a servant leader, without contextualizing the wider intersectional power relations subordinating the real 'servants' (Liu, 2019b).

A critical agenda emerging around leadership for diversity in and across organizations is one that rests on an ethical commitment to radical democratic politics and intersectionality, taking its cues from grassroots organizing, feminist alliances, and a collective ethical responsibility for social change (Pullen, Rhodes, McEwen, & Liu, 2019). Leadership (and entrepreneurship) are thus repoliticized, reclaimed, and 'redeemed' in feminist and anti-racist terms, through a renewed appreciation of how leadership has oppressed and excluded to date, and for the need to break from a hegemonic leader ideal rooted in patriarchy, capitalism, imperialism, and white supremacy (Liu, 2020).

Diversity, Activism, and Social Movements

Where taking critical action on behalf of diversity and equality perhaps becomes most collective, but also most fluid across traditional organizational boundaries, is in terms of activism and social movements, themselves a form of organizing.

Social activism in and around organizations typically involves insiders and outsiders seeking to influence target organizations with which they have varying qualities of relationship, deploying a range of mechanisms and tactics to bring about both societal change and changes in organizational policies and practices (Briscoe & Gupta, 2017). As mentioned earlier in this chapter, trade unions provide change agency and leadership for diversity and equality but are also often considered in terms of activism as well. Diverse and intersectional women trade union activists self-organize to provide a platform of collective action to represent their consciousness, identities, and interests (Colgan & Ledwith, 2000).

Working-class women working part-time in service sectors, for example, are engaged in activism on several fronts, including flexible working, childcare provisions, and recruiting and training new members to the cause (Conley, 2005). Huge progress has been made in terms of gender equality, representation, and democracy, with support networks and strategies evolving to introduce more women's issues onto the mainstream agendas, albeit with considerable variation by union, and much unfinished business (Kirton, 2015). More recent equality and equal pay legislation have opened up opportunities for unions to achieve change, but these are strained by political conservatism and tensions between individual rights-based legislation and collective voluntarist traditions of union organizing and collective bargaining (Conley, 2014). All in all, in the UK at least, after fifty years of considerable overall progress dating back to the 1968 Ford women workers' strike, further progress still depends on equality and class-based bargaining agendas being more closely integrated, improved representation of BAME membership, and making outcomes of activism and campaigns more visible (Kirton, 2019).

Alongside unions, related but independent notions of activism come from academia and universities. Guided by feminist theories and principles, groups of women are coming together in European universities, working amid top-down administrative agendas and managerial forces to carve out collaborative spaces and renewed efforts to 'manage the management' from the bottom up (Bendl & Schmidt, 2012). Feminist activism in universities represents a potential model for other organizations to achieve change toward gender equality, through influencing managerial responses to equality issues and adapting governance structures across phases of institutional change (Bendl, Danowitz, & Schmidt, 2014).

For their part, individual critical scholars working in business schools can be called upon to draw on feminist and postcolonial ideas and put their power in service of social justice; an intellectual activism that faces up to positions, demands, and issues associated with finding alternatives in response to economic, political and ethical crises (Contu, 2018). Activist academics can respond to the times, producing new forms of knowledge, endeavoring to change structures and cultures, and lend their voices to calls to action about what needs to change in the times in which we live and work (Bell, Meriläinen, Taylor, & Tienari, 2019). Diversity and equality 'scholar-activism' is more than publishing scholarship – it involves partnership with activists, translating academic work to interested publics, and calling out hypocrisies and false equivalences (Holmes IV, 2019).

Indeed, beyond the walls of academia are many currents of activism for scholars to participate in. In a study of a Brazilian and a Canadian community organization, Barros (2010) worked closely with the organizations to understand how they practiced values of emancipatory management in cultural context. The study revealed ways of learning from the limits, contradictions, and tensions between the individual selfinterest and internal inequalities of organizations on the one hand, and the collective and external practices of fulfillment and solidarity on the other (Barros, 2010).

As well as striving to create more humane and fulfilling experiences in specific organizations, Craddock (2017) considers women's community groups in the UK city of Nottingham; set up to resist a broader national policy of austerity and government cuts, in crucial respects a feminist issue as it disproportionately affects women. This is important given that the gendered dimensions of local movements are not always made as visible within wider campaigns. Feminist activism has a complex gendered relationship with the notion of care work and an ethic of care, with a need to direct more attention, value, and collective responsibility to care needs and interdependence in public life (Craddock, 2017).

In a similar vein, international studies of gender activism and movements in and around organizations in particular industry and sector contexts continue to emerge. Often the opposition and dissent is against forms of precarity, inequality, and exploitation exacerbated in part by the global financial crisis and its lasting impacts. A case study of antimining protests in Greece highlighted the role of affective embodiment in feminist activism, as protestors put their bodies on the line in clashes with neoliberal forces threatening their way of life, community spaces, and the natural environment (Fotaki & Daskalaki, 2020). Women also acted as front-line, rank-and-file change agents in the Vietnamese garment manufacturing industry, their informal grassroots and unsanctioned gendered activism between 2010 and 2016 shaping progressive labor relations in a patriarchal, Global South context, with wildcat strikes leading to changes in minimum wages, sanitation, rest breaks, and flexible working hours (Chi & van den Broek, 2020). Even under highly oppressed and marginalized conditions, it would clearly be a mistake to think of women and other minorities as docile or passive when it comes to activism and change agency.

In the case of racial diversity and ethnicity, we can turn back in history to the antislavery activism and society organizations in America and the UK in the late 18th and early 19th centuries, their change agency shaped by mass media and religious and theological discourses - the press and the pulpit (King & Haveman, 2008). It is the repeated communications, affiliations, interactions, and messages associated with influential institutions that bind these change movements and their collective identities. Various African countries and states in the twentieth century and into the twenty-first century are following disruptive postcolonial change trajectories in working toward the economic empowerment of a majority of black citizens emerging from a legacy of suffering and discrimination (Decker, 2010). The Africanization of management in foreign-owned organizations has been slow and painful, characterized by social and cultural distance, vicious self-fulfilling cycles of under-performance, and poverty and education barriers (Decker, 2010). Tribal leaders (chiefs) and the complexity of precolonial organization and centralization continue to shape postcolonial regional development within and across African countries, alongside more developed and modernized locales, in a 'dual' ethnic and national environment (Michalopoulos & Papaioannou, 2015).

Studies relating today's ethnic diversity to activism and social movements shed light on a variety of contexts with critical implications for organizing and organizations. In 2008, in Cape Town, South Africa, when outbreaks of xenophobic violence led to thousands of displaced 'refugees' in government 'safety camps', an AIDS activist organization responded to this humanitarian aid crisis, shaping a social movement in streets, courts, and the media to put pressure on the state to address health and survival needs in the population (Human & Robins, 2014). In London, migrant domestic workers, previously thought 'unorganizable', used a variety of mechanisms to overcome barriers to collective mobilization and transform the framing of their predicament from isolated 'laborers of love' to 'workers with rights' in self-help groups and with links to formal organizations (Jiang & Korczynski, 2016).

On a more problematic note, and in conflict with other forms of organized labor, North American police unions have constructed 'blue solidarity' through 'Blue Lives Matter' campaigns; to counter racial justice movements and working class resistance to austerity, while contributing to rising right-wing populism (Thomas & Tufts, 2020). These examples start to illuminate more of the fluid, interactive, and collaborative or contested dynamics of diversity and equality activism and social movements. Blue Lives Matter in American police forces is in part a response and reaction to the corresponding Black Lives Matter movement and international network of chapters, which turned five years' old in 2020 but continues to struggle to build support for realizing racial justice and the demands enshrined in its 'Vision for Black Lives' (Szetela, 2020). Activists and scholars of even the most passionate and urgent movements have to reckon with reflexivity, charges of exceptionalism, achievability discrepancies between theory and practice, and fragmented voices across the political Left (Szetela, 2020).

A final point here then concerns the wider change dynamics of social movements. As 'inhabited ecosystems' (DeJordy, Scully, Ventresca, & Creed, 2020), the activism in social movements flows in, through, across, and around organizations in their organizing, and this social complexity is indicative of their diversity and democracy, whether the focus is feminism, racial justice, class, the environment, or all of the above. More localized activities, such as women's movements in London and Mumbai, may be able to have some success in improving representation at the local government and city level, with tight civil society networks and awareness of the most disadvantaged (Barry, Honour, & Palnitkar, 2004). Theorization of social movements tends to focus on their 'movement', in terms of how they process identities, relationships, and resources in pursuit of various aims (Barry et al., 2004). Similarly, there are also recurrent debates about whether women's movements go through periods of 'abeyance' and 'resurgence', as forms and levels of support and mobilization appear to wax and wane over time (Barry, Chandler, & Berg, 2007). However, Barry and colleagues (2007) conclude that:

> [i]t is the capacity for the everyday struggles and practices of women, as well as supportive fellow travellers, which provide the justification for seeing such practices and values as part of a women's movement for change, even if any advances made are modest, difficult to measure, subject to reversal and beset with contradictions. (p. 364)

Online twenty-first century movements like the Everyday Sexism Project can provide platforms with some of the remarkable ethical and political richness and reach needed for building empathy and solidarity in addressing systemic sexism (Vachhani & Pullen, 2019). The fact that movements have to work through their own internal diversity and politics of experience is critical to reflexive practice, and it does not need to divide and disengage people, but it does require cultivation and sensitivity to become as inclusive as possible (Vachhani & Pullen, 2019). The broader vision at this point for feminist movements is perhaps one that involves local, global, and intersectional experiments in radical democracy and dissent, where feminine differences are reasserted through a sense of shock, accountability, and the disruption of spaces (Vachhani, 2020).

Ultimately, many organizations can arguably engage more effectively with social change by learning from activism and social movements. In an interview with Ruth Hunt, former CEO of Stonewall, a leading UK LGBT charity, her experiences of driving social change involved:

> managing the tensions between an assimilation and liberation approach to social change, promoting intersectionality and positive action to enhance inclusion, the challenges and opportunities of sharing power and the skills of facilitation, boundary-spanning and working relationally that constitute the everyday practice of leadership in complex and contested landscapes. (Bolden, Williams, & O'Regan, 2020, p. 1)

Conclusion

This chapter has reviewed a range of works relating to various sources and forms of critical pro-diversity change agency and social change efforts, as well as some of the debates surrounding their struggles, contradictions, and conditions of possibility. Hopefully this chapter can be seen to forge some closer and more coherent links between diversity, equality, and social justice-related change in organizations as a result.

The processes of diversity and equality changes in organizations are shifting, complex, and uncertain, often notable by their absence or charged with superficiality. As noted at the outset of this chapter, most social and organizational change is inevitably embedded and pragmatic, being neither totally free nor totally constrained (Farjoun, Ansell, & Boin, 2015). The ontology and epistemology of organizational change interact with experiences of praxis and performativity, which is why change (and stability) can be constituted in organizations in so many different ways. From a pragmatic point of view, change agency need not always serve a strong critical position or direct action but rather a future-oriented process of questioning, underpinned by curiosity, dialogue, and democracy, which may have a more realistic chance at changing habits and mindsets in particular situations (Keleman, Rumens, & Vo, 2019).

This should be compatible with and complemented by Contu's (2020) notions of intellectual activism, where scholars concerned with diversity and equality strive to create more concrete engagement and solidarity across diverse, intersectional communities affected by forms of crisis, injustice, and hegemonic power – from 'theorizing' to 'doing' and 'building'. One example of such activism is Vida, a progressive and grassroots association of hundreds of critical management scholars working in business schools around the world, engaged with speaking truth to power, inequality, and exploitation (Contu, 2020).

Feminism remains marginalized in prestigious 'malestream' management and organizational journals as a form of knowledge production, reminding us of the ongoing need for personal, political, and epistemological change in scholarly fields and communities (Bell, Meriläinen, Taylor, & Tienari, 2020). Similarly, notions of social scientific rigor and methodological techniques can be seen as founded on Western neo-imperialism and colonialism, as revealed by peripheral locations such as India, where indigenous forms of knowledge can serve to denaturalize and decolonize narrow and isomorphic global norms of knowledge production (Bell, Kothiyal, & Willmott, 2017).

Critical diverse voices are therefore gaining momentum to some extent in seeking to change the international hierarchies built into business schools and management knowledge. This appears in the form of calling for action in decolonizing them, acknowledging their racist and post-colonial foundations, and establishing support networks for dismantling their white and Global North/West power structures and inequalities (Abreu-Pederzini & Suárez-Barraza, 2020; Dar, Liu, Martinez Dy, & Brewis 2020; Girei, 2017; Naude, 2019). These changes have the potential to empower more local, indigenous experiences, voices and contexts, allowing their organizing, diversity, and well-being to flourish. It also encourages understanding and engagement with the power relations and dynamics of social and institutional change in developing countries in more cross-cultural, feminist, and context-sensitive ways (Karam & Jamali, 2017).

Meanwhile, in the internal politics and exploitation of more traditional, established organizations, minority actors have to struggle with the partial knowledge and power that goes with their position and standpoint, limited to pitching social issues for change in a functionalist marketplace where ideas are bought and sold, accepted and resisted (Wickert & de Bakker, 2016). Without greater activism, democracy, and self-organizing movements, the absence of change has to be reckoned with – the silence, loyalty, and tolerance that inhibits greater voice about poor conditions and inequalities (Dean & Greene, 2017). Such conditions also refer us back to important questions of how to construct better forms of allyship from majority actors, avoiding the pitfalls of individualized remedies and diminished responsibility (Sumerau, Forbes, Grollman, & Mathers, 2020). One recent example of an answer is by adopting Creary's (2020) LEAP framework for being an ally to black colleagues (listen/learn, engage, ask, provide).

13 Imagining Diverse Futures

This chapter focuses on critical conceptions of futures in relation to diversity in organizations. While futures can be thought of more or less literally, they also represent a speculative and imaginative frontier of critical thought, drawing on interdependencies with the past and the present to carve out spaces of (im)possibility for organizational lives and forms. Organizations and diversity come into contact with projected ideas, images, ideals, fictions, ideologies, scenarios, and landscapes of salvation and tyranny.

This might seem fanciful and far-fetched, but we should consider the cultural and political influence of imaginative and diverse orientations toward possible and alternative futures – not because of how realistic or feasible they are, but because they constitute a symbolic and meaningful connection with the present and any diverse desires to break with it. For example, we might dream of a future with significantly greater levels of equality in employment – but there are considerable mediations between the abstract and concrete details of such a vision to be thought through, and that thinking through in itself might be conceived of as valuable. There is equality of a relative and absolute character; equality regarding proportionate representation, opportunities, efforts, and rewards across individuals, groups, contracts, jobs, and sectors to consider, along with the design and implementation of radical policies to achieve such goals (Eichler, 1989).

Similarly, a political vision of more democratic or labor-managed organizations requires sorting through a multitude of cooperative principles and reconciling them with competing utopian images of anarchism, liberalism, conservatism, and radicalism, as well as the legitimate basis for collective and rational decision-making (Luhman, 2006). Whatever managers in organizations do, they are still managing, and this creates a social puzzle around how to combat feelings of individualized and utilitarian alienation with restored forms of organic, moral, and democratic community (Johnson & Duberley, 2011).

Imagining Organizational Futures and Alternatives

Understanding diverse visions of the future requires understanding the corresponding philosophical foundations (and biases) of management on which they might be built. These have often been dominated by Western themes of heroism, rationalism, positivism, romanticism, existentialism, and postmodernism (Joullié, 2016). For organizations and institutions to survive, and indeed to reckon with issues of diversity and inequality lurking behind economic and social crises, they need to think about the relationship between their imaginative capabilities and charting alternative futures. The works of the Greek-French philosopher Cornelius Castoriadis, for example, can be used to propose a situated and political view of imagination surrounding organizations, where imagination can be considered a profoundly generative and psychosocial force for overcoming dualisms and giving form and meaning to novel representations (Komporozos-Athanasiou, & Fotaki, 2015).

In an extension of the previous chapter of this book, dealing with multiple crises of "economic, financial, food, water, energy, climate, migration and security" (Fotaki, Altman, & Koning, 2020, p. 7) resources requires dealing with an underlying crisis or failure of our collective imagination around change, diversity, and organizations. In questioning existing paradigms and fragmentation, and seeking to break new political and intellectual ground toward transcendence, thus spirituality, symbolism and storytelling take on renewed importance in challenging mainstream thinking to provide more public and ethical relevance (Fotaki et al., 2020). Our myths define and sustain us in our present, while also suggesting alternative paths to our futures. At the same time, this reckoning with imagination and fantasy must also reckon with conflict – as the 'differences in the world' co-constitute social and organizational orders, with ethico-political consequences for work and life (Contu, 2019). Facing up to conflict responsibly means facing up to ideology – systems of ideas and beliefs with a variety of contents and functions, but which can conceal or reveal diverse group realities and interests, as "concerned with *domination, legitimation, critique and/or fantasy*" (Seeck, Sturdy, Boncori, & Fougère, 2020, p. 68).

This again turns us back to imagination and storytelling to a degree, because novels and fiction can help us experience, imagine, and mediate between diverse and critical modes of representation and organizing. For living and working in the twenty-first century, engaging more with diverse novels and narratives in business ethics education represents a case based on growing evidence that more reading of novels among business students can produce better, more responsible business people (Martin, Edwards, & Sayers, 2018; Michaelson, 2016). To be inclusive, this should involve gender, postcolonial and queer engagements with literary expression too; beyond predominantly male and Western authors and

222 *Implications of Critical Perspectives*

traditions and toward novels that "provoke a different sensibility and new ways of seeing" (Beyes, Costas, & Ortmann, 2019, p. 1799).

The significant difficulty in orienting towards diverse organizational futures lies in the weight of the past, the present, and of capitalist dominance, where we need new economic vocabularies to allow consideration of ruptures, new beginnings, and possibilities of difference that are not reducible to degrees of adjustment extending the status quo (Fournier, 2006). Ironically, executives and corporate elites are not very diverse and, despite much managerial talk of revolutions, scenarios, and change, are also not very engaged with imagining and preparing for long-term futures beyond cycles of staying on top of 'business as usual' (Berg Johansen & De Cock, 2018). Although more common to philosophy, thought experiments – what would happen if imagined, open-ended scenarios were real – might help organizational researchers and practitioners to problematize serious current issues in stimulating ways (Kornberger & Mantere, 2020). Well-known examples of thought experiments include what visitors from another planet would make of our organizations (and inequalities), and making more just and equal moral and social contracts from behind a 'veil of ignorance', with no regard to what our own starting position or ability would be (Kornberger & Mantere, 2020).

Many of these ideas relate to utopianism, a tradition of thought dating back to Thomas More in the sixteenth century. Utopias or 'eutopias' refer to non-existent good places where people are conceived of as living in communities with transformed everyday lives, institutions, and political and economic systems – later complemented by critical anti-utopian and dystopian (bad places) traditions and critiques (Sargent, 2010). These notions relate to diversity because they often cross it with issues of common ownership, far-reaching equality, and cycles of hope, failure, and improvement for the organizations and societies we build (Sargent, 2010). Martin Parker has reflected on utopias as matter or plans for launching alternative forms of organization and organizing in the broadest of terms, but in ways that consciously depart from market managerialism and recognize the beleaguered nature of the concept (Parker, 2002b, 2017). Perhaps the most important aspect of struggling with utopias is how to render them responsive to fluidity, diversity, and difference, and to situate them more concretely in time, place, and the sensuality of being – an invitation to 'show' in the here and now rather than 'tell' about the future (Parker, 2017).

When it comes to organizations, we can be rightly suspicious from a critical perspective about any current organizational discourses of Shangri-La and lands of milk and honey but also without being anti-utopian – we just need to keep issues of power and identity in mind (McCabe, 2004). Utopias are instructive in terms of how they try, fail, and partially succeed in representing possible futures; clearing spaces and working out what might happen with diversity and technology as they go, as demonstrated by the considerable body of work in the science fiction genre and studies of that genre (Jameson, 2005). Indeed, science fiction actively goes beyond a realist organizational present, breaking free of today's constraints to try and show us what could be real but has not yet come about (De Cock, 2009).

Critical themes of diversity and inequality appear in much science fiction, shaped by the ethnic, feminist, and other identity concerns of the authors. For example, Octavia Butler's work deals with racial and gendered conflicts by experimenting with identity and community in ways that make our current narratives and realities seem less familiar and fixed (Miller, 1998). Working backwards and forwards from apocalyptic events, crises, and totalitarian regimes weaves together critical concerns around diversity, equality, and the boundaries of organizing. Dystopian novels of the twentieth century like *1984* and *Brave New World* are still relevant to how we anticipate emerging forms of technological and cultural control today, and how we might critique and resist them (Klinger, 2018). Margaret Atwood, author of *The Handmaid's Tale*, coined the term 'ustopia' as a fusion of utopia and dystopia, because along relative lines of difference, every utopia is organized as someone else's dystopia, and vice versa (Hendershot, 2018).

Lest the real-world resonance of such ideas be doubted, we should recall that (real) women in many parts of the world donned (fictional) handmaid's outfits in 2018 to protest against laws and policies oppressive to women, as life imitated art (Beaumont & Holpuch, 2018). Additionally, although not science fiction, the 1975 Icelandic women's strike, or Women's Day Off, was and remains a protest of great power and imagination, in inviting everyone to consider the prospect of economies and societies bereft of the indispensable yet undervalued work of women (Brewer, 2015).

On its own, the word 'future' and its many variants (futures, futurology, foresight) are perhaps captured best under the umbrella 'futures studies' when it comes to describing alternative futures, but we also need to remember historical and cultural discourses about futures, and the necessary roles of complexity, diversity, scepticism, and connection to the present (Sardar, 2010). In the corporate mainstream of futures thinking and more radical critical variants, there is a prevailing interest in what will happen to work, technology, and organization in the future, although this is often framed in general socio-economic terms rather than in terms of diversity per se.

After the economic predictions of Keynes and later from the 1970s onwards, there have been repeated concerns with ensuring the dignity of future work and leisure, but far less focus on gender and diversity, and problems with writers eschewing descriptive prediction in favor of normative prescription (Bergman & Karlsson, 2011). Technological work futures remain at something of a sociomaterial or socio-technical impasse as well; with workers caught between the physical and the virtual, the manual and the automated, and the empowering and the controlling, across a range of working trends (e.g. Bailey, Leonardi, & Bailey, 2012; Zuboff, 2019). The more radical leap is into a future where there is a relative or absolute end of work and the ushering in of a post-work world, with theses rooted in critical social theory, invoking heady elements of utopia, Marx, automation, leisure, creativity, globalization, welfare, consumption, ethics, and de-materializing, de-industrializing forms of work (Granter, 2016). However, despite enthusiastic discussion, many of these agendas lack credibility as they are disconnected from the empirical realities of more pressing progressive economic concerns around worsening inequalities, saving jobs, and improving the quality of existing work (Thompson, 2020).

Rather than 'futures', critical management studies scholars have increasingly focused upon the more grounded, less idealistic notion of 'alternative' organizations and organizing, where literary, historical, and contemporary movements, communities, and visions do suggest an impressive array of alternative organizing forms apart from market managerialism (Parker, Fournier, & Reedy, 2007). Business education can follow suit by challenging the view that a managed corporation pursuing wealth, status, and competitive power in a neoliberal economy is the only, best, or most desirable option for an organization (Reedy & Learmonth, 2009). Of course, in another sense, this challenges the market managerial foundations of modern business schools themselves, where a 'School for Organizing' would arguably represent a more radical alternative moniker (Parker, 2018).

A manifesto for alternative organizations has been proposed as needing to rest on threefold principles of autonomy, solidarity, and responsibility, along with an understanding that reconciling these principles is not easy, requiring careful politics, co-production, and a spirit of experimentation (Parker, Cheney, Fournier, & Land, 2014b). In the case of a small sustainable financial services organization in North America, Parker and Parker (2017) also show how this can be a model for critical research; for maintaining a middle ground between radical critique of an organization and simply accommodating its managerialism.

In sum, alternative organizations do seem to suggest more diverse organizations, and furthermore, more diverse organizations that address inequalities from more authentic and committed critical stances. These include ecofeminism, antiracism, anticapitalism, human rights, therapy, profit sharing, anarchism, or any other number of organizing projects by, for, and with marginalized groups. Much depends on how future generations of hopeful and diverse organizers and scholars come together to carry them out.

Utopias

A general introduction to the idea of utopias was provided earlier, but some further, more specific links between utopianism, organizations, and diversity can be teased out here as well. These "social and political philosophies about how the world should best be arranged" (Grey & Garsten, 2002, p. 9) can seem impractical but are historically and so-cially situated in collective hopes and horrors, shaped by tensions be-tween order and chaos, regulation and markets, totalitarianism and anarchism, responsibility and freedom.

There are probably several ways to link diversity, equality, and in-clusion to utopian thinking. One is simply to write and experiment with a sense of diversity as a 'new beginning' – of minorities choosing to live and organize differently, and to amplify and extend that (Lightfoot & Lilley, 2002). Another might be to embrace a form of anarchist or grassroots organizing that allows diversity to flourish freely in conditions of possibility apart from existing hierarchies, authorities and market inequalities (Reedy, 2002; Vournier, 2002). Yet another way still might be to take some emphasis off economic growth and consumption, and restore a sense of time and place for locally diverse communities to care for one another and the environment. In protecting and sharing re-sources for common and public goods – various romantic, bucolic, and pastoral images of tended gardens with natural and equal gatherings of diversity come to mind (Burrell & Dale, 2002; Munro, 2002). That said, the possibility of majority power and state control is always a threat to utopia, and we should beware of 'crypto-utopias' that present themselves as real, pragmatic, modern, and free of ideological vision, while pre-cluding alternative forms of social change (Jacques, 2002). The American Dream of fighting to protect democracy around the world is one potent example, the scientific theory of evolution is another (Jacques, 2002).

Fittingly enough then, utopias on behalf of diversity therefore need to studiously avoid presumption and accept the notion of highly plural, mutable, multiple utopias (Grey & Garsten, 2002). This makes uto-pianism a collective action problem of framing issues and mobilizing resources, as well as one of exercising moral imagination in ways sen-sitive to practical demands and the social help and harm implied in contradictory institutional arrangements (Hargrave, 2009). All else being well, this should lead to morally imaginative outcomes and diverse or-ganizational forms and communities when viewed through the lens of moral economy. A perspective of moral economy foregrounds concerns about unfettered markets and disconnected capitalism, highlighting how they can and need to be reconnected with forms of reciprocity, com-munity and normative political struggles addressing the human and vulnerable character of work and employment (Bolton & Laaser, 2013).

However, more critical research and vision are needed to build on and update these agendas. Critical organization studies can work to concretize and problematize more specific contemporary arrays and moral visions of diversity and utopian organizing, drawing together the fictional, imaginary, and historical to inform the present and the future. Racial diversity poses a particular problem for utopian organization because of the dangers of conceiving mono-racial utopias. However, since the 1970s science fiction has continued to imagine better worlds where the link between race and culture has been broken and "oppression and discrimination can no longer target visibly defined categories of people...a world without the possibility of racial profiling or biologically determined identity" (Chan, 2006, p. 473). Similarly but focusing on disabilities, the musician, actor, activist, and thalidomide survivor Mat Fraser asked in a recent radio documentary 'what if everyone was disabled?', provoking discussions around a better world with inclusive design and spaces where nobody would need to be reminded of impairments as not normal or disabling (Fraser, 2020). At the very least, utopian thought experiments and fictions invite us to ask what would be needed to make a better reality happen, and why the limits of liberal democracies do not enable it.

The 1983 anarchist, anti-capitalist utopian text *Bolo'bolo* by Swiss writer Hans Widmer (pseudonym P.M.) describes a worldwide network of small, diverse communities or large communistic households (*bolos*), which can be read as a concrete response to calls for a more open society redeemed from the apocalyptic ravages of industrialism and colonization (Hatzenberger, 2003). The challenge with utopian learning communities can be described in terms of solidarity, in connecting the micro-politics of group life with the macro-politics of more extended forms of solidarity, where we make consensual and moral choices about identifying with diverse others, via thinkers such as Durkheim and Rorty (Reedy, 2003).

In gender terms, utopian aspirations can involve women seeking alternatives to patriarchal identities and idealized managerial masculinities. Kosmala (2008) looks at the critical artistic practices of women working in the visual arts and finds dominant masculine values of managing and producing replaced by collectivism, play, and relational transmission. Invisible and diverse ways of working are thus made more visible as political and cultural alternatives; different ways of living, defining economic value, and expressing one's identity (Kosmala, 2008). Indeed, women have often sought out alternative sectors and movements to achieve emancipation from role definitions based on gender binaries, with a strain of utopianism in their organizing coming far closer to equality and eliminating discrimination than many traditional sectors and organizations (Kück, 1985). A gender utopia is not simply one where women have equality, opportunity, and neutrality in a man's world, it is a more radical overhaul of social systems (education, healthcare, home, law, politics) designed and dominated by men that revisits basic masculine and feminine qualities and how they are respected, utilized, and valued (Chary, 2017).

Furthermore, gender can channel utopian and transformative impulses and organizing potentials through writing differently. 'Feminine' writing has the disruptive feminist potential to break masculine rationality and order, and for reclaiming ethical and political discourses of love more attuned to care and justice (Pullen & Rhodes, 2015; Vachhani, 2015). Similarly, Donna Haraway's 'cyborg' writing acts as a site for social transformation by disrupting Enlightenment ideals of duality, objectivity, and rationality in order to think through the politics of a post-gender world, writing differently – playfully, metaphorically, intimately – about diverse bodies, subjectivities, and technologies (Prasad, 2016).

It may be that many large, complex organizations are still trying to constrain difference and diversity through a one-dimensional utopian ideal of acting as a well-oiled machine – one with high performance, reliability, control, resilience, and an ability to rise to the challenge of increasingly tough demands. However, questioning the need for this particular design – in size, structure, ownership – or its legitimacy is again a turn to diverse utopian alternatives. For instance, Torchia (2016) describes the inclusion, affordability, community, and friendship of a small British fan-owned football club (5000 members), formed as a reaction to the individualistic standard business model prevailing in commercial football. Whether judged entirely successful as an alternative or not, FC United of Manchester represents a desire to organize in ways that are pre- or anti- in stance relative to the emergent global corporate order of liquid modernity and liberal consumption, a desire to try and rediscover some of the solidity and order of community engagement (Torchia, 2016).

Two Polish cooperative organizations have been used as examples for enacting possibilities of 'disalienation' at work, instead of the more common 'alienation' where managed workers don't feel at home, themselves or in control of their work (Kociatkiewicz, Kostera, & Parker, 2020). In contrast, disalienated work is organized through a nonprofit, value-driven orientation and despite acknowledged difficulties, with personalized, democratic relationships, and horizontal principles of togetherness, meaningfulness, ownership, communal space, and purposefulness (Kociatkiewicz et al., 2020). Taken together, alternative organizations and social movements that reject managerialism and neoliberalism embrace diversity by replacing corporate 'individualism' with a more collective 'individuation' in pursuit of autonomous selves. In this way, alternative organizations are actually prefiguring new social forms of utopia by linking organizing, politics, and identity in the here and now (Reedy, King, & Coupland, 2016). The creative and communal use of space, the forging of social bonds for mutual aid, and creative political expression are familiar themes, but ones that coexist alongside conflicts and compromises with more brute material needs and precarity (Reedy et al., 2016).

Many of these movements and alternatives are surely more egalitarian than traditional organizations, although it may be reasonable to wonder about whether they can sustain diversity and inclusion as part of a wider, interdependent economy and society, even if that is not the precise utopian intention. Ideals and principles are likely to remain fragile and elusive as they come into contact with the flux of material and discursive realities. We could question, for example, whether utopian-type organizations and organizers are authentic in the threefold sense of upholding consistency, conformity, and connection across their identities, values, and constituents (Lehman, O'Connor, Kovács, & Newman, 2019). In Bryer's (2020) case study of a Spanish cooperative selling books and clothing and its very practical discussions of financial targets and budgets, she uses the work of Brunot Latour and anthropological notions of belonging to show how true openness and inclusion in organizations emerges by keeping them 'liveable' in context. Belonging and inclusion take hard work as actors work through difficulties – reflexively and empathically – between competing social aims (sustainability, fund allocations, and alliances) and the need to survive in competitive market conditions, seeking to minimize exclusionary tendencies (Bryer, 2020).

Many may take scornful or fearful, fatalistic views of attempts to try to devise and sustain more inclusive, equal organizations aimed at creating a better world for diverse groups as simply too impractical or likely to be subject to serious failures – an anti-utopian or dystopian position. Yet for others the counterarguments are likely to be that it is precisely the difficulties and failures which make utopian alternatives worth striving for. It is the hope and determination to make more inclusive, egalitarian, humane alternatives work that energizes solidarity and community across diversity, whether short-lived and fragile or not. In addition, various socio-political events and crises such as Brexit and Trump may be conceived of as opening up a space for fresh utopian thinking and imagination, a space for confronting more starkly the contradictions that divide the social and organizational order (De Cock, Just, & Husted, 2018).

Dystopias

As the dark side of utopias, dystopias are intimately related to utopias as the flaws in the latter are revealed or viewed from a different perspective, although dystopias are also most commonly associated with late industrial and technological catastrophes and regimes (Jacques, 2002). If a little bleak and despairing, they have affective value as cynical cautionary tales, using similar rules of logic, time and space as utopias, but instead of offering hope for a Heavenly ideal state, offering caution and admonishment against Hellish destruction and suffering (Jacques, 2002).

Even as early as in the fifth century, writings about angels meditated on issues of order, obedience, and the tyranny of vertical organizational hierarchies, intimating common sense ideas of the dystopian and monstrous in the popular ordering of differences, although fallen rebel angel metaphors might be recast as actors who have simply chosen to escape hierarchies (Parker, 2009). In ways not dissimilar to Heaven and Hell, many organizations reach dystopian-type states of antipathy and deadlock, where particular identity groups are influenced by fantasies of difference that portray a dominant identity as hegemonic and objectively superior, while other identities are subject to 'othering' and scapegoating (Lok & Willmott, 2014). Loosening or breaking a diversity deadlock or impasse entails the difficult process of uncovering fantasies of opposition, balancing differences with equivalences, and pursuing areas of common ground and mutual accommodation with more constructive criticism (Lok & Willmott, 2014).

Dystopias would also appear to be useful for naming, labeling, and providing some of the 'monstrous' contradictions that technological developments and forms of social organization foreshadow in terms of diversity and inequalities (Bloomfield & Vurdubakis, 2014). Two examples of this would be 'designer babies' from genetic and reproductive procedures, or 'algorithmic prisons' where particular people are oppressed by technological decisions over which they have no freedom or right to contest. Dystopian language, imagery and scenarios thus all invite us to vividly imagine minorities' experiences of oppression, injustice, and suffering, connecting tragedies of the past and problems of the present with warnings of futures that would make things even worse.

Simulations like zombie apocalypses show us how we might behave in a dystopian setting or a global crisis, helping us to understand dangerous and extreme contexts from the relative safety of fictional and narrative speculation, but with genuine lessons on the dark side of diverse group behavior, survival and collaboration (Hällgren & Buchanan, 2020). In a less extreme way, organizations can resemble dystopias where they are experienced as maddening, irrational or absurd, although the stress and confusion can be countered if leaders and followers alike recognize the inevitability of some irrationality and disorder, and take solace and comfort in humility and relinquishing some control (McCabe, 2016). Absurd dystopias have a long artistic, historical and philosophical tradition, and offer compelling, theatrical spaces for critiquing harmful fantasies complicit in explaining away inequalities as inconvenient truths (Starkey, Tempest, & Cinque, 2019).

The main project of critical management studies since at least the 1990s has been defined as addressing dystopian ideas of corporations as aspiring to be totalitarian entities controlling the minds and bodies of employees through any cultural or technological means possible (Fleming, 2013). Today, diversity and difference remain one of the horizons of this battle of control and resistance. The language and liberal economic appropriation of diversity in business represents just one more form of subjection and self-discipline necessitating newer forms of resistance and dissent (Fleming, 2013). Organizational dystopias like those found in Kafka's fiction change form but do not seem to go away, suggesting we need powerful reminders and calls to action around where bureaucratic controls erase difference and create perilous, inhumane experiences that only ever reinforce inequalities (Warner, 2007).

Dystopias often draw on an aesthetic of 'ruin' to make a strong impression, something that could be harnessed more in critical studies of diversity and organization to "connect to a dystopian future...[and] conjure up overlooked people, places and processes in a world that is slowly reverting" (De Cock & O'Doherty, 2017, p. 137). Dystopias force us to look at, imagine, and experience things that under other aesthetic and organizational conditions are too easy to remain blind to when we should perhaps be more unsettled – waste, wreckage, pollution, poverty, and destruction (De Cock & O'Doherty, 2017). Today's organizations, in some instances, may well be creating tomorrow's ruins. Academics working in neoliberal business schools are increasingly thinking of their work environments as another case of tyranny, alienation, and despair in some respects, but collectively calling it out and confronting it represents a modest step toward a critical survival strategy (Fleming, 2019a).

For some time, there has been a view that 'bad' management theories have a performative, self-fulfilling impact in creating 'bad' managers and practices in the real world, raising the troubling possibility that education and writing – suffering from a lack of diversity – reproduce dystopian tendencies as well (Ghoshal, 2005). In critical views of organization, managerialism is a lead contender for a defining feature of organizational dystopia. Managerialism has been relentlessly and globally exported and enacted via Taylorism, America, business schools, MBA graduates, and executives of the largest corporations; colonizing human life as something to be measured and managed to spur economic growth and destroy the planet (Clegg, 2014). Hope lies in diverse forms of resistance, reform, and alternatives.

Similarly, organizations and institutions structuring their practices around the free market are highly implicated in rising global inequalities, to the point where even mainstream management cannot entirely ignore the problem. The dystopian flavor of this follows from the notion that free market organizations are actively creating and maintaining these inequalities, embedding them ever more deeply along the lines of gender, race, class, and other intersections (Amis, Munir, & Lawrence, 2018).

Organizations that reinforce systemic discrimination through inter-locking hiring, role allocation, promotion, compensation, and struc-turing practices and myths of global efficiency and meritocracy have become veritable machines that are highly effective at reproducing in-equalities, feeding off them and constituting them (Amis, Mair, & Munir, 2020).

This also leaves many workers in a relatively dystopian state of pre-cariousness and anxiety, facing a Darwinian struggle to turn their un-dercompensated work and hopes into something more secure and worthwhile (Mackenzie & McKinlay, 2020). Collective and diverse re-sistance and subversion of these neoliberal subjectivities of self-exploitation and individualistic responsibility will be essential to avoiding a dystopia based on a human capital hoax. Human capital advocates promise humans returns on their investments in themselves, but instead are leading us into "growing economic insecurity, low pro-ductivity, diminished autonomy and worrying levels of personal debt" (Fleming, 2017, p. 691). Unfortunately, advanced technology may be compounding inequalities by diminishing the sort of time available for work that might be needed to support high-quality and creative colla-boration, such that averting an 'endtime' futuristic doomsday scenario will require policies that restore time for reflection and less detached social interactions (Jarvenpaa & Valikangas, 2020).

These high-level dystopian narratives are inherently gloomy, but more work linking them more specifically to diversity might restore some hope and agency, although there needs to be real urgency and engagement for a positive and timely impact, one suspects. For instance, women are disappearing from software development in Europe and the US, and we need to urgently understand the masculine discourses that exclude them if we are to prevent a future where the algorithms and software which affect us are not written and developed by a diverse and inclusive community of professionals (Tassabehji, Harding, Lee, & Dominguez-Pery, 2020). To mention science fiction again, this emphasis on tech-nology and the future reconnects with the twentieth century feminist dystopias of writers such as Marge Piercy, which put dystopias and utopias in dialogue with one another according to freedom from gender stratifications and how technology is contested and diversified (Booker, 1994). From some feminist perspectives, the relative patriarchal dom-inance, commodification, and gendering of parenthood, surrogacy, and family itself represents a dystopia, to be overthrown by manifestoes that make caring for all children a more inclusive and collective responsibility (Gatto, 2020; Lewis, 2019).

Where race relations and organizations are concerned, what dystopias reveal are the mythical, zero-sum deadlocks that sustain racism and end up hurting everyone. This is one message behind *Noughts & Crosses,* a series of young adult novels by British author Malorie Blackman, which portray an inverted world ruled by Black people and sub-Saharan African culture, where white Europeans are the ones being colonized and oppressed in their work and lives (Thompson, 2020). These alternate realities and speculative fictions challenge us to wake up to racism – and the duty of care to address it and choose anti-racism – by presenting it in a surprising form that is nevertheless familiar and tragic in its irrational hatred and tribal psychology (Thompson, 2020). Similarly, black people suffer disproportionately from police violence but so do poor working-class white people – and the democratic and organizing dilemma becomes how to build solidarity across common threats to both, where so many forces would see them divided (Rothman & Fields, 2020).

In 2020, the COVID-19 pandemic has the potential to trigger some fresh and renewed bouts of interest in dystopia and inequalities. In this regard, a final important function of dystopia should be emphasized here – the focusing of attention on the 'strange tales' of those who are always already most vulnerable and worst affected, already living in a dystopia regardless of whether, how, or when it might be arriving for the rest of us (Saraiva & Vinholi Rampazo, 2020). This refers to the modern slavery of millions of women and other minority workers worldwide, enmeshed in an abject necropolitics where their bodies are denied a more dignified existence and who are simply expected to be more likely to die at and in their work (Caruana, Crane, Gold, & LeBaron, 2020; Crane, 2013; Saraiva & Vinholi Rampazo, 2020). It is hard to imagine a more vivid and harsh dystopia than that.

Heterotopias

As well as utopias and dystopias, the concept of heterotopia(s) also bears some consideration here, although it is generally a less commonly used term than the other two, and perhaps more rooted in the present than the future. Heterotopias also tend to have even stronger spatial and geographical connotations that relate back to an earlier chapter of this book (see Chapter 10).

However, heterotopias are nevertheless concerned with alternative spaces of difference, where the unifying power of Western modernity gives way to a more accepting and playful view of scattered fragments, less optimistic than utopias but less pessimistic than dystopias (Jacques, 2002). Exploring heterotopias is also proposed as a key method or tactic of critical performativity in organization studies – exploring other places for being and doing things differently, deviating from what is considered normal or unitary with more or less realized alternatives, and a touch of struggle and realism (Spicer et al., 2009).

Heterotopias as a concept originate with Foucault but have various creative and artistic connotations of radical otherness. In critical terms, entrepreneurship and playful creativity in everyday practices can be thought of as creating heterotopias or spaces for play in ways that temporarily transform work activities and surprise management, not unlike children playing in an office, breaking the monotony and sameness of a working day (Hjorth, 2005). Geographers can find Foucault's original treatment of the concept confusing and frustrating, but 'heterotopias of difference' remain a way for diversity to critically reassert itself with alternative orders of crisis and deviance in public spaces and cities - such as the Sunday congregations of Filipina maids in the business plazas of Hong Kong (Cenzatti, 2008).

A strength of heterotopias for showing us futures of diversity and organization is their distinctive aesthetic – redistributing existing places, identities and capacities, including those of work, such that they are open to enjoyment and use in undisciplined and thought-provoking ways (Rancière, 2010). Where utopias and dystopias are more unitary and absolute to a degree, heterotopian understandings remind us that organizations are 'imperfect Pantopicons'; they do not exert total control over time/space and offer more complex, ambiguous, and pragmatic realities for thinking/acting differently (Cairns, McInnes, & Roberts, 2003). While we cannot change the world, we can create and tend diverse gardens together. In this respect, Steyaert (2010) shows how sexual minorities 'queer' sexual spaces through heterotopological practices, using the example of the artist Derek Jarman, whose garden and gardening acted as a transitional space and project for dealing with his HIV and continuing to sharpen his queer activism and politics with new connections.

Indeed, although heterotopias can be sketchy in spatio-temporal terms and bewildering in their diversity, they insist on making difference in spaces, showing us the local and multifaceted geographical organizing of diversity – gardens, museums, architecture, landscapes, installations, malls, cemeteries, temples, ships, and camps being just some examples (Johnson, 2013). Heterotopias are vulnerable to critique in terms of how they account for the relations between the totality of space-time and its multiple, uneven and changing properties (Saldanha, 2008). However, at the same time, we might not be too hindered by this critique, given that, as in Johnson's (2013) persuasive concluding phrase, heterotopias "have no axe to grind, just scissors to cut" (p. 800).

To the extent that there are new sites to occupy and new sights to see, heterotopias help us to see the diverse spaces where the contingent and improvisational breaching of norms and assumptions concerning organizational space-time tend to take place (O'Doherty, De Cock, Rehn, & Ashcraft, 2013). This includes unchartered territories of organization beyond western imperial ambition, and unconventional but influential topics such as children and childhood, rogue states, refugee camps, bland spaces of mundanity, buildings that 'speak' and dreams of travel and mobility (O'Doherty et al., 2013).

Despite its fairly significant use across disciplines, it seems safe to say that the concept of heterotopias and its potential value remain under-explored and under-utilized in management and organization studies. In their review, Bazin and Naccache (2016) argue it has value as a heuristic concept for understanding non-hegemonic areas that can signify exclusion but question the domination of modern globalized capitalism, such as the social movements that take place in global cities, entrepreneurial innovations serving communities, and other hidden spaces in organizations. Social movements in particular suggest various forms of heterotopia – contained, mobile, virtual, encounters, self-organizing – that challenge routine politics by doing things that are 'wrong' from the perspectives of the state and capital (Beckett, Bagguley, & Campbell, 2017).

At a more intimate level, diverse individuals can be said to experience heterotopias as a form of self-transformation, where thought and self-hood dissolve and rupture to a degree, giving way to feelings of groundlessness and moral-psychological change (Locke, 2020). While it is important not to idealize heterotopias as always giving rise to triumphant sites of freedom and liberation, we need to understand how they might represent sites of organizing whereby diversity can escape harmful forms of power and move towards inclusion (Beckett et al., 2017).

In research to date, there are not many cumulative or connected organizational examples of diversity and heterotopias. Meininger (2013) outlines how we can think of social spaces of encounter and dialogue between people with and without intellectual disability in everyday life as heterotopias, because they represent niches for possible inclusion and alternative social ordering of relations. One advantage of this is it shifts focus beyond the unhelpful building up and tearing down of utopian/dystopian institutional spaces such as care residences, apart from 'normal' life, and toward the normalizing attitudes and structures that sustain exclusion (Meininger, 2013). This turns inclusion into more of a journey; starting from familiar surroundings and moving toward a more uncertain future (Meininger, 2013).

Other examples tend to involve educational settings and spaces as heterotopias for diversity and inclusion concerns. Gender studies classrooms at Canadian universities, for example, function as heterotopic 'other places' from which to reflect, challenge, and view differently the 'regular places' outside of the academy, rendering power and identity dynamics more visible through the student experience (Kannen, 2014). In management education and business schools, Foucault can be combined with Lefebvre to reflect on experimental, heterotopological teaching projects and practices as spatial interventions, where students use their imaginations to critically produce future cities and organizational spaces that wrestle with inclusion, encounters, and connections (Beyes & Michels, 2011). However, although independent universities can be thought of us heterotopic spaces (e.g. ivory towers), they are also heteronomic spaces (e.g. sites of neoliberal entrepreneurship), and these strategies intermingle in relation to the performativity surrounding other discourses and counterdiscourses, such as academic excellence and gender equality (Wieners & Weber, 2020).

In a relatively unusual development of heterotopic thinking, and in an organizational setting rather than an educational one, Vidaillet and Bousalham (2020) studied several coworking spaces in France and Belgium occupied by diverse professionals, entrepreneurs, freelancers, and self-employed individuals. They developed the novel concept of 'syntopia' to better capture how these spaces actually play an active role in articulating, integrating, and arranging the economic diversity that characterizes a 'post capitalocentric' economy, where diverse actors follow values and logics that diverge from private accumulation and profit maximization (Vidaillet & Bousalham, 2020). In this way, today's heterotopias could be tomorrow's more inclusive and egalitarian syntopias.

The Future of Diverse and Diversity Futures

There are many general ideas around how we imagine diverse futures, alternatives, and utopian, dystopian, and heterotopian possibilities relating to equality, diversity, and inclusion. However, some further future directions for continuing to build on and extend notions of diverse futures for diversity can also be highlighted.

One is simply to keep imagining what these futures may or may not look like, and the implications that follow from such exercises. Hearn (2014b) proposes various future scenarios for gender, sexualities and organizational forms, based on evolutions of patriarchy and late capitalism, as well as the impact of globalization and socio-technologies, on convergence, divergence, blurring, differentiation, and (in)equalities. Organizations also have a moral and ethical responsibility to future generations as intergenerational diversity extends into the future, shaping debates around finite energy sources and biodiversity, although present governments and markets are not always best placed to protect these future interests from threats and inequalities (Jeurissen & Keijzers, 2004). Large shareholder-owner corporations are gradually declining in the twenty-first century and giving rise to a more diverse range of low-cost, small-scale and technologically-supported alternatives that can be considered more local, democratic, and non-corporate in how they deliver products and services (Davis, 2016). However, this does present decoupling challenges, where policies and practices and means and ends become more characterized by gaps and disconnects from influences of monitoring and evaluation (Bromley & Powell, 2012).

Diversity and inequalities reveal the big problems big organizations and capitalism have both contributed to and been unable to fully solve.

Thus, the future fate of organizational diversity is tied to the notion of alternative economic futures, with socioeconomic structures that better support human flourishing and address problems of market competition, wage employment, levels of government involvement and forms of ownership and governance (Adler, 2016). Sadly, these are familiar and persistent problems but appear with a renewed sense of urgency across multiple progressive management agendas. Another example is the calls for management to understand and tackle 'grand challenges', which invariably involve global inequalities and instabilities associated with diversity and organizational forms (George, Howard-Grenville, Joshi, & Tihanyi, 2016).

Critical organizational scholars are perhaps more forthright in declaring agendas based on post-capitalist and anti-capitalist politics, which is crucial for encouraging forms of imaginary and praxis that challenge how the dark side of capitalism oppresses forms of diversity (Zanoni, Contu, Healy, & Mir, 2017). An immanent post-capitalist future can be understood in relation to a longer-term anti-capitalist horizon, with the 'de-mediation' of social relations revealing and calling into question the locations of crises and struggles of political economy (Zanoni, 2020). These de-mediations of market, state, wages, value, money, and class represent possibilities for alternative values and economic relations. A key shift for diversity lies in futures that promote alternative ideas of caring that are not based simply on autonomy, responsibility, capability, and merit but frame caring in terms of equality and justice by sharpening criticism of prevailing conditions and uncaring futures (Aulenbacher & Riegraf, 2018). Then there are complex public policy experiments around making 'universal' care and living standards as truly equal and free in supporting organizing and work as possible. These include the universal basic income (UBI) idea of unconditional welfare payment systems (D'Mello, 2019), and compulsory universal unionization to establish more basic safeguards and 'floors' for protecting employee rights, below which employers cannot sink (Reiff, 2020).

The future of diversity and technology is also intertwined, not least because the big technology companies such as those in Silicon Valley keep vowing to diversify their workforces but have shown dismal track records and failings to date (Banjo & Bass, 2020). Artificial intelligence (AI) and algorithms in organizations – running on software devised largely by relatively homogeneous men – are an emerging phenomenon for future research (Von Krogh, 2018). These technological systems are troubled by bad press stories of systems biased against diversity, and only time will tell whether interested change agents and stakeholders can steer them toward acceptable transparency and the promotion of diversity and inclusion (Daugherty, Wilson, & Chowdhury, 2019; Miller, Katz, & Gans, 2018).

In terms of job losses, organization studies suggest that robots, AI, and automation will not lead to a mass disappearance of jobs but are more likely to produce 'bounded automation', eroding skills, pay, and responsibilities in a myriad of partial socio-organizational ways, which will require communities to address social justice concerns (Fleming, 2019b). Specific organizational products such as sex robots raise feminist concerns over how they appear to reinforce male domination in ways similar to slavery and prostitution, although feminist new materialist readings suggest queer, liberated alternatives if diverse design options and inclusive design decisions are supported (Kubes, 2019).

A full discussion of environmentalist futures is beyond the scope of this book, but as our shared home, the future of the planet has considerable utopian/dystopian implications for how any environmental crises and initiatives might affect groups and minorities unequally around the world and over time. Planetary-scale efforts such as geoengineering involve collective but controversial attempts to imagine distant futures, with imaginaries developing through the critiques and alternatives of diverse engagements, which can affect the moral convictions, worldviews, concreteness, and credibility attached to them as 'as if' futures (Augustine, Soderstrom, Milner, & Weber, 2019). The sustainable development goals are a huge potential rallying point for organized diversity and inclusion efforts at the global level, although efforts need to be coordinated and directed judiciously at so-called 'Goldilocks' problems, making genuine progress with problems neither too big nor too small (Howard-Grenville et al., 2019). In addition, the growing congestion of large urban environments is suggestive of the need to pay greater attention to how they interface with rural communities and diverse forms of rural entrepreneurship and organization, which "hold rich promise for deeper, more inclusive and diversified understandings of...space, time, values, sociality, and communities" (Hunt, Townsend, Korsgaard, & Naar, 2020, p. 16).

Whichever aspects of diverse futures are under discussion, we might do well to ask how such futures will be minority-led or minority-organized. Women professionals working in information and communications technology sectors are embedded in wider discourses of skills shortages and gender imbalances in late modern society, and concerned with problematizing gendered futures, anticipating challenges and opportunities (Moore, Griffiths, Richardson, & Adam, 2008). Imagining new feminist futures through contemporary feminist social movements and CSR means resisting cooptation by corporate, neoliberal, and privatized agendas and reconnecting with wider social change programmes, taking advantage of distinct political opportunities, elite allies, and NGO tactics for contesting more establishment interests and power relations (Grosser & McCarthy, 2019).

Afrofuturist feminism suggests progressive and transgressive futures where black feminist identities and diasporic relationships are central to "critiquing conventional systems of power and dominance and offering futurist solutions based on cooperation and egalitarian ethics" (Morris, 2012, p. 155). Disability and disabled futures are ones in which there is "broader collective access to resources and alternate understandings of bodies and ability" (Obourn, 2013, p. 109). These futures can also be described as "dis-topias" based not on progress, but on new pathways for living, uncovered not through evoking the familiar imaginaries of curing, eliminating, or overcoming disability but through incorporating experiences of embodied difference into time" (Rice et al., 2017, p. 213). If diversity is to have a future, diverse voices need to be allowed to imagine, embody, re-story, and reorganize their futures as more livable places, drawing on their own distinct histories, legacies, and struggles in the present (Rice et al., 2017).

Finally, diverse futures of diversity in organizations will probably be underpinned by different futures for disciplines, methods, practices and learning experiences. The idea that organizations should be fascinated about imagining and shaping indeterminate futures is a relatively modern one. There is a shift afoot from the organizational adoption of fairly conservative planning practices toward more problematizing, open-ended 'future-making' practices in relation to "prevalent discourses such as climate change, digital transformation, and post-truth politics" (Wenzel, Krämer, Koch, & Reckwitz, 2020, p. 1).

For the study of how organizational actors produce and enact futures to connect with diversity, it needs to be practised in conjunction with inclusive notions of learning with and through difference. Ethnographic reading, writing, and research as 'alterethnography' is one way to achieve this – a method that breaks with dominant scientific practice and the authorial ego to radically and reflexively "embrace otherness as to-getherness" (Ericsson & Kostera, 2020, p. 2). Such a project is inherently nonconformist and difficult to define and imagine under traditional realist and scientific paradigms but is suggestive of the kind of bold, transgressive moves needed for researchers to break with linear, patri-archal, and repressive modes of knowledge production and envisage the messy Otherness of diverse futures (Ericsson & Kostera, 2020; Wenzel et al., 2020).

This also corresponds to the ongoing calls to reimagine management education, such that future managers will be able to experience and experiment with intervening in everyday life more creatively and spon-taneously, paying more attention to atmospheres of difference and in-equality (Michels, Hindley, Knowles & Ruth, 2020). To do this, habits need to be broken, and managers need to wander around as strangers and encounter organizational environments more sensuously and visc-erally – their boundaries and constraints, their routines and alternatives (Michels et al., 2020). Again, perhaps this is hard to imagine by com-parison with the intense, techno-bureaucratic work of much management today, but this is precisely what makes it more alive and meaningful to difference and futures.

Conclusion

This chapter has surveyed a loose array of critical organizational work on connected themes of imagination, futures, alternatives, and types of 'space' where diversity and difference might be lived and experienced very differently, in and around (future) organizations. Sometimes these topics are inherently far-reaching and speculative, and they are not always concretely related to issues of difference, equality, and inclusion in organizations. However, in many ways they bring this book full circle, returning to a sense of urgency around the types of paradigm and perspective needed to resolve crises of diversity as they extend across the temporal imagination and a sense of past, present and future.

There is much doubt around how positivistic, scientistic understandings of diversity alone can bring about better futures and organizations for the many, or even help to fend off disastrous and oppressive ones. This is not just around particular methods and techniques but also social scientific institutions such as academic journals, which could themselves improve in future by addressing inconsistencies and inequalities in their editing, reviewing, and writing practices (Starbuck, 2016). There are scholars who would contend that the discipline and field is in crisis, sustained in many cases by a pretence of doing important work while truly important issues and the purpose of advancing knowledge are neglected (Tourish, 2020). These debates are likely to continue through the very same problematic frameworks and practices that are themselves being debated, but they will affect critical and mainstream scholars alike to a degree and may provide opportunities for new alliances to flourish, with diversity being part of the solution rather than part of the problem.

Hopefully, some of the pessimism is offset by a growing awareness of the need for egalitarian, diverse alternatives and change processes. Those in business schools seeking to provide a new model based on the public good, for example, can engage systemic, institutional change by being part of an iterative process, highlighting new directions informed by substantive and purposeful values (Kitchener & Delbridge, 2020). Critical perspectives on diversity in organizations can and should feed into such processes. Furthermore, and although troubling in some respects and more reactive than proactive in the responses generated, a sense of crisis may act as an external shock and trigger for more positive and necessary change. The language of the 'Anthropocene' places human activities and business interests at the heart of a crisis of planetary disruption, underpinned by profound cycles of inclusion and exclusion, necessitating new, less anthropocentric forms of imagination and reasoning in order to slow down or break such harmful cycles (Gasparin et al., 2020). In turn, the Corona crisis and global pandemic engendered by the spread of the COVID-19 virus has also thrown the role of organizations in society and societal economic inequality into sharp relief, making a 'societal turn' or the 'societalization' of mainstream management something more acknowledged than before (Bapuji, Patel, Ertug, & Allen, 2020; Brammer, Branicki, & Linnenluecke, 2020).

In part, these responses seem to reflect a struggle to hold critical social scientific and sociological work together with the mainstream of management, with broader crises calling previously separate logics, codes, and boundaries into question in a battle for civil reforms and reconfigured cultural and institutional spheres of life (Alexander, 2018). A similar point might be made with respect to the relationship between diversity and technology, as it appeared in this chapter. A plethora of advanced technological shifts – broadly captured by AI, automation, the gig economy, and the digital transformation of business strategies – is looking increasingly likely to shake up how different groups of diversity scholars and employees frame and define the effects of digital inequalities and technologically inflected group representation (Ozkazanc-Pan, 2019; Schneider & Sting, 2019).

Finally, this chapter also contained suggestions of what the character of future theories and perspectives on diversity and organization might be like. A realization that the future may be unknowable and that progress towards it is not very consciously or rationally directed can prompt a look to the margins, such as systems psychodynamic perspectives, where the oppressed and repressed aspects of organizations are denied but resurface, revealing the persistence of dysfunctional and stifling problems (Petriglieri & Petriglieri, 2020). Rationality in its utility-driven, mass commodified form can be re-radicalized by re-introducing a sense of epistemological doubt, which in turn can be ethically and politically mobilized to ensure critical thinking and a questioning of majority or exclusionary visions of progress and future (Landfester & Metelmann, 2020). Irrationality is also being confronted more directly in theories of organizational paradoxes, although it is often minorities or those with less power who end up being trapped in a paradox, as imposed on them in particular organizational situations where they can neither fully obey nor resist (Berti & Simpson, 2020).

Linking the present to the future with theory that is engaged with societal problem-solving and practical relevance requires drawing on institutionalist and pragmatist strains in combination. This integrative approach links the descriptive and the normative, by showing the empirical reality while also morally reflecting on how things could/should be valued differently (Risi, 2020). Another way to do this is to contrast conventional managerial and capitalist organizations with alternative anarchist and anti-capitalist ones, to show that the latter are not impossible and can be called organizations, with once again the more diverse and egalitarian hopes critically self-organizing from the margins (Reedy, 2020). Ultimately, questions of organizational futures and diversity rest on collective exercises in hope and imagination, but rather than abstract fantasies and nightmares, they need to be stories that feel real and generative, precisely so that diverse futures can be rebuilt, reclaimed, and repurposed, by the diverse people empowered to imagine them (Parker, 2020).

Concluding Remarks

It seems fair to say that this book has privileged breadth over depth in surveying research and writing on diversity in organizations, but this was largely the intention, so that two main meta-theoretical contributions could be made. First, a key aim was to present some of the distinctions and tensions between more 'mainstream' (e.g. psychological, managerial, positivist) and more 'critical' (e.g. sociological, emancipatory, social constructionist) perspectives on diversity in organizations. Second, a further aim was to present a range of specific critical concepts and approaches to understanding diversity in organizations across an array of subsequent chapters.

Ideally, these two main contributions should play a modest role in shaping future research and practice on diversity and organizations. In the first instance, this might be in terms of how self-defined critical and mainstream scholars and stakeholders relate to one another, perhaps with some greater engagement over mutual limitations, overlaps, and complementarities. In the second instance, this might be in terms of how scholars and stakeholders continue to deploy and develop some of the agendas of some of the chapters in this book in international, interdisciplinary, innovative, and inclusive combinations.

This book is very different from many existing books on diversity and organizations that might focus on specific disciplines, theories, contexts, laws, practices, policies, and axes of difference. It can be painful trying to incorporate and address so much valid work on diversity and equality while inevitably having to make some omissions in failing to pick up specific topics and issues in more detail. However, the chapters should represent insightful currents of critical thought that can continue to be applied to more specific concerns. In various ways, the chapters also underscore the interdisciplinary importance of the arts, humanities, and social sciences in constituting critical perspectives on diversity in organizations. Indeed, one great opportunity arising from the critical perspectives covered in this book is the opportunity to read and practice 'diversity' and 'organization' through diverse disciplinary, conceptual and topical lenses and concerns.

Underlying almost all of the material in this book is the weighty philosophical dialectic between diversity and sameness, or difference and identity, and how that is understood, experienced, and enacted in organizations in innumerable ways. In turn, critical perspectives provide various ways of making us more aware of these tensions between sameness and difference, and how to reflect on them and act on them to secure greater equality and inclusion, despite how difficult and contingent it can seem. This notion of sameness and diversity is heavily implied within and across the mainstream and critical perspectives themselves, as presented over the course of the chapters. To a significant extent, the future of universities and business schools rests on how they encourage dynamic organizing and reflecting for addressing societal diversity, ethically and politically. In addition, a spectrum of political positions across left, center, and right continues to exert a constitutive influence on academic and organizational subjectivities. If researchers and organizations are to reckon with the diversity of which they are a part, they must renew their efforts to critically attend to concepts such as ideology, reflexivity, evidence, practice, and impact.

Critical perspectives on diversity in organizations tend to bring philosophy, politics, sociology, and culture more systematically to bear on the subject and its contextualization than mainstream perspectives, but this on its own is not the whole story. There is a healthy pluralism and variety of critical approaches in evidence, but efforts to work through conflicts and to mediate and consolidate proliferating critical positions and projects are still needed to build solidarity and social change beyond academic communities themselves. As critical schools of thought on diversity and organization continue to evolve, we can expect them to continue to surprise and engage us in diverse ways, while reminding us to stay vigilant and responsive to their many layers, limits, and contradictions. Therapeutic solutions, activist solutions, pedagogical solutions, performative solutions, arts-based solutions, and anti-capitalist solutions are just some of the avenues touched upon in this book. These agendas exist alongside more intellectual exercises of deconstruction and phenomenology, as well as more materialist struggles for social justice relating to political economy and inequalities.

It will be vital and interesting to see how critical diversity scholarship continues to engage crises and challenges across organizations and societies in the next decade and generation of research and practice. There is the challenge of speaking to the complex global systems of multiple, differentiated institutions and regimes of inequality that do not accord straightforwardly with the notion of discrete nation-states (Walby, 2020). There is the challenge of how critical scholars can engage strategically with more mainstream organizational stances – such as essentialism and the business case – to achieve more accepted change through practical engagement with those stances (Prasad, 2012; Rhodes, 2017).

We might also expect and hope for increasing integration and re-conciliation between decades of critical management studies, pragmatist and business ethics research, where issues around capitalism, diversity, and inequality are clearly common concerns (Prasad & Mills, 2010; Visser, 2019). In an era of post-truth politics and the conspiracies and polarization that can accompany that, we need to ask what constitutes effective platforms for democratic debate and critique on diversity, such that affective communities can come together and change each other's minds on highly contested issues (Baird & Calvard, 2019; Parker & Racz, 2020). When working with minorities and diverse communities, critical researchers are encouraged to practice 'reflexive theorizing' by weaving together discursive practices in ways that change how we have conversations for change between Self and Other and mutual recognition of difference (Cutcher, Hardy, Riach, & Thomas, 2020). This helps to avoid "people talking past each other and, in doing so, excluding countless others from the conversation...different discursive practices... open conversations up to a wider range of voices, where respect and generosity are evident and where forms of knowledge emerge in dia-logue" (Cutcher et al., 2020, p. 16).

These questions of how to carry out critical diversity research in or-ganizations, and the associated challenges and outcomes, continue to be asked and answered in fruitful ways. The future of critical diversity scholarship has the potential to be more evidence-based, engaged, and relational, focused on "mutual co-construction, equal partnerships and reciprocation between researchers, practitioners and the community (researched), and the fusion of methodologies and paradigms" (Bleijenbergh, Booysen, & Mills, 2018, p. 214). The hope is that this book can play its part in helping advance some of these worthy con-cluding aims and futures.

References

Abreu-Pederzini, G. D., & Suárez-Barraza, M. F. (2020). Just let us be: Domination, the postcolonial condition, and the global field of business schools. *Academy of Management Learning & Education, 19*(1), 40–58. doi: 10.5465/amle.2018.0116.

Acker, J. (1990). Hierarchies, jobs, bodies: A theory of gendered organizations. *Gender & Society, 4*(2), 139–158. doi: 10.1177/089124390004002002.

Acker, J. (2012). Gendered organizations and intersectionality: Problems and possibilities. *Equality, Diversity and Inclusion: An International Journal, 31*(3), 214–224. doi: 10.1108/02610151211209072.

Adam, I., & Rea, A. (2018). The three "i" s of workplace accommodation of Muslim religious practices: Instrumental, internal, and informal. *Ethnic and Racial Studies, 41*(15), 2711–2730. doi: 10.1080/01419870.2017.1409430.

Adamson, M. (2014). Reflexivity and the construction of competing discourses of masculinity in a female-dominated profession. *Gender, Work & Organization, 21*(6), 559–572. doi: 10.1111/gwao.12058.

Adamson, M., & Johansson, M. (2016). Compositions of professionalism in counselling work: An embodied and embedded intersectionality framework. *Human Relations, 69*(12), 2201–2223. doi: 10.1177/0018726716639118.

Adewunmi, B. (2014, April 2). *Kimberlé Crenshaw on intersectionality: "I wanted to come up with an everyday metaphor that anyone could use"*. New Statesman. Retrieved from https://www.newstatesman.com/lifestyle/2014/04/kimberl-crenshaw-intersectionality-i-wanted-come-everyday-metaphor-anyone-could.

Adler, N. J. (1983). Organizational development in a multicultural environment. *The Journal of Applied Behavioral Science, 19*(3), 349–365. doi: 10.1177/002188638301900311.

Adler, P. S. (2007). The future of critical management studies: A paleo-Marxist critique of labour process theory. *Organization Studies, 28*(9), 1313–1345. doi: 10.1177/0170840607080743.

Adler, P. S. (2016). Alternative economic futures: A research agenda for progressive management scholarship. *Academy of Management Perspectives, 30*(2), 123–128. doi: 10.5465/amp.2016.0054.

Adler, P. S., Forbes, L. C., & Willmott, H. (2007). Critical management studies. *The Academy of Management Annals, 1*(1), 119–179. doi: 10.1080/078559808.

Agar, C. C., & Manolchev, C. (2020). Migrant labour as space: Rhythm analysing the agri-food industry. *Organization, 27*(2), 251–271. doi: 10.1177/1350508419883379.

Agocs, C. (1997). Institutionalized resistance to organizational change: Denial, inaction and repression. *Journal of Business Ethics, 16*(9), 917–931. doi: 10.1023/A:1017939404578.

Ahmed, S. (2007). 'You end up doing the document rather than doing the doing': Diversity, race equality and the politics of documentation. *Ethnic and Racial Studies, 30*(4), 590–609. doi: 10.1080/01419870701356015.

Ahmed, S. (2012). *On being included: Racism and diversity in institutional life.* Durham, NC: Duke University Press.

Ahmed, S., & Swan, E. (2006). Doing diversity work'. *Policy Futures in Education, 4*(2), 1–10. doi: 10.2304/pfie.2006.4.2.96.

Ahonen, P., & Tienari, J. (2009). United in diversity? Disciplinary normalization in an EU project. *Organization, 16*(5), 655–679. doi: 10.1177/1350508409338434.

Ahonen, P., Tienari, J., Meriläinen, S., & Pullen, A. (2014). Hidden contexts and invisible power relations: A Foucauldian reading of diversity research. *Human Relations, 67*(3), 263–286. doi: 10.1177/0018726713491772.

Ailon, G., & Kunda, G. (2009). The one-company approach': Transnationalism in an Israeli—Palestinian subsidiary of a multinational corporation. *Organization Studies, 30*(7), 693–712. doi: 10.1177/0170840609104808.

Ainsworth, S., & Hardy, C. (2004). Critical discourse analysis and identity: Why bother? *Critical Discourse Studies, 1*(2), 225–259. doi: 10.1080/17405900042000302085.

Ainsworth, S., Knox, A., & O'Flynn, J. (2010). 'A blinding lack of progress': Management rhetoric and affirmative action. *Gender, Work & Organization, 17*(6), 658–678. doi: 10.1111/j.1468-0432.2009.00479.x.

Al Ariss, A., Özbilgin, M., Tatli, A., & April, K. (2014). Tackling whiteness in organizations and management. *Journal of Managerial Psychology, 29*(4), 362–369. doi: 10.1108/JMP-10-2013-0331.

Alexander, J. C. (2018). The societalization of social problems: Church pedophilia, phone hacking, and the financial crisis. *American Sociological Review, 83*(6), 1049–1078. doi: 10.1177/0003122418803376.

Alexander-Floyd, N. G. (2012). Disappearing Acts: Reclaiming Intersectionality in the Social Sciences in a Post—Black Feminist Era. *Feminist Formations, 24*(1), 1–25. doi: 10.1353/ff.2012.0003.

Allard-Poesi, F. (2005). The paradox of sensemaking in organizational analysis. *Organization, 12*(2), 169–196. doi: 10.1177/1350508405051187.

Allen, N. J., Stanley, D. J., Williams, H. M., & Ross, S. J. (2007). Assessing the impact of nonresponse on work group diversity effects. *Organizational Research Methods, 10*(2), 262–286. doi: 10.1177/1094428106/294731.

Allison, R., & Banerjee, P. (2014). Intersectionality and social location in organization studies, 1990-2009. *Race, Gender & Class, 21*(3/4), 67–87.

Alonso González, P. (2016). The organization of commemorative space in postcolonial Cuba: From Civic Square to Square of the Revolution. *Organization, 23*(1), 47–70. doi: 10.1177/1350508415605100.

Al-Rasheed, M. (2013). *A most masculine state: Gender, politics and religion in Saudi Arabia.* Cambridge, UK: Cambridge University Press.

Altermark, N. (2017). The post-institutional era: Visions of history in research on intellectual disability. *Disability & Society, 32*(9), 1315–1332. doi: 10. 1080/09687599.2017.1322497.

Al-Tuwalah, A. (2017, May 9). *Girl drives minibus to save driver's life.* Saudi Gazette. Retrieved from http://saudigazette.com.sa/saudi-arabia/girl-drives-minibus-save-drivers-life/.

Alvesson, M. (2010). Self-doubters, strugglers, storytellers, surfers and others: Images of self-identities in organization studies. *Human Relations, 63*(2), 193–217. doi: 10.1177/0018726709350372.

Alvesson, M., & Billing, Y. D. (1992). Gender and organization: Towards a differentiated understanding. *Organization Studies, 13*(1), 73–103. doi: 10. 1177/017084069201300107.

Alvesson, M., & Gabriel, Y. (2013). Beyond formulaic research: In praise of greater diversity in organizational research and publications. *Academy of Management Learning & Education, 12*(2), 245–263. doi: 10.5465/amle.2012.0327.

Alvesson, M., & Kärreman, D. (2000). Varieties of discourse: On the study of organizations through discourse analysis. *Human Relations, 53*(9), 1125–1149. doi: 10.1177/0018726700539002.

Alvesson, M., & Kärreman, D. (2007). Constructing mystery: Empirical matters in theory development. *Academy of Management Review, 32*(4), 1265–1281. doi: 10.5465/AMR.2007.26586822.

Alvesson, M., & Kärreman, D. (2011). Decolonializing discourse: Critical reflections on organizational discourse analysis. *Human Relations, 64*(9), 1121–1146. doi: 10.1177/0018726711408629.

Alvesson, M., & Spicer, A. (2012). A stupidity-based theory of organizations. *Journal of Management Studies, 49*(7), 1194–1220. doi: 10.1111/j.1467-6486.2012.01072.x.

Alvesson, M., & Spicer, A. (2018). *Neo-institutional theory and organization studies: A mid-life crisis? Organization Studies,* Online First. doi: 10.1177/ 0170840618772610.

Alvesson, M., & Willmott, H. (1992). On the idea of emancipation in management and organization studies. *Academy of Management Review, 17*(3), 432–464. doi: 10.5465/amr.1992.4281977.

Amin, A. (2004). Multi-ethnicity and the idea of Europe. *Theory, Culture & Society, 21*(2), 1–24. doi: 10.1177/0263276404042132.

Amis, J. M., Mair, J., & Munir, K. A. (2020). The organizational reproduction of inequality. *Academy of Management Annals, 14*(1), 195–230. doi: 10.5465/ annals.2017.0033.

Amis, J. M., Munir, K. A., Lawrence, T. B., Hirsch, P., & McGahan, A. (2018). Inequality, institutions and organizations. *Organization Studies, 39*(9), 1131–1152. doi: 10.1177/0170840618792596.

Anand, R., & Winters, M. F. (2008). A retrospective view of corporate diversity training from 1964 to the present. *Academy of Management Learning & Education, 7*(3), 356–372. doi: 10.5465/AMLE.2008.34251673.

André, R. (1995). Diversity stress as morality stress. *Journal of Business Ethics, 14*(6), 489–496. doi: 10.1007/BF00872089.

Anthias, F. (1999). Institutional racism, power and accountability. *Sociological Research Online, 4*(1), 1–9. doi: 10.5153/sro.239.

Anthony, B. M. (1980). Parallels, particularities, problems and positive possibilities related to institutional sexism and racism. *Women's Studies International Quarterly, 3*(4), 339–346. doi: 10.1016/S0148-0685(80)91058-1.

Arekapudi, N. (2018, May 9). *Over 100 countries still bar women from working in specific jobs*. LSE Business Review. Retrieved from http://blogs.lse.ac.uk/businessreview/2018/05/09/over-100-countries-still-bar-women-from-working-in-specific-jobs/.

Aromaa, E., Eriksson, P., Mills, J. H., Hiltunen, E., Lammassaari, M., & Mills, A. J. (2019). Critical sensemaking: Challenges and promises. *Qualitative Research in Organizations and Management: An International Journal, 14*(3), 356–376. doi: 10.1108/QROM-05-2018-1645.

Ashcraft, K. (2000). Empowering "professional" relationships: Organizational communication meets feminist practice. *Management Communication Quarterly, 13*(3), 347–392. doi: 10.1177/0893318900133001.

Ashcraft, K. L. (2018). Critical complicity: The feel of difference at work in home and field. *Management Learning, 49*(5), 613–623. doi: 10.1177/1350507618774151.

Ashcraft, K., & Allen, B. J. (2003). The racial foundation of organizational communication. *Communication Theory, 13*(1), 5–38. doi: 10.1111/j.1468-2885.2003.tb00280.x.

Ashcraft, K. L., Kuhn, T. R., & Cooren, F. (2009). Constitutional amendments: "Materializing" organizational communication. *Academy of Management Annals, 3*(1), 1–64. doi: 10.5465/19416520903047186.

Ashley, L. (2010). Making a difference? The use (and abuse) of diversity management at the UK's elite law firms. *Work, Employment and Society, 24*(4), 711–727. doi: 10.1177/0950017010380639.

Ashley, L., & Empson, L. (2013). Differentiation and discrimination: Understanding social class and social exclusion in leading law firms. *Human Relations, 66*(2), 219–244. doi: 10.1177/0018726712455833.

Atewologun, D. and Sealy, R. (2014). Experiencing privilege at ethnic, gender and senior intersections. *Journal of Managerial Psychology, 29*(4), 423–439. doi: 10.1108/JMP-02-2013-0038.

Augustine, G., Soderstrom, S., Milner, D., & Weber, K. (2019). Constructing a distant future: Imaginaries in geoengineering. *Academy of Management Journal, 62*(6), 1930–1960. doi: 10.5465/amj.2018.0059.

Aulenbacher, B., & Riegraf, B. (2018). Between dystopias and alternative ideas of caring. *Equality, Diversity and Inclusion: An International Journal, 37*(4), 314–317. doi: 10.1108/EDI-03-2018-0048.

Aydin, E., & Colgan, F. (2020). LGBTQ research in management and institutions: Broadening the lens. *Journal of Organizational Change Management, 33*(3), 449–455. doi: 10.1108/JOCM-05-2020-494.

Bailey, D. E., Leonardi, P. M., & Barley, S. R. (2012). The lure of the virtual. *Organization Science, 23*(5), 1485–1504. doi: 10.1287/orsc.1110.0703.

Baird, C., & Calvard, T. S. (2019). Epistemic vices in organizations: Knowledge, truth, and unethical conduct. *Journal of Business Ethics, 160*(1), 263–276. doi: 10.1007/s10551-018-3897-z.

Bairstow, S. (2007). 'There isn't supposed to be a speaker against!' Investigating tensions of 'safe space' and intra-group diversity for trade union lesbian and gay organization. *Gender, Work & Organization*, 14(5), 393–408. doi: 10. 1111/j.1468-0432.2007.00357.x.

Bakken, T., & Hernes, T. (2006). Organizing is both a verb and a noun: Weick meets Whitehead. *Organization Studies*, 27(11), 1599–1616. doi: 10.1177/ 0170840606068335.

Balch, A., & Balabanova, E. (2011). A system in chaos? Knowledge and sense-making on immigration policy in public debates. *Media, Culture & Society*, 33(6), 885–904. doi: 10.1177/0163443711411007.

Banerjee, S. B., & Linstead, S. (2001). Globalization, multiculturalism and other fictions: Colonialism for the new millennium? *Organization*, 8(4), 683–722. doi: 10.1177/135050840184006.

Banjo, S. & Bass, D. (2020, August 3). *On diversity, Silicon Valley failed to think different*. Bloomberg Businessweek. Online article. Retrieved from https:// www.bloomberg.com/news/articles/2020-08-03/silicon-valley-didn-t-inherit-discrimination-but-replicated-it-anyway.

Bansal, P., Kim, A., & Wood, M. O. (2018). Hidden in plain sight: The importance of scale in organizations' attention to issues. *Academy of Management Review*, 43(2), 217–241. doi: 10.5465/amr.2014.0238.

Bansal, P., & Knox-Hayes, J. (2013). The time and space of materiality in organizations and the natural environment. *Organization & Environment*, 26(1), 61–82. doi: 10.1177/1086026612475069.

Bapuji, H., Patel, C., Ertug, G., & Allen, D. G. (2020). Corona crisis and inequality: Why management research needs a societal turn. *Journal of Management*, 46(7), 1205–1222. doi: 10.1177/0149206320925881.

Barinaga, E. (2007). 'Cultural diversity' at work: 'National culture' as a discourse organizing an international project group. *Human Relations*, 60(2), 315–340. doi: 10.1177/0018726707075883.

Barragan, S., Paludi, M. I., & Mills, A. (2017). Top women managers as change agents in the machista context of Mexico. *Equality, Diversity and Inclusion: An International Journal*, 36(4), 321–339. doi: 10.1108/EDI-08-2016-0065.

Barros, M. (2010). Emancipatory management: The contradiction between practice and discourse. *Journal of Management Inquiry*, 19(2), 166–184. doi: 10.1177/1056492609357825.

Barry, B. (2001). The muddles of multiculturalism. *New Left Review*, 8(1), 49–71.

Barry, B., & Bateman, T. S. (1996). A social trap analysis of the management of diversity. *Academy of Management Review*, 21(3), 757–790. doi: 10.5465/ amr.1996.9702100314.

Barry, D., & Meisiek, S. (2010). Seeing more and seeing differently: Sensemaking, mindfulness, and the work arts. *Organization Studies*, 31(11), 1505–1530. doi: 10.1177/0170840610380802.

Barry, J., Berg, E., & Chandler, J. (2007). Women's movements: Abeyant or still on the move? *Equal Opportunities International*, 26(4), 352–369. doi: 10. 1108/02610150710749449.

Barry, J., Honour, T., & Palnitkar, S. (2004). Social movement, action and change: The influence of women's movements on city government in Mumbai and London. *Gender, Work & Organization*, 11(2), 143–162. doi: 10.1111/j. 1468-0432.2004.00226.x.

Basbøll, T. (2010). Softly constrained imagination: Plagiarism and misprision in the theory of organizational sensemaking. *Culture and Organization*, 16(2), 163–178. doi: 10.1080/14759551003769318.

Basu, K., & Palazzo, G. (2008). Corporate social responsibility: A process model of sensemaking. *Academy of Management Review*, 33(1), 122–136. doi: 10. 5465/amr.2008.27745504.

Bates, L. (2016). *Everyday sexism: The project that inspired a worldwide movement*. London: Macmillan.

Bates, R. (2018, April 17). *France's autism problem – and its roots in psychoanalysis*. The Conversation. Retrieved from https://theconversation.com/frances-autism-problem-and-its-roots-in-psychoanalysis-94210.

Battilana, J., Leca, B., & Boxenbaum, E. (2009). How actors change institutions: Towards a theory of institutional entrepreneurship. *Academy of Management Annals*, 3(1), 65–107. doi: 10.5465/19416520903053598.

Bazin, Y., & Naccache, P. (2016). The emergence of heterotopia as a heuristic concept to study organization. *European Management Review*, 13(3), 225–233. doi: 10.1111/emre.12082.

BBC News (2018, May 26). *Irish abortion referendum: Ireland overturns abortion ban*. BBC News website. Retrieved from https://www.bbc.co.uk/news/world-europe-44256152.

Beard, M. (2017). *Women and power: A manifesto*. London, England: Profile Books.

Beaumont, P. & Holpuch, A. (2018, August 3). *How The Handmaid's Tale dressed protests across the world*. The Guardian. Retrieved from https://www.theguardian.com/world/2018/aug/03/how-the-handmaids-tale-dressed-protests-across-the-world.

Beck, U. (2008). Reframing power in the globalized world. *Organization Studies*, 29(5), 793–804. doi: 10.1177/0170840608090096.

Beckett, A. E., Bagguley, P., & Campbell, T. (2017). Foucault, social movements and heterotopic horizons: Rupturing the order of things. *Social Movement Studies*, 16(2), 169–181. doi: 10.1080/14742837.2016.1252666.

Beiner, R. (1984). Walter Benjamin's philosophy of history. *Political Theory*, 12(3), 423–434. doi: 10.1177/0090591784012003005.

Bell, J. B. (2002). The organization of Islamic terror: The global jihad. *Journal of Management Inquiry*, 11(3), 261–266. doi: 10.1177/1056492602113009.

Bell, M. P., Connerley, M. L., & Cocchiara, F. K. (2009). The case for mandatory diversity education. *Academy of Management Learning & Education*, 8(4), 597–609. doi: 10.5465/amle.8.4.zqr597.

Bell, E., Kothiyal, N., & Willmott, H. (2017). Methodology-as-Technique and the meaning of rigour in globalized management research. *British Journal of Management*, 28(3), 534–550. doi: 10.1111/1467-8551.12205.

Bell, E., Meriläinen, S., Taylor, S., & Tienari, J. (2019). Time's up! Feminist theory and activism meets organization studies. *Human Relations*, 72(1), 4–22. doi: 10.1177/0018726718790067.

Bell, E., Meriläinen, S., Taylor, S., & Tienari, J. (2020). Dangerous knowledge: The political, personal, and epistemological promise of feminist research in management and organization studies. *International Journal of Management Reviews*, 22(2), 177–192. doi: 10.1111/ijmr.12221.

Bell, S. T., Villado, A. J., Lukasik, M. A., Belau, L., & Briggs, A. L. (2011). Getting specific about demographic diversity variable and team performance relationships: A meta-analysis. *Journal of Management, 37*(3), 709–743. doi: 10.1177/0149206310365001.

Bendl, R., Danowitz, M. A., & Schmidt, A. (2014). Recalibrating management: Feminist activism to achieve equality in an evolving university. *British Journal of Management, 25*(2), 320–334. doi: 10.1111/1467-8551.12008.

Bendl, R., Fleischmann, A., & Walenta, C. (2008). Diversity management discourse meets queer theory. *Gender in Management, 23*(6), 382–394. doi: 10.1108/17542410810897517.

Bendl, R., & Schmidt, A. (2010). From 'Glass Ceilings' to 'Firewalls'—different metaphors for describing discrimination. *Gender, Work & Organization, 17*(5), 612–634. doi: 10.1111/j.1468-0432.2010.00520.x.

Bendl, R., & Schmidt, A. (2012). Revisiting feminist activism at managerial universities. *Equality, Diversity and Inclusion: An International Journal, 31*(5/6), 484–505. doi: 10.1108/02610151211235488.

Benhabib, S. (1999). The liberal imagination and the four dogmas of multiculturalism. *The Yale Journal of Criticism, 12*(2), 401–413. doi: 10.1353/yale.1999.0018.

Bennett, J., Pitt, M., & Price, S. (2012). Understanding the impact of generational issues in the workplace. *Facilities, 30*(7-8), 278–288. doi: 10.1108/02632771211220086.

Benschop, Y., & Doorewaard, H. (1998). Covered by equality: The gender subtext of organizations. *Organization Studies, 19*(5), 787–805. doi: 10.1177/017084069801900504.

Benschop, Y., van den Brink, M., Doorewaard, H., & Leenders, J. (2013). Discourses of ambition, gender and part-time work. *Human Relations, 66*(5), 699–723. doi: 10.1177/0018726712466574.

Berg Johansen, C., & De Cock, C. (2018). Ideologies of time: How elite corporate actors engage the future. *Organization, 25*(2), 186–204. doi: 10.1177/1350508417725592.

Bergman, A., & Karlsson, J. C. (2011). Three observations on work in the future. *Work, Employment and Society, 25*(3), 561–568. doi: 10.1177/0950017011407974.

Berlin, I. (2015). *The long emancipation: The demise of slavery in the United States.* Harvard, MA: Harvard University Press.

Bernstein, R. S., Bulger, M., Salipante, P., & Weisinger, J. Y. (2019). *From diversity to inclusion to equity: A theory of generative interactions. Journal of Business Ethics.* Advance online publication. doi: 10.1007/s10551-019-04180-1.

Berry, J. W. (2011). Integration and multiculturalism: Ways towards social solidarity. *Papers on Social Representations, 20*(1), 2.1–2.21. Retrieved from http://psr.iscte-iul.pt/index.php/PSR/article/view/414.

Berti, M., & Simpson, A. (2019). *The dark side of organizational paradoxes: The dynamics of disempowerment. Academy of Management Review.* Advance online publication. doi: 10.5465/amr.2017.0208.

Bertossi, C. (2011). National models of integration in Europe: A comparative and critical analysis. *American Behavioral Scientist, 55*(12), 1561–1580. doi: 10.1177/0002764211409560.

Besharov, M. L., & Smith, W. K. (2014). Multiple institutional logics in organizations: Explaining their varied nature and implications. *Academy of Management Review*, 39(3), 364–381. doi: 10.5465/amr.2011.0431.

Beyes, T., Costas, J., & Ortmann, G. (2019). Novel thought: Towards a literary study of organization. *Organization Studies*, 40(12), 1787–1803. doi: 10.1177/0170840619874458.

Beyes, T., & Michels, C. (2011). The production of educational space: Heterotopia and the business university. *Management Learning*, 42(5), 521–536. doi: 10.1177/1350507611400001.

Beyes, T., & Steyaert, C. (2012). Spacing organization: Non-representational theory and performing organizational space. *Organization*, 19(1), 45–61. doi: 10.1177/1350508411401946.

Beyes, T., & Steyaert, C. (2013). Strangely familiar: The uncanny and unsiting organizational analysis. *Organization Studies*, 34(10), 1445–1465. doi: 10.1177/0170840613495323.

Bhopal, K. (2018). *White privilege: The myth of a post-racial society*. Bristol, England: Policy Press.

Billing, Y. D. (2011). Are women in management victims of the phantom of the male norm? *Gender, Work & Organization*, 18(3), 298–317. doi: 10.1111/j.1468-0432.2010.00546.x.

Bird, S. (2007). Sensemaking and identity: The interconnection of storytelling and networking in a women's group of a large corporation. *The Journal of Business Communication*, 44(4), 311–339. doi: 10.1177/0021943607306135.

Bishop, D. G., Treviño, L. K., Gioia, D., & Kreiner, G. E. (2019). Leveraging a recessive narrative to transform Joe Paterno's image: Media sensebreaking, sensemaking, and sensegiving during scandal. *Academy of Management Discoveries*. Advance online publication. doi: 10.5465/amd.2019.0108.

Bleijenbergh, I. (2018). Transformational change towards gender equality: An autobiographical reflection on resistance during participatory action research. *Organization*, 25(1), 131–138. doi: 10.1177/1350508417726547.

Bleijenbergh, I. L., Booysen, L., & Mills, A. J. (2018). The challenges and outcomes of critical diversity scholarship. *Qualitative Research in Organizations and Management. An International Journal*, 13(3), 206–217. doi: 10.1108/QROM-09-2018-597.

Bleijenbergh, I., Peters, P., & Poutsma, E. (2010). Diversity management beyond the business case. *Equality, Diversity and Inclusion: An International Journal*, 29(5), 413–421. doi: 10.1108/02610151011052744.

Bloemraad, I., Korteweg, A., & Yurdakul, G. (2008). Citizenship and immigration: Multiculturalism, assimilation, and challenges to the nation-state. *Annual Review of Sociology*, 34, 153–179. doi: 10.1146/annurev.soc.34.040507.134608.

Bloemraad, I., & Wright, M. (2014). "Utter failure" or unity out of diversity? Debating and evaluating policies of multiculturalism. *International Migration Review*, 48(1_suppl), S292–S334. doi: 10.1111/imre.12135.

Blommaert, J., & Verschueren, J. (2002). *Debating diversity: Analysing the discourse of tolerance*. London, England: Routledge.

Bloomfield, B., & Vurdubakis, T. (2014). On the naming of monsters: Organization,(in) equality and diversity in the age of technological reproduction. *Equality, Diversity and Inclusion: An International Journal, 33*(7), 575–594. doi: 10.1108/EDI-04-2012-0028.

Boje, D. M. (1994). Organizational storytelling: The struggles of pre-modern, modern and postmodern organizational learning discourses. *Management Learning, 25*(3), 433–461. doi: 10.1177/135050769402500304.

Boje, D. M., Oswick, C., & Ford, J. D. (2004). Language and organization: The doing of discourse. *Academy of Management Review, 29*(4), 571–577. doi: 10.5465/amr.2004.14497609.

Bolden, R., Williams, R., & O'Regan, N. (2020). *Leading to achieve social change: An interview with Ruth Hunt, former Chief Executive Officer of Stonewall. Journal of Management Inquiry.* Advance online publication. doi: 10.1177/1056492620935192.

Bolton, S. C., & Laaser, K. (2013). Work, employment and society through the lens of moral economy. *Work, Employment and Society, 27*(3), 508–525. doi: 10.1177/0950017013479828.

Boogaard, B., & Roggeband, C. (2010). Paradoxes of intersectionality: Theorizing inequality in the Dutch police force through structure and agency. *Organization, 17*(1), 53–75. doi: 10.1177/1350508409350042.

Booker, M. K. (1994). Woman on the edge of a genre: The feminist dystopias of Marge Piercy. *Science Fiction Studies, 21*(3), 337–350. https://www.jstor.org/stable/4240370.

Boucher, F., & Maclure, J. (2018). Moving the debate forward: Interculturalism's contribution to multiculturalism. *Comparative Migration Studies, 6*(1), 16. doi: 10.1186/s40878-018-0078-2.

Bourne, J. (2001). The life and times of institutional racism. *Race & Class, 43*(2), 7–22. doi: 10.1177/0306396801432002.

Bouvier, G., & Machin, D. (2018). Critical Discourse Analysis and the challenges and opportunities of social media. *Review of Communication, 18*(3), 178–192. doi: 10.1080/15358593.2018.1479881.

Bowen, F., & Blackmon, K. (2003). Spirals of silence: The dynamic effects of diversity on organizational voice. *Journal of Management Studies, 40*(6), 1393–1417. doi: 10.1111/1467-6486.00385.

Bowers, C. A., Pharmer, J. A., & Salas, E. (2000). When member homogeneity is needed in work teams: A meta-analysis. *Small Group Research, 31*(3), 305–327. doi: 10.1177/104649640003100303.

Bowling, B. (2018, April 19). *Stephen Lawrence: His death changed British law forever but trust in police has yet to recover.* The Conversation. Retrieved from https://theconversation.com/stephen-lawrence-his-death-changed-british-law-forever-but-trust-in-police-has-yet-to-recover-95091.

Brahm Levey, G. (2019). The Bristol school of multiculturalism. *Ethnicities, 19*(1), 200–226. doi: 10.1177/1468796818787413.

Brammer, S., Branicki, L., & Linnenluecke, M. (2020). COVID-19, societalization and the future of business in society. *Academy of Management Perspectives.* Advance online publication. doi: 10.5465/amp.2019.0053.

Brewer, K. (2015, October 23). *The day Iceland's women went on strike.* BBC News. Retrieved from https://www.bbc.co.uk/news/magazine-34602822.

Brewis, D. N. (2017). Social justice 'lite'? Using emotion for moral reasoning in diversity practice. *Gender, Work & Organization*, *24*(5), 519–532. doi: 10. 1111/gwao.12171.

Brewis, D. N. (2019). Duality and fallibility in practices of the self: The 'inclusive subject' in diversity training. *Organization Studies*, *40*(1), 93–114. doi: 10. 1177/0170840618765554.

Briner, R. B., Denyer, D., & Rousseau, D. M. (2009). Evidence-based management: Concept cleanup time? *The Academy of Management Perspectives*, *23*(4), 19–32. doi: 10.5465/AMP.2009.45590138.

Briscoe, F., & Gupta, A. (2016). Social activism in and around organizations. *The Academy of Management Annals*, *10*(1), 671–727. doi: 10.1080/ 19416520.2016.1153261.

Bristow, A., & Robinson, S. (2018). Brexiting CMS. *Organization*, *25*(5), 636–648. doi: 10.1177/1350508418786057.

Broadbridge, A., & Hearn, J. (2008). Gender and management: New directions in research and continuing patterns in practice. *British Journal of Management*, *19*(s1), S38–S49. doi: 10.1111/j.1467-8551.2008.00570.x.

Broadfoot, K. J., Cockburn, T., Cockburn-Wootten, C., do Carmo Reis, M., Gautam, D. K., Malshe, A., ... Srinivas, N. (2008). A mosaic of visions, daydreams, and memories: Diverse inlays of organizing and communicating from around the globe. *Management Communication Quarterly*, *22*(2), 322–350. doi: 10.1177/0893318908323574.

Broadfoot, K. J., & Munshi, D. (2007). Diverse voices and alternative rationalities: Imagining forms of postcolonial organizational communication. *Management Communication Quarterly*, *21*(2), 249–267. doi: 10.1177/ 0893318907306037.

Bromley, P., & Powell, W. W. (2012). From smoke and mirrors to walking the talk: Decoupling in the contemporary world. *Academy of Management Annals*, *6*(1), 483–530. doi: 10.5465/19416520.2012.684462.

Brown, A. D. (2004). Authoritative sensemaking in a public inquiry report. *Organization Studies*, *25*(1), 95–112. doi: 10.1177/0170840604038182.

Brown, A. D., Colville, I., & Pye, A. (2015). Making sense of sensemaking in organization studies. *Organization Studies*, *36*(2), 265–277. doi: 10.1177/ 0170840614559259.

Brown, A. D., & Humphreys, M. (2006). Organizational identity and place: A discursive exploration of hegemony and resistance. *Journal of Management Studies*, *43*(2), 231–257. doi: 10.1111/j.1467-6486.2006.00589.x.

Brown, A. D., & Jones, M. (2000). Honourable members and dishonourable deeds: Sensemaking, impression management and legitimation in the 'Arms to Iraq Affair'. *Human Relations*, *53*(5), 655–689. doi: 10.1177/ 0018726700535003.

Brown, G., Lawrence, T. B., & Robinson, S. L. (2005). Territoriality in organizations. *Academy of Management Review*, *30*(3), 577–594. doi: 10.5465/ amr.2005.17293710.

Bruni, A., Gherardi, S., & Poggio, B. (2004). Doing gender, doing entrepreneurship: An ethnographic account of intertwined practices. *Gender, Work & Organization*, *11*(4), 406–429. doi: 10.1111/j.1468-0432.2004.00240.x.

Bryant, L., & Jaworski, K. (2011). Gender, embodiment and place: The gendering of skills shortages in the Australian mining and food and beverage processing industries. *Human Relations*, 64(10), 1345–1367. doi: 10.1177/ 0018726711415130.

Bryer, A. (2020). Making organizations more inclusive: The work of belonging. *Organization Studies*, 41(5), 641–660. doi: 10.1177/0170840618814576.

Bullough, A., & Renko, M. (2017). A different frame of reference: Entrepreneurship and gender differences in the perception of danger. *Academy of Management Discoveries*, 3(1), 21–41. doi: 10.5465/amd.2015.0026.

Burchiellaro, O. (2020). *Queering control and inclusion in the contemporary organization: On 'LGBT-friendly control' and the reproduction of (queer) value*. *Organization Studies*. Advance online publication. doi: 10.1177/ 0170840620944557.

Burrell, G. (1988). Modernism, postmodernism and organizational analysis 2: The contribution of Michel Foucault. *Organization Studies*, 9(2), 221–235. doi: 10.1177/017084068800900205.

Burrell, G., & Dale, K. (2002). Utopiary: Utopias, gardens and organization. *The Sociological Review*, 50(1_suppl), 106–127. doi: 10.1111/j.1467-954X.2002. tb03581.x.

Buzzanell, P. M., Meisenbach, R., Remke, R., Liu, M., Bowers, V., & Conn, C. (2005). The good working mother: Managerial women's sensemaking and feelings about work–family issues. *Communication Studies*, 56(3), 261–285. doi: 10.1080/10510970500181389.

Buzzanell, P. M., Meisenbach, R., Remke, R., Sterk, H., & Turner, L. H. (2009). Positioning gender as fundamental in applied communication research. In L. Frey & K. Cissna (Eds.), *Routledge handbook of applied communication research* (pp. 457–478). New York, NY: Routledge.

Bygnes, S. (2013). Ambivalent multiculturalism. *Sociology*, 47(1), 126–141. doi: 10.1177/0038038512448560.

Cabantous, L., & Gond, J. P. (2011). Rational decision making as performative praxis: Explaining rationality's Éternel Retour. *Organization Science*, 22(3), 573–586. doi: 10.1287/orsc.1100.0534.

Cabantous, L., Gond, J. P., Harding, N., & Learmonth, M. (2016). Critical essay: Reconsidering critical performativity. *Human Relations*, 69(2), 197–213. doi: 10.1177/0018726715584690.

Caidor, P., & Cooren, F. (2018). The appropriation of diversity discourses at work: A ventriloquial approach. *Journal of Business Diversity*, 18(4), 22–41. doi: 10.33423/jbd.v18i4.244.

Cairns, G., McInnes, P., & Roberts, P. (2003). Organizational space/time: From imperfect panoptical to heterotopian understanding. *Ephemera*, 3(2), 126–139. Retrieved from https://eprints.qut.edu.au/101925/1/101925.pdf.

Caldwell, R. (2005). Things fall apart? Discourses on agency and change in organizations. *Human Relations*, 58(1), 83–114. doi: 10.1177/ 0018726705050937.

Callahan, J. L., & Elliott, C. (2020). Fantasy spaces and emotional derailment: Reflections on failure in academic activism. *Organization*, 27(3), 506–514. doi: 10.1177/1350508419831925.

Calton, J. M., & Payne, S. L. (2003). Coping with paradox: Multistakeholder learning dialogue as a pluralist sensemaking process for addressing messy problems. *Business & Society*, 42(1), 7–42. doi: 10.1177/0007650302250505.

Calvard, T. S. (2015). Integrating organization studies and community psychology: A process model of an organizing sense of place in working lives. *Journal of Community Psychology, 43*(6), 654–686. doi: 10.1002/jcop.21754.

Calvard, T., O'Toole, M., & Hardwick, H. (2020). Rainbow lanyards: Bisexuality, queering and the corporatisation of LGBT inclusion. *Work, Employment and Society, 34*(2), 356–368. doi: 10.1177/0950017019865686.

Calvard, T. S., & Sang, K. J. (2017). Complementing psychological approaches to employee well-being with a socio-structural perspective on violence in the workplace: An alternative research agenda. *The International Journal of Human Resource Management, 28*(16), 2256–2274. doi: 10.1080/09585192. 2017.1314976.

Campbell, M. L. (2016). Intersectionality, policy-oriented research and the social relations of knowing. *Gender, Work & Organization, 23*(3), 248–260. doi: 10.1111/gwao.12083.

Campbell, S. M., Twenge, J. M., & Campbell, W. K. (2017). Fuzzy but useful constructs: Making sense of the differences between generations. *Work, Aging and Retirement, 3*(2), 130–139. doi: 10.1093/workar/wax001.

Campion, M. A., Guerrero, L., & Posthuma, R. (2011). Reasonable human resource practices for making employee downsizing decisions. *Organizational Dynamics, 40*(3), 174–180. doi: 10.1016/j.orgdyn.2011.04.004.

Carastathis, A. (2014). The concept of intersectionality in feminist theory. *Philosophy Compass, 9*(5), 304–314. doi: 10.1111/phc3.12129.

Carbado, D. W., Crenshaw, K. W., Mays, V. M., & Tomlinson, B. (2013). Intersectionality: Mapping the movements of a theory. *Du Bois Review: Social Science Research on Race, 10*(2), 303–312. doi: 10.1017/ S1742058X13000349.

Carrillo Arciniega, L. (2020). *Selling diversity to white men: How disentangling economics from morality is a racial and gendered performance. Organization.* Advance online publication. doi: 10.1177/1350508420930341.

Carrim, N. M. H., & Nkomo, S. M. (2016). Wedding intersectionality theory and identity work in organizations: South African Indian women negotiating managerial identity. *Gender, Work & Organization, 23*(3), 261–277. doi: 10. 1111/gwao.12121.

Carroll, B., & Firth, J. (2020). *Leading or led? A critical exploration of youth leadership development. Management Learning.* Advance online publication. doi: 10.1177/1350507620917849.

Carroll, A. B., & Shabana, K. M. (2010). The business case for corporate social responsibility: A review of concepts, research and practice. *International Journal of Management Reviews, 12*(1), 85–105. doi: 10.1111/j.1468-2370. 2009.00275.x.

Caruana, R., Crane, A., Gold, S., & LeBaron, G. (2020). Modern slavery in business: The sad and sorry state of a non-field. *Business & Society.* Advance online publication. doi: 10.1177/0007650320930417.

Castor, T. R. (2005). Constructing social reality in organizational decision making: Account vocabularies in a diversity discussion. *Management Communication Quarterly, 18*(4), 479–508. doi: 10.1177/0893318904273689.

Cavico, F. J., Muffler, S. C., & Mujtaba, B. G. (2013). Appearance discrimination in employment: Legal and ethical implications of "lookism" and "lookphobia." *Equality, Diversity and Inclusion: An International Journal,* 32(1), 89–119. doi: 10.1108/02610151311305632.

Cederström, C., & Spicer, A. (2014). Discourse of the real kind: A post-foundational approach to organizational discourse analysis. *Organization,* 21(2), 178–205. doi: 10.1177/1350508412473864.

Cenzatti, M. (2008). Heterotopias of difference. In M. Dehaene & L. De Cauter (Eds.), *Heterotopia and the city: Public space in a postcivil society* (pp. 75–86). London, England: Routledge.

Cha, S. E., & Roberts, L. M. (2019). Leveraging minority identities at work: An individual-level framework of the identity mobilization process. *Organization Science,* 30(4), 735–760. doi: 10.1287/orsc.2018.1272.

Chan, E. K. (2006). Utopia and the problem of race: Accounting for the remainder in the imagination of the 1970s utopian subject. *Utopian Studies,* 17(3), 465–490. https://www.jstor.org/stable/20718854.

Chang, R. S., & Culp Jr, J. M. (2002). After intersectionality. *UMKC Law Review,* 71, 485–492.

Chanlat, J. F. (2006). Space, organization and management thinking: A socio-historical perspective. In S. Clegg and M. Kornberger (Eds.), *Space, organization and management theory* (pp. 17–43). Oslo, Norway: Liber.

Chary, S. N. (2017). Gender equality: A view from India. *Journal of Management Inquiry,* 26(1), 108–111. doi: 10.1177/1056492616664853.

Chattopadhyay, P., George, E., & Ng, C. K. (2016). Hearts and minds: Integrating regulatory focus and relational demography to explain responses to dissimilarity. *Organizational Psychology Review,* 6(2), 119–144. doi: 10.1177/2041386615574540.

Chi, D. Q., & van den Broek, D. (2020). *Gendered labour activism in the Vietnamese manufacturing industry. Gender, Work & Organization.* Advance online publication. doi: 10.1111/gwao.12452.

Chiang, S. Y. (2015). Cultural adaptation as a sense-making experience: International students in China. *Journal of International Migration and Integration,* 16(2), 397–413. doi: 10.1007/s12134-014-0346-4.

Cho, S., Crenshaw, K. W., & McCall, L. (2013). Toward a field of inter-sectionality studies: Theory, applications, and praxis. *Signs: Journal of Women in Culture and Society,* 38(4), 785–810. doi: 10.1086/669608.

Choo, H. Y., & Ferree, M. M. (2010). Practicing intersectionality in sociological research: A critical analysis of inclusions, interactions, and institutions in the study of inequalities. *Sociological Theory,* 28(2), 129–149. doi: 10.1111/j.1467-9558.2010.01370.x.

Chouliaraki, L., & Fairclough, N. (2010). Critical discourse analysis in organizational studies: Towards an integrationist methodology. *Journal of Management Studies,* 47(6), 1213–1218. doi: 10.1111/j.1467-6486.2009.00883.x.

Christensen, J. F., & Muhr, S. L. (2018). Desired diversity and symptomatic anxiety: Theorising failed diversity as Lacanian lack. *Culture and Organization,* 24(2), 114–133. doi: 10.1080/14759551.2017.1407764.

Christian, M., Seamster, L., & Ray, V. (2019). New directions in critical race theory and sociology: Racism, white supremacy, and resistance. *American Behavioral Scientist,* 63(13), 1731–1740. doi: 10.1177/0002764219842623.

Christiansen, T. J., & Just, S. N. (2012). Regularities of diversity discourse: Address, categorization, and invitation. *Journal of Management & Organization, 18*(3), 398–411. doi: 10.1017/S1833367200000870.

Chrobot-Mason, D., Hoobler, J. M., & Burno, J. (2019). Lean in versus the literature: An evidence-based examination. *Academy of Management Perspectives, 33*(1), 110–130. doi: 10.5465/amp.2016.0156.

Chwastiak, M. (2015). Torture as normal work: The Bush Administration, the Central Intelligence Agency and 'Enhanced Interrogation Techniques'. *Organization, 22*(4), 493–511. doi: 10.1177/1350508415572506.

Clark, P., & Rowlinson, M. (2004). The treatment of history in organisation studies: Towards an 'historic turn'? *Business History, 46*(3), 331–352. doi: 10.1080/0007679042000219175.

Clegg, S. R. (2006). Why is organization theory so ignorant? The neglect of total institutions. *Journal of Management Inquiry, 15*(4), 426–430. doi: 10.1177/1056492606294640.

Clegg, S. (2014). Managerialism: Born in the USA. *Academy of Management Review, 39*(4), 566–576. doi: 10.5465/amr.2014.0129.

Clegg, S., e Cunha, M. P., & Rego, A. (2012). The theory and practice of utopia in a total institution: The pineapple panopticon. *Organization Studies, 33*(12), 1735–1757. doi: 10.1177/0170840612464611.

Clegg, S., Geppert, M., & Hollinshead, G. (2018). Politicization and political contests in and around contemporary multinational corporations: An introduction. *Human Relations, 71*(6), 745–765. doi: 10.1177/0018726718755880.

Clegg, S., & Kornberger, M. (Eds.). (2006). *Space, organizations and management theory*. Oslo, Norway: Liber.

Coghlan, D. (2011). Action research: Exploring perspectives on a philosophy of practical knowing. *Academy of Management Annals, 5*(1), 53–87. doi: 10.5465/19416520.2011.571520.

Cole, E. R. (2009). Intersectionality and research in psychology. *American Psychologist, 64*(3), 170–180. doi: 10.1037/a0014564.

Cole, B. M., & Salimath, M. S. (2013). Diversity identity management: An organizational perspective. *Journal of Business Ethics, 116*(1), 151–161. doi: 10.1007/s10551-012-1466-4.

Colgan, F. (2011). Equality, diversity and corporate responsibility. *Equality, Diversity and Inclusion: An International Journal, 30*(8), 719–734. doi: 10.1108/02610151111183225.

Colgan, F., Creegan, C., McKearney, A., & Wright, T. (2007). Equality and diversity policies and practices at work: Lesbian, gay and bisexual workers. *Equality, Diversity and Inclusion: An International Journal, 26*(6), 590–609. doi: 10.1108/02610150710777060.

Colgan, F., & Ledwith, S. (2000). Diversity, identities and strategies of women trade union activists. *Gender, Work & Organization, 7*(4), 242–257. doi: 10.1111/1468-0432.00112.

Collins, S. M. (2011). From affirmative action to diversity: Erasing inequality from organizational responsibility. *Critical Sociology, 37*(5), 517–520. doi: 10.1177/0896920510380072.

Collins, P. H. (2015). Intersectionality's definitional dilemmas. *Annual Review of Sociology, 41,* 1–20. doi: 10.1146/annurev-soc-073014-112142.

Colombo, E. (2015). Multiculturalisms: An overview of multicultural debates in western societies. *Current Sociology, 63*(6), 800–824. doi: 10.1177/0011392115586802.

Colville, I., Brown, A. D., & Pye, A. (2012). Simplexity: Sensemaking, organizing and storytelling for our time. *Human Relations, 65*(1), 5–15. doi: 10.1177/0018726711425617.

Colville, I., Pye, A., & Brown, A. D. (2016). Sensemaking processes and Weickarious learning. *Management Learning, 47*(1), 3–13. doi: 10.1177/1350507615616542.

Colville, I., Pye, A., & Carter, M. (2013). Organizing to counter terrorism: Sensemaking amidst dynamic complexity. *Human Relations, 66*(9), 1201–1223. doi: 10.1177/0018726712468912.

Comas, J., Shrivastava, P., & Martin, E. C. (2015). Terrorism as formal organization, network, and social movement. *Journal of Management Inquiry, 24*(1), 47–60. doi: 10.1177/1056492614538486.

Compton, C. A. (2016). Managing mixed messages: Sexual identity management in a changing US workplace. *Management Communication Quarterly, 30*(4), 415–440. doi: 10.1177/0893318916641215.

Conley, H. (2005). Front line or all fronts? Women's trade union activism in retail services. *Gender, Work & Organization, 12*(5), 479–496. doi: 10.1111/j.1468-0432.2005.00285.x.

Conley, H. (2014). Trade unions, equal pay and the law in the UK. *Economic and Industrial Democracy, 35*(2), 309–323. doi: 10.1177/0143831X13480410.

Contu, A. (2018). '… The point is to change it'–Yes, but in what direction and how? Intellectual activism as a way of 'walking the talk' of critical work in business schools. *Organization, 25*(2), 282–293. doi: 10.1177/1350508417740589.

Contu, A. (2019). Conflict and organization studies. *Organization Studies, 40*(10), 1445–1462. doi: 10.1177/0170840617747916.

Contu, A. (2020). Answering the crisis with intellectual activism: Making a difference as business schools scholars. *Human Relations, 73*(5), 737–757. doi: 10.1177/0018726719827366.

Conway, P. R. (2020). The folds of coexistence: Towards a diplomatic political ontology, between difference and contradiction. *Theory, Culture & Society, 37*(3), 23–47. doi: 10.1177/0263276419885004.

Cook, A., & Glass, C. (2014). Women and top leadership positions: Towards an institutional analysis. *Gender, Work & Organization, 21*(1), 91–103. doi: 10.1111/gwao.12018.

Cooke, B. (1999). Writing the left out of management theory: The historiography of the management of change. *Organization, 6*(1), 81–105. doi: 10.1177/135050849961004.

Cooke, B. (2003). The denial of slavery in management studies. *Journal of Management Studies, 40*(8), 1895–1918. doi: 10.1046/j.1467-6486.2003.00405.x.

Cooper, R., & Burrell, G. (1988). Modernism, postmodernism and organizational analysis: An introduction. *Organization Studies, 9*(1), 91–112. doi: 10.1177/017084068800900112.

Cooren, F., Kuhn, T., Cornelissen, J. P., & Clark, T. (2011). Communication, organizing and organization: An overview and introduction to the special issue. *Organization Studies, 32*(9), 1149–1170. doi: 10.1177/0170840611410836.

Cornelius, N., Lucio, M. M., Wilson, F., Gagnon, S., MacKenzie, R., & Pezet, E. (2010). Ethnicity, equality and voice: The ethics and politics of representation and participation in relation to equality and ethnicity. *Journal of Business Ethics, 97*(1), 1–7. doi: 10.1007/s10551-011-1072-x.

Cornelissen, J. P., Mantere, S., & Vaara, E. (2014). The contraction of meaning: The combined effect of communication, emotions, and materiality on sensemaking in the Stockwell shooting. *Journal of Management Studies, 51*(5), 699–736. doi: 10.1111/joms.12073.

Cornelissen, J. P., & Werner, M. D. (2014). Putting framing in perspective: A review of framing and frame analysis across the management and organizational literature. *The Academy of Management Annals, 8*(1), 181–235. doi: 10.1080/19416520.2014.875669.

Costas, J. (2013). Problematizing mobility: A metaphor of stickiness, non-places and the kinetic elite. *Organization Studies, 34*(10), 1467–1485. doi: 10.1177/0170840613495324.

Courpasson, D., Dany, F., & Clegg, S. (2012). Resisters at work: Generating productive resistance in the workplace. *Organization Science, 23*(3), 801–819. doi: 10.1287/orsc.1110.0657.

Courtney, S. J. (2014). Inadvertently queer school leadership amongst lesbian, gay and bisexual (LGB) school leaders. *Organization, 21*(3), 383–399. doi: 10. 1177/1350508413519762.

Cox Jr, T. (1991). The multicultural organization. *Academy of Management Perspectives, 5*(2), 34–47. doi: 10.5465/ame.1991.4274675.

Cox, T. (1994). A comment on the language of diversity. *Organization, 1*(1), 51–58. doi: 10.1177/135050849400100109.

Craddock, E. (2017). Caring about and for the cuts: A case study of the gendered dimension of austerity and anti-austerity activism. *Gender, Work & Organization, 24*(1), 69–82. doi: 10.1111/gwao.12153.

Crane, A. (2013). Modern slavery as a management practice: Exploring the conditions and capabilities for human exploitation. *Academy of Management Review, 38*(1), 49–69. doi: 10.5465/amr.2011.0145.

Crawford, W. S., Thompson, M. J., & Ashforth, B. E. (2019). Work-life events theory: Making sense of shock events in dual-earner couples. *Academy of Management Review, 44*(1), 194–212. doi: 10.5465/amr.2016.0432.

Crawley, A., & Sinclair, A. (2003). Indigenous human resource practices in Australian mining companies: Towards an ethical model. *Journal of Business Ethics, 45*(4), 361–373. doi: 10.1023/A:1024123721202.

Creary, S. (2020, July 8). *How to be a better ally to your Black colleagues.* Harvard Business Review. Online article. Retrieved from https://hbr.org/2020/07/how-to-be-a-better-ally-to-your-black-colleagues.

Creed, W. D., DeJordy, R., & Lok, J. (2010). Being the change: Resolving institutional contradiction through identity work. *Academy of Management Journal, 53*(6), 1336–1364. doi: 10.5465/amj.2010.57318357.

Creed, W. D., & Scully, M. A. (2000). Songs of ourselves: Employees' deployment of social identity in workplace encounters. *Journal of Management Inquiry*, 9(4), 391–412. doi: 10.1177/105649260000900410.

Creegan, C., Colgan, F., Charlesworth, R., & Robinson, G. (2003). Race equality policies at work: Employee perceptions of the 'implementation gap' in a UK local authority. *Work, Employment and Society*, 17(4), 617–640. doi: 10.1177/0950017003174002.

Crenshaw, K. (1989). *Demarginalizing the intersection of race and sex: A black feminist critique of antidiscrimination doctrine, feminist theory and antiracist politics.* University of Chicago Legal Forum, 1989, 139–167.

Crenshaw, K. (1991). Mapping the margins: Identity politics, intersectionality, and violence against women. *Stanford Law Review*, 43(6), 1241–1299.

Critical Management (2016, April 23). *About CMS. What is CMS?* Critical Management website (UK). Retrieved from http://www.criticalmanagement.org/content/about-cms.

Cukier, W., Gagnon, S., Roach, E., Elmi, M., Yap, M., & Rodrigues, S. (2017). Trade-offs and disappearing acts: Shifting societal discourses of diversity in Canada over three decades. *The International Journal of Human Resource Management*, 28(7), 1031–1064. doi: 10.1080/09585192.2015.1128459.

Cullen, P., & Murphy, M. P. (2018). Leading the debate for the business case for gender equality, perilous for whom? *Gender, Work & Organization*, 25(2), 110–126. doi: 10.1111/gwao.12199.

Cumbers, A., Shaw, D., Crossan, J., & McMaster, R. (2018). The work of community gardens: Reclaiming place for community in the city. *Work, Employment and Society*, 32(1), 133–149. doi: 10.1177/0950017017695042.

Cunha, M. P. E., Clegg, S. R., & Kamoche, K. (2006). Surprises in management and organization: Concept, sources and a typology. *British Journal of Management*, 17(4), 317–329. doi: 10.1111/j.1467-8551.2005.00470.x.

Cunliffe, A., & Coupland, C. (2012). From hero to villain to hero: Making experience sensible through embodied narrative sensemaking. *Human Relations*, 65(1), 63–88. doi: 10.1177/0018726711424321.

Cunliffe, A. L., & Locke, K. (2019). *Working with differences in everyday interactions through anticipational fluidity: A hermeneutic perspective.* Organization Studies. Advance online publication. doi: 10.1177/0170840619831035.

Cunliffe, A. L., & Scaratti, G. (2017). Embedding impact in engaged research: Developing socially useful knowledge through dialogical sensemaking. *British Journal of Management*, 28(1), 29–44. doi: 10.1111/1467-8551.12204.

Curtis, W. M. (2007). Liberals and pluralists: Charles Taylor vs John Gray. *Contemporary Political Theory*, 6(1), 86–107. doi: 10.1057/palgrave.cpt.9300260.

Cutcher, L., Hardy, C., Riach, K., & Thomas, R. (2020). *Reflections on reflexive theorizing: The need for a little more conversation.* Organization Theory, 1(3). doi: 10.1177/2631787720944183.

Czarniawska, B. (2005). Karl Weick: Concepts, style and reflection. *The Sociological Review*, 53(1_suppl), 267–278. doi: 10.1111/j.1467-954X.2005.00554.x.

Czech, H. (2018). Hans Asperger, National Socialism, and "race hygiene" in Nazi-era Vienna. *Molecular Autism*, 9(1), 29. doi: 10.1186/s13229-018-0208-6.

Dale, K., & Burrell, G. (2008). *The spaces of organisation and the organisation of space: Power, identity and materiality at work.* Basingstoke, England: Palgrave Macmillan.

Dale, K., Kingma, S. F., & Wasserman, V. (Eds.). (2018). *Organisational space and beyond: The significance of Henri Lefebvre for organisation studies.* London, England: Routledge.

Dar, S., Liu, H., Martinez Dy, A., & Brewis, D. N. (2020). *The business school is racist: Act up!. Organization.* Advance online publication. doi: 10.1177/1350508420928521.

Dashtipour, P., & Rumens, N. (2018). Entrepreneurship, incongruence and affect: Drawing insights from a Swedish anti-racist organisation. *Organization, 25*(2), 223–241. doi: 10.1177/1350508417720022.

Daskalaki, M., & Kokkinidis, G. (2017). Organizing solidarity initiatives: A socio-spatial conceptualization of resistance. *Organization Studies, 38*(9), 1303–1325. doi: 10.1177/0170840617709304.

Dass, P., & Parker, B. (1999). Strategies for managing human resource diversity: From resistance to learning. *Academy of Management Perspectives, 13*(2), 68–80. doi: 10.5465/ame.1999.1899550.

Daugherty, P. R., Wilson, H. J., & Chowdhury, R. (2019). Using artificial intelligence to promote diversity. *MIT Sloan Management Review, 60*(2). Online article. Retrieved from https://sloanreview.mit.edu/article/using-artificial-intelligence-to-promote-diversity/.

Davies, C. (1989). Goffman's concept of the total institution: Criticisms and revisions. *Human studies, 12*(1–2), 77–95. doi: 10.1007/BF00142840.

Davis, G. F. (2016). Can an economy survive without corporations? Technology and robust organizational alternatives. *Academy of Management Perspectives, 30*(2), 129–140. doi: 10.5465/amp.2015.0067.

Davis, K. (1973). The case for and against business assumption of social responsibilities. *Academy of Management Journal, 16*(2), 312–322. doi: 10.5465/255331.

Davis, K. (2008). Intersectionality as buzzword: A sociology of science perspective on what makes a feminist theory successful. *Feminist Theory, 9*(1), 67–85. doi: 10.1177/1464700108086364.

Dawson, J. (2012). Measurement of work group diversity. *Doctoral Thesis, Aston University.* Retrieved from http://publications.aston.ac.uk/16437/1/Measurement+of+work+group+diversity(2012).pdf.

Decker, S. (2010). Postcolonial transitions in Africa: Decolonization in West Africa and present day South Africa. *Journal of Management Studies, 47*(5), 791–813. doi: 10.1111/j.1467-6486.2010.00924.x.

Cock, C. D. (2009). Jumpstarting the future with Fredric Jameson: Reflections on capitalism, science fiction and Utopia. *Journal of Organizational Change Management, 22*(4), 437–449. doi: 10.1108/09534810910967198.

De Cock, C., & Böhm, S. (2007). Liberalist fantasies: Žižek and the impossibility of the open society. *Organization, 14*(6), 815–836. doi: 10.1177/1350508407082264.

De Cock, C., Just, S. N., & Husted, E. (2018). What's he building? Activating the utopian imagination with Trump. *Organization, 25*(5), 671–680. doi: 10.1177/1350508418784393.

De Cock, C., & O'Doherty, D. (2017). Ruin and organization studies. *Organization Studies*, 38(1), 129–150. doi: 10.1177/0170840616640311.

Dean, D., & Greene, A. M. (2017). How do we understand worker silence despite poor conditions–as the actress said to the woman bishop. *Human Relations*, 70(10), 1237–1257. doi: 10.1177/0018726717694371.

Deetz, S. (1996). Crossroads—Describing differences in approaches to organization science: Rethinking Burrell and Morgan and their legacy. *Organization Science*, 7(2), 191–207. doi: 10.1287/orsc.7.2.191.

Deetz, S. (2000). Putting the community into organizational science: Exploring the construction of knowledge claims. *Organization Science*, 11(6), 732–738. doi: 10.1287/orsc.11.6.732.12536.

De Jaegher, H., & Di Paolo, E. (2007). Participatory sense-making. *Phenomenology and the Cognitive Sciences*, 6(4), 485–507. doi: 10.1007/s11097-007-9076-9.

De Jong, S. (2016). Converging logics? Managing migration and managing diversity. *Journal of Ethnic and Migration Studies*, 42(3), 341–358. doi: 10.1080/1369183X.2015.1074857.

DeJordy, R., Scully, M., Ventresca, M. J., & Creed, W. D. (2020). *Inhabited ecosystems: Propelling transformative social change between and through organizations*. Administrative Science Quarterly. Advance online publication. doi: 10.1177/0001839219899613.

De la Chaux, M., Haugh, H., & Greenwood, R. (2018). Organizing refugee camps: "Respected space" and "listening posts". *Academy of Management Discoveries*, 4(2), 155–179. doi: 10.5465/amd.2017.0040.

Delaney, D. (2002). The space that race makes. *The Professional Geographer*, 54(1), 6–14. doi: 10.1111/0033-0124.00309.

Delbridge, R., & Edwards, T. (2013). Inhabiting institutions: Critical realist refinements to understanding institutional complexity and change. *Organization Studies*, 34(7), 927–947. doi: 10.1177/0170840613483805.

Delbridge, R., Hauptmeier, M., & Sengupta, S. (2011). Beyond the enterprise: Broadening the horizons of International HRM. *Human Relations*, 64(4), 483–505. doi: 10.1177/0018726710396388.

Dennissen, M., Benschop, Y., & van den Brink, M. (2019). Diversity networks: Networking for equality? *British Journal of Management*, 30(4), 966–980. doi: 10.1111/1467-8551.12321.

Dennissen, M., Benschop, Y., & van den Brink, M. (2020). Rethinking diversity management: An intersectional analysis of diversity networks. *Organization Studies*, 41(2), 219–240. doi: 10.1177/0170840618800103.

de Rond, M., Holeman, I., & Howard-Grenville, J. (2019). Sensemaking from the body: An enactive ethnography of rowing the Amazon. *Academy of Management Journal*, 62(6), 1961–1988. doi: 10.5465/amj.2017.1417.

de Souza, E.M., & Parker, M. (2020). *Practices of freedom and the disruption of binary genders: Thinking with trans*. Organization. Advance online publication. doi: 10.1177/1350508420935602.

De Vaujany, F. X., & Vaast, E. (2014). If these walls could talk: The mutual construction of organizational space and legitimacy. *Organization Science*, 25(3), 713–731. doi: 10.1287/orsc.2013.0858.

de Waal, T. (2018). Is the post-multicultural era pro-diversity? *Comparative Migration Studies*, 6(1), 15. doi: 10.1186/s40878-018-0084-4.

Dhamoon, R. K. (2011). Considerations on mainstreaming intersectionality. *Political Research Quarterly*, 64(1), 230–243. doi: 10.1177/1065912910379227.

Dick, P., & Cassell, C. (2002). Barriers to managing diversity in a UK constabulary: The role of discourse. *Journal of Management Studies*, 39(7), 953–976. doi: 10.1111/1467-6486.00319.

Dick, P., & Cassell, C. (2004). The position of policewomen: A discourse analytic study. *Work, Employment and Society*, 18(1), 51–72. doi: 10.1177/0950017004040762.

Diochon, P. F., & Nizet, J. (2019). Ethics as a fabric: An emotional reflexive sensemaking process. *Business Ethics Quarterly*, 29(4), 461–489. doi: https://doi.org/10.1017/beq.2019.11.

D'Mello, J. F. (2019). Universal basic income and entrepreneurial pursuit in an autonomous society. *Journal of Management Inquiry*, 28(3), 306–310. doi: 10.1177/1056492619827381.

Dobusch, L. (2017a). Diversity discourses and the articulation of discrimination: The case of public organisations. *Journal of Ethnic and Migration Studies*, 43(10), 1644–1661. doi: 10.1080/1369183X.2017.1293590.

Dobusch, L. (2017b). Gender, dis-/ability and diversity management: Unequal dynamics of inclusion?. *Gender, Work & Organization*, 24(5), 487–505. doi: 10.1111/gwao.12159.

Doldor, E., Sealy, R., & Vinnicombe, S. (2016). Accidental activists: Headhunters as marginal diversity actors in institutional change towards more women on boards. *Human Resource Management Journal*, 26(3), 285–303. doi: 10.1111/1748-8583.12107.

Dortants, M., & Knoppers, A. (2016). The organization of diversity in a boxing club: Governmentality and entangled rationalities. *Culture and Organization*, 22(3), 245–261. doi: 10.1080/14759551.2016.1157804.

Dougherty, D. S., & Goldstein Hode, M. (2016). Binary logics and the discursive interpretation of organizational policy: Making meaning of sexual harassment policy. *Human Relations*, 69(8), 1729–1755. doi: 10.1177/0018726715624956.

Dougherty, D., & Smythe, M. J. (2004). Sensemaking, organizational culture, and sexual harassment. *Journal of Applied Communication Research*, 32(4), 293–317. doi: 10.1080/0090988042000275998.

Dover, T. L., Kaiser, C. R., & Major, B. (2020). Mixed signals: The unintended effects of diversity initiatives. *Social Issues and Policy Review*, 14(1), 152–181. doi: 10.1111/sipr.12059.

Dowding, K. (2006). Three-dimensional power: A discussion of Steven Lukes' Power: A radical view. *Political Studies Review*, 4(2), 136–145. doi: 10.1111/j.1478-9299.2006.000100.x.

Drori, G. S. (2019). *Hasn't institutional theory always been critical?!*. *Organization Theory*, 1(1). doi: 10.1177/2631787719887982.

Dunne, S., Grady, J., & Weir, K. (2017). Organization studies of inequality, with and beyond Piketty. *Organization*, 25(2), 165–185. doi: 10.1177/1350508417714535.

Durand, R., & Thornton, P. H. (2018). Categorizing institutional logics, institutionalizing categories: A review of two literatures. *Academy of Management Annals*, 12(2), 631–658. doi: 10.5465/annals.2016.0089.

Dy, A. M., Marlow, S., & Martin, L. (2017). A Web of opportunity or the same old story? Women digital entrepreneurs and intersectionality theory. *Human Relations*, 70(3), 286–311. doi: 10.1177/0018726716650730.

Eastman, W., & Santoro, M. (2003). The importance of value diversity in corporate life. *Business Ethics Quarterly*, 13(4), 433–452. https://www.jstor.org/stable/3857966.

Eddo-Lodge, R. (2018). *Why I'm no longer talking to white people about race.* London, England: Bloomsbury Publishing.

Eichler, M. (1989). Equality in employment. *Equal Opportunities International*, 8(6), 26–31. doi: 10.1108/eb010519.

Elfer, J. (June 15, 2018). *When organisations take more than they give to the equality agenda.* LSE Business Review Blog. Retrieved from https://blogs.lse.ac.uk/businessreview/2018/06/15/when-organisations-take-more-than-they-give-to-the-equality-agenda/.

Ellem, B. (2016). Geographies of the labour process: Automation and the spatiality of mining. *Work, Employment and Society*, 30(6), 932–948. doi: 10.1177/0950017015604108.

Elmes, M. B., Jiusto, S., Whiteman, G., Hersh, R., & Guthey, G. T. (2012). Teaching social entrepreneurship and innovation from the perspective of place and place making. *Academy of Management Learning & Education*, 11(4), 533–554. doi: 10.5465/amle.2011.0029.

Elmes, M. B., Mendoza-Abarca, K., & Hersh, R. (2016). Food banking, ethical sensemaking, and social innovation in an era of growing hunger in the United States. *Journal of Management Inquiry*, 25(2), 122–138. doi: 10.1177/1056492615589651.

Ely, R. J. & Thomas, D. A. (2001). Cultural diversity at work: The effects of diversity perspectives on work group processes and outcomes. *Administrative Science Quarterly*, 46(2), 229–273. doi: 10.2307/2667087.

Eräranta, K., & Kantola, J. (2016). The Europeanization of Nordic gender equality: A Foucauldian analysis of reconciling work and family in Finland. *Gender, Work & Organization*, 23(4), 414–430. doi: 10.1111/gwao.12136.

Erel, U. (2010). Migrating cultural capital: Bourdieu in migration studies. *Sociology*, 44(4), 642–660. doi: 10.1177/0038038510369363.

Ericsson, D., & Kostera, M. (2020). *Alterethnography: Reading and writing otherness in organizations. Gender, Work & Organization*. Advance online publication. doi: 10.1111/gwao.12503.

Erskine, S. E., & Bilimoria, D. (2019). White allyship of Afro-Diasporic women in the workplace: A transformative strategy for organizational change. *Journal of Leadership & Organizational Studies*, 26(3), 319–338. doi: 10.1177/1548051819848993.

Evans, A. E. (2007). School leaders and their sensemaking about race and demographic change. *Educational Administration Quarterly*, 43(2), 159–188. doi: 10.1177/0013161X06294575.

Evans, C. (2014). Diversity management and organizational change: What can institutional theory contribute to our understanding of the lack of radical change? *Equality, Diversity and Inclusion: An International Journal*, 33(6), 482–493. doi: 10.1108/EDI-09-2013-0072.

Eveline, J., Bacchi, C., & Binns, J. (2009). Gender mainstreaming versus diversity mainstreaming: Methodology as emancipatory politics. *Gender, Work & Organization*, 16(2), 198–216. doi: 10.1111/j.1468-0432.2008.00427.x.

Fairclough, N. (2005). Discourse analysis in organization studies: The case for critical realism. *Organization Studies*, 26(6), 915–939. doi: 10.1177/0170840605054610.

Fairhurst, G. T., & Putnam, L. (2004). Organizations as discursive constructions. *Communication Theory*, 14(1), 5–26. doi: 10.1111/j.1468-2885.2004.tb00301.x.

Fairhurst, G. T., & Putnam, L. L. (2019). An integrative methodology for organizational oppositions: Aligning grounded theory and discourse analysis. *Organizational Research Methods*, 22(4), 917–940. doi: 10.1177/1094428118776771.

Farjoun, M., Ansell, C., & Boin, A. (2015). Pragmatism in organization studies: Meeting the challenges of a dynamic and complex world. *Organization Science*, 26(6), 1787–1804. doi: 10.1287/orsc.2015.1016.

Fenwick, T. (2005). Ethical dilemmas of critical management education: Within classrooms and beyond. *Management Learning*, 36(1), 31–48. doi: 10.1177/1350507605049899.

Ferdman, B. M. (2017). Paradoxes of inclusion: Understanding and managing the tensions of diversity and multiculturalism. *The Journal of applied behavioral science*, 53(2), 235–263. doi: 10.1177/0021886317702608.

Filatotchev, I., Wei, L. Q., Sarala, R. M., Dick, P., & Prescott, J. E. (2020). Connecting Eastern and Western Perspectives on management: Translation of practices across organizations, institution and geographies. *Journal of Management Studies*, 57(1), 1–24. doi: 10.1111/joms.12526.

Fisher, D. H., & Fowler, S. B. (1995). Reimagining moral leadership in business: Image, identity and difference. *Business Ethics Quarterly*, 5(1), 29–42. doi: 10.2307/3857270.

Fitzsimmons, S. R. (2013). Multicultural employees: A framework for understanding how they contribute to organizations. *Academy of Management Review*, 38(4), 525–549. doi: 10.5465/amr.2011.0234.

Fleetwood, S. (2005). Ontology in organization and management studies: A critical realist perspective. *Organization*, 12(2), 197–222. doi: 10.1177/1350508405051188.

Fleming, P. (2007). Sexuality, power and resistance in the workplace. *Organization Studies*, 28(2), 239–256. doi: 10.1177/0170840606068307.

Fleming, P. (2013). 'Down with Big Brother!' The end of 'corporate culturalism'?. *Journal of Management Studies*, 50(3), 474–495. doi: 10.1111/j.1467-6486.2012.01056.x.

Fleming, P. (2017). The human capital hoax: Work, debt and insecurity in the era of Uberization. *Organization Studies*, 38(5), 691–709. doi: 10.1177/0170840616686129.

Fleming, P. (2019a). *Dark academia: Despair in the neoliberal business school*. *Journal of Management Studies*. Advance online publication. doi: 10.1111/joms.12521.

Fleming, P. (2019b). Robots and organization studies: Why robots might not want to steal your job. *Organization Studies*, *40*(1), 23–38. doi: 10.1177/0170840618765568.

Fleming, P., & Spicer, A. (2008). Beyond power and resistance: New approaches to organizational politics. *Management Communication Quarterly*, *21*(3), 301–309. doi: 10.1177/0893318907309928.

Fleming, P., & Spicer, A. (2014). Power in management and organization science. *The Academy of Management Annals*, *8*(1), 237–298. doi: 10.1080/19416520.2014.875671.

Flynn, M., Upchurch, M., Muller-Camen, M., & Schroder, H. (2013). Trade union responses to ageing workforces in the UK and Germany. *Human Relations*, *66*(1), 45–64. doi: 10.1177/0018726712464801.

Fodor, É., Glass, C., & Nagy, B. (2019). Transnational business feminism: Exporting feminism in the global economy. *Gender, Work & Organization*, *26*(8), 1117–1137. doi: 10.1111/gwao.12302.

Foldy, E. G. (2006). Dueling schemata: Dialectical sensemaking about gender. *The Journal of Applied Behavioral Science*, *42*(3), 350–372. doi: 10.1177/0021886306290309.

Ford, J. D., Ford, L. W., & D'Amelio, A. (2008). Resistance to change: The rest of the story. *Academy of Management Review*, *33*(2), 362–377. doi: 10.5465/amr.2008.31193235.

Foster, D. (2018). The health and well-being at work agenda: Good news for (disabled) workers or Just a capital idea? *Work, Employment and Society*, *32*(1), 186–197. doi: 10.1177/0950017016682458.

Foster, C., & Harris, L. (2005). Easy to say, difficult to do: Diversity management in retail. *Human Resource Management Journal*, *15*(3), 4–17. doi: 10.1111/j.1748-8583.2005.tb00150.x.

Fotaki, M., Altman, Y., & Koning, J. (2020). Spirituality, symbolism and storytelling in twenty first century organizations: Understanding and addressing the crisis of imagination. *Organization Studies*, *41*(1), 7–30. doi: 10.1177/0170840619875782.

Fotaki, M., & Daskalaki, M. (2020). *Politicizing the body in the anti-mining protest in Greece. Organization Studies.* Advance online publication. doi: 10.1177/0170840619882955.

Fotaki, M., & Prasad, A. (2015). Questioning neoliberal capitalism and economic inequality in business schools. *Academy of Management Learning & Education*, *14*(4), 556–575. doi: 10.5465/amle.2014.0182.

Fournier, V. (2002). Utopianism and the cultivation of possibilities: Grassroots movements of hope. *The Sociological Review*, *50*(1_suppl), 189–216. doi: 10.1111/j.1467-954X.2002.tb03585.x.

Fournier, V. (2006). Breaking from the weight of the eternal present: Teaching organizational difference. *Management Learning*, *37*(3), 295–311. doi: 10.1177/1350507606067167.

Fournier, V., & Grey, C. (2000). At the critical moment: Conditions and prospects for critical management studies. *Human Relations*, *53*(1), 7–32. doi: 10.1177/0018726700531002.

Fowers, B. J., & Richardson, F. C. (1996). Why is multiculturalism good? *American Psychologist*, *51*(6), 609. doi: 10.1037/0003-066X.51.6.609.

Fox, C. O., & Ore, T. E. (2010). (Un) covering normalized gender and race subjectivities in LGBT "safe spaces". *Feminist Studies*, 36(3), 629–649. Retrieved from www.jstor.org/stable/27919125.

Fraser, M. (2020, July 16). *What if everyone was disabled?* BBC Radio 4 Documentary. Retrieved from https://www.bbc.co.uk/programmes/m000-kx1l#:~:text=The%20writer%2C%20actor%20and%20rights,if%20everybody%20had%20a%20disability.&text=Mat%20invites%20designers%2C%20ar-chitects%2C%20advisers,great%20examples%20of%20inclusive%20design.

Freeman, M. (1975). Sociology and Utopia: Some reflections on the social philosophy of Karl Popper. *The British Journal of Sociology*, 26(1), 20–34. doi: 10.2307/589240.

Frémeaux, S. (2020). A common good perspective on diversity. *Business Ethics Quarterly*, 30(2), 200–228. doi: 10.1017/beq.2019.37.

Frenkel, M. (2008). The multinational corporation as a third space: Rethinking international management discourse on knowledge transfer through Homi Bhabha. *Academy of Management Review*, 33(4), 924–942. doi: 10.5465/amr.2008.34422002.

Frenkel, M., & Shenhav, Y. (2006). From binarism back to hybridity: A postcolonial reading of management and organization studies. *Organization Studies*, 27(6), 855–876. doi: 10.1177/0170840606064086.

Friedland, R., & Alford, R. R. (1991). Bringing society back in: Symbols, practices and institutional contradictions. In W. W. Powell & P. J. DiMaggio (Eds.), *The new institutionalism in organizational analysis* (pp. 232–267). Chicago, IL: University of Chicago Press.

Friedman, S., O'Brien, D., & Laurison, D. (2017). 'Like skydiving without a parachute': How class origin shapes occupational trajectories in British acting. *Sociology*, 51(5), 992–1010. doi: 10.1177/0038038516629917.

Fujimoto, Y., Rentschler, R., Le, H., Edwards, D., & Härtel, C. E. (2014). Lessons learned from community organizations: Inclusion of people with disabilities and others. *British Journal of Management*, 25(3), 518–537. doi: 10.1111/1467-8551.12034.

Gabriel, Y. (1995). The unmanaged organization: Stories, fantasies and subjectivity. *Organization Studies*, 16(3), 477–501. doi: 10.1177/017084069501600305.

Gabriel, Y. (2000). *Storytelling in organizations: Facts, fictions, and fantasies*. Oxford, England: Oxford University Press.

Gabriel, Y. (2012, September 10). *The Other and Othering – A short introduction* [Blog]. Retrieved from http://www.yiannisgabriel.com/2012/09/the-other-and-othering-short.html#!/2012/09/the-other-and-othering-short.html.

Gagnon, S., & Collinson, D. (2017). Resistance through difference: The co-constitution of dissent and inclusion. *Organization Studies*, 38(9), 1253–1276. doi: 10.1177/0170840616685362.

Gallo, E., & Scrinzi, F. (2019). Migrant masculinities in-between private and public spaces of reproductive labour: Asian porters in Rome. *Gender, Place & Culture*, 26(11), 1632–1653. doi: 10.1080/0966369X.2019.1586653.

Galloway, L., Kapasi, I., & Sang, K. (2015). Entrepreneurship, leadership, and the value of feminist approaches to understanding them. *Journal of Small Business Management*, 53(3), 683–692. doi: 10.1111/jsbm.12178.

Garrett, L. E., Spreitzer, G. M., & Bacevice, P. A. (2017). Co-constructing a sense of community at work: The emergence of community in coworking spaces. *Organization Studies*, *38*(6), 821–842. doi: 10.1177/0170840616685354.

Garry, A. (2011). Intersectionality, metaphors, and the multiplicity of gender. *Hypatia*, *26*(4), 826–850. doi: 10.1111/j.1527-2001.2011.01194.x.

Gasparin, M., Brown, S. D., Green, W., Hugill, A., Lilley, S., Quinn, M., ... Zalasiewicz, J. (2020). *The business school in the Anthropocene: Parasite logic and pataphysical reasoning for a working earth. Academy of Management Learning & Education.* Advance online publication. doi: 10.5465/amle.2019.0199.

Gatrell, C. (2019). Boundary creatures? Employed, breastfeeding mothers and 'abjection as practice'. *Organization Studies*, *40*(3), 421–442. doi: 10.1177/0170840617736932.

Gatto, M. (2020). *Parenthood demands: Resisting a dystopia in the workplace. Human Resource Development International*, 1–17. doi: 10.1080/13678868.2020.1735832.

Gebert, D., Buengeler, C., & Heinitz, K. (2017). Tolerance: A neglected dimension in diversity training? *Academy of Management Learning & Education*, *16*(3), 415–438. doi: 10.5465/amle.2015.0252.

George, G., Howard-Grenville, J., Joshi, A., & Tihanyi, L. (2016). Understanding and tackling societal grand challenges through management research. *Academy of Management Journal*, *59*(6), 1880–1895. doi: 10.5465/amj.2016.4007.

Geppert, M. (2015). Reflections on the methods of how we present and compare the political contents of our research: A prerequisite for critical institutional research. *Journal of Management Inquiry*, *24*(1), 100–104. doi: 10.1177/1056492614545305.

Ghosh, A. (2015). LGBTQ activist organizations as 'respectably queer' in India: Contesting a Western view. *Gender, Work & Organization*, *22*(1), 51–66. doi: 10.1111/gwao.12068.

Ghosh, R. (2018). Multiculturalism in a comparative perspective: Australia, Canada and India. *Canadian Ethnic Studies*, *50*(1), 15–36. doi: 10.1353/ces.2018.0002.

Ghoshal, S. (2005). Bad management theories are destroying good management practices. *Academy of Management Learning & Education*, *4*(1), 75–91. doi: 10.5465/amle.2005.16132558.

Giazitzoglu, A. (2020). This Sporting Life: The intersection of hegemonic masculinities, space and emotions among rugby players. *Gender, Work & Organization*, *27*(1), 67–81. doi: 10.1111/gwao.12367.

Gibson-Graham, J. K. (1996). Queer (y) ing capitalist organization. *Organization*, *3*(4), 541–545. doi: 10.1177/135050849634011.

Gilbert, J. A., Stead, B. A., & Ivancevich, J. M. (1999). Diversity management: A new organizational paradigm. *Journal of Business Ethics*, *21*(1), 61–76. doi: 10.1023/A:1005907602028.

Gilmore, S., Harding, N., Helin, J., & Pullen, A. (2019). Writing differently. *Management Learning*, *50*(1), 3–10. doi: 10.1177/1350507618811027.

Gilroy, P. (2012). 'My Britain is fuck all': Zombie multiculturalism and the race politics of citizenship. *Identities, 19*(4), 380–397. doi: 10.1080/1070289X. 2012.725512.

Giorgi, S., Lockwood, C., & Glynn, M. A. (2015). The many faces of culture: Making sense of 30 years of research on culture in organization studies. *The Academy of Management Annals, 9*(1), 1–54. doi: 10.1080/19416520.2015. 1007645.

Girei, E. (2017). Decolonising management knowledge: A reflexive journey as practitioner and researcher in Uganda. *Management Learning, 48*(4), 453–470. doi: 10.1177/1350507617697867.

Giroux, H. (1995). National identity and the politics of multiculturalism. *College Literature, 22*(2), 42–57. Retrieved from http://www.jstor.org/stable/25112186.

Glass, C., & Cook, A. (2020). *Performative contortions: How white women and people of color navigate elite leadership roles. Gender, Work & Organization.* Advance online publication. doi: 10.1111/gwao.12463.

Glazer, N. (1998). *We are all multiculturalists now.* Harvard, MA: Harvard University Press.

Godfrey, P. C., Hassard, J., O'Connor, E. S., Rowlinson, M., & Ruef, M. (2016). What is organizational history? Toward a creative synthesis of history and organization studies. *Academy of Management Review, 41*(4), 590–608. doi: 10.5465/amr.2016.0040.

Godfrey, R., Lilley, S., & Brewis, J. (2012). Biceps, bitches and borgs: Reading *Jarhead's* representation of the construction of the (masculine) military body. *Organization Studies, 33*(4), 541–562. doi: 10.1177/0170840612443458.

Gond, J. P., Cabantous, L., Harding, N., & Learmonth, M. (2016). What do we mean by performativity in organizational and management theory? The uses and abuses of performativity. *International Journal of Management Reviews, 18*(4), 440–463. doi: 10.1111/ijmr.12074.

Grant, D., Keenoy, T., & Oswick, C. (2001). Organizational discourse: Key contributions and challenges. *International Studies of Management & Organization, 31*(3), 5–24. doi: 10.1080/00208825.2001.11656818.

Granter, E. (2016). *Critical social theory and the end of work.* New York, NY: Routledge.

Gray, J. (2017, April 24). *Oxford University accused of targeting autistic students after claiming lack of eye contact is 'racist'.* Huff Post. Retrieved from http://www.huffingtonpost.co.uk/entry/oxford-university-autistic-students-eye-contact-racist_uk_58fdd466e4b06b9cb9182362.

Green, A. I., Follert, M., Osterlund, K., & Paquin, J. (2010). Space, place and sexual sociality: Towards an 'atmospheric analysis'. *Gender, Work & Organization, 17*(1), 7–27. doi: 10.1111/j.1468-0432.2007.00378.x.

Greene, A. M., & Kirton, G. (2011). Diversity management meets downsizing: The case of a government department. *Employee Relations, 33*(1), 22–39. doi: 10.1108/01425451111091636.

Greenwood, R., Raynard, M., Kodeih, F., Micelotta, E. R., & Lounsbury, M. (2011). Institutional complexity and organizational responses. *Academy of Management Annals, 5*(1), 317–371. doi: 10.5465/19416520.2011.590299.

Grey, C. (2007). Possibilities for critical management education and studies. *Scandinavian Journal of Management, 23*(4), 463–471. doi: 10.1016/j. scaman.2007.08.006.

Grey, C. (2018). Does Brexit mean the end for critical management studies in Britain? *Organization, 25*(5), 662–670. doi: 10.1177/1350508418757567.

Grey, C., & Garsten, C. (2002). Organized and disorganized utopias: An essay on presumption. *The Sociological Review, 50*(1_suppl), 9–23. doi: 10.1111/j.1467-954X.2002.tb03576.x.

Grey, C., & O'Toole, M. (2018). The placing of identity and the identification of place: "Place-Identity" in community lifeboating. *Journal of Management Inquiry, 29*(2), 206–219. doi: 10.1177/1056492618768696.

Grimes, D. S. (2002). Challenging the status quo? Whiteness in the diversity management literature. *Management Communication Quarterly, 15*(3), 381–409. doi: 10.1177/0893318902153003.

Gress, D. R., & Paek, J. (2014). Differential spaces in Korean places? Feminist geography and female managers in South Korea. *Gender, Work & Organization, 21*(2), 165–186. doi: 10.1111/gwao.12028.

Grint, K. (1994). Reengineering history: Social resonances and business process reengineering. *Organization, 1*(1), 179–201. doi: 10.1177/135050849400100116.

Grint, K., & Case, P. (1998). The violent rhetoric of re-engineering: Management consultancy on the offensive. *Journal of Management Studies, 35*(5), 557–577. doi: 10.1111/1467-6486.00109.

Grisoni, L., & Beeby, M. (2007). Leadership, gender and sense-making. *Gender, Work & Organization, 14*(3), 191–209. doi: 10.1111/j.1468-0432.2007.00339.x.

Gross, N. (2017, February 9). *How to do social science without data. The New York Times*. Retrieved from https://www.nytimes.com/2017/02/09/opinion/sunday/how-to-do-social-science-without-data.html?_r=0.

Grosser, K., & McCarthy, L. (2019). Imagining new feminist futures: How feminist social movements contest the neoliberalization of feminism in an increasingly corporate-dominated world. *Gender, Work & Organization, 26*(8), 1100–1116. doi: 10.1111/gwao.12267.

Guillaume, Y. R., Dawson, J. F., Woods, S. A., Sacramento, C. A., & West, M. A. (2013). Getting diversity at work to work: What we know and what we still don't know. *Journal of Occupational and Organizational Psychology, 86*(2), 123–141. doi: 10.1111/joop.12009.

Guimond, L., & Desmeules, A. (2018). Indigenous minorities on major northern worksites: Employment, space of encounter, sense of place. *Geoforum, 97*, 219–230. doi: 10.1016/j.geoforum.2018.09.007.

Guthey, G. T., Whiteman, G., & Elmes, M. (2014). Place and sense of place: Implications for organizational studies of sustainability. *Journal of Management Inquiry, 23*(3), 254–265. doi: 10.1177/1056492613517511.

Gutmann, A. (1993). The challenge of multiculturalism in political ethics. *Philosophy & Public Affairs, 22*(3), 171–206.

Hällgren, M., & Buchanan, D. A. (2020). *The dark side of group behavior: Zombie apocalypse lessons. Academy of Management Perspectives*. Advance online publication. doi: 10.5465/amp.2019.0007.

Halsall, R. (2008). From 'business culture' to 'brand state': Conceptions of nation and culture in business literature on cultural difference. *Culture and Organization, 14*(1), 15–30. doi: 10.1080/14759550701863290.

Halsall, R. (2009). The discourse of corporate cosmopolitanism. *British Journal of Management*, 20(S1), S136–S148. doi: 10.1111/j.1467-8551.2008.00637.x.

Hamel, S. A. (2009). Exit, voice, and sensemaking following psychological contract violations: Women's responses to career advancement barriers. *The Journal of Business Communication*, 46(2), 234–261. doi: 10.1177/0021943608328079.

Han, J., Han, J., & Brass, D. J. (2014). Human capital diversity in the creation of social capital for team creativity. *Journal of Organizational Behavior*, 35(1), 54–71. doi: 10.1002/job.1853.

Hancock, P., Sullivan, K., & Tyler, M. (2015). A touch too much: Negotiating masculinity, propriety and proximity in intimate labour. *Organization Studies*, 36(12), 1715–1739. doi: 10.1177/0170840615593592.

Haque, E. (2010). Homegrown, Muslim and other: Tolerance, secularism and the limits of multiculturalism. *Social Identities*, 16(1), 79–101. doi: 10.1080/13504630903465902.

Harding, N., Ford, J., & Fotaki, M. (2013). Is the 'F'-word still dirty? A past, present and future of/for feminist and gender studies in Organization. *Organization*, 20(1), 51–65. doi: 10.1177/1350508412460993.

Harding, N. H., Ford, J., & Lee, H. (2017). Towards a performative theory of resistance: Senior managers and revolting subject (ivitie) s. *Organization Studies*, 38(9), 1209–1232. doi: 10.1177/0170840616685360.

Hardy, C. (2001). Researching organizational discourse. *International Studies of Management & Organization*, 31(3), 25–47. doi: 10.1080/00208825.2001.11656819.

Hardy, C., & Thomas, R. (2015). Discourse in a material world. *Journal of Management Studies*, 52(5), 680–696. doi: 10.1111/joms.12113.

Hargrave, T. J. (2009). Moral imagination, collective action, and the achievement of moral outcomes. *Business Ethics Quarterly*, 19(1), 87–104. doi: 10.5840/beq20091914.

Harris, K. L. (2017). Re-situating organizational knowledge: Violence, intersectionality and the privilege of partial perspective. *Human Relations*, 70(3), 263–285. doi: 10.1177/0018726716654745.

Harrison, D. A., & Klein, K. J. (2007). What's the difference? Diversity constructs as separation, variety, or disparity in organizations. *Academy of Management Review*, 32(4), 1199–1228. doi: 10.5465/AMR.2007.26586096.

Harrison, D. A., Price, K. H. and Bell, M. P. (1998). Beyond relational demography: Time and the effects of surface-and deep-level diversity on work group cohesion. *Academy of Management Journal*, 41(1), 96–107. doi: 10.2307/256901.

Haslam, S. A., Eggins, R. A., & Reynolds, K. J. (2003). The ASPIRe model: Actualizing social and personal identity resources to enhance organizational outcomes. *Journal of Occupational and Organizational Psychology*, 76(1), 83–113. doi: 10.1348/096317903321208907.

Hassard, J., & Parker, M. (Eds.). (1993). *Postmodernism and organizations*. London, England: Sage.

Hatzenberger, A. (2003). Open society and bolos: A utopian reading of Bergson's 'final remarks'. *Culture and Organization*, 9(1), 43–58. doi: 10.1080/14759550302796.

Hayes, N., Introna, L. D., & Kelly, P. (2017). *Institutionalizing Inequality: Calculative practices and regimes of inequality in international development. Organization Studies*, OnelineFirst. doi: 10.1177/0170840617694067.

Hayward, C., & Lukes, S. (2008). Nobody to shoot? Power, structure, and agency: A dialogue. *Journal of Power*, *1*(1), 5–20. doi: 10.1080/ 17540290801943364.

Healy, G., Kirton, G., Özbilgin, M., & Oikelome, F. (2010). Competing rationalities in the diversity project of the UK judiciary: The politics of assessment centres. *Human Relations*, *63*(6), 807–834. doi: 10.1177/ 0018726709343335.

Healy, G., Tatli, A., Ipek, G., Özturk, M., Seierstad, C., & Wright, T. (2018). In the steps of Joan Acker: A journey in researching inequality regimes and intersectional inequalities. *Gender, Work & Organization*. Early Online Version. doi: 10.1111/gwao.12252.

Hearn, J. (1989). Leading questions for men: Men's leadership, feminist challenges, and men's responses. *Equal Opportunities International*, *8*(1), 3–11. doi: 10.1108/eb010495.

Hearn, J. (2014a). On men, organizations and intersectionality: Personal, working, political and theoretical reflections (Or how organization studies met profeminism). *Equality, Diversity and Inclusion: An International Journal*, *33*(5), 414–428. doi: 10.1108/EDI-07-2013-0051.

Hearn, J. (2014b). Sexualities, organizations and organization sexualities: Future scenarios and the impact of socio-technologies (a transnational perspective from the global 'north'). *Organization*, *21*(3), 400–420. doi: 10.1177/ 1350508413519764.

Heath, R. G. (2007). Rethinking community collaboration through a dialogic lens: Creativity, democracy, and diversity in community organizing. *Management Communication Quarterly*, *21*(2), 145–171. doi: 10.1177/ 0893318907306032.

Helms Mills, J. (2005). Organizational change and representations of women in a North American utility company. *Gender, Work & Organization*, *12*(3), 242–269. doi: 10.1111/j.1468-0432.2005.00272.x.

Helms Mills, J., & Mills, A. J. (2009). Critical sensemaking and workplace inequities. In M. Özbilgin (ed.) *Equality, Diversity and Inclusion at Work: Theory and Scholarship* (pp. 171–178). Cheltenham, England: Edward Elgar.

Hendershot, H. (2018). The Handmaid's Tale as ustopian allegory: "Stars and stripes forever, baby". *Film Quarterly*, *72*(1), 13–25. doi: 10.1525/fq.2018.72.1.13.

Hennekam, S., Bacouel-Jentjens, S., & Yang, I. (2019). *Perceptions of diversity management practices among first-versus second-generation migrants. Work, Employment and Society*. Advance online publication. doi: 10.1177/ 0950017019887335.

Hernes, T., & Weik, E. (2007). Organization as process: Drawing a line between endogenous and exogenous views. *Scandinavian Journal of Management*, *23*(3), 251–264. doi: 10.1016/j.scaman.2007.06.002.

Herod, A., Rainnie, A., & McGrath-Champ, S. (2007). Working space: Why incorporating the geographical is central to theorizing work and employment practices. *Work, Employment and Society*, *21*(2), 247–264. doi: 10.1177/ 0950017007076633.

Hill, R. J. (2009). Incorporating queers: Blowback, backlash, and other forms of resistance to workplace diversity initiatives that support sexual minorities. *Advances in Developing Human Resources, 11*(1), 37–53. doi: 10.1177/1523422308328128.

Hirsch, P., & Lounsbury, M. (2015). Toward a more critical and "powerful" institutionalism. *Journal of Management Inquiry, 24*(1), 96–99. doi: 10.1177/1056492614545297.

Hirst, A., & Humphreys, M. (2013). Putting power in its place: The centrality of edgelands. *Organization Studies, 34*(10), 1505–1527. doi: 10.1177/0170840613495330.

Hjorth, D. (2005). Organizational entrepreneurship: With de Certeau on creating heterotopias (or spaces for play). *Journal of Management Inquiry, 14*(4), 386–398. doi: 10.1177/1056492605280225.

Hodgson, G. M. (2007). Institutions and individuals: Interaction and evolution. *Organization Studies, 28*(1), 95–116. doi: 10.1177/0170840607067832.

Holck, L., & Muhr, S. L. (2017). Unequal solidarity? Towards a norm-critical approach to welfare logics. *Scandinavian Journal of Management, 33*(1), 1–11. doi: 10.1016/j.scaman.2016.11.001.

Holck, L., Muhr, S. L., & Villeseche, F. (2016). Identity, diversity and diversity management: On theoretical connections, assumptions and implications for practice. *Equality, Diversity and Inclusion: An International Journal, 35*(1), 48–64. doi: 10.1108/EDI-08-2014-0061.

Holland, R. (1999). Reflexivity. *Human Relations, 52*(4), 463–484. doi: doi.org/10.1177/001872679905200403.

Holmes IV, O. (2019). For diversity scholars who have considered activism when scholarship isn't enough! *Equality, Diversity and Inclusion: An International Journal, 38*(6), 668–675. doi: 10.1108/EDI-08-2017-0170.

Holt, R., den Hond, F., & Reay, T. (2016). X and organization studies. *Organization Studies, 37*(7), 901–902. doi: 10.1177/0170840616645491.

Holt, R., & Cornelissen, J. (2014). Sensemaking revisited. *Management Learning, 45*(5), 525–539. doi: 10.1177/1350507613486422.

Holvino, E. (2010). Intersections: The simultaneity of race, gender and class in organization studies. *Gender, Work & Organization, 17*(3), 248–277. doi: 10.1111/j.1468-0432.2008.00400.x.

Holvino, E., & Kamp, A. (2009). Diversity management: Are we moving in the right direction? Reflections from both sides of the North Atlantic. *Scandinavian Journal of Management, 25*(4), 395–403. doi: 10.1016/j.scaman.2009.09.005.

Hoobler, J. M. (2005). Lip service to multiculturalism: Docile bodies of the modern organization. *Journal of Management Inquiry, 14*(1), 49–56. doi: 10.1177/1056492604270798.

Hoque, K., & Noon, M. (2004). Equal opportunities policy and practice in Britain: Evaluating the 'empty shell' hypothesis. *Work, Employment and Society, 18*(3), 481–506. doi: 10.1177/0950017004045547.

Horwitz, S. K., & Horwitz, I. B. (2007). The effects of team diversity on team outcomes: A meta-analytic review of team demography. *Journal of Management, 33*(6), 987–1015. doi: 10.1177/0149206307308587.

Hotho, J., & Saka-Helmhout, A. (2017). In and between societies: Reconnecting comparative institutionalism and organization theory. *Organization Studies*, 38(5), 647–666. doi: 10.1177/0170840616655832.

Howard-Grenville, J., Davis, G. F., Dyllick, T., Miller, C. C., Thau, S., & Tsui, A. S. (2019). Sustainable development for a better world: Contributions of leadership, management, and organizations. *Academy of Management Discoveries*, 5(4), 355–366. doi: 10.5465/amd.2019.0275.

Howitt, D., & Owusu-Bempah, J. (1990). The pragmatics of institutional racism: Beyond words. *Human Relations*, 43(9), 885–899. doi: 10.1177/001872679004300905.

Hubbard, P., Kitchin, R., & Valentine, G. (Eds.). (2004). *Key thinkers on space and place*. London Sage.

Hughes, M. (2010). *Managing change: A critical perspective*. London: Kogan Page Publishers.

Hughes, M. (2018). Reflections: Studying organizational change leadership as a subfield. *Journal of Change Management*, 18(1), 10–22. doi: 10.1080/14697017.2017.1387219.

Human, O., & Robins, S. (2014). Social movements and biopolitical states: A study of humanitarian aid in Cape Town 2008. *Culture and Organization*, 20(2), 121–134. doi: 10.1080/14759551.2011.651388.

Hunt, R. A., Townsend, D., Korsgaard, S., & Naar, A. (2019). Urban farmers and cowboy coders: Re-imagining rural venturing in the 21st century. *Academy of Management Perspectives*. Advance online publication. doi: 10.5465/amp.2017.0157.

Hunter, S. D. J., & Swan, S. E. (2007). Oscillating politics and shifting agencies: Equalities and diversity work and actor network theory. *Equal Opportunities International*, 26(5), 402–419. doi: 10.1108/02610150710756621.

Husted, E., & Plesner, U. (2017). Spaces of open-source politics: Physical and digital conditions for political organization. *Organization*, 24(5), 648–670. doi: 10.1177/1350508417713215.

Iggers, G. G. (1995). Historicism: The history and meaning of the term. *Journal of the History of Ideas*, 56(1), 129–152. doi: 10.2307/2710011.

Iggers, G. G. (2005). Historiography in the twentieth century. *History and Theory*, 44(3), 469–476. doi: 10.1111/j.1468-2303.2005.00337.x.

Ind, M., Iglesias, O. & Schultz, M. (2015, August 24). *How Adidas found its second wind*. Strategy+business magazine. Retrieved from https://www.strategy-business.com/article/00352?gko=75bcd.

Introna, L. D. (2019). On the making of sense in sensemaking: Decentred sensemaking in the meshwork of life. *Organization Studies*, 40(5), 745–764. doi: 10.1177/0170840618765579.

Irving, S., & Helin, J. (2018). A world for sale? An ecofeminist reading of sustainable development discourse. *Gender, Work & Organization*, 25(3), 264–278. doi: 10.1111/gwao.12196.

Isotalus, E., & Kakkuri-Knuuttila, M. L. (2018). Ethics and intercultural communication in diversity management. *Equality, Diversity and Inclusion: An International Journal*, 37(5), 450–469. doi: 10.1108/EDI-01-2017-0019.

Jack, G. A., Calás, M. B., Nkomo, S. M., & Peltonen, T. (2008). Critique and international management: An uneasy relationship? *Academy of Management Review*, *33*(4), 870–884. doi: 10.5465/amr.2008.34421991.

Jack, G., Riach, K., & Bariola, E. (2019). Temporality and gendered agency: Menopausal subjectivities in women's work. *Human Relations*, *72*(1), 122–143. doi: 10.1177/0018726718767739.

Jackson, N., & Carter, P. (1993). 'Paradigm wars': A response to Hugh Willmott. *Organization Studies*, *14*(5), 721–725.

Jacques, R. S. (2002). What is a crypto-utopia and why does it matter? *The Sociological Review*, *50*(1_suppl), 24–39. doi: 10.1111/j.1467-954X.2002.tb03577.x.

Jamali, D., Abdallah, H., & Hmaidan, S. (2010). The challenge of moving beyond rhetoric: Paradoxes of diversity management in the Middle East. *Equality, Diversity and Inclusion: An International Journal*, *29*(2), 167–185. doi: 10.1108/02610151011024484.

James, F. A. (2016). Introduction: Some significances of the two cultures debate. *Interdisciplinary Science Reviews*, *41*(2–3), 107–117. doi: 10.1080/03080188.2016.1223651.

James, E. H., & Wooten, L. P. (2006). Diversity crises: How firms manage discrimination lawsuits. *Academy of Management Journal*, *49*(6), 1103–1118. doi: 10.5465/amj.2006.23478091.

Jameson, F. (2005). *Archaeologies of the future: The desire called utopia and other science fictions*. London: Verso.

Jammaers, E., Zanoni, P., & Hardonk, S. (2016). Constructing positive identities in ableist workplaces: Disabled employees' discursive practices engaging with the discourse of lower productivity. *Human Relations*, *69*(6), 1365–1386. doi: 10.1177/0018726715612901.

Janssens, M., & Zanoni, P. (2005). Many diversities for many services: Theorizing diversity (management) in service companies. *Human Relations*, *58*(3), 311–340. doi: 10.1177/0018726705053424.

Janssens, M., & Zanoni, P. (2014). Alternative diversity management: Organizational practices fostering ethnic equality at work. *Scandinavian Journal of Management*, *30*(3), 317–331. doi: 10.1016/j.scaman.2013.12.006.

Janssens, M., & Steyaert, C. (2019a). A practice-based theory of diversity: Respecifying (in) equality in organizations. *Academy of Management Review*, *44*(3), 518–537. doi: 10.5465/amr.2017.0062.

Janssens, M., & Steyaert, C. (2019b). The site of diversalizing: The accomplishment of inclusion in intergenerational dance. *Journal of Management Studies*. Advance online publication. doi: 10.1111/joms.12524.

Jarvenpaa, S. L., & Valikangas, L. (2020). Advanced technology and endtime in organizations: A doomsday for collaborative creativity? *Academy of Management Perspectives*. Advance online publication. doi: 10.5465/amp.2019.0040.

Jaya, P. S. (2001). Do we really 'know'and 'profess'? Decolonizing management knowledge. *Organization*, *8*(2), 227–233. doi: 10.1177/1350508401082008.

Jayne, M.E. & Dipboye, R.L. (2004). Leveraging diversity to improve business performance: Research findings and recommendations for organizations. *Human Resource Management*, *43*(4), 409–424. doi: 10.1002/hrm.20033.

Jensen, T., & Sandström, J. (2019). *Organizing rocks: Actor–network theory and space*. *Organization*. OnlineFirst. doi: 10.1177/1350508419842715.

Jeong, H. S., & Brower, R. S. (2008). Extending the present understanding of organizational sensemaking: Three stages and three contexts. *Administration & Society*, 40(3), 223–252. doi: 10.1177/0095399707313446.

Jeurissen, R., & Keijzers, G. (2004). Future generations and business ethics. *Business Ethics Quarterly*, 14(1), 47–69. doi: 10.5840/beq20041415.

Jiang, Z., & Korczynski, M. (2016). When the 'unorganizable' organize: The collective mobilization of migrant domestic workers in London. *Human Relations*, 69(3), 813–838. doi: 10.1177/0018726715600229.

Johansson, M., & Ringblom, L. (2017). The business case of gender equality in swedish forestry and mining-Restricting or enabling organizational change. *Gender, Work & Organization*, 24(6), 628–642. doi: 10.1111/gwao.12187.

Johns, G. (2017). Reflections on the 2016 Decade Award: Incorporating context in organizational research. *Academy of Management Review*, 42(4), 577–595. doi: 10.5465/amr.2017.0044.

Johnson, P. (2013). The geographies of heterotopia. *Geography Compass*, 7(11), 790–803. doi: 10.1111/gec3.12079.

Johnson, P., & Duberley, J. (2011). Anomie and culture management: Reappraising Durkheim. *Organization*, 18(4), 563–584. doi: 10.1177/1350508410392435.

Johnstone-Louis, M. (2017). Corporate social responsibility and women's entrepreneurship: Towards a more adequate theory of "work". *Business Ethics Quarterly*, 27(4), 569–602. doi: 10.1017/beq.2017.6.

Jones, D. (2004). Screwing diversity out of the workers? Reading diversity. *Journal of Organizational Change Management*, 17(3), 281–291. doi: 10.1108/09534810410538333.

Jones, D. (2007). Change agents, double agents, secret agents: EEO in New Zealand. *Equal Opportunities International*, 26(5), 387–401. doi: 10.1108/02610150710756612.

Jones, N., Novicevic, M. M., Hayek, M., & Humphreys, J. H. (2012). The first documents of emancipated African American management: The letters of Benjamin Montgomery (1865-1870). *Journal of Management History*, 18(1), 46–60. doi: 10.1108/17511341211188646.

Jones, T., & Ram, M. (2007). Re-embedding the ethnic business agenda. *Work, Employment and Society*, 21(3), 439–457. doi: 10.1177/0950017007080007.

Joppke, C. & Lukes, S. (eds) (1999). *Multicultural questions*. Oxford: Oxford University Press.

Joshi, A., Liao, H., & Roh, H. (2011). Bridging domains in workplace demography research: A review and reconceptualization. *Journal of Management*, 37(2), 521–552. doi: 10.1177/0149206310372969.

Joshi, A., & Roh, H. (2009). The role of context in work team diversity research: A meta-analytic review. *Academy of Management Journal*, 52(3), 599–627. doi: 10.5465/AMJ.2009.41331491.

Joullié, J. E. (2016). The philosophical foundations of management thought. *Academy of Management Learning & Education*, 15(1), 157–179. doi: 10.5465/amle.2012.0393.

Joy, A., & Haynes, B. (2011). Office design for the multi-generational knowledge workforce. *Journal of Corporate Real Estate*, 13(4), 216–232. doi: 10.1108/14630011111214428.

Joy, S., & Poonamallee, L. (2013). Cross-cultural teaching in globalized management classrooms: Time to move from functionalist to postcolonial approaches? *Academy of Management Learning & Education, 12*(3), 396–413. doi: 10.5465/amle.2012.0205.

Kachtan, D., & Wasserman, V. (2015). (Un) dressing masculinity: The body as a site of ethno-gendered resistance. *Organization, 22*(3), 390–417. doi: 10.1177/1350508413517408.

Kalonaityte, V. (2010). The case of vanishing borders: Theorizing diversity management as internal border control. *Organization, 17*(1), 31–52. doi: 10.1177/1350508409350238.

Kanji, S., & Cahusac, E. (2015). Who am I? Mothers' shifting identities, loss and sensemaking after workplace exit. *Human Relations, 68*(9), 1415–1436. doi: 10.1177/0018726714557336.

Kannen, V. (2014). These are not 'regular places': Women and gender studies classrooms as heterotopias. *Gender, Place & Culture, 21*(1), 52–67. doi: 10.1080/0966369X.2012.759910.

Kaplan, S. (2020). Beyond the business case for social responsibility. *Academy of Management Discoveries, 6*(1), 1–4. doi: 10.5465/amd.2018.0220.

Karam, C. M., & Jamali, D. (2017). A cross-cultural and feminist perspective on CSR in developing countries: Uncovering latent power dynamics. *Journal of Business Ethics, 142*(3), 461–477. doi: 10.1007/s10551-015-2737-7.

Karhunen, P., Kankaanranta, A., Louhiala-Salminen, L., & Piekkari, R. (2018). Let's talk about language: A review of language-sensitive research in international management. *Journal of Management Studies, 55*(6), 980–1013. doi: 10.1111/joms.12354.

Kelemen, M., Rumens, N., & Vo, L. C. (2019). Questioning and organization studies. *Organization Studies, 40*(10), 1529–1542. doi: 10.1177/0170840618783350.

Keltner, D. (2017). *The power paradox: How we gain and lose influence*. London, England: Penguin.

Kenny, E. J., & Briner, R. B. (2007). Ethnicity and behaviour in organizations: A review of British research. *Journal of Occupational and Organizational Psychology, 80*(3), 437–457. doi: 10.1348/096317906X156313.

Kenny, K. (2016). Organizations and violence: The child as abject-boundary in Ireland's industrial schools. *Organization Studies, 37*(7), 939–961. doi: 10.1177/0170840615622069.

Kenny, M. (2007). Gender, institutions and power: A critical review. *Politics, 27*(2), 91–100. doi: 10.1111/j.1467-9256.2007.00284.x.

Kenny, M., & Mackay, F. (2009). Already doin' it for ourselves? Skeptical notes on feminism and institutionalism. *Politics & Gender, 5*(2), 271–280. doi: 10.1017/S1743923X09000221.

Kersten, A. (2000). Diversity management. *Journal of Organizational Change Management, 13*(3), 235–248. doi: 10.1108/09534810010330887.

Kersten, A., & Abbott, C. (2012). Unveiling the global spectacle: Difference, identity and community. *Culture and Organization, 18*(4), 323–335. doi: 10.1080/14759551.2012.705532.

Kilduff, M., & Kelemen, M. (2001). The consolations of organization theory. *British Journal of Management, 12*(3), S55–S59. doi: 10.1111/1467-8551.12.s1.7.

King, E., Dawson, J., Jensen, J., & Jones, K. (2017). A socioecological approach to relational demography: How relative representation and respectful coworkers affect job attitudes. *Journal of Business and Psychology, 32*(1), 1–19. doi: 10.1007/s10869-016-9439-8.

King Jr, J. E. (2008). (Dis) missing the obvious: Will mainstream management research ever take religion seriously? *Journal of Management Inquiry, 17*(3), 214–224. doi: 10.1177/1056492608314205.

King, M. D., & Haveman, H. A. (2008). Antislavery in America: The press, the pulpit, and the rise of antislavery societies. *Administrative Science Quarterly, 53*(3), 492–528. doi: 10.2189/asqu.53.3.492.

Kirby, E. L., & Harter, L. M. (2003). Speaking the language of the bottom-line: The metaphor of "obliquity, waysetting and managing diversity". *The Journal of Business Communication (1973), 40*(1), 28–49. doi: 10.1177/002194360304000103.

Kirton, G. (2015). Progress towards gender democracy in UK unions 1987–2012. *British Journal of Industrial Relations, 53*(3), 484–507. doi: 10.1111/bjir.12052.

Kirton, G. (2019). Unions and equality: 50 years on from the fight for fair pay at Dagenham. *Employee Relations: The International Journal, 41*(2), 344–356. doi: 10.1108/ER-09-2018-0239.

Kirton, G., & Greene, A. M. (2006). The discourse of diversity in unionised contexts: Views from trade union equality officers. *Personnel Review, 35*(4), 431–448. doi: 10.1108/00483480610670599.

Kirton, G., & Greene, A. M. (2009). The costs and opportunities of doing diversity work in mainstream organisations. *Human Resource Management Journal, 19*(2), 159–175. doi: 10.1111/j.1748-8583.2009.00091.x.

Kirton, G. & Greene, A.M. (2010). *The dynamics of managing diversity*. London, England: Routledge.

Kirton, G., & Greene, A. M. (2019). Telling and selling the value of diversity and inclusion—External consultants' discursive strategies and practices. *Human Resource Management Journal, 29*(4), 676–691. doi: 10.1111/1748-8583.12253.

Kirton, G., Greene, A. M., & Dean, D. (2007). British diversity professionals as change agents–radicals, tempered radicals or liberal reformers?. *The International Journal of Human Resource Management, 18*(11), 1979–1994. doi: 10.1080/09585190701638226.

Kirton, G., & Healy, G. (2012). 'Lift as you rise': Union women's leadership talk. *Human Relations, 65*(8), 979–999. doi: 10.1177/0018726712448202.

Kitchener, M., & Delbridge, R. (2020). *Lessons from creating a business school for public good: Obliquity, waysetting and wayfinding in substantively rational change. Academy of Management Learning & Education*. Advance online publication. doi: 10.5465/amle.2019.0195.

Klikauer, T. (2015a). Critical management studies and critical theory: A review. *Capital & Class, 39*(2), 197–220. doi: 10.1177/0309816815581773.

Klikauer, T. (2015b). What is managerialism? *Critical Sociology, 41*(7–8), 1103–1119. doi: 10.1177/0896920513501351.

Klinger, C. (2018). An essay on life, care and death in the Brave New World after 1984. *Equality, Diversity and Inclusion: An International Journal, 37*(4), 318–331. doi: 10.1108/EDI-12-2017-0269.

Klotz, A., & Bolino, M. C. (2020). *Bringing the great outdoors into the workplace: The energizing effect of biophilic work design. Academy of Management Review.* Advance online publication. doi: 10.5465/amr. 2017.0177.

Knight, E., & Tsoukas, H. (2018). When Fiction Trumps Truth: What 'post-truth' and 'alternative facts' mean for management studies. *Organization Studies, 40*(2), 183–197. doi: 10.1177/0170840618814557.

Knights, D., & Omanović, V. (2016). (Mis) managing diversity: Exploring the dangers of diversity management orthodoxy. *Equality, Diversity and Inclusion: An International Journal, 35*(1), 5–16. doi: 10.1108/EDI-03-2014-0020.

Knoppers, A., Claringbould, I., & Dortants, M. (2015). Discursive managerial practices of diversity and homogeneity. *Journal of Gender Studies, 24*(3), 259–274. doi: 10.1080/09589236.2013.833086.

Kociatkiewicz, J., Kostera, M., & Parker, M. (2020). *The possibility of dis-alienated work: Being at home in alternative organizations. Human Relations.* Advance online publication. doi: 10.1177/0018726720916762.

Köllen, T. (2016). Acting out of compassion, egoism, and malice: A Schopenhauerian view on the moral worth of CSR and diversity management practices. *Journal of Business Ethics, 138*(2), 215–229. doi: 10.1007/s10551-015-2599-z.

Köllen, T. (2019). *Diversity management: A critical review and agenda for the future. Journal of Management Inquiry.* Advance online publication. doi: 10. 1177/1056492619868025.

Köllen, T., Kakkuri-Knuuttila, M. L., & Bendl, R. (2018). An indisputable "holy trinity"? On the moral value of equality, diversity, and inclusion. *Equality, Diversity and Inclusion: An International Journal, 37*(5), 438–449. doi: 10. 1108/EDI-04-2018-0072.

Koltko-Rivera, M. E. (2004). The psychology of worldviews. *Review of General Psychology, 8*(1), 3–58. doi: 10.1037/1089-2680.8.1.3.

Komporozos-Athanasiou, A., & Fotaki, M. (2015). A theory of imagination for organization studies using the work of Cornelius Castoriadis. *Organization Studies, 36*(3), 321–342. doi: 10.1177/0170840614559258.

Kondra, A. Z., & Hinings, C. R. (1998). Organizational diversity and change in institutional theory. *Organization Studies, 19*(5), 743–767. doi: 10.1177/017084069801900502.

Korn, J. B. (1995). Institutional sexism: Responsibility and intent. *Texas Journal of Women & Law, 4*, 83–124.

Kornberger, M., Leixnering, S., Meyer, R. E., & Höllerer, M. A. (2018). Rethinking the sharing economy: The nature and organization of sharing in the 2015 refugee crisis. *Academy of Management Discoveries, 4*(3), 314–335. doi: 10.5465/amd.2016.0138.

Kornberger, M., & Mantere, S. (2020). *Thought experiments and philosophy in organizational research. Organization Theory, 1*(3). doi: 10.1177/2631787720942524.

Kosmala, K. (2008). Women on work, women at work: Visual artists on labour exploitation. *British Journal of Management, 19*(S1), S85–S98. doi: 10.1111/j.1467-8551.2008.00574.x.

Kossek, E., Lewis, S., & Hammer, L. B. (2010). Work–life initiatives and organizational change: Overcoming mixed messages to move from the margin to the mainstream. *Human Relations, 63*(1), 3–19. doi: 10.1177/0018726709352385.

Kubes, T. (2019). New materialist perspectives on sex robots: A feminist dystopia/utopia? *Social Sciences, 8*(8), 224–238. doi: 10.3390/socsci8080224.

Kück, M. (1985). Women's opportunities in the alternative sector. *Equal Opportunities International, 4*(2), 1–4. doi: 10.1108/eb010418.

Kulik, C. T. (2014). Working below and above the line: The research–practice gap in diversity management. *Human Resource Management Journal, 24*(2), 129–144. doi: 10.1111/1748-8583.12038.

Kymlicka, W. (2007). Multicultural odysseys. *Ethnopolitics, 6*(4), 585–597. doi: 10.1080/17449050701659789.

Kymlicka, W. (2015). Solidarity in diverse societies: Beyond neoliberal multiculturalism and welfare chauvinism. *Comparative Migration Studies, 3*(1), 17. doi: 10.1186/s40878-015-0017-4.

Labelle, R., Francoeur, C., & Lakhal, F. (2015). To regulate or not to regulate? Early evidence on the means used around the world to promote gender diversity in the boardroom. *Gender, Work & Organization, 22*(4), 339–363. doi: 10.1111/gwao.12091.

Labelle, R., Gargouri, R. M., & Francoeur, C. (2010). Ethics, diversity management, and financial reporting quality. *Journal of Business Ethics, 93*(2), 335–353. doi: 10.1007/s10551-009-0225-7.

Lacerda, D. S., Meira, F. B., & Brulon, V. (2020). Spatial ethics beyond the North–South dichotomy: Moral dilemmas in favelas. *Journal of Business Ethics*. Advance online publication. doi: 10.1007/s10551-020-04467-8.

Landfester, U., & Metelmann, J. (2020). *Back to the roots: Why academic business schools should re-radicalize rationality. Academy of Management Learning & Education*. Advance online publication. doi: 10.5465/amle.2019.0212.

Lau, D. C., & Murnighan, J. K. (1998). Demographic diversity and faultlines: The compositional dynamics of organizational groups. *Academy of Management Review, 23*(2), 325–340. doi: 10.5465/AMR.1998.533229.

Lauring, J. (2013). International diversity management: Global ideals and local responses. *British Journal of Management, 24*(2), 211–224. doi: 10.1111/j.1467-8551.2011.00798.x.

Lauwo, S. (2016). Challenging masculinity in CSR disclosures: Silencing of women's voices in Tanzania's mining industry. *Journal of Business Ethics, 149*(3), 689–706. doi: 10.1007/s10551-016-3047-4.

Lawley, S. (2019). Spaces and laces: Insights from LGBT initiatives in sporting institutions. *Journal of Organizational Change Management, 33*(3), 502–514. doi: 10.1108/JOCM-11-2018-0342.

Lawrence, B. S. (1997). Perspective—The black box of organizational demography. *Organization Science, 8*(1), 1–22. doi: 10.1287/orsc.8.1.1.

Lawrence, T. B., & Dover, G. (2015). Place and institutional work: Creating housing for the hard-to-house. *Administrative Science Quarterly, 60*(3), 371–410. doi: 10.1177/0001839215589813.

Lawrence, T. B., Leca, B., & Zilber, T. B. (2013). Institutional work: Current research, new directions and overlooked issues. *Organization Studies, 34*(8), 1023–1033. doi: 10.1177/0170840613495305.

Lawrence, T., Suddaby, R., & Leca, B. (2011). Institutional work: Refocusing institutional studies of organization. *Journal of Management Inquiry, 20*(1), 52–58. doi: 10.1177/1056492610387222.

Lawrence, B. S., & Zyphur, M. J. (2011). Identifying organizational faultlines with latent class cluster analysis. *Organizational Research Methods, 14*(1), 32–57. doi: 10.1177/1094428110376838.

Leclercq-Vandelannoitte, A. (2011). Organizations as discursive constructions: A Foucauldian approach. *Organization Studies, 32*(9), 1247–1271. doi: 10. 1177/0170840611411395.

Lee, M. Y., Mazmanian, M., & Perlow, L. (2020). Fostering positive relational dynamics: The power of spaces and interaction scripts. *Academy of Management Journal, 63*(1), 96–123. doi: 10.5465/amj.2016.0685.

Lefebvre, H. (1991). *The production of space*. Oxford, England: Blackwell.

Lehman, D. W., O'Connor, K., Kovács, B., & Newman, G. E. (2019). Authenticity. *Academy of Management Annals, 13*(1), 1–42. doi: 10.5465/ annals.2017.0047.

Leitch, S., & Palmer, I. (2010). Analysing texts in context: Current practices and new protocols for critical discourse analysis in organization studies. *Journal of Management Studies, 47*(6), 1194–1212. doi: 10.1111/j.1467-6486.2009. 00884.x.

Lentin, A. (2014). Post-race, post politics: The paradoxical rise of culture after multiculturalism. *Ethnic and Racial Studies, 37*(8), 1268–1285. doi: 10.1080/ 01419870.2012.664278.

Leslie, L. M. (2017). A status-based multilevel model of ethnic diversity and work unit performance. *Journal of Management, 43*(2), 426–454. doi: 10. 1177/0149206314535436.

Leslie, L. M. (2019). Diversity initiative effectiveness: A typological theory of unintended consequences. *Academy of Management Review, 44*(3), 538–563. doi: 10.5465/amr.2017.0087.

Lewis, P. (2008). Emotion work and emotion space: Using a spatial perspective to explore the challenging of masculine emotion management practices. *British Journal of Management, 19*, S130–S140. doi: 10.1111/j.1467-8551.2008. 00578.x.

Lewis, P., Benschop, Y., & Simpson, R. (2017). Postfeminism, gender and or-ganization. *Gender, Work & Organization, 24*(3), 213–225. doi: 10.1111/ gwao.12175.

Lewis, R., Marine, S., & Kenney, K. (2018). I get together with my friends and try to change it'. Young feminist students resist 'laddism', 'rape culture' and 'everyday sexism'. *Journal of Gender Studies, 27*(1), 56–72. doi: 10.1080/ 09589236.2016.1175925.

Lewis, S. (2019). *Full surrogacy now: Feminism against family*. London, England: Verso Books.

Liff, S., & Wajcman, J. (1996). 'Sameness' and 'difference' revisited: Which way forward for equal opportunity initiatives? *Journal of Management Studies, 33*(1), 79–94. doi: 10.1111/j.1467-6486.1996.tb00799.x.

Lightfoot, G., & Lilley, S. (2002). Writing utopia. *The Sociological Review, 50*(1_suppl), 155–168. doi: 10.1111/j.1467-954X.2002.tb03583.x.

Lindsay, S., Jack, G., & Ambrosini, V. (2018). A critical diversity framework to better educate students about strategy implementation. *Academy of Management Learning & Education*, *17*(3), 241–258. doi: 10.5465/amle. 2017.0150.

Lindsay, C., Munro, A., & Wise, S. (2007). Making equalities work? Scottish trade unions' approaches to equal opportunities. *Equal Opportunities International*, *26*(5), 465–481. doi: 10.1108/02610150710756667.

Litvin, D. R. (1997). The discourse of diversity: From biology to management. *Organization*, *4*(2), 187–209. doi: 10.1177/135050849742003.

Liu, H. (2017a). Beneath the white gaze: Strategic self-Orientalism among Chinese Australians. *Human Relations*, *70*(7), 781–804. doi: 10.1177/ 0018726716676323.

Liu, H. (2017b). Undoing whiteness: The Dao of anti-racist diversity practice. *Gender, Work & Organization*, *24*(5), 457–471. doi: 10.1111/gwao.12142.

Liu, H. (2017c). The masculinisation of ethical leadership dis/embodiment. *Journal of Business Ethics*, *144*(2), 263–278. doi: 10.1007/s10551-015-2831-x.

Liu, H. (2018). Re-radicalising intersectionality in organisation studies. *Ephemera*, *18*(1), 81–101.

Liu, H. (2019a). An embarrassment of riches: The seduction of postfeminism in the academy. *Organization*, *26*(1), 20–37. doi: 10.1177/1350508418763980.

Liu, H. (2019b). Just the servant: An intersectional critique of servant leadership. *Journal of Business Ethics*, *156*(4), 1099–1112. doi: 10.1007/s10551-017-3633-0.

Liu, H. (2020). *Redeeming leadership: An anti-racist feminist intervention*. Bristol, England: Bristol University Press.

Liu, H., Cutcher, L., & Grant, D. (2015). Doing authenticity: The gendered construction of authentic leadership. *Gender, Work & Organization*, *22*(3), 237–255. doi: 10.1111/gwao.12073.

Liu, Y., & Grey, C. (2018). History, gendered space and organizational identity: An archival study of a university building. *Human Relations*, *71*(5), 640–667. doi: 10.1177/0018726717733032.

Locke, J. (2020). Being in-between and becoming undone: Bardos, heterotopias, and nepantla. *The Journal of Speculative Philosophy*, *34*(2), 113–140. doi: 10. 5325/jspecphil.34.2.0113.

Lockett, A., Currie, G., Finn, R., Martin, G., & Waring, J. (2014). The influence of social position on sensemaking about organizational change. *Academy of Management Journal*, *57*(4), 1102–1129. doi: 10.5465/amj.2011.0055.

Lok, J. (2019). Why (and how) institutional theory can be critical: Addressing the challenge to institutional theory's critical turn. *Journal of Management Inquiry*, *28*(3), 335–349. doi: 10.1177/1056492617732832.

Lok, J., & Willmott, H. (2014). Identities and identifications in organizations: Dynamics of antipathy, deadlock, and alliance. *Journal of Management Inquiry*, *23*(3), 215–230. doi: 10.1177/1056492613504461.

Lorbiecki, A. (2001). Changing views on diversity management: The rise of the learning perspective and the need to recognize social and political contradictions. *Management Learning*, *32*(3), 345–361. doi: 10.1177/ 1350507601323004.

Lorbiecki, A., & Jack, G. (2000). Critical turns in the evolution of diversity management. *British Journal of Management, 11*(3), S17–S31. doi: 10.1111/1467-8551.11.s1.3.

Louis, M. R. (1980). *Surprise and sense making: What newcomers experience in entering unfamiliar organizational settings. Administrative Science Quarterly,* 226–251. doi: 10.2307/2392453.

Lowe, S., Hwang, K. S., & Moore, F. (2011). Sensemaking and sojourner adjustment among Korean entrepreneurs in London (UK). *Culture and Organization, 17*(1), 31–46. doi: 10.1080/14759551.2011.530743.

Lowndes, V. (2014). How are things done around here? Uncovering institutional rules and their gendered effects. *Politics & Gender, 10*(4), 685–691. doi: 10.1017/S1743923X1400049X.

Lozano, J. F., & Escrich, T. (2017). Cultural diversity in business: A critical reflection on the ideology of tolerance. *Journal of Business Ethics, 142*(4), 679–696. doi: 10.1007/s10551-016-3113-y.

Lücke, G., Kostova, T., & Roth, K. (2014). Multiculturalism from a cognitive perspective: Patterns and implications. *Journal of International Business Studies, 45*(2), 169–190. doi: 10.1057/jibs.2013.53.

Luhman, J. T. (2006). Theoretical postulations on organization democracy. *Journal of Management Inquiry, 15*(2), 168–185. doi: 10.1177/1056492605275419.

Lukes, S. (1997). Toleration and recognition. *Ratio Juris, 10*(2), 213–222. doi: 10.1111/1467-9337.00056.

Lukes, S. (2003). *Liberals and cannibals: The implications of diversity.* London, England: Verso.

Luna, Z. (2016). "Truly a women of color organization": Negotiating sameness and difference in pursuit of intersectionality. *Gender & Society, 30*(5), 769–790. doi: 10.1177/0891243216649929.

Luo, Y., & Shenkar, O. (2006). The multinational corporation as a multilingual community: Language and organization in a global context. *Journal of International Business Studies, 37*(3), 321–339. doi: 10.1057/palgrave.jibs. 8400197.

Lyons, S., Urick, M., Kuron, L., & Schweitzer, L. (2015). Generational differences in the workplace: There is complexity beyond the stereotypes. *Industrial and Organizational Psychology, 8*(3), 346–356. doi: 10.1017/iop.2015.48.

McBride, A., Hebson, G., & Holgate, J. (2015). Intersectionality: Are we taking enough notice in the field of work and employment relations? *Work, Employment and Society, 29*(2), 331–341. doi: 10.1177/0950017014538337.

McCabe, D. (2004). 'A land of milk and honey'? Reengineering the 'past' and 'present' in a call centre. *Journal of Management Studies, 41*(5), 827–856. doi: 10.1111/j.1467-6486.2004.00455.x.

McCabe, D. (2016). 'Curiouser and curiouser!': Organizations as Wonderland–a metaphorical alternative to the rational model. *Human Relations, 69*(4), 945–973. doi: 10.1177/0018726715618453.

McCabe, D., & Knights, D. (2016). Learning to listen? Exploring discourses and images of masculine leadership through corporate videos. *Management Learning, 47*(2), 179–198. doi: 10.1177/1350507615586334.

McCabe, J. (2011). Doing multiculturalism: An interactionist analysis of the practices of a multicultural sorority. *Journal of Contemporary Ethnography*, 40(5), 521–549. doi: 10.1177/0891241611403588.

McCall, L. (2005). The complexity of intersectionality. *Signs*, 30(3), 1771–1800. doi: 10.1086/426800.

McCarthy, L. (2017). Empowering women through corporate social responsibility: A feminist Foucauldian critique. *Business Ethics Quarterly*, 27(4), 603–631. doi: 10.1017/beq.2017.28.

McCarthy, T. & Jacobs, B. (2016, July 19). *Melania Trump convention speech seems to plagiarise Michelle Obama*. The Guardian. Retrieved from https://www.theguardian.com/us-news/2016/jul/19/melania-trump-republican-convention-plagiarism-michelle-obama.

Macey, D. (2001). *The Penguin dictionary of critical theory*. London, England: Penguin.

MacIntosh, R., Beech, N., Bartunek, J., Mason, K., Cooke, B., & Denyer, D. (2017). Impact and management research: Exploring relationships between temporality, dialogue, reflexivity and praxis. *British Journal of Management*, 28(1), 3–13. doi: 10.1111/1467-8551.12207.

Mackay, F. (2011). Conclusion: Towards a feminist institutionalism? In M.L. Krook and F. Mackay (Eds.) *Gender, Politics and Institutions* (pp. 181–196). London, England: Palgrave Macmillan.

McKay, P. F., & Avery, D. R. (2005). Warning! Diversity recruitment could backfire. *Journal of Management Inquiry*, 14(4), 330–336. doi: 10.1177/1056492605280239.

Mackay, F., Kenny, M., & Chappell, L. (2010). New institutionalism through a gender lens: Towards a feminist institutionalism? *International Political Science Review*, 31(5), 573–588. doi: 10.1177/0192512110388788.

Mackenzie, E., & McKinlay, A. (2020). Hope labour and the psychic life of cultural work. *Human Relations*. Advance online publication. doi: 10.1177/0018726720940777.

Maclean, M., Harvey, C., & Chia, R. (2012). Sensemaking, storytelling and the legitimization of elite business careers. *Human Relations*, 65(1), 17–40. doi: 10.1177/0018726711425616.

Mahmood, B. (2020, July 28). *Exclusive: Ex-equalities commissioners say calling out racism cost them their jobs*. Newsweek. Online article. Retrieved from https://www.newsweek.com/equality-race-racism-ehrc-equalities-human-rights-commission-1520714.

Maitlis, S., & Christianson, M. (2014). Sensemaking in organizations: Taking stock and moving forward. *Academy of Management Annals*, 8(1), 57–125. doi: 10.5465/19416520.2014.873177.

Maitlis, S., & Sonenshein, S. (2010). Sensemaking in crisis and change: Inspiration and insights from Weick (1988). *Journal of Management Studies*, 47(3), 551–580. doi: 10.1111/j.1467-6486.2010.00908.x.

Maitlis, S., Vogus, T. J., & Lawrence, T. B. (2013). Sensemaking and emotion in organizations. *Organizational Psychology Review*, 3(3), 222–247. doi: 10.1177/2041386613489062.

Malik, S., Chapain, C., & Comunian, R. (2017). Rethinking cultural diversity in the UK film sector: Practices in community filmmaking. *Organization, 24*(3), 308–329. doi: 10.1177/1350508416689094.

Mantel, H. (2009, 17 October). *Booker winner Hilary Mantel on dealing with history in fiction.* The Guardian. Retrieved from https://www.theguardian. com/books/2009/oct/17/hilary-mantel-author-booker.

Marcus, A. A. (1987). US firms' responses to regulation: Stonewalling and opportunism. *Long Range Planning, 20*(3), 98–104. doi: 10.1016/0024-6301(87)90077-X.

Maréchal, G., Linstead, S., & Munro, I. (2013). The territorial organization: History, divergence and possibilities. *Culture and Organization, 19*(3), 185–208. doi: 10.1080/14759551.2013.812703.

Marfelt, M. M. (2016). Grounded intersectionality: Key tensions, a methodological framework, and implications for diversity research. *Equality, Diversity and Inclusion: An International Journal, 35*(1), 31–47. doi: 10.1108/EDI-05-2014-0034.

Markard, L., & Dähnke, I. (2017). Contested discourses on diversity and practices of diversity incorporation in political parties in Germany. *Ethnic and Racial Studies, 40*(5), 809–829. doi: 10.1080/01419870.2016.1259490.

Marshall, N., & Rollinson, J. (2004). Maybe Bacon had a point: The politics of interpretation in collective sensemaking. *British Journal of Management, 15*(S1), 71–86. doi: 10.1111/j.1467-8551.2004.00401.x.

Martí, I., & Fernández, P. (2013). The institutional work of oppression and resistance: Learning from the Holocaust. *Organization Studies, 34*(8), 1195–1223. doi: 10.1177/0170840613492078.

Martin, L. A., Edwards, M., & Sayers, J. G. (2018). A "novel" discovery: Exploring women's literary fiction for use in management and leadership education. *Academy of Management Learning & Education, 17*(1), 24–40. doi: 10.5465/amle.2016.0369.

Masood, A. (2019). Doing gender, modestly: Conceptualizing workplace experiences of Pakistani women doctors. *Gender, Work & Organization, 26*(2), 214–228. doi: 10.1111/gwao.12308.

Masood, A., & Nisar, M. A. (2020). Speaking out: A postcolonial critique of the academic discourse on far-right populism. *Organization, 27*(1), 162–173. doi: 10.1177/1350508419828572.

Maznevski, M. L., & Chudoba, K. M. (2000). Bridging space over time: Global virtual team dynamics and effectiveness. *Organization Science, 11*(5), 473–492. doi: 10.1287/orsc.11.5.473.15200.

Mease, J. J. (2016). Embracing discursive paradox: Consultants navigating the constitutive tensions of diversity work. *Management Communication Quarterly, 30*(1), 59–83. doi: 10.1177/0893318915604239.

Meer, N., & Modood, T. (2012). How does interculturalism contrast with multiculturalism?. *Journal of Intercultural Studies, 33*(2), 175–196. doi: 10. 1080/07256868.2011.618266.

Meininger, H. P. (2013). Inclusion as heterotopia: Spaces of encounter between people with and without intellectual disability. *Journal of Social Inclusion, 4*(1), 24–44. doi: 10.36251/josi.61.

Mena, S., Rintamäki, J., Fleming, P., & Spicer, A. (2016). On the forgetting of corporate irresponsibility. *Academy of Management Review*, *41*(4), 720–738. doi: 10.5465/amr.2014.0208.

Mertes, H. (2015). Does company-sponsored egg freezing promote or confine women's reproductive autonomy? *Journal of Assisted Reproduction and Genetics*, *32*(8), 1205–1209. doi: 10.1007/s10815-015-0500-8.

Mestyan, A. (2018, April 25). *Was Cairo's grand opera house a tool of cultural imperialism? Aeon*. Online magazine. Retrieved from https://aeon.co/ideas/was-cairos-grand-opera-house-a-tool-of-cultural-imperialism.

Metcalfe, B. D., & Woodhams, C. (2012). Introduction: New directions in gender, diversity and organization theorizing–re-imagining feminist post-colonialism, transnationalism and geographies of power. *International Journal of Management Reviews*, *14*(2), 123–140. doi: 10.1111/j.1468-2370. 2012.00336.x.

Meyerson, D. E., & Scully, M. A. (1995). Tempered radicalism and the politics of ambivalence and change. *Organization Science*, *6*(5), 585–600. doi: 10. 1287/orsc.6.5.585.

Michaelson, C. (2016). A novel approach to business ethics education: Exploring how to live and work in the 21st century. *Academy of Management Learning & Education*, *15*(3), 588–606. doi: 10.5465/amle.2014.0129.

Michalopoulos, S., & Papaioannou, E. (2015). On the ethnic origins of African development: Chiefs and precolonial political centralization. *Academy of Management Perspectives*, *29*(1), 32–71. doi: 10.5465/amp.2012.0162.

Michels, C., Hindley, C., Knowles, D., & Ruth, D. (2020). *Learning atmospheres: Re-imagining management education through the dérive. Management Learning*. Advance online publication. doi: 10.1177/ 1350507620906673.

Mikkelsen, E. N., & Wåhlin, R. (2020). Dominant, hidden and forbidden sensemaking: The politics of ideology and emotions in diversity management. *Organization*, *27*(4), 557–577. doi: 10.1177/1350508419830620.

Miller, F. A., Katz, J. H., & Gans, R. (2018). The OD imperative to add inclusion to the algorithms of artificial intelligence. *OD Practitioner*, *50*(1), 8–12. Retrieved from https://www.researchgate.net/profile/Roger_Gans2/publication/323830092_AI_x_I_AI2_The_OD_imperative_to_add_inclusion_to_the_algorithms_of_artificial_intelligence/links/5aad244e0-f7e9b4897be932a/AI-x-I-AI2-The-OD-imperative-to-add-inclusion-to-the-algorithms-of-artificial-intelligence.pdf.

Miller, G. E., & Rowney, J. I. (1999). Workplace diversity management in a multicultural society. *Women in Management Review*, *14*(8), 307–315. doi: 10.1108/09649429910301670.

Miller, J. (1998). Post-apocalyptic hoping: Octavia Butler's dystopian/utopian vision. *Science Fiction Studies*, *25*(2), 336–360. https://www.jstor.org/stable/4240705.

Milliken, F. J. and Martins, L. L. (1996). Searching for common threads: Understanding the multiple effects of diversity in organizational groups. *Academy of Management Review*, *21*(2), 402–433. doi: 10.5465/AMR.1996. 9605060217.

Mills, C. W. (1959/2000). *The sociological imagination*. Oxford, England: Oxford University Press.

Mills, C. (2002). The hidden dimension of blue-collar sensemaking about workplace communication. *The Journal of Business Communication (1973)*, *39*(3), 288–313. doi: 10.1177/002194360203900301.

Mills, A. J. (2008). Getting critical about sensemaking. In D. Barry & H. Hansen (Eds.), *The Sage handbook of new approaches to organization studies* (pp. 29–30). London, England: Sage.

Mills, A. J., & Chiaramonte, P. (1991). Organization as gendered communication act. *Canadian Journal of Communication*, *16*(3), 381–398. doi: 10.22230/cjc.1991v16n3a624.

Mills, J. H., Thurlow, A., & Mills, A. J. (2010). Making sense of sensemaking: The critical sensemaking approach. *Qualitative Research in Organizations and Management: An International Journal*, *5*(2), 182–195. doi: 10.1108/17465641011068857.

Milner, S. (2017). Trade unions, equality and diversity: An inconsistent record of transformative action. *Work, Employment & Society*, *31*(1), 191–196. doi: 10.1177/0950017016650622.

Mir, R., & Mir, A. (2013). The colony writes back: Organization as an early champion of non-Western organizational theory. *Organization*, *20*(1), 91–101. doi: 10.1177/1350508412461003.

Mirchandani, K. (2003). Challenging racial silences in studies of emotion work: Contributions from anti-racist feminist theory. *Organization Studies*, *24*(5), 721–742. doi: 10.1177/0170840603024005003.

Mitchell, T. D. (2014). How service-learning enacts social justice sensemaking. *Journal of Critical Thought and Praxis*, *2*(2), 1–26. doi: 10.31274/jctp-180810-22.

Modood, T. (2007). *Multiculturalism. The Blackwell encyclopedia of sociology* (Online edition). doi: 10.1002/9781405165518.wbeosm129.pub2.

Moen, P. (2015). An institutional/organizational turn: Getting to work–life quality and gender equality. *Work and Occupations*, *42*(2), 174–182. doi: 10.1177/0730888414568085.

Mohammed, S. and Angell, L. C. (2004). Surface-and deep-level diversity in workgroups: Examining the moderating effects of team orientation and team process on relationship conflict. *Journal of Organizational Behavior*, *25*(8), 1015–1039. doi: 10.1002/job.293.

Moisander, J. K., Hirsto, H., & Fahy, K. M. (2016). Emotions in institutional work: A discursive perspective. *Organization Studies*, *37*(7), 963–990. doi: 10.1177/0170840615613377.

Monro, S. (2007). New institutionalism and sexuality at work in local government. *Gender, Work & Organization*, *14*(1), 1–19. doi: 10.1111/j.1468-0432.2007.00329.x.

Mooney, S. (2016). 'Nimble' intersectionality in employment research: A way to resolve methodological dilemmas. *Work, Employment and Society*, *30*(4), 708–718. doi: 10.1177/0950017015620768.

Moore, G., & Grandy, G. (2017). Bringing morality back in: Institutional theory and MacIntyre. *Journal of Management Inquiry*, *26*(2), 146–164. doi: 10.1177/1056492616670754.

Moore, K., Griffiths, M., Richardson, H., & Adam, A. (2008). Gendered futures? Women, the ICT workplace and stories of the future. *Gender, Work & Organization, 15*(5), 523–542. doi: 10.1111/j.1468-0432.2008.00416.x.

Morgan, G. (1997). *Images of organization* (2nd ed.). Thousand Oaks, CA: Auflage.

Morrell, K. (2012). Evidence-based dialectics. *Organization, 19*(4), 461–479. doi: 10.1177/1350508411414229.

Morris, S. M. (2012). Black girls are from the future: Afrofuturist feminism in Octavia E. Butler's "Fledgling". *Women's Studies Quarterly, 40*(3/4), 146–166. doi: 10.1353/wsq.2013.0034.

Moufahim, M., Reedy, P., & Humphreys, M. (2015). The Vlaams Belang: The rhetoric of organizational identity. *Organization Studies, 36*(1), 91–111. doi: 10.1177/0170840614546149.

Muhr, S. L. (2012). Strangers in familiar places–using generic spaces in cross-cultural identity work. *Culture and Organization, 18*(1), 51–68. doi: 10.1080/14759551.2011.631340.

Mulholland, K. (2004). Workplace resistance in an Irish call centre: Slammin', scammin' smokin' an' leavin'. *Work, Employment and Society, 18*(4), 709–724. doi: 10.1177/0950017004048691.

Mullen, J., Vladi, N., & Mills, A. J. (2006). Making sense of the Walkerton crisis. *Culture and Organization, 12*(3), 207–220. doi: 10.1080/14759550600865933.

Mumby, D. K. (1998). Organizing men: Power, discourse, and the social construction of masculinity (s) in the workplace. *Communication Theory, 8*(2), 164–183. doi: 10.1111/j.1468-2885.1998.tb00216.x.

Mumby, D. K. (2005). Theorizing resistance in organization studies: A dialectical approach. *Management Communication Quarterly, 19*(1), 19–44. doi: 10.1177/0893318905276558.

Mumby, D. K. (2016). Organizing beyond organization: Branding, discourse, and communicative capitalism. *Organization, 23*(6), 884–907. doi: 10.1177/1350508416631164.

Mumby, D. K., & Putnam, L. L. (1992). The politics of emotion: A feminist reading of bounded rationality. *Academy of Management Review, 17*(3), 465–486. doi: 10.5465/amr.1992.4281983.

Mumby, D. K., Thomas, R., Martí, I., & Seidl, D. (2017). Resistance redux. *Organization Studies, 38*(9), 1157–1183. doi: 10.1177/0170840617717554.

Munir, K. A. (2015). A loss of power in institutional theory. *Journal of Management Inquiry, 24*(1), 90–92. doi: 10.1177/1056492614545302.

Munir, K. A. (2019). Challenging institutional theory's critical credentials. *Organization Theory, 1*(1). doi: 10.1177/2631787719887975.

Munro, I., & Jordan, S. (2013). 'Living Space' at the Edinburgh Festival Fringe: Spatial tactics and the politics of smooth space. *Human Relations, 66*(11), 1497–1525. doi: 10.1177/0018726713480411.

Munro, R. (2002). The consumption of time and space: Utopias and the English romantic garden. *The Sociological Review, 50*(1_suppl), 128–154. doi: 10.1111/j.1467-954X.2002.tb03582.x.

Murji, K. (2007). Sociological engagements: Institutional racism and beyond. *Sociology, 41*(5), 843–855. doi: 10.1177/0038038507080440.

Murphy, A. (2001). The flight attendant dilemma: An analysis of communication and sensemaking during in-flight emergencies. *Journal of Applied Communication Research*, 29(1), 30–53. doi: 10.1080/00909880128100.

Murray, T. (2014). *Is judging Islamic culture possible?* Philosophy Now. Online magazine. Retrieved from https://philosophynow.org/issues/102/Is_Judging_ Islamic_Culture_Possible.

Murray, P., & Syed, J. (2005). Critical issues in managing age diversity in Australia. *Asia Pacific Journal of Human Resources*, 43(2), 210–224. doi: 10. 1177/1038411105055059.

Musson, G., & Tietze, S. (2004). Places and spaces: The role of metonymy in organizational talk. *Journal of Management Studies*, 41(8), 1301–1323. doi: 10.1111/j.1467-6486.2004.00476.x.

Mutch, A. (2018). Practice, substance, and history: Reframing institutional logics. *Academy of Management Review*, 43(2), 242–258. doi: 10.5465/amr. 2015.0303.

Nadiv, R., & Kuna, S. (2020). Diversity management as navigation through organizational paradoxes. *Equality, Diversity and Inclusion: An International Journal*, 39(4), 355–377. doi: 10.1108/EDI-12-2018-0236.

Nash, J. C. (2017). Intersectionality and its discontents. *American Quarterly*, 69(1), 117–129. doi: 10.1353/aq.2017.0006.

Nash, L. (2018). Gendered places: Place, performativity and flânerie in the City of London. *Gender, Work & Organization*, 25(6), 601–620. doi: 10.1111/ gwao.12241.

Nash, L. (2020). Performing place: A rhythmanalysis of the city of London. *Organization Studies*, 41(3), 301–321. doi: 10.1177/0170840618789161.

Naude, P. (2019). Decolonising knowledge: Can Ubuntu ethics save us from coloniality?. *Journal of Business Ethics*, 159(1), 23–37. doi: 10.1007/s10551- 017-3763-4.

Nemetz, P. L., & Christensen, S. L. (1996). The challenge of cultural diversity: Harnessing a diversity of views to understand multiculturalism. *Academy of Management Review*, 21(2), 434–462. doi: 10.5465/amr.1996.9605060218.

Nentwich, J. C., Özbilgin, M. F., & Tatli, A. (2015). Change agency as performance and embeddedness: Exploring the possibilities and limits of Butler and Bourdieu. *Culture and Organization*, 21(3), 235–250. doi: 10.1080/ 14759551.2013.851080.

Ng, E. S., & Bloemraad, I. (2015). A SWOT Analysis of multiculturalism in Canada, Europe, Mauritius, and South Korea. *American Behavioral Scientist*, 59(6), 619–636. doi: 10.1177/0002764214566500.

Ng, E. S., & Metz, I. (2015). Multiculturalism as a strategy for national competitiveness: The case for Canada and Australia. *Journal of Business Ethics*, 128(2), 253–266. doi: 10.1007/s10551-014-2089-8.

Ng, K., Niven, K., & Hoel, H. (2019). 'I could help, but…': A dynamic sensemaking model of workplace bullying bystanders. *Human Relations*. Advance online publication. doi: 10.1177/0018726719884617.

Nielsen, R. P. (1993). Organization ethics from a perspective of praxis. *Business Ethics Quarterly*, 3(2), 131–152. doi: 10.2307/3857368.

Nielsen, S. (2010). Top management team diversity: A review of theories and methodologies. *International Journal of Management Reviews*, 12(3), 301–316. doi: 10.1111/j.1468-2370.2009.00263.x.

Nishii, L. H., Khattab, J., Shemla, M., & Paluch, R. M. (2018). A multi-level process model for understanding diversity practice effectiveness. *Academy of Management Annals*, 12(1), 37–82. doi: 10.5465/annals.2016.0044.

Nkomo, S. M. (2011). A postcolonial and anti-colonial reading of 'African' leadership and management in organization studies: Tensions, contradictions and possibilities. *Organization*, 18(3), 365–386. doi: 10.1177/1350508411398731.

Nkomo, S. M., Bell, M. P., Roberts, L. M., Joshi, A., & Thatcher, S. M. (2019). Diversity at a critical juncture: New theories for a complex phenomenon. *Academy of Management Review*, 44(3), 498–517. doi: 10.5465/amr.2019.0103.

Nkomo, S., & Hoobler, J. M. (2014). A historical perspective on diversity ideologies in the United States: Reflections on human resource management research and practice. *Human Resource Management Review*, 24(3), 245–257. doi: 10.1016/j.hrmr.2014.03.006.

Noon, M. (2007). The fatal flaws of diversity and the business case for ethnic minorities. *Work, Employment and Society*, 21(4), 773–784. doi: 10.1177/0950017007082886.

Noon, M. (2010). The shackled runner: Time to rethink positive discrimination?. *Work, Employment and Society*, 24(4), 728–739. doi: 10.1177/0950017010380648.

Noon, M. (2012). Simply the best? The case for using 'threshold selection' in hiring decisions. *Human Resource Management Journal*, 22(1), 76–88. doi: 10.1111/j.1748-8583.2011.00168.x.

Noon, M. (2018). Pointless diversity training: Unconscious bias, new racism and agency. *Work, Employment and Society*, 32(1), 198–209. doi: 10.1177/0950017017719841.

Nwonka, C. J., & Malik, S. (2018). Cultural discourses and practices of in-stitutionalised diversity in the UK film sector: 'Just get something black made'. *The Sociological Review*. Advance online publication. doi: 10.1177/0038026118774183.

Nye, J. S. (2011). *The future of power*. New York, NY: Public Affairs.

Obourn, M. (2013). Octavia Butler's disabled futures. *Contemporary Literature*, 54(1), 109–138. doi: 10.1353/cli.2013.0001.

O'Doherty, D., De Cock, C., Rehn, A., & Lee Ashcraft, K. (2013). New sites/sights: Exploring the white spaces of organization. *Organization Studies*, 34(10), 1427–1444. doi: 10.1177/0170840613499654.

Ojha, A.K. (2005). Sensemaking and identity development. *Journal of Intercultural Communication* 10 (December) (Online article). Retrieved from http://www.immi.se/intercultural/nr10/ojha.htm.

Okin, S. M. (1998a). Feminism and multiculturalism: Some tensions. *Ethics*, 108(4), 661–684. doi: 10.1086/233846.

Okin, S. M. (1998b). Feminism, women's human rights, and cultural differences. *Hypatia*, 13(2), 32–52. doi: 10.1111/j.1527-2001.1998.tb01224.x.

O'Leary, M., & Chia, R. (2007). Epistemes and structures of sensemaking in organizational life. *Journal of Management Inquiry*, 16(4), 392–406. doi: 10.1177/1056492607310976.

Ortlieb, R., & Sieben, B. (2013). Diversity strategies and business logic: Why do companies employ ethnic minorities?. *Group & Organization Management*, *38*(4), 480–511. doi: 10.1177/1059601113497094.

O'Shea, S. C. (2018). This girl's life: An autoethnography. *Organization*, *25*(1), 3–20. doi: 10.1177/1350508417703471.

O'Shea, S. C. (2019). Cutting my dick off. *Culture and Organization*, *25*(4), 272–283. doi: 10.1080/14759551.2019.1608203.

Osland, J. S., & Bird, A. (2000). Beyond sophisticated stereotyping: Cultural sensemaking in context. *Academy of Management Perspectives*, *14*(1), 65–77. doi: 10.5465/ame.2000.2909840.

Ostendorp, A., & Steyaert, C. (2009). How different can differences be (come)?: Interpretative repertoires of diversity concepts in Swiss-based organizations. *Scandinavian Journal of Management*, *25*(4), 374–384. doi: 10.1016/j.scaman.2009.09.003.

Oswick, C., Fleming, P., & Hanlon, G. (2011). From borrowing to blending: Rethinking the processes of organizational theory building. *Academy of Management Review*, *36*(2), 318–337. doi: 10.5465/amr.2009.0155.

Oswick, C., & Noon, M. (2014). Discourses of diversity, equality and inclusion: Trenchant formulations or transient fashions? *British Journal of Management*, *25*(1), 23–39. doi: 10.1111/j.1467-8551.2012.00830.x.

Özbilgin, M. F., Beauregard, T. A., Tatli, A., & Bell, M. P. (2011). Work–life, diversity and intersectionality: A critical review and research agenda. *International Journal of Management Reviews*, *13*(2), 177–198. doi: 10.1111/j.1468-2370.2010.00291.x.

Özbilgin, M. F., Syed, J., Ali, F., & Torunoglu, D. (2012). International transfer of policies and practices of gender equality in employment to and among Muslim majority countries. *Gender, Work & Organization*, *19*(4), 345–369. doi: 10.1111/j.1468-0432.2010.00515.x.

Özbilgin, M., & Tatli, A. (2005). Understanding Bourdieu's contribution to organization and management studies. *The Academy of Management Review*, *30*(4), 855–869. doi: 10.5465/amr.2005.18378882.

Özbilgin, M., & Tatli, A. (2011). Mapping out the field of equality and diversity: Rise of individualism and voluntarism. *Human Relations*, *64*(9), 1229–1253. doi: 10.1177/0018726711413620.

Özkazanç-Pan, B. (2008). International management research meets "the rest of the world". *Academy of Management Review*, *33*(4), 964–974. doi: 10.5465/amr.2008.34422014.

Özkazanç-Pan, B. (2019). *Diversity and future of work: Inequality abound or opportunities for all? Management Decision*. Advance online publication. doi: 10.1108/MD-02-2019-0244.

Ozturk, M. B., & Rumens, N. (2014). Gay male academics in UK business and management schools: Negotiating heteronormativities in everyday work life. *British Journal of Management*, *25*(3), 503–517. doi: 10.1111/1467-8551.12061.

Pache, A. C., & Santos, F. (2010). When worlds collide: The internal dynamics of organizational responses to conflicting institutional demands. *Academy of Management Review*, *35*(3), 455–476. doi: 10.5465/amr.35.3.zok455.

Page, M., Grisoni, L., & Turner, A. (2014). Dreaming fairness and re-imagining equality and diversity through participative aesthetic inquiry. *Management Learning, 45*(5), 577–592. doi: 10.1177/1350507613486425.

Pal, M. (2016). Organization at the margins: Subaltern resistance of Singur. *Human Relations, 69*(2), 419–438. doi: 10.1177/0018726715589797.

Park, C. L. (2010). Making sense of the meaning literature: An integrative review of meaning making and its effects on adjustment to stressful life events. *Psychological Bulletin, 136*(2), 257–301. doi: 10.1037/a0018301.

Parker, M. (1993). *Postmodernism and organizations*. London, England: Sage.

Parker, M. (2002a). Queering management and organization. *Gender, Work & Organization, 9*(2), 146–166. doi: 10.1111/1468-0432.00153.

Parker, M. (2002b). Utopia and the organizational imagination: Outopia. *The Sociological Review, 50*(1_suppl), 1–8. doi: 10.1111/j.1467-954X.2002. tb03575.x.

Parker, M. (2009). Angelic organization: Hierarchy and the tyranny of heaven. *Organization Studies, 30*(11), 1281–1299. doi: 10.1177/0170840609339828.

Parker, M. (2016). Queering queer. *Gender, Work & Organization, 23*(1), 71–73. doi: 10.1111/gwao.12106.

Parker, M. (2017). No future. Utopia now! *Ephemera, 17*(4), 933–936. Online article, retrieved from: http://www.ephemerajournal.org/sites/default/files/pdfs/contribution/17-4parker_0.pdf.

Parker, M. (2018). *Shut down the business school: What's wrong with management education*. London, England: Pluto Press.

Parker, M. (2020, June 4). Where did the grandeur go? *Aeon* (Online article). Retrieved from https://aeon.co/essays/superlative-projects-are-made-possible-by-great-collective-efforts.

Parker, M., Cheney, G., Fournier, V., & Land, C. (eds.). (2014a). *The Routledge companion to alternative organization*. London, England: Routledge.

Parker, M., Cheney, G., Fournier, V., & Land, C. (2014b). The question of organization: A manifesto for alternatives. *Ephemera: Theory and Politics in Organization, 14*(4), 623–638. Online article. Retrieved from http://www.ephemerajournal.org/contribution/question-organization-manifesto-alternatives.

Parker, M., Fournier, V., & Reedy, P. (2007). *The dictionary of alternatives: Utopianism and organization*. London: Zed Books.

Parker, M., & Jary, D. (1995). The McUniversity: Organization, management and academic subjectivity. *Organization, 2*(2), 319–338. doi: 10.1177/135050849522013.

Parker, S., & Parker, M. (2017). Antagonism, accommodation and agonism in Critical Management Studies: Alternative organizations as allies. *Human Relations, 70*(11), 1366–1387. doi: 10.1177/0018726717696135.

Parker, S., & Racz, M. (2020). Affective and effective truths: Rhetoric, normativity and critical management studies. *Organization, 27*(3), 454–465. doi: 10.1177/1350508419855717.

Pasquero, J. (1997). Business ethics and national identity in Quebec: Distinctiveness and directions. *Journal of Business Ethics, 16*(6), 621–633. doi: 10.1023/A:1005702126961.

Pathak, P. (2008). Making a case for multiculture: From the politics of piety to the politics of the secular? *Theory, Culture & Society, 25*(5), 123–141. doi: 10. 1177/0263276408095219.

Patil, V. (2013). From patriarchy to intersectionality: A transnational feminist assessment of how far we've really come. *Signs: Journal of Women in Culture and Society, 38*(4), 847–867. doi: 10.1086/669560.

Pelled, L. H., Eisenhardt, K. M., & Xin, K. R. (1999). Exploring the black box: An analysis of work group diversity, conflict and performance. *Administrative Science Quarterly, 44*(1), 1–28. doi: doi.org/10.2307/2667029.

Peretz, T. (2017). Engaging diverse men: An intersectional analysis of men's pathways to antiviolence activism. *Gender & Society, 31*(4), 526–548. doi: 10. 1177/0891243217717181.

Peretz, T. (2019). *Why Atlanta? A case study of how place produces intersectional social movement groups. Gender, Place & Culture.* Advance online publication. doi: 10.1080/0966369X.2019.1693340.

Petani, F. J. (2019). Confessions of an organizational space writer. *Organization, 26*(6), 961–971. doi: 10.1177/1350508418821010.

Petriglieri, G., & Petriglieri, J. L. (2020). The return of the oppressed: A systems psychodynamic approach to organization studies. *Academy of Management Annals, 14*(1), 411–449. doi: 10.5465/annals.2017.0007.

Pfeffer, J. (1985). Organizational demography: Implications for management. *California Management Review, 28*(1), 67–81. doi: 10.2307/41165170.

Pfeffer, J. (1992). *Managing with power: Politics and influence in organizations.* Harvard, MA: Harvard Business Press.

Phillips, N., & Oswick, C. (2012). Organizational discourse: Domains, debates, and directions. *Academy of Management Annals, 6*(1), 435–481. doi: 10. 5465/19416520.2012.681558.

Pieterse J. N. (1997) Multiculturalism and museums: Discourse about others in the age of globalization. *Theory, Culture & Society 14*(4): 123–146. doi: 10. 1177/026327697014004006.

Pieterse, J. N. (2001). Hybridity, so what?. *Theory, Culture & Society, 18*(2–3), 219–245. doi: 10.1177/026327640101800211.

Pio, E., & Essers, C. (2014). Professional migrant women decentring otherness: A transnational perspective. *British Journal of Management, 25*(2), 252–265. doi: 10.1111/1467-8551.12003.

Pio, E., & Syed, J. (2018). To include or not to include? A poetics perspective on the Muslim workforce in the West. *Human Relations, 71*(8), 1072–1095. doi: 10.1177/0018726717733529.

Pio, E., & Syed, J. (2020). Stelae from ancient India: Pondering anew through historical empathy for diversity. *Management Learning, 51*(1), 109–129. doi: 10.1177/1350507619841213.

Plaut, V. C. (2014). Diversity science and institutional design. *Policy Insights from the Behavioral and Brain Sciences, 1*(1), 72–80. doi: 10.1177/ 2372732214550164.

Pless, N., & Maak, T. (2004). Building an inclusive diversity culture: Principles, processes and practice. *Journal of Business Ethics, 54*(2), 129–147. doi: 10. 1007/s10551-004-9465-8.

Porter, J., & Oliver, R. (2016). Rethinking lactation space: Working mothers, working bodies, and the politics of inclusion. *Space and Culture, 19*(1), 80–93. doi: 10.1177/1206331215596488.

Powell, W. W., & DiMaggio, P. J. (Eds.). ([1991] 2012). *The new institutionalism in organizational analysis.* Chicago, IL: University of Chicago Press.

Prasad, A. (2012). Beyond analytical dichotomies. *Human Relations, 65*(5), 567–595. doi: 10.1177/0018726711432183.

Prasad, A. (2016). Cyborg writing as a political act: Reading Donna Haraway in organization studies. *Gender, Work & Organization, 23*(4), 431–446. doi: 10. 1111/gwao.12128.

Prasad, A., & Mills, A. J. (2010). Critical management studies and business ethics: A synthesis and three research trajectories for the coming decade. *Journal of Business Ethics, 94*(2), 227–237. doi: 10.1007/s10551-011-0753-9.

Prasad, A., Prasad, P., & Mir, R. (2011). 'One mirror in another': Managing diversity and the discourse of fashion. *Human Relations, 64*(5), 703–724. doi: 10.1177/0018726710386511.

Pratt, M. G. (2000). Building an ideological fortress: The role of spirituality, encapsulation and sensemaking. *Studies in Cultures, Organizations and Societies, 6*(1), 35–69. doi: 10.1080/10245280008523537.

Prichard, C., & Benschop, Y. (2018). It's time for Acting Up! *Organization, 25*(1), 98–105. doi: 10.1177/1350508417741501.

Pringle, J. K., & Ryan, I. (2015). Understanding context in diversity management: A multi-level analysis. *Equality, Diversity and Inclusion: An International Journal, 34*(6), 470–482. doi: 10.1108/EDI-05-2015-0031.

Prügl, E. (2011). Diversity management and gender mainstreaming as technologies of government. *Politics & Gender, 7*(1), 71–89. doi: 10.1017/ S1743923X10000565.

Pullen, A., & Rhodes, C. (2015). Writing, the feminine and organization. *Gender, Work & Organization, 22*(2), 87–93. doi: 10.1111/gwao.12084.

Pullen, A., Rhodes, C., McEwen, C., & Liu, H. (2019). *Radical politics, intersectionality and leadership for diversity in organizations. Management Decision.* Advance online publication. doi: 10.1108/MD-02-2019-0287.

Pullen, A., Rhodes, C., & Thanem, T. (2017). Affective politics in gendered organizations: Affirmative notes on becoming-woman. *Organization, 24*(1), 105–123. doi: 10.1177/1350508416668367.

Pullen, A., Thanem, T., Tyler, M., & Wallenberg, L. (2016). Sexual politics, organizational practices: Interrogating queer theory, work and organization. *Gender, Work & Organization, 23*(1), 1–6. doi: 10.1111/gwao.12123.

Pullen, A., & Vachhani, S. J. (2020). *Feminist ethics and women leaders: From difference to intercorporeality. Journal of Business Ethics,* 1–11. doi: 10.1007/ s10551-020-04526-0.

Pullen, A., Vachhani, S., Gagnon, S., & Cornelius, N. (2017). Critical diversity, philosophy and praxis. *Gender, Work & Organization, 24*(5), 451–456. doi: 10.1111/gwao.12192.

Putnam, L. L. (2015). Unpacking the dialectic: Alternative views on the discourse–materiality relationship. *Journal of Management Studies, 52*(5), 706–716. doi: 10.1111/joms.12115.

Radoynovska, N. M. (2018). Working within discretionary boundaries:

Allocative rules, exceptions, and the micro-foundations of inequ (al) ity. *Organization Studies, 39*(9), 1277–1298. doi: 10.1177/0170840617717544.

Raelin, J. A. (2008). Emancipatory discourse and liberation. *Management Learning, 39*(5), 519–540. doi: 10.1177/1350507608096039.

Raffnsøe, S., Mennicken, A., & Miller, P. (2019). The Foucault effect in organization studies. *Organization Studies, 40*(2), 155–182. doi: 10.1177/0170840617745110.

Ramarajan, L. (2014). Past, present and future research on multiple identities: Toward an intrapersonal network approach. *The Academy of Management Annals, 8*(1), 589–659. doi: 10.1080/19416520.2014.912379.

Rancière, J. (2010). The aesthetic heterotopia. *Philosophy Today, 54*(Supplement), 15–25. doi: 10.5840/philtoday201054Supplement42.

Ratner, H. (2019). *Topologies of organization: Space in continuous deformation. Organization Studies.* Advance online publication. doi: 10.1177/0170840619874464.

Rattansi, A. (2011). *Multiculturalism: A very short introduction.* Oxford: Oxford University Press.

Reaktion Books (2017). *Critical Lives.* Retrieved from http://www. reaktionbooks.co.uk/results.asp?SF1=series_exact&ST1=CRITICALLIVES& DS=Critical%20Lives&SORT=sort_title.

Reed, H. (2017). Corporations as agents of social change: A case study of diversity at Cummins Inc. *Business History, 59*(6), 821–843. doi: 10.1080/00076791.2016.1255196.

Reed, M. I. (1989). *The sociology of management.* London, England: Harvester Wheatsheaf.

Reed, M. I. (2012). Masters of the universe: Power and elites in organization studies. *Organization Studies, 33*(2), 203–221. doi: 10.1177/0170840611430590.

Reedy, P. (2002). Keeping the Black Flag flying: Anarchy, utopia and the politics of nostalgia. *The Sociological Review, 50*(1_suppl), 169–188. doi: 10.1111/j.1467-954X.2002.tb03584.x.

Reedy, P. (2003). Together we stand? An investigation into the concept of solidarity in management education. *Management Learning, 34*(1), 91–109. doi: 10.1177/1350507603034001132.

Reedy, P. (2014). Impossible organisations: Anarchism and organisational praxis. *Ephemera, 14*(4), 639–658. Retrieved from http://www.ephemerajournal.org/contribution/impossible-organisations-anarchism-and-organisational-praxis.

Reedy, P., King, D., & Coupland, C. (2016). Organizing for individuation: Alternative organizing, politics and new identities. *Organization Studies, 37*(11), 1553–1573. doi: 10.1177/0170840616641983.

Reedy, P., & Learmonth, M. (2009). Other possibilities? The contribution to management education of alternative organizations. *Management Learning, 40*(3), 241–258. doi: 10.1177/1350507609104338.

Reicher, S., Haslam, S.A. & Van Bavel, J. (2018, June 25). *Time to change the story: New evidence from the Zimbardo archives challenges everything you have taught (or been taught) about the Stanford Prison Experiment.* The

Psychologist. Retrieved from https://thepsychologist.bps.org.uk/time-change-story.

Reiff, M. R. (2020). *In the name of liberty: The argument for universal unionization*. Cambridge, England: Cambridge University Press.

Reinecke, J., & Ansari, S. (2015). What is a "fair" price? Ethics as sensemaking. *Organization Science, 26*(3), 867–888. doi: 10.1287/orsc.2015.0968.

Reitman, M. (2006). Uncovering the white place: Whitewashing at work. *Social & Cultural Geography, 7*(2), 267–282. doi: 10.1080/14649360600600692.

Rhodes, C. (2017). Ethical praxis and the business case for LGBT diversity: Political insights from Judith Butler and Emmanuel Levinas. *Gender, Work & Organization, 24*(5), 533–546. doi: 10.1111/gwao.12168.

Riach, K. (2009). Managing 'difference': Understanding age diversity in practice. *Human Resource Management Journal, 19*(3), 319–335. doi: 10.1111/j.1748-8583.2009.00096.x.

Riach, K., Rumens, N., & Tyler, M. (2014). Un/doing chrononormativity: Negotiating ageing, gender and sexuality in organizational life. *Organization Studies, 35*(11), 1677–1698. doi: 10.1177/0170840614550731.

Riach, K., Rumens, N., & Tyler, M. (2016). Towards a Butlerian methodology: Undoing organizational performativity through anti-narrative research. *Human Relations, 69*(11), 2069–2089. doi: 10.1177/0018726716632050.

Riach, K., & Wilson, F. (2014). Bodyspace at the pub: Sexual orientations and organizational space. *Organization, 21*(3), 329–345. doi: 10.1177/1350508413519767.

Riaz, S. (2015). Bringing inequality back in: The economic inequality footprint of management and organizational practices. *Human Relations, 68*(7), 1085–1097. doi: 10.1177/0018726715584803.

Rice, C., Chandler, E., Rinaldi, J., Changfoot, N., Liddiard, K., Mykitiuk, R., & Mündel, I. (2017). Imagining disability futurities. *Hypatia, 32*(2), 213–229. doi: 10.1111/hypa.12321.

Richard, O. C., Murthi, B. P., & Ismail, K. (2007). The impact of racial diversity on intermediate and long-term performance: The moderating role of environmental context. *Strategic Management Journal, 28*(12), 1213–1233. doi: 10.1002/smj.633.

Richards, J., & Sang, K. (2016). Trade unions as employment facilitators for disabled employees. *The International Journal of Human Resource Management, 27*(14), 1642–1661. doi: 10.1080/09585192.2015.1126334.

Riordan, C. M., & Wayne, J. H. (2008). A review and examination of demographic similarity measures used to assess relational demography within groups. *Organizational Research Methods, 11*(3), 562–592. doi: 10.1177/1094428106295503.

Risi, D. (2020). *Business and society research drawing on institutionalism: Integrating normative and descriptive research on values. Business & Society.* Advance online publication. doi: 10.1177/0007650320928959.

Roberson, Q., Holmes IV, O., & Perry, J. L. (2017). Transforming research on diversity and firm performance: A dynamic capabilities perspective. *Academy of Management Annals, 11*(1), 189–216. doi: 10.5465/annals.2014.0019.

Roberson, Q. M., & Stevens, C. K. (2006). Making sense of diversity in the workplace: Organizational justice and language abstraction in employees' accounts of diversity-related incidents. *Journal of Applied Psychology, 91*(2), 379–391. doi: 10.1037/0021-9010.91.2.379.

Robinson, G., & Dechant, K. (1997). Building a business case for diversity. *Academy of Management Perspectives, 11*(3), 21–31. doi: 10.5465/ame.1997. 9709231661.

Robinson, M. J., Van Esch, C., & Bilimoria, D. (2017). Bringing transgender issues into management education: A call to action. *Academy of Management Learning & Education, 16*(2), 300–313. doi: 10.5465/amle.2015.0355.

Rodner, V., Roulet, T. J., Kerrigan, F., & Vom Lehn, D. (2019). *Making space for art: A spatial perspective of disruptive and defensive institutional work in Venezuela's art world. Academy of Management Journal.* Advance online publication. doi: 10.5465/amj.2016.1030.

Rodriguez, J. K., Holvino, E., Fletcher, J. K., & Nkomo, S. M. (2016). The theory and praxis of intersectionality in work and organisations: Where do we go from here? *Gender, Work & Organization, 23*(3), 201–222. doi: 10.1111/ gwao.12131.

Romani, L., Holck, L., & Risberg, A. (2019). Benevolent discrimination: Explaining how human resources professionals can be blind to the harm of diversity initiatives. *Organization, 26*(3), 371–390. doi: 10.1177/ 1350508418812585.

Rorty, R. (1989). *Contingency, irony, and solidarity.* Cambridge, England: Cambridge University Press.

Rosenthal, L. (2016). Incorporating intersectionality into psychology: An opportunity to promote social justice and equity. *American Psychologist, 71*(6), 474. doi: 10.1037/a0040323.

Roth, L. M. (2007). Women on Wall Street: Despite diversity measures, Wall Street remains vulnerable to sex discrimination charges. *Academy of Management Perspectives, 21*(1), 24–35. doi: 10.5465/amp.2007.24286162.

Rothman, A. & Fields, B.J. (2020, July 24). *The death of Hannah Fizer.* Dissent. Online article. Retrieved from https://www.dissentmagazine.org/online_ articles/the-death-of-hannah-fizer.

Rothman, N. B., Pratt, M. G., Rees, L., & Vogus, T. J. (2017). Understanding the dual nature of ambivalence: Why and when ambivalence leads to good and bad outcomes. *Academy of Management Annals, 11*(1), 33–72. doi: 10.5465/ annals.2014.0066.

Routledge Taylor & Francis Group (2017). *Routledge Critical Thinkers.* Retrieved from https://www.routledge.com/Routledge-Critical-Thinkers/ book-series/SE0370.

Rowlinson, M. (2004). Challenging the foundations of organization theory. *Work, Employment and Society, 18*(3), 607–620. doi: 10.1177/ 0950017004045553.

Roy, A. (2016, July 21). *Melania Trump was inspired by...Michelle Obama!* newslaundry.com. Retrieved from https://www.newslaundry.com/2016/07/21/ melania-trump-was-inspired-bymichelle-obama.

Ruef, M., & Harness, A. (2009). Agrarian origins of management ideology: The Roman and Antebellum cases. *Organization Studies, 30*(6), 589–607. doi: 10. 1177/0170840609104801.

Ruiz Castro, M., & Holvino, E. (2016). Applying intersectionality in organizations: Inequality markers, cultural scripts and advancement practices in a professional service firm. *Gender, Work & Organization*, 23(3), 328–347. doi: 10.1111/gwao.12129.

Rumens, N. (2012). Queering cross-sex friendships: An analysis of gay and bisexual men's workplace friendships with heterosexual women. *Human Relations*, 65(8), 955–978. doi: 10.1177/0018726712442427.

Rumens, N. (2016). Towards queering the business school: A research agenda for advancing lesbian, gay, bisexual and trans perspectives and issues. *Gender, Work & Organization*, 23(1), 36–51. doi: 10.1111/gwao.12077.

Rumens, N. (2017). Queering lesbian, gay, bisexual and transgender identities in human resource development and management education contexts. *Management Learning*, 48(2), 227–242. doi: 10.1177/1350507616672737.

Rumens, N., De Souza, E. M., & Brewis, J. (2019). Queering queer theory in management and organization studies: Notes toward queering heterosexuality. *Organization Studies*, 40(4), 593–612. doi: 10.1177/0170840617748904.

Runté, M., & Mills, A. J. (2006). Cold War, chilly climate: Exploring the roots of gendered discourse in organization and management theory. *Human Relations*, 59(5), 695–720. doi: 10.1177/0018726706066174.

Russell, G. M., & Bohan, J. S. (2016). Institutional allyship for LGBT equality: Underlying processes and potentials for change. *Journal of Social Issues*, 72(2), 335–354. doi: 10.1111/josi.12169.

Sage, D., Justesen, L., Dainty, A., Tryggestad, K., & Mouritsen, J. (2016). Organizing space and time through relational human–animal boundary work: Exclusion, invitation and disturbance. *Organization*, 23(3), 434–450. doi: 10.1177/1350508416629449.

Saifuddin, S. (2017). Unveiling women's leadership: Identity and meaning of leadership in India. *Equality, Diversity and Inclusion: An International Journal*, 36(3), 283–286. doi: 10.1108/EDI-01-2017-0001.

Saldanha, A. (2008). Heterotopia and structuralism. *Environment and Planning A*, 40(9), 2080–2096. doi: 10.1068/a39336.

Samdanis, M., & Özbilgin, M. (2020). The duality of an atypical leader in diversity management: The legitimization and delegitimization of diversity beliefs in organizations. *International Journal of Management Reviews*, 22(2), 101–119. doi: 10.1111/ijmr.12217.

Sandberg, J., & Tsoukas, H. (2011). Grasping the logic of practice: Theorizing through practical rationality. *Academy of Management Review*, 36(2), 338–360. doi: 10.5465/amr.2009.0183.

Sandberg, J., & Tsoukas, H. (2015). Making sense of the sensemaking perspective: Its constituents, limitations, and opportunities for further development. *Journal of Organizational Behavior*, 36(S1), S6–S32. doi: 10.1002/job.1937.

Sanderson, K., Parsons, D. B., Mills, J. H., & Mills, A. J. (2010). Riding the second wave: Organizing feminism and organizational discourse—Stewardesses For women's rights. *Management & Organizational History*, 5(3-4), 360–377. doi: 10.1177/1744935910368460.

Sandberg, J., & Tsoukas, H. (2020). Sensemaking reconsidered: Towards a broader understanding through phenomenology. *Organization Theory*, 1(1). doi: 10.1177/2631787719879937.

Sang, K., Al-Dajani, H., & Özbilgin, M. (2013). Frayed careers of migrant female professors in British academia: An intersectional perspective. *Gender, Work & Organization, 20*(2), 158–171. doi: 10.1111/gwao.12014.

Saraiva, L. A. S., & Vinholi Rampazo, A. (2020). A strange tale. *Gender, Work & Organization.* Advance online publication. doi: 10.1111/gwao.12498.

Sardar, Z. (2010). The Namesake: Futures; futures studies; futurology; futuristic; foresight—What's in a name? *Futures, 42*(3), 177–184. doi: 10.1016/j.futures. 2009.11.001.

Sargent, L. T. (2010). *Utopianism: A very short introduction.* Oxford (UK): Oxford University Press.

Sartori, G. (1997). Understanding pluralism. *Journal of Democracy, 8*(4), 58–69. doi: 10.1353/jod.1997.0064.

Sayce, S. (2019). Revisiting Joan Acker's work with the support of Joan Acker. *Gender, Work & Organization, 26*(12), 1721–1729. doi: 10.1111/gwao. 12243.

Scalvini, M. (2016). A crisis of religious diversity: Debating integration in post-immigration Europe. *Discourse & Communication, 10*(6), 614–634. doi: 10. 1177/1750481316674779.

Schildt, H., Mantere, S., & Cornelissen, J. (2020). Power in sensemaking processes. *Organization Studies, 41*(2), 241–265. doi: 10.1177/ 0170840619847718.

Schneider, P., & Sting, F. J. (2019). *Employees' perspectives on digitalization-induced change: Exploring frames of Industry 4.0. Academy of Management Discoveries.* Advance online publication. doi: 10.5465/amd.2019.0012.

Schubert, J. D. (2002). Defending multiculturalism: From hegemony to symbolic violence. *American Behavioral Scientist, 45*(7), 1088–1102. doi: 10.1177/ 0002764202045007004.

Schwabenland, C. (2012). *Metaphor and dialectic in managing diversity.* London, England: Palgrave Macmillan.

Schwabenland, C., & Tomlinson, F. (2015). Shadows and light: Diversity management as phantasmagoria. *Human Relations, 68*(12), 1913–1936. doi: 10.1177/0018726715574587.

Schwandt, D. R. (2005). When managers become philosophers: Integrating learning with sensemaking. *Academy of Management Learning & Education, 4*(2), 176–192. doi: 10.5465/amle.2005.17268565.

Schwanen, T., Hardill, I., & Lucas, S. (2012). Spatialities of ageing: The co-construction and co-evolution of old age and space. *Geoforum, 43*(6), 1291–1295. doi: 10.1016/j.geoforum.2012.07.002.

Sealy, T. (2018). Multiculturalism, interculturalism, 'multiculture' and super-diversity: Of zombies, shadows and other ways of being. *Ethnicities, 18*(5), 692–716. doi: 10.1177/1468796817751575.

Seeck, H., Sturdy, A., Boncori, A. L., & Fougère, M. (2020). Ideology in management studies. *International Journal of Management Reviews, 22*(1), 53–74. doi: 10.1111/ijmr.12215.

Segal, A. (1996). Flowering feminism: Consciousness raising at work. *Journal of Organizational Change Management, 9*(5), 75–90. doi: 10.1108/ 09534819610128805.

Sekerka, L. E., & Yacobian, M. M. (2018). Fostering workplace respect in an era of anti-Muslimism and Islamophobia: A proactive approach for management. *Equality, Diversity and Inclusion: An International Journal, 37*(8), 813–831. doi: 10.1108/EDI-11-2017-0265.

Selznick, P. (1996). Institutionalism "old" and "new". *Administrative Science Quarterly, 41*(2), 270–277. doi: 10.2307/2393719.

Sewell, D. (2009). *The political gene: How Darwin's ideas changed politics.* London, England: Pan Macmillan.

Shadnam, M., Crane, A., & Lawrence, T. B. (2020). Who calls it? Actors and accounts in the social construction of organizational moral failure. *Journal of Business Ethics, 165*(4), 699–717. doi: 10.1007/s10551-018-4089-6.

Sharp, R., Franzway, S., Mills, J., & Gill, J. (2012). Flawed policy, failed politics? Challenging the sexual politics of managing diversity in engineering organizations. *Gender, Work & Organization, 19*(6), 555–572. doi: 10.1111/j.1468-0432.2010.00545.x.

Shemla, M., Meyer, B., Greer, L., & Jehn, K. A. (2016). A review of perceived diversity in teams: Does how members perceive their team's composition affect team processes and outcomes? *Journal of Organizational Behavior, 37*(S1), S89–S106. doi: 10.1002/job.1957.

Shen, J., Chanda, A., D'netto, B., & Monga, M. (2009). Managing diversity through human resource management: An international perspective and conceptual framework. *The International Journal of Human Resource Management, 20*(2), 235–251. doi: 10.1080/09585190802670516.

Shenkar, O. (1996). The firm as a total institution: Reflections on the Chinese state enterprise. *Organization Studies, 17*(6), 885–907. doi: 10.1177/017084069601700601.

Shenoy-Packer, S. (2015). Immigrant professionals, microaggressions, and critical sensemaking in the US workplace. *Management Communication Quarterly, 29*(2), 257–275. doi: 10.1177/0893318914562069.

Shetterly, M. L. (2016). *Hidden figures: The untold story of the African American women who helped win the space race.* NY: HarperCollins.

Shields, V. R., & Dervin, B. (1993). Sense-making in feminist social science research: A call to enlarge the methodological options of feminist studies. *Women's Studies International Forum 16*(1), 65–81. doi: 10.1016/0277-5395(93)90081-J.

Shimoni, B., & Bergmann, H. (2006). Managing in a changing world: From multiculturalism to hybridization—The production of hybrid management cultures in Israel, Thailand, and Mexico. *Academy of Management Perspectives, 20*(3), 76–89. doi: 10.5465/amp.2006.21903482.

Shortt, H. (2015). Liminality, space and the importance of 'transitory dwelling places' at work. *Human Relations, 68*(4), 633–658. doi: 10.1177/0018726714536938.

Shrikant, N., & Musselwhite, J. (2018). Indexing neoliberal ideology and political identities in a racially diverse business community. *Discourse & Communication, 13*(1), 119–137. doi: 10.1177/1750481318801627.

Siebert, S., Bushfield, S., Martin, G., & Howieson, B. (2018). Eroding 'respectability': Deprofessionalization through organizational spaces. *Work, Employment and Society, 32*(2), 330–347. doi: 10.1177/0950017017726948.

Siebert, S., Wilson, F., & Hamilton, J. R. (2017). "Devils may sit here:" The role of enchantment in institutional maintenance. *Academy of Management Journal*, *60*(4), 1607–1632. doi: 10.5465/amj.2014.0487.

Sim, S. (2004). *Introducing critical theory: A graphic guide*. Royston, England: Icon Books.

Skoglund, A., & Holt, R. (2020). Spatially organizing future genders: An artistic intervention in the creation of a hir-toilet. *Human Relations*. Advance online publication. doi: 10.1177/0018726719899728.

Skovgaard-Smith, I., & Poulfelt, F. (2018). Imagining 'non-nationality': Cosmopolitanism as a source of identity and belonging. *Human Relations*, *71*(2), 129–154. doi: 10.1177/0018726717714042.

Śliwa, M., & Johansson, M. (2014). The discourse of meritocracy contested/reproduced: Foreign women academics in UK business schools. *Organization*, *21*(6), 821–843. doi: 10.1177/1350508413486850.

Smith, A. (2016). The winds of change and the end of the Comprador System in the Hongkong and Shanghai Banking Corporation. *Business History*, *58*(2), 179–206. doi: 10.1080/00076791.2015.1041379.

Smith, C. W., & Mayorga-Gallo, S. (2017). The new principle-policy gap: How diversity ideology subverts diversity initiatives. *Sociological Perspectives*, *60*(5), 889–911. doi: 10.1177/0731121417719693.

Sobre-Denton, M. S. (2012). Stories from the cage: Autoethnographic sensemaking of workplace bullying, gender discrimination, and white privilege. *Journal of Contemporary Ethnography*, *41*(2), 220–250. doi: 10.1177/0891241611429301.

Söderlund, J., & Borg, E. (2018). Liminality in management and organization studies: Process, position and place. *International Journal of Management Reviews*, *20*(4), 880–902. doi: 10.1111/ijmr.12168.

Solebello, N., Tschirhart, M., & Leiter, J. (2016). The paradox of inclusion and exclusion in membership associations. *Human Relations*, *69*(2), 439–460. doi: 10.1177/0018726715590166.

Sonenshein, S. (2007). The role of construction, intuition, and justification in responding to ethical issues at work: The sensemaking-intuition model. *Academy of Management Review*, *32*(4), 1022–1040. doi: 10.5465/amr.2007.26585677.

Soni-Sinha, U. (2013). Intersectionality, subjectivity, collectivity and the union: A study of the 'locked-out' hotel workers in Toronto. *Organization*, *20*(6), 775–793. doi: 10.1177/1350508412453364.

Spedale, S. (2019). Deconstructing the 'older worker': Exploring the complexities of subject positioning at the intersection of multiple discourses. *Organization*, *26*(1), 38–54. doi: 10.1177/1350508418768072.

Spence, C., Carter, C., Belal, A., Husillos, J., Dambrin, C., & Archel, P. (2016). Tracking habitus across a transnational professional field. *Work, Employment and Society*, *30*(1), 3–20. doi: 10.1177/0950017015574824.

Spicer, A. (2006). Beyond the convergence–divergence debate: The role of spatial scales in transforming organizational logic. *Organization Studies*, *27*(10), 1467–1483. doi: 10.1177/0170840606067515.

Spicer, A., Alvesson, M., & Kärreman, D. (2009). Critical performativity: The unfinished business of critical management studies. *Human Relations*, 62(4), 537–560. doi: 10.1177/0018726708101984.

Spoelma, T. M., & Ellis, A. P. (2017). Fuse or fracture? Threat as a moderator of the effects of diversity faultlines in teams. *The Journal of Applied Psychology*, 102(9), 1344–1359. doi: 10.1037/apl0000231.

Stainback, K., Kleiner, S., & Skaggs, S. (2016). Women in power: Undoing or redoing the gendered organization? *Gender & Society*, 30(1), 109–135. doi: 10.1177/0891243215602906.

Starbuck, W. H. (2015). Karl E. Weick and the dawning awareness of organized cognition. *Management Decision*, 53(6), 1287–1299. doi: 10.1108/MD-04-2014-0183.

Starbuck, W. H. (2016). 60th anniversary essay: How journals could improve research practices in social science. *Administrative Science Quarterly*, 61(2), 165–183. doi: 10.1177/0001839216629644.

Starkey, K., Tempest, S., & Cinque, S. (2019). Management education and the theatre of the absurd. *Management Learning*, 50(5), 591–606. doi: 10.1177/1350507619875894.

Steel, D., & Bolduc, N. (2020). *A closer look at the business case for diversity: The tangled web of equity and epistemic benefits. Philosophy of the Social Sciences*. Advance online publication. doi: 10.1177/0048393120911130.

Steingard, D. S. (2005). Spiritually-informed management theory: Toward profound possibilities for inquiry and transformation. *Journal of Management Inquiry*, 14(3), 227–241. doi: 10.1177/1056492605276841.

Stephenson, K. A., Kuismin, A., Putnam, L. L., & Sivunen, A. (2020). *Process studies of organizational space. Academy of Management Annals*. Advance online publication. doi: 10.5465/annals.2018.0146.

Stevens, F. G., Plaut, V. C., & Sanchez-Burks, J. (2008). Unlocking the benefits of diversity: All-inclusive multiculturalism and positive organizational change. *The Journal of applied behavioral science*, 44(1), 116–133. doi: 10.1177/0021886308314460.

Stewman, S. (1988). Organizational demography. *Annual Review of Sociology*, 14(1), 173–202. doi: 10.1146/annurev.so.14.080188.001133.

Steyaert, C. (2010). Queering space: Heterotopic life in Derek Jarman's garden. *Gender, Work & Organization*, 17(1), 45–68. doi: 10.1111/j.1468-0432.2008.00404.x.

Steyaert, C., & Janssens, M. (2013). Multilingual scholarship and the paradox of translation and language in management and organization studies. *Organization*, 20(1), 131–142. doi: 10.1177/1350508412460998.

Stobbe, L. (2005). Doing machismo: Legitimating speech acts as a selection discourse. *Gender, Work & Organization*, 12(2), 105–123. doi: 10.1111/j.1468-0432.2005.00265.x.

Stokke, C., & Lybæk, L. (2018). Combining intercultural dialogue and critical multiculturalism. *Ethnicities*, 18(1), 70–85. doi: 10.1177/1468796816674504.

Strike, V. M., & Rerup, C. (2016). Mediated sensemaking. *Academy of Management Journal*, 59(3), 880–905. doi: 10.5465/amj.2012.0665.

Styhre, A. (2014). Gender equality as institutional work: The case of the church of Sweden. *Gender, Work & Organization, 21*(2), 105–120. doi: 10.1111/gwao.12024.

Styhre, A. (2016). What David Foster Wallace can teach management scholars. *Academy of Management Review, 41*(1), 170–183. doi: 10.5465/amr.2015.0250.

Styhre, A., & Eriksson-Zetterquist, U. (2008). Thinking the multiple in gender and diversity studies: Examining the concept of intersectionality. *Gender in Management: An International Journal, 23*(8), 567–582. doi: 10.1108/17542410810912690.

Suddaby, R. (2015). Can institutional theory be critical? *Journal of Management Inquiry, 24*(1), 93–95. doi: 10.1177/1056492614545304.

Suddaby, R., Bruton, G. D., & Walsh, J. P. (2018). What we talk about when we talk about inequality: An introduction to the Journal of Management Studies Special Issue. *Journal of Management Studies, 55*(3), 381–393. doi: 10.1111/joms.12333.

Suddaby, R., & Foster, W. M. (2017). History and organizational change. *Journal of Management, 43*(1), 19–38. doi: 10.1177/0149206316675031.

Sumerau, J. E., Forbes, T. D., Grollman, E. A., & Mathers, L. A. (2020). Constructing allyship and the persistence of inequality. *Social Problems.* Advance online publication. doi: 10.1093/socpro/spaa003.

Sutcliffe, K. M., Brown, A. D., & Putnam, L. L. (2006). Introduction to the special issue 'Making sense of organizing: In honor of Karl Weick'. *Organization Studies, 27*(11), 1573–1578. doi: 10.1177/0170840606068327.

Swan, E. (2010). Commodity diversity: Smiling faces as a strategy of containment. *Organization, 17*(1), 77–100. doi: 10.1177/1350508409350043.

Swan, E. (2017). What are white people to do? Listening, challenging ignorance, generous encounters and the 'not yet' as diversity research praxis. *Gender, Work & Organization, 24*(5), 547–563. doi: 10.1111/gwao.12165.

Swan, E., & Fox, S. (2010). Playing the game: Strategies of resistance and co-optation in diversity work. *Gender, Work & Organization, 17*(5), 567–589. doi: 10.1111/j.1468-0432.2010.00524.x.

Swinkels, M., & van Meijl, T. (2020). Performing as a professional: Shaping migrant integration policy in adverse times. *Culture and Organization, 26*(1), 61–74. doi: 10.1080/14759551.2018.1475480.

Syed, J. (2011). Akbar's multiculturalism: Lessons for diversity management in the 21st century. *Canadian Journal of Administrative Sciences/Revue Canadienne des Sciences de l'Administration, 28*(4), 402–412. doi: 10.1002/cjas.185.

Syed, J., & Kramer, R. (2009). Socially responsible diversity management. *Journal of Management & Organisation, 15*(5), 639–651. doi: 10.5172/jmo.15.5.639.

Syed, J., & Özbilgin, M. (2009). A relational framework for international transfer of diversity management practices. *The International Journal of Human Resource Management, 20*(12), 2435–2453. doi: 10.1080/09585190903363755.

Szetela, A. (2020). Black Lives Matter at five: Limits and possibilities. *Ethnic and Racial Studies, 43*(8), 1358–1383. doi: 10.1080/01419870.2019.1638955.

Tapia, M., & Alberti, G. (2019). Unpacking the category of migrant workers in trade union research: A multi-level approach to migrant intersectionalities. *Work, Employment and Society*, *33*(2), 314–325. doi: 10.1177/0950017018780589.

Tasheva, S., & Hillman, A. J. (2019). Integrating diversity at different levels: Multilevel human capital, social capital, and demographic diversity and their implications for team effectiveness. *Academy of Management Review*, *44*(4), 746–765. doi: 10.5465/amr.2015.0396.

Tassabehji, R., Harding, N., Lee, H., & Dominguez-Pery, C. (2020). *From female computers to male computo͛ rs: Or why there are so few women writing algorithms and developing software. Human Relations*. Advance online publication. doi: 10.1177/0018726720914723.

Tatli, A. (2011). A multi-layered exploration of the diversity management field: Diversity discourses, practices and practitioners in the UK. *British Journal of Management*, *22*(2), 238–253. doi: 10.1111/j.1467-8551.2010.00730.x.

Tatli, A., Nicolopoulou, K., Özbilgin, M., Karatas-Ozkan, M., & Öztürk, M. B. (2015). Questioning impact: Interconnection between extra-organizational resources and agency of equality and diversity officers. *The International Journal of Human Resource Management*, *26*(9), 1243–1258. doi: 10.1080/09585192.2014.934893.

Tatli, A., & Özbilgin, M. F. (2012). An emic approach to intersectional study of diversity at work: A Bourdieuan framing. *International Journal of Management Reviews*, *14*(2), 180–200. doi: 10.1111/j.1468-2370.2011.00326.x.

Tatli, A., Özbilgin, M., & Karatas-Ozkan, M. (Eds.). (2015). *Pierre Bourdieu, organization, and management*. London, England: Routledge.

Tatli, A., Vassilopoulou, J., Ariss, A. A., & Özbilgin, M. (2012). The role of regulatory and temporal context in the construction of diversity discourses: The case of the UK, France and Germany. *European Journal of Industrial Relations*, *18*(4), 293–308. doi: 10.1177/0959680112461092.

Taylor, S., & Spicer, A. (2007). Time for space: A narrative review of research on organizational spaces. *International Journal of Management Reviews*, *9*(4), 325–346. doi: 10.1111/j.1468-2370.2007.00214.x.

Taylor, P., Warhurst, C., Thompson, P., & Scholarios, D. M. (2009). On the front line. *Work, Employment and Society*, *23*(1), 7–11. doi: 10.1177/0950017008099774.

Teasdale, N. (2013). Fragmented sisters? The implications of flexible working policies for professional women's workplace relationships. *Gender, Work & Organization*, *20*(4), 397–412. doi: 10.1111/j.1468-0432.2012.00590.x.

Tedmanson, D., Verduyn, K., Essers, C., & Gartner, W. (2012). Critical perspectives in entrepreneurship research. *Organization*, *19*(5), 531–541. doi: 10.1177/1350508412458495.

Tetrault, J. E., Bucerius, S. M., & Haggerty, K. D. (2020). Multiculturalism under confinement: Prisoner race relations inside Western Canadian prisons. *Sociology*, *54*(3), 534–555. doi: 10.1177/0038038519882311.

Thanem, T. (2008). Embodying disability in diversity management research. *Equal Opportunities International*, *27*(7), 581–595. doi: 10.1108/02610150810904292.

Thanem, T., & Wallenberg, L. (2016). Just doing gender? Transvestism and the power of underdoing gender in everyday life and work. *Organization, 23*(2), 250–271. doi: 10.1177/1350508414547559.

The Economist (2017, May 4). *Down and out in Cairo and Beirut: The sorry state of Arab men.* Retrieved from http://www.economist.com/news/middle-east-and-africa/21721651-they-are-clinging-patriarchy-comfort-sorry-state-arab-men.

Thijssen, P. (2012). From mechanical to organic solidarity, and back: With Honneth beyond Durkheim. *European Journal of Social Theory, 15*(4), 454–470. doi: 10.1177/1368431011423589.

Thomas, M. P., & Tufts, S. (2020). Blue solidarity: Police unions, race and authoritarian populism in North America. *Work, Employment and Society, 34*(1), 126–144. doi: 10.1177/0950017019863653.

Thomas, P., Busher, J., Macklin, G., Rogerson, M., & Christmann, K. (2018). Hopes and Fears: Community cohesion and the 'White working class' in one of the 'failed spaces' of multiculturalism. *Sociology, 52*(2), 262–281. doi: 10.1177/0038038516676775.

Thomas, R. R. (1990). From affirmative action to affirming diversity. *Harvard Business Review, 68*(2), 107–117.

Thomas, R., & Davies, A. (2005). What have the feminists done for us? Feminist theory and organizational resistance. *Organization, 12*(5), 711–740. doi: 10.1177/1350508405055945.

Thompson, P. (2020). Capitalism, technology and work: Interrogating the tipping point thesis. *The Political quarterly, 91*(2), 299–309. doi: 10.1111/1467-923X.12787.

Thompson, P., and McHugh, D. (1990). *Work organisations: A critical introduction.* London: Macmillan.

Thompson, T. (2020, August 5). What Noughts and Crosses taught me about myths behind race and Brexit. *Prospect.* Online article. Retrieved from https://www.prospectmagazine.co.uk/philosophy/noughts-and-crosses-race-racism-uk-brexit-black-lives-matter-essay.

Thomson, J. (2018). Resisting gendered change: Feminist institutionalism and critical actors. *International Political Science Review, 39*(2), 178–191. doi: 10.1177/0192512116677844.

Thuesen, F. (2017). Linguistic barriers and bridges: Constructing social capital in ethnically diverse low-skill workplaces. *Work, Employment and Society, 31*(6), 937–953. doi: 10.1177/0950017016656321.

Tomlinson, F. (2010). Marking difference and negotiating belonging: Refugee women, volunteering and employment. *Gender, Work & Organization, 17*(3), 278–296. doi: 10.1111/j.1468-0432.2008.00399.x.

Tomlinson, F., & Egan, S. (2002a). Organizational sensemaking in a culturally diverse setting: Limits to the 'valuing diversity' discourse. *Management Learning, 33*(1), 79–97. doi: 10.1177/1350507602331004.

Tomlinson, F., & Egan, S. (2002b). From marginalization to (dis) empowerment: Organizing training and employment services for refugees. *Human Relations, 55*(8), 1019–1043. doi: 10.1177/0018726702055008182.

Tomlinson, F., & Schwabenland, C. (2010). Reconciling competing discourses of diversity? The UK non-profit sector between social justice and the business case. *Organization, 17*(1), 101–121. doi: 10.1177/1350508409350237.

Tomlinson, J., Valizade, D., Muzio, D., Charlwood, A., & Aulakh, S. (2018). *Privileges and penalties in the legal profession: An intersectional analysis of career progression. The British Journal of Sociology.* Early Online Version. doi: 10.1111/1468-4446.12375.

Torchia, D. (2016). An alternative football club in a liquid modernity: FC United of Manchester. *Culture and Organization, 22*(3), 203–220. doi: 10.1080/14759551.2016.1161625.

Tormos, F. (2017). Intersectional solidarity. *Politics, Groups, and Identities, 5*(4), 707–720. doi: 10.1080/21565503.2017.1385494.

Tourish, D. (2020). The triumph of nonsense in management studies. *Academy of Management Learning & Education, 19*(1), 99–109. doi: 10.5465/amle.2019.0255.

Tourish, D., & Robson, P. (2006). Sensemaking and the distortion of critical upward communication in organizations. *Journal of Management Studies, 43*(4), 711–730. doi: 10.1111/j.1467-6486.2006.00608.x.

Tourse, R. W., Hamilton-Mason, J., & Wewiorski, N. J. (2018). The infrastructure of racism: The institutional dimensions. In *Systemic Racism in the United States* (pp. 79–99). Cham, Switzerland: Springer.

Toyoki, S., & Brown, A. D. (2014). Stigma, identity and power: Managing stigmatized identities through discourse. *Human Relations, 67*(6), 715–737. doi: 10.1177/0018726713503024.

Tremblay, A. (2018). *Diversity in Decline?: The Rise of the Political Right and the Fate of Multiculturalism.* London: Springer.

Trittin, H., & Schoeneborn, D. (2017). Diversity as polyphony: Reconceptualizing diversity management from a communication-centered perspective. *Journal of Business Ethics, 144*(2), 305–322. doi: 10.1007/s10551-015-2825-8.

Tsui, A. S., Egan, T. D., & O'Reilly III, C. A. (1992). Being different: Relational demography and organizational attachment. *Administrative Science Quarterly, 37*(4), 549–579. doi: 10.2307/2393472.

Tsui, A. S., & O'reilly, C. A. (1989). Beyond simple demographic effects: The importance of relational demography in superior-subordinate dyads. *Academy of Management Journal, 32*(2), 402–423. doi: 10.2307/256368.

Tyler, M. (2019). Reassembling difference? Rethinking inclusion through/as embodied ethics. *Human Relations, 72*(1), 48–68. doi: 10.1177/0018726718764264.

Tyler, M., & Cohen, L. (2010). Spaces that matter: Gender performativity and organizational space. *Organization Studies, 31*(2), 175–198. doi: 10.1177/0170840609357381.

Ulus, E. (2015). Workplace emotions in postcolonial spaces: Enduring legacies, ambivalence, and subversion. *Organization, 22*(6), 890–908. doi: 10.1177/1350508414522316.

Urciuoli, B. (2016). The compromised pragmatics of diversity. *Language & communication, 51*, 30–39. doi: 10.1016/j.langcom.2016.07.005.

Vaara, E., & Faÿ, E. (2012). Reproduction and change on the global scale: A Bourdieusian perspective on management education. *Journal of Management Studies, 49*(6), 1023–1051. doi: 10.1111/j.1467-6486.2012.01049.x.

Vaccaro, A., & Palazzo, G. (2015). Values against violence: Institutional change in societies dominated by organized crime. *Academy of Management Journal, 58*(4), 1075–1101. doi: 10.5465/amj.2012.0865.

Vachhani, S. J. (2015). Organizing love—Thoughts on the transformative and activist potential of feminine writing. *Gender, Work & Organization, 22*(2), 148–162. doi: 10.1111/gwao.12079.

Vachhani, S. J. (2020). Envisioning a democratic culture of difference: Feminist ethics and the politics of dissent in social movements. *Journal of Business Ethics, 164*(4), 745–757. doi: 10.1007/s10551-019-04403-5.

Vachhani, S. J., & Pullen, A. (2019). Ethics, politics and feminist organizing: Writing feminist infrapolitics and affective solidarity into everyday sexism. *Human Relations, 72*(1), 23–47. doi: 10.1177/0018726718780988.

van den Brink, M., & Benschop, Y. (2018). Gender interventions in the Dutch police force: Resistance as a tool for change? *Journal of Change Management, 18*(3), 181–197.doi: 10.1080/14697017.2017.1378695.

Van Dijk, T. A. (2015). Critical discourse studies: A sociocognitive approach. In R. Wodak & M. Meyer (eds.) *Methods of Critical Discourse Studies* (pp. 63–85). London: Sage.

van Hilten, A. (2019). *A theory of (research) practice makes sense in sense-making. Journal of Organizational Change Management.* Advance online publication. doi: 10.1108/JOCM-06-2019-0177.

Van Knippenberg, D., De Dreu, C. K., & Homan, A. C. (2004). Work group diversity and group performance: An integrative model and research agenda. *Journal of Applied Psychology, 89*(6), 1008–1022. doi: 10.1037/0021-9010. 89.6.1008.

Van Knippenberg, D., & Schippers, M. C. (2007). Work group diversity. *Annual Review of Psychology, 58*, 515–541. doi: 10.1146/annurev.psych.58.110405. 085546.

Van Laer, K. (2018). The role of co-workers in the production of (homo) sexuality at work: A Foucauldian approach to the sexual identity processes of gay and lesbian employees. *Human Relations, 71*(2), 229–255. doi: 10.1177/ 0018726717711236.

Van Laer, K., Jammaers, E., & Hoeven, W. (2020). *Disabling organizational spaces: Exploring the processes through which spatial environments disable employees with impairments. Organization.* Advance online publication. doi: 10.1177/1350508419894698.

Van Laer, K., & Janssens, M. (2017). Agency of ethnic minority employees: Struggles around identity, career and social change. *Organization, 24*(2), 198–217. doi: 10.1177/1350508416664143.

Van Maanen, J., Sørensen, J. B., & Mitchell, T. R. (2007). The interplay between theory and method. *Academy of Management Review, 32*(4), 1145–1154. doi: 10.5465/AMR.2007.26586080.

Van Marrewijk, A., & Yanow, D. (Eds.). (2010). *Organizational spaces: Rematerializing the workaday world.* Cheltenham, UK: Edward Elgar Publishing.

Varman, R., & Al-Amoudi, I. (2016). Accumulation through derealization: How corporate violence remains unchecked. *Human Relations, 69*(10), 1909–1935. doi: 10.1177/0018726716628970.

Vaughan, D. (1999). The dark side of organizations: Mistake, misconduct, and disaster. *Annual Review of Sociology*, 25(1), 271–305. doi: 10.1146/annurev. soc.25.1.271.

Vertovec, S. (2010). Towards post-multiculturalism? Changing communities, conditions and contexts of diversity. *International Social Science Journal*, 61(199), 83–95. doi: 10.1111/j.1468-2451.2010.01749.x.

Vertovec, S. (2018). [reprint from 2010] Towards post-multiculturalism? Changing communities, conditions and contexts of diversity. *International Social Science Journal*, 68(227-228), 167–178. doi: 10.1111/issj.12191.

Vickers, M. H. (2007). Autoethnography as sensemaking: A story of bullying. *Culture and Organization*, 13(3), 223–237. doi: 10.1080/14759550701486555.

Vidaillet, B., & Bousalham, Y. (2020). Coworking spaces as places where economic diversity can be articulated: Towards a theory of syntopia. *Organization*, 27(1), 60–87. doi: 10.1177/1350508418794003.

Villesèche, F., Muhr, S. L., & Śliwa, M. (2018). From radical black feminism to postfeminist hashtags: Re-claiming intersectionality. *Ephemera*, 18(1), 1–16.

Vince, R. (2019). Institutional illogics: The unconscious and institutional analysis. *Organization Studies*, 40(7), 953–973. doi: 10.1177/0170840618765866.

Vinnicombe, S., & Singh, V. (2002). Women-only management training: An essential part of women's leadership development. *Journal of Change Management*, 3(4), 294–306. doi: 10.1080/714023846.

Violi, P. (2012). Trauma site museums and politics of memory: Tuol Sleng, Villa Grimaldi and the Bologna Ustica Museum. *Theory, Culture & Society*, 29(1), 36–75. doi: 10.1177/0263276411423035.

Visser, M. (2019). Pragmatism, critical theory and business ethics: Converging lines. *Journal of Business Ethics*, 156(1), 45–57. doi: 10.1007/s10551-017-3564-9.

Volpp, L. (2001). Feminism versus multiculturalism. *Columbia Law Review*, 101(5), 1181–1218. Retrieved from https://ssrn.com/abstract=277712.

Von Bergen, C. W., Soper, B., & Foster, T. (2002). Unintended negative effects of diversity management. *Public Personnel Management*, 31(2), 239–251. doi: 10.1177/009102600203100209.

Von Krogh, G. (2018). Artificial intelligence in organizations: New opportunities for phenomenon-based theorizing. *Academy of Management Discoveries*, 4(4), 404–409. doi: 10.5465/amd.2018.0084.

Vora, D., Martin, L., Fitzsimmons, S. R., Pekerti, A. A., Lakshman, C., & Raheem, S. (2019). Multiculturalism within individuals: A review, critique, and agenda for future research. *Journal of International Business Studies*, 50(4), 499–524. doi: 10.1057/s41267-018-0191-3.

Vough, H. C., Bataille, C. D., Noh, S. C., & Lee, M. D. (2015). Going off script: How managers make sense of the ending of their careers. *Journal of Management Studies*, 52(3), 414–440. doi: 10.1111/joms.12126.

Waites, M. (2017). LGBTI organizations navigating imperial contexts: The Kaleidoscope Trust, the Commonwealth and the need for a decolonizing, intersectional politics. *The Sociological Review*, 65(4), 644–662. doi: 10.1111/1467-954X.12424.

Walby, S. (2020). *Developing the concept of society: Institutional domains, regimes of inequalities and complex systems in a global era. Current Sociology.* Advance online publication. doi: 10.1177/0011392120932940.

Walby, S., Armstrong, J., & Strid, S. (2012). Intersectionality: Multiple inequalities in social theory. *Sociology, 46*(2), 224–240. doi: 10.1177/0038038511416164.

Wall, T. D., & Wood, S. J. (2005). The romance of human resource management and business performance, and the case for big science. *Human Relations, 58*(4), 429–462. doi: 10.1177/0018726705055032.

Wallace, S. E. (Ed.) (1971). *Total institutions.* Piscataway, NJ: Transaction Publishers.

Waller, W., & Jennings, A. (1990). On the possibility of a feminist economics: The convergence of institutional and feminist methodology. *Journal of Economic Issues, 24*(2), 613–622. doi: 10.1080/00213624.1990.11505060.

Ward, K. (2007). Thinking geographically about work, employment and society. *Work, Employment and Society, 21*(2), 265–276. doi: 10.1177/0950017007076634.

Ward, C., Gale, J., Staerklé, C., & Stuart, J. (2018). Immigration and multiculturalism in context: A framework for psychological research. *Journal of Social Issues, 74*(4), 833–855. doi: 10.1111/josi.12301.

Ward, J., & Winstanley, D. (2003). The absent presence: Negative space within discourse and the construction of minority sexual identity in the workplace. *Human Relations, 56*(10), 1255–1280. doi: 10.1177/00187267035610005.

Warner, L. R. (2008). A best practices guide to intersectional approaches in psychological research. *Sex Roles, 59*(5-6), 454–463. doi: 10.1007/s11199-008-9504-5.

Warner, M. (2007). Kafka, Weber and organization theory. *Human Relations, 60*(7), 1019–1038. doi: 10.1177/0018726707081156.

Warren, B., Ballenger, C., Ogonowski, M., Rosebery, A. S., & Hudicourt-Barnes, J. (2001). Rethinking diversity in learning science: The logic of everyday sense-making. *Journal of Research in Science Teaching: The Official Journal of the National Association for Research in Science Teaching, 38*(5), 529–552. doi: 10.1002/tea.1017.

Wasserman, V., & Frenkel, M. (2011). Organizational aesthetics: Caught between identity regulation and culture jamming. *Organization Science, 22*(2), 503–521. doi: 10.1287/orsc.1100.0583.

Wasserman, V., & Frenkel, M. (2015). Spatial work in between glass ceilings and glass walls: Gender-class intersectionality and organizational aesthetics. *Organization Studies, 36*(11), 1485–1505. doi: 10.1177/0170840615593583.

Webber, S. S., & Donahue, L. M. (2001). Impact of highly and less job-related diversity on work group cohesion and performance: A meta-analysis. *Journal of Management, 27*(2), 141–162. doi: 10.1016/S0149-2063(00)00093-3.

Weber, L. J. (1993). Ethics and the praise of diversity. *Business Ethics Quarterly, 3*(1), 87–96. doi: 10.2307/3857387.

Weber, K., & Glynn, M. A. (2006). Making sense with institutions: Context, thought and action in Karl Weick's theory. *Organization Studies, 27*(11), 1639–1660. doi: 10.1177/0170840606068343.

Webster, W. (2018, April 18). Windrush generation: The history of unbelonging.

The Conversation. Retrieved from https://theconversation.com/windrush-generation-the-history-of-unbelonging-95021.

Weick, K. E. (1995). *Sensemaking in organizations*. Thousand Oaks, CA: Sage.

Weick, K. E. (2005). Managing the unexpected: Complexity as distributed sensemaking. In R. R. McDaniel Jr. & D. J. Driebe (Eds.), *Uncertainty and surprise in complex systems: Questions on working with the unexpected* (pp. 51–65). Berlin: SpringerVerlag.

Weick, K. E. (2010). Comment on 'softly constrained imagination'. *Culture and Organization, 16*(2), 179. doi: 10.1080/14759551003769326.

Weick, K. E. (2012). Organized sensemaking: A commentary on processes of interpretive work. *Human Relations, 65*(1), 141–153. doi: 10.1177/0018726711424235.

Weick, K. E. (2015a). Karl E. Weick (1979), the social psychology of organizing. *M@n@gement, 18*(2), 189–193. doi: 10.3917/mana.182.0189.

Weick, K. E. (2015b). Ambiguity as grasp: The reworking of sense. *Journal of Contingencies and Crisis Management, 23*(2), 117–123. doi: 10.1111/1468-5973.12080.

Weick, K. E. (2016). 60th anniversary essay: Constrained comprehending: The experience of organizational inquiry. *Administrative Science Quarterly, 61*(3), 333–346. doi: 10.1177/0001839216633453.

Weick, K. E. (2020). Book review. Thomas B. Lawrence and Nelson Phillips. Constructing Organizational Life: How Social-Symbolic Work Shapes Selves, Organizations, and Institutions. *Administrative Science Quarterly*. Advance online publication. doi: 10.1177/0001839219896664.

Weick, K. E., Sutcliffe, K. M., & Obstfeld, D. (2005). Organizing and the process of sensemaking. *Organization Science, 16*(4), 409–421. doi: 10.1287/orsc.1050.0133.

Weick, K. E., & Westley, F. (1996). Organizational learning: Affirming an oxymoron. In S. R. Clegg, C. Hardy, & W. R. Nord (Eds.), *Handbook of organization studies* (pp. 440–458). Thousand Oaks, CA: Sage.

Weinfurtner, T. U., & Seidl, D. (2019). Towards a spatial perspective: An integrative review of research on organisational space. *Scandinavian Journal of Management, 35*(2), 1–30. doi: 10.1016/j.scaman.2018.02.003.

Wenzel, M., Krämer, H., Koch, J., & Reckwitz, A. (2020). *Future and organization studies: On the rediscovery of a problematic temporal category in organizations*. *Organization Studies*. Advance online publication. doi: 10.1177/0170840620912977.

Werbner, P. (2005). The translocation of culture: 'Community cohesion' and the force of multiculturalism in history. *The Sociological Review, 53*(4), 745–768. doi: 10.1111/j.1467-954X.2005.00594.x.

Werbner, P. (2013). Everyday multiculturalism: Theorising the difference between 'intersectionality' and 'multiple identities'. *Ethnicities, 13*(4), 401–419. doi: 10.1177/1468796813483728.

West, I. (2018). Queer perspectives in communication studies. *Oxford Research Encyclopedia of Communication*. Feb. doi:10.1093/acrefore/9780190228613.013.81.

White, R. J., & Green, A. E. (2015). The importance of socio-spatial influences in shaping young people's employment aspirations: Case study evidence from three British cities. *Work, Employment and Society, 29*(2), 295–313. doi: 10. 1177/0950017014561334.

Whitty, M. T., & Carr, A. N. (2003). Cyberspace as potential space: Considering the web as a playground to cyber-flirt. *Human Relations, 56*(7), 869–891. doi: 10.1177/00187267030567005.

Wieners, S., & Weber, S. M. (2020). Athena's claim in an academic regime of performativity: Discursive organizing of excellence and gender at the intersection of heterotopia and heteronomia. *Management Learning.* Advance online publication. doi: 10.1177/1350507620915198.

Wiersema, M. F., & Bird, A. (1993). Organizational demography in Japanese firms: Group heterogeneity, individual dissimilarity, and top management team turnover. *Academy of Management Journal, 36*(5), 996–1025. doi: 10. 2307/256643.

Wickert, C., & De Bakker, F. G. (2018). Pitching for social change: Toward a relational approach to selling and buying social issues. *Academy of Management Discoveries, 4*(1), 50–73. doi: 10.5465/amd.2015.0009.

Wilhoit, E. D. (2018). Space, place, and the communicative constitution of organizations: A constitutive model of organizational space. *Communication Theory, 28*(3), 311–331. doi: 10.1093/ct/qty007.

Williams, G. (2020). Management Millennialism: Designing the New Generation of Employee. *Work, Employment and Society, 34*(3), 371–387. doi: 10.1177/ 0950017019836891.

Williams, J. (1985). Redefining institutional racism. *Ethnic and Racial Studies, 8*(3), 323–348. doi: 10.1080/01419870.1985.9993490.

Williams, J. B. (2017). Breaking down bias: Legal mandates vs. corporate interests. *Washington Law Review, 92*(3), 1473–1513. Retrieved from https:// search.proquest.com/docview/1960284835?accountid=10673.

Williams, R. R. (2010). Space for God: Lived religion at work, home, and play. *Sociology of Religion, 71*(3), 257–279. doi: 10.1093/socrel/srq048.

Williamson, D. (2002). Forward from a critique of Hofstede's model of national culture. *Human Relations, 55*(11), 1373–1395. doi: 10.1177/ 00187267025511006.

Willmott, H. (Ed.). (1992). *Critical management studies.* London: Sage.

Willmott, H. (2015). Why institutional theory cannot be critical. *Journal of Management Inquiry, 24*(1), 105–111. doi: 10.1177/1056492614545306.

Willmott, H. (2018). *Can it? On expanding institutional theory by disarming critique. Journal of Management Inquiry,* Online First. doi: 10.1177/ 1056492617744893.

Wilton, R., & Schuer, S. (2006). Towards socio-spatial inclusion? Disabled people, neoliberalism and the contemporary labour market. *Area, 38*(2), 186–195. doi: 10.1111/j.1475-4762.2006.00668.x.

Wise, A. (2016). Convivial labour and the 'joking relationship': Humour and everyday multiculturalism at work. *Journal of Intercultural Studies, 37*(5), 481–500. doi: 10.1080/07256868.2016.1211628.

Wise, A., & Velayutham, S. (2014). Conviviality in everyday multiculturalism: Some brief comparisons between Singapore and Sydney. *European Journal of Cultural Studies, 17*(4), 406–430. doi: 10.1177/1367549413510419.

Wise, A., & Velayutham, S. (2020). Humour at work: Conviviality through language play in Singapore's multicultural workplaces. *Ethnic and Racial Studies*, 43(5), 911–929. doi: 10.1080/01419870.2019.1588341.

Witte, A. E. (2012). Making the case for a post-national cultural analysis of organizations. *Journal of Management Inquiry*, 21(2), 141–159. doi: 10.1177/1056492611415279.

Woodhams, C., & Danieli, A. (2000). Disability and diversity-a difference too far? *Personnel Review*, 29(3), 402–417. doi: 10.1108/00483480010324779.

Woodward, R., & Winter, P. (2006). Gender and the limits to diversity in the contemporary British Army. *Gender, Work & Organization*, 13(1), 45–67. doi: 10.1111/j.1468-0432.2006.00295.x.

Wooten, L. P., & James, E. H. (2004). When firms fail to learn: The perpetuation of discrimination in the workplace. *Journal of Management Inquiry*, 13(1), 23–33. doi: 10.1177/1056492603259059.

Wrench, J. (2005). Diversity management can be bad for you. *Race & Class*, 46(3), 73–84. doi: 10.1177/0306396805050019.

Wright, C. R., Manning, M. R., Farmer, B., & Gilbreath, B. (2000). Resourceful sensemaking in product development teams. *Organization Studies*, 21(4), 807–825. doi: 10.1177/0170840600214006.

Wright, A. L., Meyer, A. D., Reay, T., & Staggs, J. (2020). *Maintaining places of social inclusion: Ebola and the emergency department. Administrative Science Quarterly*. Advance online publication. doi: 10.1177/0001839220916401.

Wrzesniewski, A., Dutton, J. E., & Debebe, G. (2003). Interpersonal sensemaking and the meaning of work. *Research in Organizational Behavior*, 25, 93–135. doi: 10.1016/S0191-3085(03)25003-6.

Yack, B. (2002). Multiculturalism and the political theorists. *European Journal of Political Theory*, 1(1), 107–119.

Yadav, S., & Lenka, U. (2020). *Diversity management: A systematic review. Equality, Diversity and Inclusion: An International Journal*. Advance online publication. doi: 10.1108/EDI-07-2019-0197.

Yang, I., & Bacouel-Jentjens, S. (2019). Identity construction in the workplace: Different reactions of ethnic minority groups to an organizational diversity policy in a French manufacturing company. *Organization*, 26(3), 410–431. doi: 10.1177/1350508418812547.

Yang, Y., & Konrad, A. M. (2011). Understanding diversity management practices: Implications of institutional theory and resource-based theory. *Group & Organization Management*, 36(1), 6–38. doi: 10.1177/1059601110390997.

Zabrodska, K., Ellwood, C., Zaeemdar, S., & Mudrak, J. (2016). Workplace bullying as sensemaking: An analysis of target and actor perspectives on initial hostile interactions. *Culture and Organization*, 22(2), 136–157. doi: 10.1080/14759551.2014.894514.

Zander, U., Zander, L., Gaffney, S., & Olsson, J. (2010). Intersectionality as a new perspective in international business research. *Scandinavian Journal of Management*, 26(4), 457–466. doi: 10.1016/j.scaman.2010.09.011.

Zanoni, P. (2011). Diversity in the lean automobile factory: Doing class through gender, disability and age. *Organization*, 18(1), 105–127. doi: 10.1177/1350508410378216.

Zanoni, P. (2020). Prefiguring alternatives through the articulation of post-and anti-capitalistic politics: An introduction to three additional papers and a reflection. *Organization*, 27(1), 3–16. doi: 10.1177/1350508419894699.

Zanoni, P., Contu, A., Healy, S., & Mir, R. (2017). Post-capitalistic politics in the making: The imaginary and praxis of alternative economies. *Organization*, 24(5), 575–588. doi: 10.1177/1350508417713219.

Zanoni, P., Janssens, M., Benschop, Y., & Nkomo, S. (2010). Guest editorial: Unpacking diversity, grasping inequality: Rethinking difference through critical perspectives. *Organization*, 17(1), 9–29. doi: 10.1177/ 1350508409350344.

Zanoni, P., & Janssens, M. (2004). Deconstructing difference: The rhetoric of human resource managers' diversity discourses. *Organization Studies*, 25(1), 55–74. doi: 10.1177/0170840604038180.

Zanoni, P., & Janssens, M. (2007). Minority employees engaging with (diversity) management: An analysis of control, agency, and micro-emancipation. *Journal of Management Studies*, 44(8), 1371–1397. doi: 10.1111/j.1467-6486.2007. 00700.x.

Zanoni, P., & Janssens, M. (2015). The power of diversity discourses at work: On the interlocking nature of diversities and occupations. *Organization Studies*, 36(11), 1463–1483. doi: 10.1177/0170840615593584.

Zickar, M. J. (2015). Digging through dust: Historiography for the organizational sciences. *Journal of Business and Psychology*, 30(1), 1–14. doi: 10. 1007/s10869-013-9339-0.

Zietsma, C., Groenewegen, P., Logue, D. M., & Hinings, C. R. (2017). Field or fields? Building the scaffolding for cumulation of research on institutional fields. *Academy of Management Annals*, 11(1), 391–450. doi: 10.5465/annals. 2014.0052.

Žižek 2001 Žižek, S. (2001). *Did somebody say totalitarianism?* London: Verso.

Zoogah, D. B., Peng, M. W., & Woldu, H. (2015). Institutions, resources, and organizational effectiveness in Africa. *The Academy of Management Perspectives*, 29(1), 7–31. doi: 10.5465/amp.2012.0033.

Zuboff, S. (2019). *The age of surveillance capitalism: The fight for a human future at the new frontier of power*. London: Profile Books.

Zundel, M., Holt, R., & Cornelissen, J. (2013). Institutional work in The Wire: An ethological investigation of flexibility in organizational adaptation. *Journal of Management Inquiry*, 22(1), 102–120. doi: 10.1177/1056492612440045.

Zyphur, M. J. (2009). When mindsets collide: Switching analytical mindsets to advance organization science. *Academy of Management Review*, 34(4), 677–688. doi: 10.5465/amr.34.4.zok677.

Index

Printed in the United States
by Baker & Taylor Publisher Services